FIVE LIVES IN MUSIC

Five Lives in Music

*Women Performers, Composers,
and Impresarios from the
Baroque to the Present*

CECELIA HOPKINS PORTER

UNIVERSITY OF ILLINOIS PRESS
URBANA, CHICAGO, AND SPRINGFIELD

First Illinois paperback, 2014
© 2012 by the Board of Trustees
of the University of Illinois
All rights reserved
Manufactured in the United States of America
1 2 3 4 5 C P 5 4 3 2 1
♾ This book is printed on acid-free paper.

The Library of Congress cataloged the cloth edition as follows:
Porter, Cecelia Hopkins.
Five lives in music: women performers, composers, and impresarios
from the baroque to the present / Cecelia Hopkins Porter.
    p.   cm.
Includes bibliographical references and index.
ISBN 978-0-252-03701-6 (cloth: alk. paper)
1. Women musicians—Biography. 2. Women composers—Biography.
3. Sophie Elisabeth, Duchess, consort of August, Duke of
Braunschweig-Lüneburg, 1613–1676. 4. Jacquet de La Guerre,
Elisabeth-Claude, 1665–1729. 5. Lang, Josephine, 1815–1880.
6. Bach, Maria, 1896–1978. 7. Schein, Ann. 8. Musicians—Biography.
9. Composers—Biography.
I. Title. II. Title: 5 lives in music. III. Title: Lives in music.
ML82.P675   2012
780.92′52—dc23   2011051102

PAPERBACK ISBN 978-0-252-08009-8

For Douglas and our children,

Rebecca, Elizabeth, Bartholomew, and Lawrence

And in loving memory of Charlotte Untersteiner-Bittner

CONTENTS

LIST OF FIGURES

PREFACE

I began writing for the *Washington Post* as a music critic in 1963, a few days before John F. Kennedy's assassination. With time away for raising a family and obtaining a doctoral degree, I resumed reviewing for the *Post,* totaling over two-and-a-half decades so far. During that time, I have covered hundreds of concerts, recitals, operas, and other musical events. In the early years, I seldom encountered compositions by women or concerts publicized as "music by women." Indeed, in conversations with audience members, including musically enlightened listeners, I was asked not infrequently, "Have there ever been any really good women composers?" or "Where do we go to hear women's music?" These questions may sound shocking today, though at times they still crop up. When I mentioned some women composers' names in those days, I had to admit that music by these women was rarely performed before general audiences in public concert halls.

Additional questions arise: What kind of sound do we expect to hear from women instrumentalists and singers? Is their musical expressivity distinguishable from men's? With solo vocal music written for a female voice and settings for women's choruses, we assume a certain kind of sonority and range. Consider, for instance, the wide span of pitches and timbres identified with coloratura or mezzo sopranos and contraltos as contrasted with countertenors, tenors, baritones, and basses. The questions continue to multiply. What level of skill and stylistic interpretation do we anticipate in performances by a "woman violinist" or a "woman pianist"? Or, what do we listen for while hearing a "woman's composition"? For that matter, why do we not speak in gender-specific terms of "men's music"?

As time passed, such queries also stirred questions of my own: Why do we not hear more compositions by women? And, for that matter, what *is* "women's music"? A number of these questions remain unanswered today, at least for the general public as distinguished from scholars voicing specific feminist issues in music. I have sought to address some of these questions in this book, for even today—though less so than in the past—many concert audiences and readers tend to think of music, especially composition, as primarily men's domain.

Besides these issues, others have surfaced, such as appraisals of women's physical and mental—that is, creative—capabilities. And the matter goes deeper than in music alone, as the following comment illustrates. A certain Mrs. Jameson wrote in 1846, "The intellect of woman bears the same relation to that of man as her physical organization, [that is,] it is inferior in power, and different in kind. ... In men the intellectual faculties exist more self-poised and self-directed— more independent of the rest of the character, than we ever find them in women, with whom talent, however predominant, is in a much greater degree modified by the sympathies and moral qualities."[1] Such a view diminishes the potential role of women in creative—that is, in all intellectual—pursuits, including the domestic ones.

Chance played a crucial part in this book. Because the subject of cultural contexts has long been a major interest of mine, I was inspired a few years ago by the suggestion of William A. Frohlich, the director of Northeastern University Press, that I consider writing a work "about the role of selected women in music over several centuries set in the context of the social traditions and restrictions of each era." After reflecting on Bill's remark, I decided to take him up on his proposal and set out on the road that led to this book. My intention was bolstered by my own professional and personal experiences as a critic, scholar, musician, wife, and mother of four. I felt ready to begin a search for women who would meet Bill's criteria. Fortified by the important critical arguments put forth by leading feminist musicologists, I set about choosing the specific women whose musical roles I would explore for this undertaking. My wholesale foray into the literature on women seriously engaged in music required surveying page by page numerous older and more recent biographical dictionaries, personal memoirs, library archives, court records, autographs and published scores, monographs on women composers and performers, and the bibliographies listed in these studies, music histories, professional music journals, concert reviews and other articles, extensive interviews, and, of course, the wide open spaces of the Internet.[2] Then began this portrayal of the role of five women in creating music through five centuries.

ACKNOWLEDGMENTS

The inspiration to embark on this book and to sustain my determination while doing the research and writing has depended to a great extent on the encouragement and support of many people—scholars, editors, and journalists in various aspects of music and not a few music lovers in other professions. The list of these benefactors is therefore long. Above all, I thank my husband, Douglas R. Porter, and our four children—Rebecca, Elizabeth, Bartholomew, and Lawrence—who have contributed to this book in countless ways through thick and thin, including editing and computer issues, which they solved at times with a great deal of patience and not a little wit.

I owe much to Laurie Matheson, my editor at the University of Illinois Press, who worked closely with me on this undertaking over several years; and to William A. Frohlich, director of the Northeastern University Press, who helped me crystallize my original concept of the book. The staff of the Council for the International Exchange of Scholars in Washington, D.C. provided much assistance; and Lonnie R. Johnson, director of the Austrian-American Education Commission (Fulbright Commission) in Vienna, awarded me a Senior Scholar grant for my research in that city on the Viennese composer Maria Bach. Mary Cyr, the University of Guelph, Ontario, read the entire manuscript and provided detailed scholarly commentary, especially regarding Elisabeth-Claude Jacquet de La Guerre. Anne E. MacNeil, the University of North Carolina, also read the manuscript and provided numerous valuable comments. Christoph Wolff, Harvard University, gave me considerable support for my research on Maria Bach. Teresa Indjein-Untersteiner, of the Bundesministerium in Vienna and the Embassy of Austria, Washington, D.C., and Charlotte Untersteiner-Bittner, Vienna, sustained me in many ways. I also appreciate the encouragement of John Ward and Jack Stein, Harvard University, and John Daverio, Boston University. Baritone and musicologist Thomas Hampson, Zürich, gave me important insight into the music of twentieth-century American women composers, thereby deepening my perspective on American music in that century and the twenty-first.

Those listed below provided me with information and support for a particular chapter, although some of them also aided me in other parts of the book.

Chapter 1 (Duchess Sophie-Elisabeth of Braunschweig-Lüneburg): Christian Hogrefe, Herzog August Bibliothek, Wolfenbüttel; the staff of the Heimatsmuseum Bibliothek, Güstrow-Mecklenburg; Ulrich Schwarz and Rainer Kustak, Niedersächsisches Landesarchiv-Staatsarchiv, Wolfenbüttel; and Karl Christian Gärtner, Stadtarchiv-und Stadtbibliothek, Braunschweig.

Chapter 2 (Elisabeth-Claude Jacquet de La Guerre): Anne Young, Indianapolis Museum of Art, Indianapolis; Alan Rubin, the Pelham Galleries, London; Ronald Broude, Broude Brothers Limited, Williamstown, Mass.; also Cait Miller and Lawrence Appelbaum, Library of Congress, Music Division, Washington, D.C.; and Mary Cyr, the University of Guelph, Ontario.

Chapter 3 (Josephine Lang): Harald Krebs and Sharon Krebs, the University of Victoria, British Columbia; Felix Heinzer, Reiner Nägeli, Magdalena Popp-Grilli, Martina Rommel, and Dagmar Bunk, the Württembergische Landesbibliothek, Stuttgart; Dieter Spatschek, the Bayerische Staatsbibliothek, Munich; Birgit Lodes and Ulrike Keil, the Institut für Musikwissenschaft, the University of Munich; Otto Biba, Monika Greipel, and Ilse Kosz, the Archiv der Gesellschaft der Musikfreunde, Vienna; the staff of the Nationalbibliothek, Vienna; Babette Angelaeas, the Theatermuseum, Munich; Elena Ostleitner, the Institut für Musiksoziologie, Universität für Musik und Darstellende Kunst, Vienna; Werner Grünzweig, Stiftung Archiv der Akademie der Künste, Berlin; Margareta Ploder, Embassy of Austria, Washington, D.C.; Horst Weise, Munich; Helmut Hell, the Staatsbibliothek Preussischer Kulturbesitz, Berlin; Trautlieb Hülz, Irmgard Maria Fellner, and Petra-Studert-Goeller, Embassy of the Federal Republic of Germany, Washington, D.C.

Chapter 4 (Maria Bach): Margareta Ploder, Andrea Schrammel, Karl Schrammel, and Eleonora Windisch, the Embassy of Austria, Washington, D.C.; Sylvia Mattl-Wurm, Wiener Stadtbibliothek im Rathaus, Vienna; Madeleine Delarue, Geneva; Elena Ostleitner, Institut für Musiksoziologie, Universität für Musik und Darstellende Kunst, Vienna; the staff of the Österreichische Nationalbibliothek, Vienna; Walter Obermaier and Thomas Aigner, the Wiener Stadtbibliothek im Rathaus (formerly the Wiener Stadt-und Landesbibliothek), Vienna; the staff of the Archiv Wiener Konzerthaus, Vienna; Wolfgang Schaufler, Susanne Amann, Heike Mangold, and Andrea Kohl, MICA (Music Information Center Austria), Vienna; Gerold W. Gruber, the Universität für Musik und Darstellende Kunst, Vienna; Gabriele Allgaier, Austromechana, Vienna; Gerda M. Eiselmair, Vienna; Horst Weise, Munich; Michael Bladerer and Tibor Kovac, the Vienna Philharmonic Orchestra; Primavera Gruber, the Orpheus Trust, Vienna.

Chapter 5 (Ann Schein): Ann Schein Carlyss and Earl Carlyss, Westport, Conn.; Tim Page, the *Washington Post,* Washington, D.C.; Linda Schein Greenebaum, Amherst, Mass.; Elisabeth Adkins, the National Symphony Orchestra, Washington, D.C.; Jerome Barry, the Embassy Series, Washington, D.C.; the staff of the New York Public Library.

FIVE LIVES IN MUSIC

Introduction

In 1792, British author Mary Wollstonecraft published *A Vindication of the Rights of Women,* arguing women's right to vote. The book was a small but important part of the numerous waves of feminism that have continued to focus attention on improving the role and status of women in the evolution of civilization. Feminist musicologists and others active in the musical world, especially during the last decades of the twentieth century into the twenty-first, have focused on issues concerning the place of women in music.[1] These scholars point out that specifically in music, Mrs. Jameson's (see preface) outlook continues to reign in many quarters as proverbial truth—that is, "women's place is in the home." Women's creativity is conceived (though perhaps not with as rigid a bias as in Mrs. Jameson's times) chiefly in terms of gender identification (pairing each sex with certain art forms) and hence of her biological, or specifically domestic, function; as, for example, in the idealized image of the dutiful wife devoted to begetting and raising children or even overseeing an entire household.[2] Women are still seen in some quarters as lacking the mental capacity to compose large-scale musical works or conduct an orchestra. Perhaps worse, a woman pursuing a major professional career is often viewed as "neglecting" her family.[3] Cast in the language of body imagery, this notion of total domesticity has also spawned other ramifications: for example, one hears that women supposedly have little or no time, and therefore less liberty, to follow creative pursuits; their day is too long to include performing, composing, painting, or writing activities because their responsibilities lie chiefly in the realm of "homemaking." Men's creativity, however, has been assumed to be basically an aspect of a male's mental domain and physical brawn unhindered by family responsibilities.[4]

Even now, relatively few names of women in the "classical" music world (as opposed to the arena of pop and jazz) have been part of society's household language. We have heard of divas such as Jenny Lind, Maria Callas, Renée Fleming, and Cecilia Bartoli, all celebrated for their astonishing vocal art. And much notice, though to a lesser extent, has been given to certain "star" women instrumentalists of relatively recent times, such as the pianist Myra Hess, cellist Jacqueline du Pré, or violinist Anne-Sophie Mutter. At the same time, only a handful of women composers from the past are familiar to the majority of the public today, and then only modestly: for instance, the composers Hildegard von Bingen, Clara Schumann, Fanny Mendelssohn Hensel, Amy Beach, and perhaps Alma Mahler. How many members of the music-minded public know the names of today's women composers?

This book is intended to shed light on five women—four of them composers, all of them performers—working in five centuries, who have made distinguished contributions to their art. My purpose has been to expand the perceptions of the general public about the opportunities, restraints, and accomplishments of talented women in music.

For an arts-minded lay audience, I have attempted here to keep music's more abstract technical terms to a minimum without sacrificing the kind of evidence that a scholarly audience demands. I also envision some of my readers as music students (in music history, music theory, performance, and composition classes) who need to widen their perspectives past more traditional music courses emphasizing history's "master" composers and their works. I do recognize, in addition, the contributions made by the many valuable historical surveys of women in music that have appeared in the last several decades, as well as those vital critical studies concerned with a single woman throughout.

In my career as a journalist and musicologist, I have long been drawn to the issue of music in its cultural-historical contexts.[5] In this book, I have portrayed each woman and her musical accomplishments as reflections of the particular time, place, and society in which she lived and worked with the hope of deepening our perspective on the history of music as a whole. Indeed all the arts summon and embody, even internalize, a society's response to itself both in its past and present. This process is a circular one engaging "feedback" in the process of drawing out and playing back the issues and character of its time and place.[6]

I have sought to include areas of music studied by feminist theorists over the last few decades—not least, the issue of "genre-gendering." Accordingly, I have described music written by the four women composers examined here in terms of scale (that is, whether a work is a solo song, cantata, sonata, opera, or allegorical-mythological stage representation, to name a few genres); the size and intended nature of the "performing body," touching on gender if specific; the traditional musical concerns, such as whether a work is vocal, instrumental, or both; the melodic style; the degree of skill shown, for example, by the harmonic and contrapuntal writing; and the reception history of each woman's compositions and performance skill.

In addition, little attention has been paid to the gendering of musical education for women of the past. Institutional musical training for women began to improve only toward the later nineteenth century. By no means less important were a woman's class status and other socioeconomic factors in her particular society, time, and place—an issue additionally encompassing the financial resources available to her pursuit of professional standing in a musical art. There is also the matter of public reception to women's compositions and performance. What type of audience could a pianist or composer, for example, anticipate—a small cluster of listeners in a generally private setting (such as an intimate salon or a royal court chamber), or perhaps a multitude of urban dwellers in a sizable hall or other large public venue. Reception, of course, includes concert reviews of musical performances by professional music critics and assessments of compositions by the daily press and other knowledgeable commentators. For two of the women in this book, I have included reviews by musical journalists, for I have found that they often affect the courses of careers.

In my long search for subjects, I found five women, each worthy of a chapter, who are relatively unknown to the public at large, or to most scholars in the case of three of them—a basic step taken to counteract cultural amnesia. (See p. 4.) Their lives and works in music extend over a broad, diverse scope of sociohistorical periods from the baroque to the present day. Also, the women represent a wide spectrum of cultures ranging from the nobility to the professional ranks of the middle classes. Because my objective has been to expand the arts-minded, general public's perceptions of women in music, I have discussed the work of my five musical artists in the particular environment in which they lived and worked, identifying circumstances and traditions in the sociohistorical milieu of each artist that, to some extent, either allowed her career to flourish or hindered her from realizing her full potential.

Threading through the stories of each of the five women I have chosen from the seventeenth to the twenty-first century are several primary themes affecting her musical pursuits. First, the family history of professional, or at least serious, music making and that family's network of influence and support. Second, the nature of private and/or institutional education these women received, especially in music. Third, the extent and quality of opportunities made available for professional advancement based on the class status and financial situation of each woman's natal and extended family. Fourth, the specific personal challenges and domestic responsibilities—such as marriage and raising children—faced during both youth and adulthood. Fifth, sociopolitical conditions framing each woman's lifetime.[7]

Of the five women I selected for this book, four were published composers, and all five have been recognized as performers to varying degrees. Excellent studies, primarily in German, have been published on Duchess Sophie-Elisabeth of Braunschweig-Lüneburg (chapter 1), Elisabeth-Claude Jacquet de La Guerre (chapter 2), examined and discussed in French and English publications, Josephine Lang (chapter 3) in German and English, and Maria Bach (chapter 4), principally in German. But these studies have been addressed chiefly or even exclusively to musicologists and other professionals in music. The ongoing career of Ann Schein (chapter 5) has yet to be documented thoroughly in a history of performance, though her professional work continues to be remarkable.

The brilliant accomplishments of all five of these women, moreover, need to be introduced to English-speaking lay readers and concert audiences in books, essays, and even program notes; and this information calls for presentation on a broad cultural and sociohistorical basis. Because a relatively extensive amount of material has already been published on Clara Schumann, Fanny Mendelssohn-Hensel, and Amy Beach, they are referred to in this book only in passing. With equal regret, I also had to exclude the countless music patronesses, wonderful cultural "agents" without whom musical life as we know it would be sadly bereft. Consider, for example, such benevolent American patronesses as Elizabeth Sprague Coolidge and Gertrude Clark Whittall, both of whom made incomparable contributions to American culture. If they had been included here, each would have required a whole chapter, if only in light of her magnanimous gifts to the Library of Congress in Washington, D.C.

"Cultural Amnesia"

Over the centuries, countless generations of women musical artists have won varying degrees of success in performing and composing even while charged with the responsibilities of marriage, motherhood, and other types of family caregiving. But, on the whole, only a relatively small number of commendable women in music, especially in composing, have won any substantial notice of their accomplishments. They have worked unaware of, and therefore uninspired by, their female precursors' achievements, most of which have gone unrecorded in major, comprehensive historical annals. The resulting absence of role models from the past combined with a lack of any significant public exposure, such as that offered by large concert halls, has left potential women musical performers and composers—generation after generation—unaware of their female forebears' accomplishments.[8]

This "cultural amnesia" regarding the past (as Jacqueline Letzter and Robert Adelson have termed it recently) has also left the musically minded general public—both concert audiences and readers—equally uninformed and thus confined to a warped concept of the past. As a result of this lack of perspective, women in music have toiled alone, living with the assumption that their art, even its sublime heights, has been practiced through past centuries only by men. Such a view is hardly conducive to impelling younger women talents to carry out their creative impulses, such as composing and performing music—most crucially, at the topmost level. Although referring specifically to nineteenth-century women in music (probably including those whom Mrs. Jameson had in mind), Charles Rosen attributes their "harsh exclusion from history"—composers most of all—principally to the lack of chances to develop their compositional potential, to hear these works performed, and to experience the pride in themselves or by contemporaries and successors that would result.[9]

War

Such cultural amnesia can also result, both directly and indirectly, from political and cultural catastrophes caused by nature or by human malice. At times, such events have driven multitudes—including musicians, artists, and millions in all fields—into exile or simply into annihilation. The devastating ravages and deprivations of war have affected artists throughout the ages. World War II forced Maria Bach (chapter 4) into semi-exile, or perhaps one could say self-exile, in the Vienna Woods. She was allowed, however, to continue composing, confined in an isolated, cramped house with an artist companion. Occasionally, she performed as a piano accompanist of her own works in the Austrian capital itself, though she did so under stringent official observation. (Bach was, in fact, one of a dozen women composers allowed by the Nazi regime to continue pursuing their work in and around Vienna. Other select groups of women composers enjoyed similar privileges in Berlin and Munich.) In stark contrast to Bach's circumstances, Ann Schein (chapter 5) was preparing in America for a professional career during that same global conflict. The war "made available" celebrated pianists as her devoted teachers, émigrés who had resettled in New York City and other cultural centers along the American coasts; the Nazi takeover had driven untold numbers of Europeans in the arts into other, safer countries.[10] The Nazi domination of Europe also led to another type of cultural amnesia. Untold numbers of *verfolgte* (persecuted) composers and performers were denigrated as practicing *entartete Kunst* (degenerate art). These figures included Europe's highest-ranking composers and performing artists: principally Jewish musicians and composers and others whose works were pronounced "too modern." Tragically, they were either sent en masse to death camps or simply vanished—forgotten souls who remain nameless even today. While Maria Bach was safely secluded in a Vienna suburb, for example, the gifted young violinist and conductor Alma Rosé, daughter of the famed Viennese violinist Arnold Rosé and niece of the composer Gustav Mahler, was sent to Auschwitz, the notorious concentration camp in Poland. There she conducted a women's orchestra until her death under mysterious circumstances.[11]

Duchess Sophie-Elisabeth, however, persisted in her musical activities despite living and working in the midst of a conflict, the Thirty Years' War, that stretched through decades. Like this German noblewoman, Elisabeth-Claude Jacquet de la Guerre and Josephine Lang were continually subjected to the political machinations and personal whims of influential courts ruled by sometimes feuding but long-lasting family dynasties that often were even engaged in outright battles.

Five Themes and Variations

Duchess Sophie-Elisabeth (1613–1676) inherited a noble rank with all the privileges and responsibilities that accompanied her seventeenth-century social class, especially the intent of courts on displaying prestige through the arts. On the one hand, the rich musical life of all three of the courts in which she lived provided her with some musical training and the practical knowledge for administering the musical life of her husband's court as an effective impresario. She also acquired the basic skills needed for composition and benefited from a mother and stepmothers who tutored her in other studies that enabled her to pursue literary interests in adulthood. On the other hand, the Thirty Years' War, with all its devastation and miseries, brought critical disruptions in cultural life. This catastrophic conflict forced Sophie-Elisabeth and her family into political exile at Kassel for several years and destroyed her entire inheritance in her home court of Güstrow, leaving Sophie-Elisabeth wholly dependent on her husband's financial resources. The enlightened Duke August, however, supported her musical and literary pursuits. And, while his culturally rich duchy of Wolfenbüttel/Braunschweig also suffered major war damage, his generosity allowed the duchess to spearhead the resuscitation and reorganization of court music there. Primarily because of her noble standing, she acquired the assistance of Dresden's brilliant composer and court *Kapellmeister* Heinrich Schütz, who also at times mentored her in serious composition. Owing to her background, Sophie-Elisabeth's talents as an impresario, patron, and composer provided the means to create Wolfenbüttel's elaborate court *Festspiele,* which contributed to the early development of German opera. She composed prodigiously, had her large-scale works performed, and maintained active relationships with many noted performers and composers. Sophie-Elisabeth's life and works remain largely unknown except in a few German scholarly circles.

Born into the professional bourgeoisie of the late seventeenth and early eighteenth centuries, Elisabeth-Claude Jacquet de La Guerre (1665–1729) was clearly provided with extensive musical training by her family, part of a dynasty of professional musicians among many interrelated families in the vast musical networks of Paris. Jacquet's father, a well-known harpsichord builder and keyboard artist, wasted no time in exhibiting his young daughter's prodigious talents before Louis XIV, resulting in his grant of patronage and a continued musical education under the aegis of two successive mistresses. These Versailles years, moreover, exposed Jacquet de La Guerre to the intense musical atmosphere of the Sun King's magnificent court. She later married into another extended family of musicians, requiring her return to Paris's rich cultural life, one led increasingly by its influential and music-wise urban bourgeoisie. As a result of her familiarity with the interlocking, sometimes competing, environments of Paris and Versailles, Jacquet de La Guerre successfully enlisted her copious talents to pursue a professional musical career as both a harpsichordist/organist and a recognized composer of many genres, including an opera performed in her lifetime.[12]

Josephine Lang (1815–1880) lived and worked during the height of nineteenth-century Germany's romantic era. Like Jacquet, she belonged to the professional middle class and inherited a highly visible musical family from both her mother's and father's family lines. She grew up in the midst of the Munich court's active musical life, which had recently absorbed the brilliant musicians of Mannheim. Scattered references cite her mother as her earliest music teacher, followed by an unknown number of inept tutors, a Mlle. Berlinghof, Lang's paternal grandmother (after the twelve-year-old's mother died), and a not yet identified instructor in piano employed by her stepmother.[13] Although the history of Lang's musical training is spotty at best, the repertoire offered by her teachers leaned heavily on the trivial but virtuoso repertoire of Munich's salons. Apparently, Lang missed any extensive training in the discipline of music theory, a subject essential for serious composers, as Felix Mendelssohn-Bartholdy noted in his tutoring of her in her mid-teens.

During the German romantic period, the art song had blossomed and flourished, for German lyric poetry was reaching its apex, and the revolutionary development of the piano offered dramatic new sonic possibilities. But with marriage, the intensity of Lang's composing waned and—like her mother and grandmother—she abandoned her position as an accomplished court operatic singer in Munich. The times among German-speaking areas were also unsettling, as the sociopolitical *Vormärz* (pre-March) turmoil reached its peak in the later 1840s. When Lang moved to Tübingen with her new husband, a professor at the university there, she focused on her role as a music teacher, wife, and mother, leaving little opportunity for composing or singing. Marriage, in fact, spelled the virtual end of any close attention on her part to those professions for which her cultural background had prepared her. Furthermore, she was widowed early, burdened with raising six children, some seriously ill. Yet Lang directed a salon in her home, where important figures in various arts gathered regularly.

The family of Maria Bach (1896–1978) belonged to the cultural aristocracy of Vienna. But, while the Austro-Hungarian capital continued to thrive as a brilliant cultural mecca, the empire was slowly and inexorably disintegrating. Partly owing to the decline, many Viennese were subject to a societal malaise, perhaps explaining the personal bitterness that haunted the Bachs and passed down to Maria and her sisters. Although Bach's mother was a recognized singer and her father a highly skilled amateur violinist, her parents forged a cloistered existence for their daughters. Their affluence afforded a home secluded from other children and a totally private musical and academic education assigned to family-approved tutors. Yet the Bach parents' abundant financial resources also enabled them to hold frequent Sunday musicales, whose guests included many celebrated representatives of Viennese high culture. After their early childhood, the Bach sisters were allowed to participate in the home performances. But none of the four Bach sisters ever entirely escaped the family's melancholia and apparently emotional preference for isolation from society in general, a preference that seems born of her family's inbred social elitism. Also feeding the family's malaise were Austria's defeats in two World Wars, conflicts linked by the devastating loss of imperial political power, serious inflation following the first war, then the worldwide Great Depression and the ensuing Nazi period.

Yet Maria Bach continued to perform her compositions and those of others in women's musical organizations in Vienna—at times in major concert halls—until late in life. Ironically, this relatively secluded existence also spelled eventual financial ruin for her and her sisters, for the legal expenses generated by the competing Bach sisters in their heated disputes over their family inheritance depleted most of their assets. Yet throughout the years of World War II, Maria Bach was one of a privileged group of women musicians (see p. 126) allowed to continue composing and performing in Vienna. Bach, whose musical education had always been private, never left the city, never held a professional position, and never married or had children, although she had male companions, the last and most devoted one a professional artist.

But history does not stop with the past. In an instant, the present becomes part of earlier times. This point of view, the perception of time as ever-evolving, led me to include the chapter on Ann Schein (b. 1939). I have followed her career on and off since I first heard her in a music student competition (in which I participated). But I followed her music making from a distance as a listener and later as a music critic. As I assembled the biographical histories of my other subjects, I realized that some of the major themes at play in Schein's personal and professional life were also part of my other subjects' lives and careers—themes such as her family's musical network developed over the generations, its financial resources, her musical training, the public's appreciation, or perception, of her as a talented artist, and her domestic responsibilities as an adult. The significance of those factors parallels that in the careers of many other musicians—of both genders and through history. Looking, then, at these social, political, and cultural issues in the lives of my subjects has been enlightening. The recognition of the similarities among them all brought me to include Schein as an example of the contemporary position of women in music against the backdrop of women in music over the centuries.

In contrast with the other women discussed in this book, moreover, I also wanted to include Schein as someone at the living edge of the continuum in Western society, a non-European whose career centers on public concert performance. A present-day artist, Schein can speak about herself firsthand, adding a further dimension to our understanding of her and casting light on earlier women in music in a way not possible with those of the past. It was through interviews, moreover, that I truly began to know Schein rather than observing and hearing her only from afar, unlike our knowledge of earlier women whom we know only from secondhand information. Also, Schein is one of my subjects who has continued to enjoy a successful decades-long, multifaceted career. Her success, if not Van Cliburn's and Vladimir Horowitz's versions of celebrity, deserves recognition not only by music critics, but also by historians of the arts.

These themes include the artist's immediate family and its position in the arts, particularly during the artist's youth; the economic resources available to her; the forces active in her social and historical environment; the extent of her education; the extended family's network of professional connections in her field; her own personal interactions during her lifetime; references to her domestic roles; and the public reception of her art. Consideration of these factors can contribute to our understanding not only of a specific art but, more to the point, can deepen our perception of music's place in the grand design of women in the arts overall both now and in the past.

All in all, a previous editor, William Frohlich's, idea clearly resonated with me. Accordingly, it is my hope that this account of five women and their professional musical accomplishments, seen in light of their very diverse cultures and periods in history, will contribute to a deeper understanding of musical life in Western society as a whole. As we can see with these women in music, the present illuminates the past as much as the past informs the present.

CHAPTER ONE

Duchess Sophie-Elisabeth

*Composer, Harpsichordist, and Impresario
in the North German Baroque*

Born a princess at the court of Güstrow, an active north German cultural center, Duchess Sophie-Elisabeth of Braunschweig-Lüneburg (August 20, 1613–July 12, 1676) made a distinctive mark on the course of German baroque music (fig. 1). Her noble rank and multifaceted talents gave her access to leading avenues of German cultural life, above all in music, along with a number of the most distinguished composers and performers of the seventeenth century. Yet nobility directly presented her with the challenges of a turbulent time and place in Germany and throughout Europe. An ambitious and effective impresario, an ardent arts patron, and a serious, if not exceptional, composer, she triumphed nevertheless over many adversities, managing to restructure the organization of music at her husband's court of Wolfen-büttel (and at the duchy's secondary residence at Braunschweig) in Lower Saxony and to transform the court into an important center of German musical life. She was supported in this accomplishment by her husband, Duke August the Younger, himself the founder of a magnificent library still important today. Sophie-Elisabeth also enjoyed the aid of the celebrated composer Heinrich Schütz (1585–1672) while he was *Kapellmeister* at the nearby Saxon court at Dresden, a brilliant musical center. Schütz proved a valuable older "colleague" in helping Sophie-Elisabeth to revive musical performance at Wolfenbüttel while also mentoring her in composition. She produced many *Festspiele,* large-scale staged works consisting of spoken dialogues alternating with instrumental pieces, vocal music, and dances, with massive sets and participants in costumes. The *Festspiel* genre made a modest contribution to the development of German opera. In addition, Sophie-Elisabeth composed numerous sacred songs and motets (of the Pietist devotional persuasion) despite her modest compositional skills. Born into her father's musically intense court at Güstrow, she also spent several years of her youth in wartime exile at Kassel, the culturally active court of a distant relative. Sophie-Elisabeth was therefore well prepared to administer and support musical life at her husband's court. And she did so with a strong sense of reality and initiative. She was a dedicated composer but, above all, she was a true impresario.

SERENISSIMA ET ILLUSTRISSIMA
PRINCIPISSA AC DOMINA, DOMINA
SOPHIA ELISABETHA é STIRPE MEGA,
POLIT: PROGEN: DUCISSA BRUNOVIC:
ET LUNÆBURGENS:*etc:*
G.Müller Exudit.   C.Buno fecit.*

Figure 1. Duchess Sophie-Elisabeth of Braunschweig-Lüneburg. Copper engraving by G. Müller. Lüneburg: Conrad Buno, after 1635. Courtesy of the Herzog August Bibliothek, Wolfenbüttel.

According to the eulogy given at Sophie-Elisabeth's funeral service, she had inherited a wide range of royal titles from both her ancestors and those of her husband, including the following titles of her forebears: Duke and Duchess, Margrave and Margravess, Elector and Electoress, Count and Countess, King, and Prince and Princess. Many of these forebears held multiple titles from many states or other types of territories, including Mecklenburg, Schleswig-Holstein, Sweden, Hesse, Brandenburg-Prussia, Denmark (combined with Norway), Stettin/Pomerania, Saxony, Westphalia, the Palatinate Rhineland, and Bavaria. This personal history helps explain Sophie-Elisabeth's long official title: besides gaining her husband August the Younger's realms—making her Duchess of Braunschweig-Lüneburg—her natal title was Princess and Lady Sophie-Elisabeth, Duchess of Mecklenburg, Princess of Wenden, Schwerin and Ratzeburg, Countess of Schwerin and the States of Rostock and Stargard.[1]

Yvonne Demoskoff has recently added another genealogical connection with

Sophie-Elisabeth, but this time concerning the generations following the duchess. Tracing the ancestors of England's royal Windsor line, Demoskoff claims that
Sophie-Elisabeth, among others listed, was a direct ancestor of Britain's Queen
Victoria (1819–1901). Therefore, we might add that the German duchess was also
a forebear of the current Queen Elizabeth II and her royal descendants.[2]

This chapter aims to spell out Sophie-Elisabeth's many accomplishments, as
well as the cultural legacies that surrounded her and nourished her talents.

Childhood: Three Mothers (1613–1635)

An imposing Renaissance-era castle looms over the modest north German town
of Güstrow, a two-hour drive by car northwest of Berlin. Sophie-Elisabeth's
birth and childhood were spent at this longtime ducal court. (In modern times,
Güstrow-Mecklenburg belonged to East Germany for nearly five decades until
the official German reunification in 1990.) The castle, other court edifices, and
the town's churches that she would have known have surprisingly survived
the onslaughts of war and changing regimes over many centuries. But Sophie-
Elisabeth and her cultural achievements have been virtually forgotten, except
for a recent scholarly study—accessible only to readers of German—by Karl
Wilhelm Geck. The castle in which she grew up, for example, is now a museum
that focuses on the male line of Sophie-Elisabeth's Mecklenburg family. And,
on becoming duchess, she moved to her husband's court at Wolfenbüttel, where
the paintings in the court library's entrance hall display only her husband's line
of ducal succession (fig. 2).

Princess Sophie-Elisabeth was the older daughter of Duke Johann Albrecht II
of Mecklenburg (1590–1636) and his first wife, Margarete Elisabeth (1584–1616).[3]
The duke was a Reformed (Calvinist) convert from Lutheranism. At that time,
all important Protestant disputes between German Reformed and Orthodox Lutheran churches included the concept of the Last Supper and the doctrines of
transubstantiation and predestination, as well as the degree to which art music
should function in the liturgy.

Apart from the forced exile of her family from 1628 to about 1631, Sophie-
Elisabeth spent her first two decades at Güstrow, residence of the north German
duchy of Mecklenburg. Settled c. 300 B.C.E. by the Slavic Wends and primarily
agricultural from ancient times, the area was divided during the Middle Ages
among various princes, knights, cities, and monasteries. By the mid-sixteenth
century it had become predominately Orthodox Lutheran. Although Johann
Albrecht had converted to the Reformed faith from Orthodox Lutheranism in
1611, he practiced tolerance for his Lutheran subjects.[4]

At Güstrow, Sophie-Elisabeth's father maintained a thriving musical establishment, with a sizable contingent of English virtuoso performers in its orchestra.

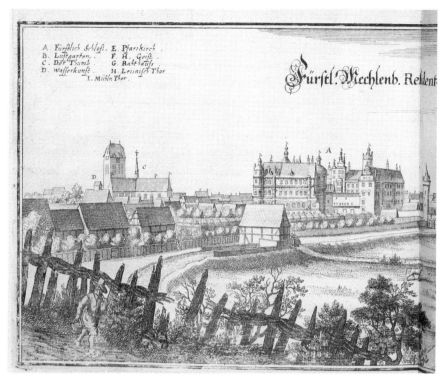

Figure 2. Güstrow-Mecklenburg, showing the ducal residence, Schloss Güstrow (1558–1589). Sophie-Elisabeth lived here until her marriage. Copper engraving by Calv. Merian, after 1650. Courtesy of the Herzog August Bibliothek, Wolfenbüttel.

Sophie-Elisabeth and her sister Christine Margarete (c. 1616–1666) thus had rich opportunities to study the lute and gamba. Their lute studies extended from 1622 to 1632 with Wilhelm Westphal; from 1625 to 1626 with John (Johann) Stanley, a distinguished English musician and later Kassel court *Kapellmeister*; and with Michael Rode c. 1626. They took gamba lessons between 1618 and 1619 with the virtuoso violinist-violist-composer William Brade, another Englishman and briefly Johann Albrecht's *Kapellmeister*. From 1626 to 1627 the sisters studied with the English violist Walter Rowe. Besides overseeing his daughters' musical training, Sophie-Elisabeth's father also played an influential role in their religious education. He was little involved, however, in their general "academic" studies.[5]

Motherless from the age of three, Sophie-Elisabeth was left in the care and tutelage of two successive stepmothers at the Güstrow court. Both of these women remained childless, which may explain the amount of time—from today's perspective—that they could devote to Sophie-Elisabeth. (This comment does not take into consideration the extraordinarily high infant mortality rate at that time. Perhaps Sophie-Elisabeth's two stepmothers gave birth, but their infants died early.) In 1618, two years after the death of Sophie-Elisabeth's mother, Johann Albrecht married Elisabeth of Hesse-Kassel (1596–1625), oldest daughter of the Calvinist and Francophile Landgrave Moritz "the Learned" of Hesse-Kassel, whose court, too, was intensely involved in cultural activities. (See p. 16.) Heir to her father's cosmopolitan outlook in intellectual and cultural matters, Elisabeth was educated privately in the liberal arts by teachers in the school founded by her father. Extraordinarily gifted, she was fluent in French, Italian, and several other languages. A "proto-Pietist," she studied theology avidly and therefore could have influenced Sophie-Elisabeth's later Pietist outlook. Elisabeth wrote poetry, composed music (though none of her compositions has survived), reportedly had a beautiful voice, and demonstrated remarkable skill on several instruments. Her tutors in music included the French lutenist Victor de Montbuysson and possibly Heinrich Schütz, one of the most important composers of the earlier German baroque. Schütz, at that time the Kassel court's promising young second organist, had returned from study in Venice in 1613. He would figure later as Sophie-Elisabeth's chief musical mentor at Wolfenbüttel.[6]

Following her personal convictions, Elisabeth of Hesse-Kassel involved herself directly for nine years in the education, including religious and musical tutoring, of the young Sophie-Elisabeth and her sister. Elisabeth's upbringing amid the intense musical activities at her father's court prepared her to be duchess at Güstrow, expanding its instrumental forces and actively encouraging festive court representations.[7] Thus as a teacher and active musical administrator, she acted as an influential role model for her young charges at Güstrow. With adulthood, Sophie-Elisabeth would follow Elisabeth's example as an important musical impresario.

Elisabeth died at twenty-nine in 1625, when Sophie-Elisabeth was thirteen. Widowed for a second time, Johann Albrecht took a third wife on May 7, 1626. His new bride was Princess Eleonore Marie (1600–1657), daughter of the Calvinist-Francophile Prince Christian I of Anhalt-Bernburg. Like Elisabeth of Hesse-Kassel, Eleonore had been well schooled in religion, languages, and music (both vocal and instrumental). This background prepared her for her new role at Güstrow in the continued education of Sophie-Elisabeth and her sister. And she assumed that role wholeheartedly. Eleonore was a founding member of the "Académie des Loyales," an exclusive Reformed society of intellectual female nobility sharing accomplishments "of womanly virtue" such as fluency in French and Italian, skill in composing poetry and performing music, and the impelling goal of contributing to a "national renewal," as Geck defines it, of German culture. Her humanistic background, therefore, closely paralleled that of Johann Albrecht's previous wives, lending some continuity to the education of his two daughters, and also providing them with a degree of domestic stability.[8]

The First Exile (1628–1632)

We see then that the young Sophie-Elisabeth was provided with consistent mothering, abundant intellectual and musical stimulation, and a well-grounded education in accordance with her times that prepared her for future roles as a musical impresario and patron, as well as a composer and poet. And it is clear that, besides the roles of his three wives, her father's own intellectual and musical leanings, as well as his very astute choice of mates, played a crucial part in his children's upbringing.

Called by some the greatest European conflict before the French Revolution, the Thirty Years' War (1618–1648), seemed at first to affect neutral Mecklenburg only slightly—that is, until the summer of 1627, when Sophie-Elisabeth was a young teenager. This war, in fact, consisted of many wars covering a wide complex of shifting political and religious alliances. The turmoil pitted Protestants against Catholics, the latter championed by the Austro-Hungarian Empire, which resisted losing areas struggling for independence from the Habsburg dynasty. Involving Germany, France, and many other northern and southern European states, the war caused massive relocations of populations and created terrifying uncertainties. Death, misery, and destruction rained down on Europe, most of all on German soil, which bore the brunt of the battles. Affecting all ranks of Europe's hierarchical society, the war severely constricted or virtually eliminated the practice of music and other arts at numerous courts, not least those of north Germany.[9] Mecklenburg, Sophie-Elisabeth's birthplace, belonged to Lower Saxony and therefore was pitted (together with the Wolfenbüttel court, Sophie-Elisabeth's future homeland) against imperial Austria. It was in the service of Austrian Emperor Ferdinand II that Duke Albrecht von Wallenstein captured Mecklenburg on December 18, 1627, establishing his residence at Güstrow.[10]

Because of the dire conditions of wartime, Johann Albrecht II fled his Güstrow realm on May 12, 1628, taking with him his wife Eleonore, Sophie-Elisabeth (now fifteen), and her sister, Christine Margarete (twelve). Conceivably, Sophie-Elisabeth as an older sister might have already been playing a maternal role in relation to her sister—that is, taking charge. The ducal family arrived, impoverished, in Magdeburg on May 16. The sisters probably were placed under the protection of their step-grandfather, Moritz "the Learned" (1572–1632; reigned 1592–1627), the Hessian Landgrave at Kassel and a member of the Reformed Church. The princesses' parents spent their exile in Lübeck. Both sisters, already twice left motherless, had lost their homeland and now were separated from their father and second stepmother at a considerable distance for nearly four years. According to today's outlook, at least, these were crucial teenage years. One wonders how much parental support Moritz provided. How alone, or even abandoned, did Sophie-Elisabeth and Christine Margarete feel at this point in their young lives?

But, with its long and distinguished musical history, the culturally intense Kassel court proved a positive factor, at least indirectly, in Sophie-Elisabeth's life. And Moritz was related by both blood and marriage to her father; his daughter Elisabeth had been Johann Albrecht II's second wife.

A sometime composer himself, Moritz was an informed patron of music and the theater.[11] Like Schütz, the young Moritz had studied composition under Kassel *Kapellmeister* Georg Otto (c. 1550–1618), and later (1598) established Kassel's Collegium Mauritianum, which Schütz, then a Kassel court choirboy (1599–1608), attended. In 1609 Moritz had even sent Schütz to Venice to study composition with St. Mark's celebrated organist Giovanni Gabrieli (c. 1553–1556 to 1612) for three years (1609–1612), after which the young composer served as Kassel's second court organist. In 1614 Schütz moved to Dresden, where he became *Kapellmeister* officially in 1619.

When Sophie-Elisabeth arrived in Kassel in 1628, Moritz had just officially abdicated his landgraveship for political reasons. His son Wilhelm V (reigned 1627–1637) actively carried on his father's passionate support of music and the theater, but a devastating plague outbreak amid the turmoil of the Thirty Years' War led to Wilhelm's premature death in 1637. And the war's impact soon brought about the dissolution of the Kassel court chapel itself.

The Moritz-Schütz relationship testifies to the vital cultural interconnections among the courts of Kassel (Hesse), Güstrow (Mecklenburg), Wolfenbüttel (Lower Saxony), and Dresden (Saxony). One might include Venice to some extent, for Karl Wilhelm Geck even claims that Moritz virtually created a "Kassel school" of composition strongly reflecting the influence of Giovanni Gabrieli's Venetian polychoral style that Schütz, among others, carried back to Germany. Moritz also corresponded with the well-known composers Michael Praetorius (1571–1621), Hans Leo Hassler (1564–1612), and John Dowland (1563–1626), all of whom served at various times at Wolfenbüttel. (In fact, the early Thirty Years' War period marked the initial infiltration of an Italianate figural style meant to meet the then-current aesthetic turn toward moving the affections and stirring emotions through music.)[12]

The Return to Güstrow and Marriage (1632–1642)

Little data has survived to tell us about Sophie-Elisabeth's personal experiences at Kassel. We cannot, in fact, pick up the threads of her life until the spring of 1632, when, about nineteen years old, she had returned with her family to the Güstrow court. (By late 1631, troops under Sweden's King Gustav Adolf had liberated her father's court from Habsburg forces, allowing Johann Albrecht II to resume control of his duchy. But the war's worst devastation was yet to visit Güstrow.) By July 1635, a degree of musical life had been temporarily reestablished there. Two of the revitalized court's musicians were former Dresden court choirboys and composition students of Schütz. He himself had probably visited the Güstrow court c. 1634, perhaps reviving some professional ties that set the stage for Sophie-Elisabeth's future connections with him.[13]

Sophie-Elisabeth's life took another important turn on July 13, 1635, when the twenty-two-year-old princess married Duke August the Younger of Braunschweig-Lüneburg (fig. 3). The duke (1579–1666) was a highly educated patron of scholarship and the arts, reigning at Wolfenbüttel, his duchy's chief residence, from 1634 to his death. His second wife, Dorothea, Princess of Anhalt-Zerbst, had died in childbirth in September 1634. At his marriage to Sophie-Elisabeth, the duke already had fathered four children.

Duke August was distantly related to Sophie-Elisabeth by blood, marriage, and political connections with her father at Güstrow and with Landgrave Moritz at Kassel. It is highly likely, therefore, that—according to centuries-old tradition—Sophie-Elisabeth's marriage had been arranged. As part of the wedding sermon, the pastor cited Genesis, Ephesians, and other well-known biblical references as commands to the young bride: for example, "love and obey your bridegroom," "subject your will to his, . . . as Sarah was to Abraham, . . . do this, as do the people who follow Christ.")[14]

Sophie-Elisabeth's marriage proved fortunate for her personally and valuable for the arts in this part of north Germany. First, the wedding and subsequent move to Wolfenbüttel spared her physically from the most devastating period experienced by her native Güstrow and the rest of the Mecklenburg duchy during

Figure 3. Duke August the Younger of Braunschweig-Lüneburg. Oil portrait by H. Boiling, 1666. Courtesy of the Herzog August Bibliothek, Wolfenbüttel.

the Thirty Years' War. With the fighting especially fierce in Mecklenburg from 1637 to 1644, the Güstrow court and its musical life, in fact, ceased to function for several years.[15] As a result, Sophie-Elisabeth even lost her dowry, becoming financially dependent completely on her husband besides assuming new domestic duties. Yet, as described later in this chapter, the duke proved responsive to many of her ideas regarding court music.

Second, as had Güstrow in Sophie-Elisabeth's early years, Wolfenbüttel and its secondary seat at nearby Braunschweig provided the new duchess with an exceptionally strong heritage of cultural life, not the least part of which included music. From his Wolfenbüttel court residence, temporarily relocated at Braunschweig from 1635 to 1643 because of the ongoing war, Duke August ruled one of the largest and most politically powerful areas of Lower Saxony.

Third, Sophie-Elisabeth's humanist background fit in perfectly with the Wolfenbüttel court, a sophisticated center of German intellectuals and literati. She participated in several of Wolfenbüttel's exclusive literary-arts societies that she had joined early in her marriage: the Académie des Loyales, the Tugendliche Gesellschaft, and the Fruchtbringende Gesellschaft, in which she was given the pseudonyms *die Fortbringende, die Gutwillige,* and *die Befreiende,* respectively.[16] Dedicated to the cultivation of works in the German language, Wolfenbüttel's Fruchtbringende Gesellschaft, however, offered full membership only to men. But with her status as Duke August's wife, Sophie-Elisabeth was thus admitted as an honorary member, one of the earliest women accepted into this society. Her participation in these organizations contributed significantly toward maintaining the Wolfenbüttel court as a major center of contemporary German and French literature; for, in the ducal family, Geck notes, "all the novels that were right in fashion were read."[17]

Sophie-Elisabeth and her husband, moreover, personally shared many ideals, not the least of which was patronage of the arts. The duchess's marriage into this dukedom expanded the "network" of courts and their interconnected cultural life to which she had access. With Wolfenbüttel and Braunschweig, for example, Sophie-Elisabeth also inherited authority over Duke August's minor residences at the musically rich towns of Lüneburg and Celle.[18]

The newlyweds, however, immediately faced grueling hardships because of developments in the Thirty Years' War. Late in this massive conflagration, Duke August was finally enabled to undertake the rebuilding of Wolfenbüttel's celebrated castle fortification, damaged by the ravages of the invading military forces. He also supervised the creation of a substantially redesigned town plan largely because he had pursued a new defensive, rather than a medieval offensive, course for Wolfenbüttel during the war years.[19] For, at the time of August's succession, his residence at Wolfenbüttel was occupied by Austrian imperial troops, forcing him and his family to live a more sheltered existence for eight years in neighboring Braunschweig.

By the early 1640s—that is, in the first decade of Sophie-Elisabeth's marriage—astute political maneuvers during the Thirty Years' War, which extended officially until 1648, had brought a separate peace treaty between Duke August and Austrian Emperor Ferdinand III, resulting in the establishment of the duchy's neutrality. In an ironic, even clever move, the Wolfenbüttel duke had thereby won the favor of the Habsburgs, securing a measure of political stability for the Guelph court.[20] As a consequence, the duke perhaps also hoped to acquire some sort of connection with Habsburg Vienna's thriving court cultural life.

Court-town relationships at Braunschweig did not always proceed smoothly. The town's citizenry—led by a Hansa-rooted burgher class—resented the ducal family's very presence as a threat to its independent status. (From the late Middle Ages, Braunschweig, only a few miles north of Wolfenbüttel, had thrived as an active Hanseatic town with a predominantly commercially oriented middle-class population of wealthy and influential merchants, brewers, and shipowners.)[21] The move to Braunschweig was the second uprooting the duchess endured from her home, Kassel being the first. One can fairly assume that the hostile local atmosphere among August's closest Braunschweig subjects could hardly have uplifted the morale of the ducal family, especially during the early years, with its growing size. Yet, in some ways, musical life in nearby Braunschweig continued to flourish. The town, for example, enjoyed the many talents of Delphin Strunck, an important composer and organist in Braunschweig in the 1640s. He, in fact, often performed Schütz's music there.[22] It was at the Wolfenbüttel establishment, therefore, that Sophie-Elisabeth came into her own in music as in other aspects of the court's cultural life.

The Hansa Legacy

In August's day, Wolfenbüttel and Braunschweig, like Sophie-Elisabeth's native Güstrow, were still enjoying a rich cultural legacy inherited from centuries-old membership in north Germany's Hanseatic League, a monopoly that from the thirteenth century on had united German merchants in a federation controlling northern European trade. Though vastly weakened by Sophie-Elisabeth's lifetime, the Hanseatic bourgeoisie had firmly established a value system centered on economic gain, with social status dependent on wealth rather than birth. And, as typically in Europe over the centuries, political power was lavishly and prestigiously displayed through the arts.[23] (In 1651, Schütz mentioned that he might take a position at "a Hanseatic city.")[24] Only sporadically paid at Dresden, the sixty-six-year-old composer saw potential in imperial and Hanseatic cities for a more lucrative professional situation. Music, even singing, in the homes of Hansa burghers—all Protestant—became a status symbol of their advanced level of education. But by Sophie-Elisabeth's lifetime, the Mecklenburg and Braunschweig dukes, like other north Germans of their rank, had gained virtually all economic and military authority over their once-independent Hansa towns.[25] Though no longer a controlling political and economic force, the Hansa had nevertheless bestowed a rich and far-reaching heritage of socioeconomic and cultural traditions on much of the north German bourgeoisie, including that of Güstrow, Wolfenbüttel, and Braunschweig. Hanseatic prosperity in both these dimensions endured through many generations, even centuries, also enriching Europe as a whole. Sophie-Elisabeth, along with her Güstrow and Wolfenbüttel families, reaped many of the benefits of this Hansa heritage.

Sophie-Elisabeth's Cultural Mecca: Wolfenbüttel/Braunschweig

The Hansa legacy had played no small part in the active cultural life that welcomed Sophie-Elisabeth at the Wolfenbüttel court. As the new duchess of this establishment, Sophie-Elisabeth gained control over a temporarily sizable ducal corps of musicians, an ensemble lavishly endowed earlier by Duke Friedrich Ulrich (reigned 1613–1634) and further developed by his son and her husband, August the Younger (ruled 1634–1666) himself.[26]

Religion, too, played a vital role in Sophie-Elisabeth's life, for Protestantism was expanding but also rapidly evolving—that is, splintering—into various subbranches of belief. The ducal residence until 1753, Wolfenbüttel had adopted a strong Reformed faith (also her father's persuasion at Güstrow, as described above) that had earlier replaced the court's Orthodox Lutheranism, this change considerably affecting musical life at Wolfenbüttel. In accordance with the rather conservative view of Reformed believers, Duke Heinrich the Younger (1489–1568) had been Luther's strongest Reformed opponent in north Germany. Therefore, according to German Calvinist practice, he restricted Wolfenbüttel's musical forces to only a small court ensemble of five trumpeters and a timpanist, thus supporting no resident instrumental or vocal ensemble of any size. In fact, only four singers, four string players, an organist, trumpeters, and timpani were allowed until 1571, early in the reign of Duke Julius (ruled 1568–1589). The following duke, Heinrich Julius (ruled 1589–1613), drew the well-known English composer-lutenist John Dowland (1563–1626) to his court briefly in 1594. This duke also tightened connections between civic, church, and court music.[27]

It was in Braunschweig, where the ducal family was lodged in exile, that Sophie-Elisabeth gave birth to three children between 1636 and 1639: Ferdinand Albrecht (b. May 22, 1636), Marie Elisabeth (b. January 27, 1638), and Christian Franz (b. August 1, 1639—d. later that same year).[28] Besides caring for her two surviving offspring, Sophie-Elisabeth assumed the responsibility of raising her husband's four children from his earlier marriages, totaling six offspring altogether for the couple. There is no record of her emotional outlook as a mother but, from today's point of view, we might assume that this particular burden alone showed Sophie-Elisabeth to have accepted her responsibilities according to the societal standards of her day. And she herself had not forgotten losing her own mother at an early age, an experience perhaps strengthening her resolve to help August's motherless children.

In 1642, six years before the Peace of Westphalia officially ended the Thirty Years' War, the ducal family could finally return to Wolfenbüttel and the castle "Dankwarderode," built in the mid-twelfth century by Duke Henry the Lion and newly restored by August. The town of Wolfenbüttel, however, had been depleted by the devastations of the Thirty Years' War; and August the Younger's court musical establishment had fallen into disarray. Sophie-Elisabeth's native duchy of Mecklenburg-Güstrow had lost two-thirds of its population. In Hesse-Kassel, her temporary asylum, half the population had either died from war-related causes such as starvation or had emigrated to safer areas. In Germany as a whole, in fact, a vast number of people had been killed, along with horrible devastation and a massive, confusing displacement of the population. In Sophie-Elisabeth's Braunschweig-Lüneburg and in Hesse-Kassel, for example, waves of Protestant Huguenot refugees, fleeing persecution and murder, poured into these areas from France, bringing with them a cultural inheritance foreign to the Germans.

A Duchess as Impresario

Three years later, in the spring of 1645, war continued to rage, wreaking further havoc in the cultural life of Güstrow, Wolfenbüttel, and elsewhere in Germany. In 1636, Heinrich Schütz had written: "The laudable art of music has not only greatly declined but at some places even been abandoned."[29] The splendid Dresden court, for example, where the famous composer was *Kapellmeister,* had lost many choral and instrumental members and was behind in paying them.[30] By 1645, musical life at Wolfenbüttel, too, had further deteriorated, the few surviving court accounting records revealing a dire financial situation. With his political prestige at stake in the eyes of competing courts, Duke August could not boast of even the minimal contingent of trumpeters and choirboys expected at that time for a court of this size.[31]

Because the war—even by 1645—was consuming so much of his attention to the court as a whole, Duke August officially transferred his administration of court music—its reorganization, revitalization, and the payment of its musicians—to his wife, whose visionary outlook and organizational gifts allowed her to play a major role in the restructuring of Wolfenbüttel's court musical establishment.[32] She had truly become Wolfenbüttel's First Lady. (One recalls the cultural role that Jacqueline Kennedy played during her husband's presidency.)

Sophie-Elisabeth, however, was actually in charge of court music before 1645 since the political forces associated with the war had left Duke August unable to fulfill all his official duties. As early as October 11, 1641, while August, his twenty-eight-year-old wife, and their children were still exiled in Braunschweig, Sophie-

Elisabeth had written her husband a request that reveals her compassionate and benevolent sense of authority for her subjects. This letter also underlines her personal spirit of initiative, perseverance, determination, and resourcefulness, as well as her formal but tactful approach to a problem. Addressing the duke with praise for his "inborn goodness and great discretion," she admitted, though reluctantly, that she was "financially completely dependent" on his resources.[33]

Therefore the duchess felt obliged to reprimand the duke politely but realistically: "Your subjects can no longer remain dispirited because of your failure to pay their salaries, for, especially among those worst off . . ., they have only enough to pay for a pair of shoes and nothing more. . . . I hope that I do not 'offend' you with this supplication [meaning her demand that he give her the money for the overdue salaries]. It is my duty to care for those who serve you. In addition, there is the danger of losing all your personnel, which you would certainly not stand for, considering your inborn goodness and great discretion. Since I . . . am now financially dependent on your gentle hand completely, I have no other choice but to turn to you."[34] (For, as explained earlier, she had lost her entire Güstrow family inheritance.)

The dire situation described in Sophie-Elisabeth's letter was not new. Even earlier, she had been involved in Wolfenbüttel's musical affairs. In 1638—only three years after her marriage—the Wolfenbüttel court had lost its *Kapellmeister*, Stephan Körner. As a result, Sophie-Elisabeth unofficially took charge of the reorganization of the court's music that eventually extended to 1648, the year the war ended.[35] And, by her official appointment in 1645, the duchess's children and stepchildren perhaps needed her attention less than in their younger years.

"Networking": Sophie-Elisabeth and Heinrich Schütz, Collaborator in the Reorganization and Composition Mentor

A classic humanist, Duchess Sophie-Elisabeth was wise in the ways of the cultural world, seeking out support wherever needed in her overseeing of the arts at Wolfenbüttel. Of all those she enlisted to fulfill this responsibility, she turned most often to Heinrich Schütz (1585–1672), a leading composer of the German baroque. Sophie-Elisabeth herself had enjoyed amicable ties with Schütz since her Güstrow youth. And he had maintained close professional ties with Wolfenbüttel since 1638, when Körner had left this court. Director of music at the nearby Dresden court, Schütz offered his help to Sophie-Elisabeth in both the reorganization of Wolfenbüttel court music and her compositional pursuits, the influential composer serving in this capacity as an occasional and persuasive mentor. Schütz scholar Hans Joachim Moser goes so far as to call Sophie-Elisabeth's relationship with the composer a relationship that Moser considers a musically successful one of like souls.[36] Schütz had possibly visited her father's court at Güstrow c. 1633, when she was about twenty.[37] And, in Schütz's youth, he had forged strong ties with

Landgrave Moritz "the Learned," that same Landgrave of Hesse (and relative) who had sheltered Sophie-Elisabeth and her sister in Kassel during their exile there.

Schütz first visited Duke August at Wolfenbüttel in 1638 (when Körner had abandoned August's court) and at various times thereafter. Crucial for the reorganization of music at that court, Schütz stayed at August's court from early 1642 to the second half of 1644 and from March to April 1645. It is puzzling, however, that he—as *Kapellmeister* of Dresden as early as 1619—would draw on his own court's poor and endangered musical resources to aid Wolfenbüttel. Schütz was also aware of other German courts, too, that sorely lacked sufficient musical forces. Yet the composer arranged to send additional Dresden singers, including some of his choirboys, and instrumentalists to Wolfenbüttel. Helping Wolfenbüttel also was made more complicated because Dresden's musical forces were mostly Italian, while, in contrast, all Wolfenbüttel's ensemble members were German.[38]

By 1638, Schütz had good reasons for seeking a collaboration with Wolfenbüttel.[39] At that time, the composer had virtually begged his patron, the Saxon elector Johann Georg, for permission to live and work for a year in Lower Saxony, which then, besides the ducal seat at Wolfenbüttel and its territory, also controlled Sophie-Elisabeth's native duchy of Mecklenburg, with which, as discussed earlier, Schütz also had had a professional connection. Among the examples of teamwork carried out jointly by Schütz and Sophie-Elisabeth was their traveling to various German cities to decide on procuring a *Positiv* (a small organ) for Braunschweig or Wolfenbüttel. After they decided on one, she was to send money for this instrument to the Dresden *Kapellmeister,* who would purchase the instrument for August's court for her.[40] And, in a letter to Sophie-Elisabeth of March 1645, Schütz, dedicated to continuing this collaboration, advised her to restructure systematically all Wolfenbüttel's musical forces, insisting that "neither *falsetti* nor eunuchs should be overlooked in reviving the court Kantorei."[41] His collaboration in this project extended into the 1650s.

In 1655, moreover, Duke August, at his wife's instigation, appointed Schütz *Kapellmeister von Haus aus* (in absentia) at his Lower Saxon court. On Schütz's recommendation as consultant on the reorganization of the court music, Duke August had named Johann Jakob Löwe "von Eisenach" (1629–1703) as resident *Kapellmeister* that same year. (Löwe had been splendidly trained in Vienna and composed early examples of *Singspiele* for Wolfenbüttel).[42] In 1655, also with Schütz's advice, August named Löwe's close friend Julius Johann Weiland (?-1663) as a court musician and, in 1660, as vice-*Kapellmeister.*

Löwe was a gifted young composer of Thuringian family background who had been educated at Vienna's imperial court, coincidentally like the composer Maria Bach's ancestors. Löwe was later a protégé of Schütz, possibly even studying with him in Dresden, this early association forging another tie with Schütz and later with Sophie-Elisabeth at Wolfenbüttel. Löwe held the Wolfenbüttel *Kapellmeister* post from 1655 to 1663, contributing significantly to the court's active repertoire. His *Singspiele*—pastoral-mythological dramas with inserted musical sections— were important in the early development of German opera. Löwe's inclusion of ballets introduced the Wolfenbüttel court to the popular French baroque *grand ballet de cour,* a genre that had impressed him while visiting the Versailles court of Louis XIV. (See chapter 2.) But after Weiland's death in 1663 and Löwe's im- mediate departure, no opera performance took place at the Wolfenbüttel court for the next two decades.[43]

Yet, the issue of money still clouded Schütz's contributions. In Sophie-Elisa- beth's letter to Schütz of January 2, 1656, she promised him that he would "always receive his stipend punctually." But this was not the case. It is not known whether Sophie-Elisabeth oversaw the details of these financial negotiations. Nevertheless, the duke, with his court in a poor financial state, did not allow Sophie-Elisabeth to pay Schütz—his income, including his travel allowance, had been overdue for sev- eral years until May 1660, although the Schütz-Wolfenbüttel relations remained cordial.[44] In another instance, Schütz did not receive two years of back pay until May 21, 1663, and, later, not until Easter 1665.[45] (Duke August died only a year later at the age of eighty-eight—an amazing lifespan for the seventeenth century. Not young herself, the duchess was then fifty-three. Schütz was eighty-one at Duke August's death.) But more payment issues followed. In a letter of January 10, 1664, to Duke August, the aging Schütz expressed his intention to send his complete published works to the duke as the Wolfenbüttel library's founder for the purpose of preserving them; he hoped, in addition, that the duke wanted his later compositions, referring to the library as "the most highly famed throughout all Europe." Was this merely a business ploy? For Schütz also said he directly would have had his newest works published but he lacked the funds because Duke August had not permitted Sophie-Elisabeth to pay him.[46] (The previous year, 1663, Johann Jakob Löwe likewise had left his Wolfenbüttel *Kapellmeister* position for the equivalent role in Zeitz. Was this move motivated by a lack of financial support, too?)

But Schütz's influential connection with the Wolfenbüttel court continued at least until the spring of 1665. The composer, for instance, sent an early version of his *Johannespassion,* dated April 10, 1665, as a delayed eighty-sixth birthday gift to Duke August, a work that the duke himself had requested for his magnificent library.

The partnership between Sophie-Elisabeth and Schütz resulted in the duchess's success in restructuring the musical life of the Wolfenbüttel court after the Thirty Years' War. For, along with Schütz's support, the duchess, as an administrator and impresario, literally set the stage for inaugurating the spectacular series of *Festspiel* productions given at the Wolfenbüttel court from 1656 to 1663—all in all, a paramount achievement of Sophie-Elisabeth as a patroness of music.

Schütz as Sophie-Elisabeth's Composition Mentor

Aside from the Wolfenbüttel court's musical reorganization, Schütz also on occasion helped Sophie-Elisabeth strengthen her modest contrapuntal skills, part of the technical language of composition that she would already have acquired had her earlier musical education been equal to that of men's. (Typically, men with musical talent grew up as cathedral choirboys with longtime musical and academic schooling.)

Sophie-Elisabeth—because she was a woman—never had been able to undertake the rigorous formal course of study, particularly in counterpoint, traditionally required of "professional" male students for composing unaccompanied choral works. Schütz is known to have required his male pupils to master counterpoint in the "*concertante*" style (that is, instrumentally accompanied vocal music with basso continuo accompaniment, as in Schütz's own *Kleine Geistliche Concerte* of 1636). But there is some evidence that Sophie-Elisabeth had studied composition formally with Stephan Körner, *Kapellmeister* at the Wolfenbüttel court through her first three years there (1635–1638). As her *Festspiel Neu erfundenes FreudenSpiel genandt FriedensSieg* reveals, she had attained only a limited level of contrapuntal skill. Also, Schütz occasionally offered Sophie-Elisabeth suggestions on improving melodic construction, use of the modes, and ways to attain more intense expression through the application of musical "figures" (musical motifs expressing certain character traits or emotions) derived from rhetorical terminology.[47] Yet this notion of the importance of rhetoric seems ironic when applied to Sophie-Elisabeth's music, for Lutheran Pietism—a theology that the duchess's sense of personal devotion anticipated—bypassed customary Orthodox Lutheran liturgy, as well as its elaborate music.

Advising the duchess from time to time on her musical compositions, Schütz did, however, offer her frequent encouragement, acknowledging her creative talents in a letter to her on October 22, 1644, from Braunschweig. Also in this letter, Schütz voiced his sense of responsibility in their student-teacher relationship. On one occasion, he took the trouble to apologize—formally by a letter—for postponing a visit to her in Wolfenbüttel because of his professional duties in Dresden. He assured her, however, that he would return "to humbly discuss without delay and with the utmost diligence the completion of the musical work that we have in hand."[48] At any rate, as late as April 10, 1661, Schütz wrote to Duke August praising Sophie-Elisabeth "as the incomparably perfect princess in all other princely virtues, especially in the praiseworthy profession of music."[49]

In addition, Schütz routinely resorted to elaborate formality and respect when he addressed Sophie-Elisabeth as "Her Serene Highness, right honorable princess and woman among women, Sophia-Elisabeth, Duchess of Braunschweig and Lüneburg, born Princess of Mecklenburg, my gracious princess and lady, serene highness, right honorable princess, gracious lady."[50] Possibly with an eye to pleasing Duke August as his true patron, Schütz referred to some arias (*Arien*) that Sophie-Elisabeth had composed: "We have safely received the new arias . . ., and we note that Your Grace has markedly improved as the result of my modest instruction, and we shall hope that this little work [unidentified] will not only receive the praise of God but will also be an eternal memorial to His honor."[51] The composer collaborated with the duchess on Schottelius's *Theatralische neü Vorstellung von der Maria Magdalena* (1644), each contributing songs; and Schütz again acted as Sophie-Elisabeth's advisor for her psalter *Christ-Fürstliches Davids-Harpfen Spiel,* published in 1667.[52]

Sophie-Elisabeth, a Pietist in Troubled Times

By the 1640s, that is, in the final years of the Thirty Years' War with its terrible carnage and destruction, Sophie-Elisabeth had become increasingly absorbed in religion, specifically in German Pietism, which had become a serious movement within the Lutheran Church by the mid-seventeenth century. In response to a request by Sophie-Elisabeth, Duke August called the respected theologian D. Joachim Lütkemann (1608–1655) to Wolfenbüttel to serve as the court's chief pastor and as general superintendent of the Lower Saxon state church.[53] Presiding at the court until his death in 1655, Pastor Lütkemann helped bolster Sophie-Elisabeth's Pietist convictions.[54]

Born into the Reformed faith (as distinct from Orthodox Lutheranism), the duchess perhaps assumed her new religious persuasion partly as a consequence of the war, for, as Hajo Holborn observes, among those in the highest German social ranks, the war had stirred much doubt regarding then-current religious beliefs.[55] Although a century had passed since the Reformation, religious issues, even among Protestants, had remained strong among Germans and other Europeans. The Pietists, for example, practiced introspection and prayer based on their own interpretation of Bible readings rather than on official Lutheran doctrine. Sophie-Elisabeth's musical works clearly testify to her increasing attention to composing sacred music and poetry intended specifically to serve as personal devotions in the private Pietist manner. The author of Sophie-Elisabeth's eulogy emphasized that she always sought to praise God and did so "also with singing and playing [instruments]."[56]

Adapting the German theologians' belief in the affective and moral power of music, Pietists cautioned that it could easily be corrupted because of its powerful effect on the human soul. The Pietists accordingly opposed the new Italianate figural style (having florid, fixed motifs symbolizing affections) and the incorporation of elaborate *concertante* works into the liturgy, which they considered ostentatious theatrical music. Similarly, they advocated singing psalms and other sacred songs only in simple unison style, condemning singing in parts. In this way, music would properly serve individual devotional sentiments ignited in Bible reading during home devotions. The Pietists also advocated that every individual Christian should own and diligently use a single Pietist hymnbook.[57] (See chapter 2 regarding a parallel case in French composer Elisabeth-Claude Jacquet de La Guerre's biblical cantatas: clerics in France then were urging women to attend more to religious devotions.)

In Orthodox Lutheran churches, the trained *Kantorei* (choir) sang complex figural music, while the congregation sang only simple hymns. But the Pietists, like the Calvinists, advocated singing only songs easy enough for the congregation to manage, allowing the individual layman to maintain a mystical relationship to God. This implied private, rather than communal, devotions. Figural music, that is, was to be excluded from the Pietist liturgy.[58]

Interestingly, Sophie-Elisabeth's religious views encompassed a broader outlook than did German Pietism, for she also drew inspiration for her poetry from the works of major church figures such as St. Augustine, Calvin, and—showing her classical humanistic upbringing—of such ancient secular figures as the Roman philosopher Seneca.[59]

Among German Lutherans, as among other northern Europeans, sacred songs were purchased much more for domestic consumption than for public performances.[60] Yet Sophie-Elisabeth was by no means alone in her Pietist convictions and music. Especially in the literary and musical academies of seventeenth-century Protestant Germany, women of royal rank typically sang this repertoire—what Robert L. Kendrick terms the "feminization of piety."[61] Even around 1700, this attitude remained common for many women of noble rank whose Pietism inspired poems voicing biblical material. For example, Sophie-Elisabeth's later contemporary Amalia Catharina (1640–1697), Countess of Erbach, wrote a collection of sixty-seven poems, some with melodies and basso continuo accompaniment and all of them composed for household devotion. It was published in 1692 at the Hildburghausen court owing to the influence of her sister, who was the wife of the reigning duke there.[62]

In Protestant north Germany of the later seventeenth century, besides the composition of sacred songs and motets, the appearance of operas on biblical subjects was perhaps intended to counter intense Pietist condemnation of staged music as the work of the devil.[63] Yet Sophie-Elisabeth, though of a Pietist persuasion, contributed extensively to the development of German opera at her court.

Showing her self-discipline and concentration, Sophie-Elisabeth's journals from 1650 (she was thirty-seven that year) reveal that she pursued Bible study through daily private devotions in her own way rather than communally—regularly reading through the entire Bible and the Apocrypha. And, as her skill in composing progressed, she set much of her own poetry (as well as some by her stepson, Anton Ulrich) for her private devotions.[64] All in all, she composed around sixty sacred songs and motets in the middle decades of the seventeenth century.

The duchess prefaced her daily Bible reading in 1650 with this commentary taken from her journal: "A brief little poem for every chapter of the Bible [most of it set with melodies] to be used in all times of need and for my and all pious Christians' edification . . . here in Wolfenbüttel."[65] Sophie-Elisabeth's creativity was flourishing with marked intensity, as evident in the following settings.[66] To begin a Bible reading, she wrote:

> "Wan wirdt die heilge schrift mit fleiss von dir gelesen
> So redet Gott mit dir, Gott zeiget dir sein wesen.
> Gott dich vermahnet selbst, und giebet Unterricht,
> Ja Gott dich selber tröst zeigt dir sein angesicht."

> (When you read the Holy Scriptures industriously,
> God speaks to you, God shows you his Being.
> God Himself advises you, and gives instruction,
> Yes, God shows you his countenance with Consolation.)[67]

On August 31, 1650, Sophie-Elisabeth wrote the following poem (a rhymed prayer), inspired by John, chapter 8. It was designed to follow this Gospel reading:

> "O licht der welt lass mich dir folgen eben,
> dass nicht die finsternüs mög ob mir schweben
> Ach mach mich frey von meinen schweren sünden
> Undt lass mich in dir rechte freiheit finden
> Halten dein wort auf dass den todt nicht sehe,
> Durch selben freudig zum leben ein gehe."

> (O light of the world, let me follow you,
> so that the darkness may not hover over me
> O make me free from my heavy sins
> And let me find true freedom in you.
> Keep your word so that I do not see death, but
> Go toward life through joy itself.)[68]

The Declining Years and Final Exile (1663–1667)

Appointed in 1660, vice-*Kapellmeister* Weiland died April 2, 1663, only a few days before the premiere of his composition *Hoffman Daniel*. His death may partially explain the departure of Löwe from Wolfenbüttel sometime after June 24, with Schütz's recommendation in hand, to become court *Kapellmeister* elsewhere. The loss of Weiland and Löwe spelled the cessation of any further opera activity at Wolfenbüttel and therefore the end of one of Sophie-Elisabeth's chief undertakings.[69]

During her final years at Wolfenbüttel (1663–1667), Sophie-Elisabeth dedicated her efforts principally to writing sacred verse. Possibly, she also composed additional song settings for *Davids-Harpfen-Spiel*. Her sister Christine Margarete, her only sibling, died on June 16, 1666, deeply saddening Sophie-Elisabeth, for the two had always enjoyed a close relationship. And the duchess's eighty-eight-year-old husband died only three months later, on September 17. (August's longevity might account for the broad scope of his accomplishments and, in these times, for a remarkably long marriage of thirty-one years, as mentioned in the eulogy for Sophie-Elisabeth.) But, with his death, a decisive and colorful era in Wolfenbüttel's music history drew to a close; for August's oldest son and successor, Rudolf August, soon completely disbanded the Wolfenbüttel court chapel musicians—barely a year after the duke's death—casting several of them into dire financial straits.[70] Not until 1685, when Rudolf's brother Anton Ulrich became coregent, could the two effectively exert their powerful influence to stimulate the resuscitation of court music, especially by supporting the development of Wolfenbüttel into an important opera center.[71]

In 1667, with the court musical establishment disbanded, Sophie-Elisabeth moved to Lüchow, a modest court under Wolfenbüttel control lying seventy miles north-northeast of her longtime home. One wonders if her leave taking had been compelled by the Wolfenbüttel establishment for reasons of political power or whether the duchess simply believed that it was time for her to step back further from her administrative duties. At any rate, the renowned Wolfenbüttel court lost its high musical status along with its principal patron, for in Sophie-Elisabeth's day, the difficult journey required at least four to five days by carriage, removing the duchess too far away to be involved significantly in the life of the chief court.

Yet she may have composed a few minor works at Lüchow up to the end of her life, including a set of three religious songs for *Davids Harpfenspiel*. Her eulogy, in fact, referred to her "special desire in composing sacred lieder."[72]

Besides continuing private devotions at Lüchow, Sophie-Elisabeth turned her little court into a refuge for financially destitute local citizens, regularly aiding the poor with money solicited from the more fortunate populace, especially for medical needs. And when the Swedish army invaded the nearby Mark of Brandenburg in 1675, she pronounced her court a political "asylum and free state," indicating that she still wielded a certain amount of administrative authority.[73] The situation may also have provided her with a maternal role, even if in a professional capacity. And, one assumes, the duchess would never have forgotten her two exiles and other losses caused by war in her younger years.

Unfortunately, Sophie-Elisabeth's son Ferdinand Albrecht brought her much trouble during her final years. He had been involved in inheritance issues with his half-brothers Rudolf August and Anton Ulrich. (These circumstances are similar to the nasty inheritance battles in which composer Maria Bach, the subject of chapter 4, was long engaged with her sisters.) Ferdinand even rushed headlong to Vienna in 1674, two years before his mother's death, hoping to win the emperor's support for his cause. (August the Younger's dukedom, like much of Germany, was officially part of imperial Austria.) This event impelled Sophie-Elisabeth to write her son an angry letter demanding that he return home to avoid dire "financial consequences" and chiding him for his "irresponsibility," calling him "unbrotherly," and telling him that she was "totally washing her hands" of the affair. She also emphasized that she personally had no material funds with which to support him.[74]

Otherwise, she attended to the traditional routine affairs of Lüchow's modest court establishment, assuring, as she had done at Wolfenbüttel, that her court staff was fairly treated and recompensed. She even participated in the family activities of her children and grandchildren (when they visited her, one assumes) as much as possible. Almost sixty-three, Sophie-Elisabeth died in Lüchow between 8 and 9 P.M. on July 12, 1676, and was buried October 6. Her eulogy cites her prolonged suffering from an unidentified illness that had led ultimately to her death.[75]

Sophie-Elisabeth's Musical Compositions

The earliest surviving collections of Sophie-Elisabeth's musical works and arrangements appear in three sizable manuscript collections now in Wolfenbüttel's Herzog-August-Bibliothek, the distinguished library founded by her husband.[76] The first manuscript collection consists chiefly of arrangements; of the 115 vocal compositions in this collection, three-fourths are arrangements of French *airs de cour* that Sophie-Elisabeth had copied from printed sources. For most of the songs, she simply replaced the original lute accompaniment with an unfigured basso continuo (a single bass line without indications of the chords to be filled in above it). Here, then, her lack of advanced compositional technique is clearly in evidence.

The second manuscript contains twenty-two compositions, chiefly sacred figural music: a style in which melodic lines are embellished by specific musical motifs suggesting certain emotions or specific word meanings. But, in this collection dating from c. 1642, only three sacred concertos (works for solo voice and basso continuo reinforced by a viola da gamba) are Sophie-Elisabeth's. While still evidencing compositional flaws, this music nevertheless exhibits a noteworthy improvement in her compositional technique. Most of the other vocal concertos in this set were composed by the court bass Abraham Friedrich.

Of the seventy-five autograph compositions making up the third manuscript, more than two-thirds are definitely Sophie-Elisabeth's: six instrumental *Sinfonien* that are important in their similarity to the evolving baroque instrumental suite; forty-four strophic songs (most with sacred texts) with basso continuo; a dance melody; and a sacred solo concerto with basso continuo accompaniment (having reference to a harpsichord filling in chords to go with a bass line doubled by a low wind or string instrument).

In addition, two published songbook collections of sacred continuo songs also can be found in the Herzog August Bibliothek: the *Vinetum evangelicum* (published in 1648 and 1651) and *ChristFürstliches Davids-Harpfen-Spiel* (published in 1667 and 1670). The *Vinetum* consists of 106 sacred songs based on poems by Joachim von Glasenapp. Eighty percent of the songs consist of the duchess's melodies combined with her husband's basso continuo settings. Duke August's contributions, in fact, far surpass Sophie-Elisabeth's in contrapuntal skill, suggesting that he had been much more thoroughly trained in music than his wife. Almost all of *ChristFürstliches Davids-Harpfen-Spiel* was composed by the duchess. It consists of sixty-three settings for voice and basso continuo based on poems by her stepson Anton Ulrich. The second edition (1670) of this music contains three new musical settings, the last collaborative work between Sophie-Elisabeth and Anton Ulrich.

These two collections of Sophie-Elisabeth's sacred music generally consist of relatively simple psalm settings in a century when psalms were central to Protestant thought both theologically and liturgically. And, as the duchess herself explicitly emphasized, this music was composed for "religious inwardness," that is, only for private devotions.[77] This type of function, therefore, explains the music's intensely subjective expressivity, some of the songs being based on a cantata-like succession of contrasting sections. In Geck's view, several examples from both the *Vinetum evangelicum* and *Davids-Harpfen-Spiel* number among the duchess's loveliest and most memorable compositions; and they show an abundance of musical imagination despite Sophie-Elisabeth's limited technical ability.[78]

The First *Festspiel* Phase (1639–1646)

As a composer, arranger, and—even more so as an impresario and patron—not infrequently in all of these roles simultaneously—Sophie-Elisabeth was involved in the production of twenty-five *Festspiele*.[79] In the duchess's multiple capacities, she contributed significantly to the development of the Wolfenbüttel court as the most important north German center of opera prior to the opening of Hamburg's public Gänsemarktoper (Goose Market Opera House) in 1678. For the first phase of her *Festspiel* compositions, Sophie-Elisabeth collaborated as a composer with Justus Georg Schottelius (1612–1676), who was also the court tutor of her children and stepchildren between 1639 and 1646. She set his librettos to music, resulting in five *Festspiele*, the poet's royal students and their elders participating as dancers in the performances.

In anticipation of the end of the Thirty Years' War, Schottelius completed the *Neu erfundenes FreudenSpiel genannt FriedensSieg* in 1642; it was published in 1648, officially the last year of the conflict. This *Festspiel* is the only Sophie-Elisabeth/Schottelius collaborative work that survives with music (fig. 4).

The solo vocal portions that she arranged or composed, moreover, show substantial progress in the techniques of composition. A prestigious composition intended

Figure 4. Title page from Sophie-Elisabeth's *Neu erfundenes FreudenSpiel genandt FriedensSieg.* Copper engraving by Conrad Buno, 1648. Composed and premiered in 1642 at the Braunschweig ducal residence. Courtesy of the Herzog August Bibliothek, Wolfenbüttel.

at least in part to bolster Duke August's declining political power, the *Festspiel* was first performed in late February 1642 before a courtly audience in the castle hall at Braunschweig. (The work was also presented there in 1648 and 1649.) In this composition, Sophie-Elisabeth's unaccompanied solo songs and instrumentally accompanied ensemble songs, both original and arranged, were performed between long segments of spoken text, the music being designed to explain or interrupt extended sections of dialogue (figs. 5 and 6). Sophie-Elisabeth's instrumental contributions to the work consist of sinfonias, intradas, and dances (two allemandes and a sarabande) in basically homophonic (noncontrapuntal) style, offering a decisive step toward the development of German opera at this court.[80] *FriedensSieg* also incorporates the prologue and epilogue from Sigmund Theophil (Gottlieb) Staden's (1607–1655) *Seelewig,* composed in 1644 at Nuremberg but not performed at Wolfenbüttel until 1654. Staden's work is considered the first extant *Singspiel.*[81]

The next *Festspiel,* the *Neue ergetzliche Vorstellung Des WaldGott Pans,* was first performed in August 1643—again at Braunschweig—because the imperial occupation forces had not completely vacated the Wolfenbüttel residence until the following month. Probably composed by Sophie-Elisabeth, the music for this *Festspiel* included six songs and instrumental interludes played between the acts.[82] (Another performance of this work took place at Wolfenbüttel in 1646.) The following *Festspiel, Die Gebuhrt unsers Heylandes,* was premiered in 1645 and contained eight songs, at least four of them composed by the duchess.

Two *Festspiele* (actually song-ballets, or masques, as Sophie-Elisabeth called them) had been performed a few years earlier than the *Festspiele* named above.

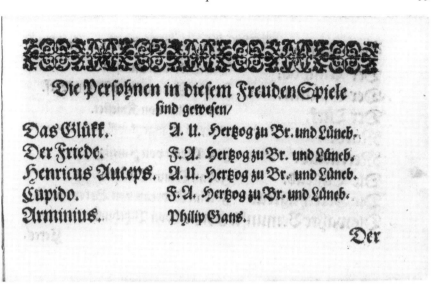

Figure 5. Cast list from the *Neu erfundenes FreudenSpiel*. Courtesy of the Herzog August Bibliothek, Wolfenbüttel.

Figure 6. View of staging showing the allegorical characters in performance for the *Neu erfundenes FreudenSpiel*. Courtesy of the Herzog August Bibliothek, Wolfenbüttel.

Given in 1639, the *Diana-Ballett* contained music, part of which included arrangements made by Sophie-Elisabeth. The *Auf die Zeit gerichtete Ballet* followed seven years later. The ducal family and lesser court members participated in these song-ballets, each one consisting of a series of dances with much vocal music embellishing the drama itself.[83]

The Second *Festspiel* Phase (1652–1656)

Ever the impresario, Sophie-Elisabeth was the driving force behind a series of seven celebratory productions of *Festspiele* that began in 1652. These elaborate "representations" involved solo and ensemble singing, instrumental music, and ballet. Most of them were written in honor of Duke August's birthday of April 10, making these clear examples of occasional music. The elements of the early baroque courtly *Festspiel*—features subsequently incorporated into the early opera presented at Wolfenbüttel—also included jousting, along with processional pageantry and dramatic action. Four of these *Festspiele* were large-scale allegorical, costumed works based, like masques, on mythological material with massive triumphal processions heightening the drama. As in the earlier *Festspiele,* these works were designed solely for the stage, with elaborate stage sets and costuming adding to the musical splendor. And again, as in previous productions, the ducal family and other court members appeared in the cast but participated only as dancers.

Götter Banquet, from 1653, was written to celebrate the wedding of the duke's daughter, Princess Clara Auguste. *Der Natur Bancket, Der Minervae Banqvet, Glükwünschende Waarsagung und Ankunft der Königin Nicaulae* followed in 1653, 1654, 1655, and 1656, respectively. (We know that *Der Natur Bancket* and the *Glükwünschende Waarsagung* were both based on Sophie-Elisabeth's libretti and, to some extent, her music.[84])

Figure 7. Opening of the final act of Sophie-Elisabeth's *Glückwünschende Freuden-darstellung,* 1652. Copper engraving by Conrad Buno. Lüneburg: Stern, 1653. Courtesy of the Herzog August Bibliothek, Wolfenbüttel.

Composed for Duke August's birthday, *Glückwünschende Freudendarstellung* is the sole *Festspiel* surviving with its music intact from the 1652–1656 era. First performed in 1652 and again in 1655, it contains a succession of five solo songs, each introduced by an instrumental sinfonia. The instrumental movement from the *Glükwünschende Freudendarstellung* is the only extant orchestral-size work that Sophie-Elisabeth herself composed among the entire series of *Festspiele* dating from 1652 to 1663 (fig. 7).

Also dating from this second phase of *Festspiele* are *Vorstellung und Glükwünschung der 7.Planeten* (1656) and *Ballet der Zeit* (1655). The *Ballet der Zeit* contains fourteen dance sections along with instrumental pieces and two songs probably composed by Sophie-Elisabeth. This song-ballet offered a foretaste of the grand ballets of Ulrich and Löwe.

The Third *Festspiel* Phase (1656–1663)

Sophie-Elisabeth was involved principally as an impresario and patron for the third set of thirteen *Festspiele*, written and performed at the Wolfenbüttel court between August 1656 and September 1663. Sophie-Elisabeth assigned Duke August's gifted son Prince Anton Ulrich (reigned 1704–1714) to write the libretti for this third phase of *Festspiele* not only because he had the eminently qualified Löwe available to set his texts to music, but also because the duchess's stepson had been highly stimulated by the brilliant theatrical representations that he had observed earlier at Louis XIV's court. (See chapter 2.) Anton Ulrich, therefore, immediately set out to emulate these productions on his return to Wolfenbüttel.

In addition, the success of these sumptuous and expensive productions at Wolfenbüttel owed in no small part to the significant rise in the performance level of the court's musicians, who had been appointed by Schütz, Löwe, and Weiland primarily because of Sophie-Elisabeth's skillful management of court musical affairs.[85] As early as November 10, 1655, the duchess had written Schütz that music making in the newly reinvigorated Wolfenbüttel chapel was taking noticeable strides.[86] The court record for the year 1658–1659, for example, reveals intensified performance standards and an expanded musical staff. (Besides Schütz and Löwe, the report named Andreas Körner, perhaps related to Stephan Körner, as organist; and it cited five unnamed instrumentalists with a modestly sized group of choirboys.) After Schütz's visit to Wolfenbüttel in June 1660, his letter of April 10, 1661, to Duke August affirmed his satisfaction with the musicians the composer had sent from Dresden to the Wolfenbüttel court. On such occasions, moreover, chapel forces were regularly augmented with nonresident musicians, forming the "pickup orchestra" of the times.

But, judging by the duchess's surviving *Festspiel* compositions, Geck postulates that the duchess's compositional technique, though improved, still fell short of court *Kapellmeister* Löwe's skill, particularly in the large-scale musical structures of these operatic Wolfenbüttel productions. The limits of Sophie-Elisabeth's compositional abilities compared with Löwe's perhaps accounts for her serious turn to writing sacred verse by the mid-1650s.

The composer and court instrumentalist Julius Johann Weiland, Löwe's close associate at Wolfenbüttel, may have collaborated somewhat with Löwe in composing music for this phase of *Festspiele,* thereby explaining Weiland's promotion in 1660 to vice-*Kapellmeister,* a position created specifically for him. Weiland's appointment was, in addition, possibly promoted by his recent dedication, only a year before, to Duchess Sophie-Elisabeth of a collection of vocal works, the *Kleine Geistliche Konzerte.* Published in 1656, these are mainly settings of German biblical texts in a style resembling Schütz's and other contemporaries' works by the same name.[87] Both Löwe and Weiland, moreover, played active roles in reestablishing the court chapel's musical repertoire.[88] (As early as the spring of 1644, Weiland had been in contact with Wolfenbüttel while a student and choirboy in Braunschweig, then the temporary court residence.)

Although barely any of the music has survived, the thirteen *Festspiele* of the 1656–1663 era are very impressive for a small princely establishment, marking both the culmination of the French grand ballet genre at the Wolfenbüttel court and the crystallization there of native German opera. The only extant music from these *Festspiele* consists of three songs taken from Sophie-Elisabeth's *Davids-Harpfen-Spiel* that had been incorporated into these compositions. At least three of Anton Ulrich's texts for these works were possibly written in collaboration with other literary-minded members (besides Sophie-Elisabeth) of the ducal family.[89]

For this third phase of the *Festspiele,* thirteen works spanned the years from 1656 to 1663. Of these, six marked birthdays of Duke August, the others celebrating weddings and a christening—all honoring members of the ducal family. Six of the thirteen were *Singspiele* (including dances)—two on an originally French libretto, one on a biblical theme; six were song-ballets (including solo songs); and one, celebrating Sophie-Elisabeth's forty-sixth birthday, was based on an Italian "tragic poem," that of Alessandro Striggio's *Orfeo,* a text used decades earlier by Claudio Monteverdi.

The titles of the thirteen are *Frühlings-Ballet* (performed August 20, 1656; *Amelinde, oder Dy triumphirende Seele* (performed April 10, 1657); *Regier-Kunst-Schatten* (performed May 1, 1658); *Ballet des Tages* (performed April 10, 1659); *Andromeda* (performed April 10, 1659); *Orpheus aus Thracien* (performed August 20, 1659); *Ballet der Natur* (performed after Easter 1660); *Masque der Hercinie* (performed after May 4, 1661); *Iphigenia* (performed May 5, 1661); *Ballet der Gestirne* (performed January 18, 1663); *Selimena* (performed January 21, 1663); *Der Hoffman Daniel* (performed April 10, 1663); and *Ballet der Diana* (performed September 20, 1663).[90]

The principal "characters" in several of these last *Festspiele* add to the importance Sophie-Elisabeth enjoyed in the duchy of Braunschweig-Lüneburg. In parts of *Amelinde,* the *Ballet des Tages,* and the *Ballet der Natur,* the allegorical-mythical female figures of Minerva, Time, and Nature, respectively, represented an idealized Sophie-Elisabeth—in Geck's opinion. These connections had even appeared in the earlier *Festspiele Der Natur Banquet* (1654) and *Der Minervae Banqvet* (1655). There is no evidence, however, that the duchess herself participated in any of these productions. Wolfenbüttel court singers performed the songs throughout; for the nobility to do so would have breached age-old court etiquette.

Conclusion

Although twice left motherless in her childhood and subjected to the horrors and indignities of a terrible war, Sophie-Elisabeth transcended the typically circumscribed orbit of a female royal spouse in her day with its rather fixed cultural and gender roles. To the contrary, this musically gifted, persevering, compassionate, and politically astute duchess contributed significantly to the cultural history of the German early baroque period. Duke August's court and his entire duchy with all its domains reached a new pinnacle of musical life even amid the ravages and vicissitudes of war, primarily because Sophie-Elisabeth dedicated herself fully to the cause of the Wolfenbüttel court's cultural life. She devoted herself diligently to this cause and likewise applied herself wholeheartedly to the art of composition.

In addition, the duchess was blessed by growing up with a wealth of musical resources at her father's court and by a mother and then two successive stepmothers who closely supervised her education (even if not institutional). After marriage, she received a generous measure of support and independence in her musical endeavors by an enlightened humanist husband, like Sophie-Elisabeth herself, although he had ultimate control in all his duchy's affairs. A tactful music administrator-impresario and also a composer, Sophie-Elisabeth managed to enlist Heinrich Schütz, one of the most influential composers of the German baroque before Bach, to advise her from time to time in composition and in the administrative reorganization of court music. This led both to Wolfenbüttel's cultural survival and to its rise in prestige and influence in the typically intense competition among German courts of Sophie-Elisabeth's time.

Among the relatively few seventeenth-century German noblewomen composers of her day, Sophie-Elisabeth was also the first German woman composer to attain performances and publication of her works while she was living. That was no small feat. Yet, despite her many accomplishments, she vanished from historical annals soon after her death, without the recognition she deservedly had won during her lifetime.

Works by Duchess Sophie-Elisabeth of Braunschweig/Lüneburg

SACRED SONGBOOKS

Vinetum evangelicum
ChristFürstliches Davids-Harpfen-Spiel

FESTSPIELE

FriedensSieg
WaldGott Pan
Die Gebuhrt unsers Heylandes
Diana-Ballett
Auf die Zeit gerichtetes Ballet
Götter Bancket
Der Natur Banquet
Der Minervae Banqvet
Glükwünschende Waarsagung und Ankunft der Königin Nicaulae
Glückwünschende Freüdensdarstellung
Vorstellung und Glükwünschung der 7.Planeten
Ballet der Zeit

OTHER WORKS, INCLUDING:

"Geistliches Konzert: Herr wie lang wiltu mein so gar vergessen"
"Der herr erhöre dich in der not"
"Was acht ich diesen leib"
"Vom himmel kombt der trost"
"Instrumentalsinfonien"
"Variiertes Strophenlied: Was tuht mich so auss mich treiben"
"Darbietungslied: Glück zu dem mehrer, der welpen stat ziret"
    Note: Manuscripts and published compositions are located in the Herzog August Bibliothek, Wolfenbüttel, and the Niedersächsisches Staatsarchiv, Wolfenbüttel.

EDITIONS

Selected examples of individual arias, choruses, and instrumental pieces from *Festspiele* by Sophie-Elisabeth, in Karl Wilhelm Geck, *Sophie Elisabeth Herzogin zu Braunschweig und Lüneburg (1613–1676) als Musikerin* (Saarbrücken: Saarbrücker Druckerei und Verlag, 1992), 427–42. These examples are printed in modern notation.

Martin Bircher and T. Burger, eds., *Alles mit Bedacht: Barockes Fürstenlob auf Herzog August (1579–1666) in Wort, Bild und Musik*. Wolfenbüttel: n.p., 1979.

Martin Bircher and T. Burger, eds., *Glückliche Freudendarstellung*, 4 vv, chorus 4 vv, 4 strings, basso continuo. 1652, 2nd ed. 1655. Facsimile, includes score.

Hans-Gert Roloff, ed., *Sophie Elisabeth, Herzogin zu Braunschweig und Lüneburg: Dichtungen, i: Spiele*. Frankfurt: Lang, 1980.

RECORDINGS

As of this writing, there are no known recordings.

CHAPTER TWO

Elisabeth-Claude Jacquet de La Guerre

Versailles and Paris in the Twilight of the Ancien Régime

If you know something of the palace of Versailles, the city of Paris, and the landscapes of Jean-Antoine Watteau, you have glimpsed the world of the French composer, harpsichordist, and organist Elisabeth-Claude Jacquet de La Guerre (1665–1729).[1] She was the first woman to have a work, her opera *Céphale et Procris,* staged at the Académie Royale de Musique, the prestigious opera house in Paris. An older contemporary of Johann Sebastian Bach and Georg Friedrich Händel, Jacquet de La Guerre was baptized on March 17, 1665, according to her church records.[2] No birth certificate has been found (fig. 8). Catherine Cessac, Jacquet's chief biographer in recent years, concludes that her baptism occurred only a few days after her birth, a common occurrence owing to the high infant mortality rate.[3] It should be noted here that besides Cessac's monograph and articles, substantial contributions to Jacquet's life and works have also been made by Mary Cyr,[4] Carol Henry Bates, Catherine Massip, Wanda R. Griffiths, and Adrian Rose, to name a number of the most prominent scholars. The seminal study of Jacquet de La Guerre in English is Edith Borroff's 1966 work: "An Introduction to Elisabeth-Claude Jacquet de La Guerre."[5] Credit for even earlier research into Jacquet de La Guerre's accomplishments also goes to Michel Brenet (Marie Bobillier), her work (in French) on Jacquet dating from the first decade of the twentieth century.

Jacquet de La Guerre's professional successes—and they were numerous—were not altogether unpredictable. She grew up in a family, both immediate and extended, of active and respected musicians; and she lived amid the rich cultural environment of Versailles and Paris. It was a time when musical life flourished at the court of Louis XIV and among the French capital's urban bourgeoisie, who were gaining considerable power and influence in cultural affairs. Jacquet de La Guerre's life and art fit neatly into the prosperity, splendor, and turbulence of the *grand siècle,* when Louis, the "Sun King," reigned (1643–1715) as an absolute monarch. During Jacquet de La Guerre's lifetime, the thriving musical life of the French court also extended, to some degree, into the Regency of Philippe,

Figure 8. Elisabeth-Claude Jacquet de La Guerre, c. 1694–1695. Oil
portrait by François de Troy (1645–1730). Jacquet de La Guerre holding a blank sheet of paper with empty musical staves and a feather
pen at the ready. She is seated at a two-manual harpsichord made
in Antwerp. Her elegant appearance gently hints at her comfortable
living circumstances. Like the composer, the painter was a protégé of
Mme. De Montespan and a leader in French portraiture in his day.
One, therefore, could reasonably assume that Jacquet de La Guerre
and de Troy knew each other. The portrait dates from the same time
period as the composer's opera, *Céphale et Procris.* Private collection,
London. Courtesy of the owner.

Duke d'Orléans (1715–1723) and the early reign of Louis XV (1723–1774). In 1682,
Louis XIV finally realized his dream of moving the court officially from Paris
to Versailles—once merely his favored hunting lodge, then vastly expanded to
serve as his court. At Louis's death in 1715, the regent, Philippe, returned the royal
establishment to Paris; but by 1723 Louis XV had resettled the court at Versailles,
where it remained until the revolution of 1789.

Versailles and Paris

Only twelve-and-a-half miles southwest of Paris, the Versailles palace speaks of noble grandeur further adorned by finely carved sculpture and stately tapestries. Even today, these highly visible features resemble a gigantic baroque stage set tempered by rococo embellishment and idealizing a cosmic sense of fantasy, delicacy, and artificiality. As more fully examined later in this chapter, the interplay between the surroundings and music of the city and court substantially influenced Jacquet de La Guerre's life and musical achievements. With the same visual extravagance as that vested in Versailles, the bucolic paintings of Jacquet's younger contemporary Antoine Watteau (1684–1721) idealize the France of Louis XIV, as, for example, in the artist's *Country Dance,* 1706–1710 (fig. 9).

Watteau's painting underscores a delight in fantastical extremes—colorfully attired peasants cast dramatically against a darkly imagined forest landscape. Watteau's work illuminates a pastoral idyll with merry-making country folk in revelry as they (including a woman) play instruments and dance to the music. The scene is bathed in the barely imaginable, though subdued, radiance of a

Figure 9. *The Country Dance,* 1706–1710, oil by Jean-Antoine Watteau (1684–1721). Here the artist invokes rococo delight in music making. Courtesy of the Indianapolis Museum of Art, Indianapolis, Indiana.

miniature rococo *fête gallant,* but is placed in a rustic setting as if to replicate a formal palace celebration engaging members of a royal household. In a sense, therefore, Watteau's lavish idealization reflects some of the pervasive luminosity and embellished splendor that distinguished Louis XIV's Versailles.[6]

The advent of this French escapist art, as Enzo Carli and others have suggested, paralleled signs of social unrest: the Paris bourgeoisie of the early eighteenth century, who had wearied of absolutist strictures, were striving to loosen rigid court etiquette in favor of a more lenient lifestyle. In painting, perhaps sooner than in music, the deities of classical mythology and heroic figures of history began yielding their primacy to contemporary scenarios and exotic worlds foreign to traditional French court protocol. Grand universal themes were being replaced by views reflecting real-life issues, as in Watteau's *Country Dance.*[7] (Jacquet de La Guerre's opera *Céphale et Procris* could be said perhaps to straddle both the old themes and the new with its powerfully delineated mythological setting and its moralistic theme of human fidelity.) To some extent, this process of change was to be paralleled in French music of the absolutist era, this art gradually being seen not only as the voice of passion but also enjoyed for its dulcet and lavishly ornate textures. The music of Jacquet de La Guerre mirrored these characteristics by idealizing an embellished but ordered grace often seen in the allegorical paintings of her day, in which emotional expression was adorned by pleasing artifice. These tendencies pervaded the extravagant musical scene at Versailles.

Jacquet de La Guerre spent her earliest, and later married, years in Paris, a vortex of French cultural life that was shifting from the exclusive domain of the French court aristocracy to a city of increasingly affluent and powerful bourgeoisie, with its complexly interlocking professional musical dynasties. The cultural supremacy of the French capital was only one aspect of the splendid times marking Jacquet de La Guerre's Paris, a teeming metropolis in many ways independent of the magnificent court of Versailles. Yet at the same time, the Paris that Jacquet de La Guerre knew was "still very much a medieval city: noisy, crowded, and malodorous," as James R. Anthony has described it.[8] It was nevertheless Europe's largest capital at this time and was undergoing a mammoth building boom, the restoration of civil order, and the establishment of additional royal academies.

All this new construction formed part of a systemization of French cultural and intellectual life imposed by the hierarchical absolutism of the French crown. The epoch was truly France's *grand siècle.* At Louis XIV's succession in 1643, Cardinal Richelieu was assigned the powerful position of regent, becoming Louis's chief minister. Despite Richelieu's support of the king's brutal wars against the Protestant Huguenots and the disruptions still being wrought by the Thirty Years' War, Richelieu immeasurably enriched the cultural life of Paris. He directed the construction of the lavish Palais Royal, the development of the Île de la Cité, and the founding of the Académie Française. He also established the Académie Royale de Peinture et de Sculpture, awarding patronage to many Frenchmen in the arts and thereby forging a "nationalization" of French high culture. During Jacquet de La Guerre's lifetime, major institutions of Paris included the Opéra Comique, the Nouvelle Comédie Italienne, the Nouveau Théâtre Italien, and the Académie Royale de Musique. The city also gained an Académie Royale de Danse (1661), an Académie Royale des Inscriptions et Belles Lettres (1663), an Académie Royale des Sciences (1666), and an Académie Royale d'Architecture (1671).[9] The state-supported Académie Royale de Musique was established in 1669 by Pierre Perrin, an appointee of Louis XIV, although it was not considered an "official" royal performance site until 1672, when Jean-Baptiste Lully was appointed to head it.

The Académie Royale de Musique came to be an important institution in Paris from Jacquet de La Guerre's lifetime on. It was the leading house for lyric drama, having come into being and fully functioning during her youth. The all-French repertoire of this institution consisted of *tragédies lyriques* (called *tragédies en musique*) and *opéras-ballets*, performances given four times weekly in winter and three in summer. During the 1670s, Lully decided on the Académie repertoire, focusing on his own *tragédies lyriques,* which continued to be performed there (albeit with revisions) throughout the eighteenth century.

The Fronde Affair and its Socio-Musical Dimensions

These achievements were all to the good of Louis XIV, who fortified his absolutist stance, thwarting the political designs of Habsburg Austria and defeating the city's xenophobic Fronde movement (1648–1653).[10] Between 1648 and 1653, almost two decades before Jacquet de La Guerre's birth, Paris underwent a disturbing series of events that subjected its citizens "to anarchy and impoverishment."[11] This convoluted embroilment intertwined opera with politics, setting the musical scene that Jacquet inherited. Bitter contention developed in Paris between musical factions regarding *le bon goût,* a competition that cut supporters of the city's musical life into two halves: the "Lullistes," supporting the Italian style versus the "Ramistes," supporting the French. (The underlying issue at stake, in fact, continued to divide the French capital until c. 1733, four years after Jacquet de La Guerre's death.) The most intense phase of the crisis dates from 1650.[12] The immediate cause of the uproar was the Italian-born Cardinal Mazarin's (d. 1661) politically motivated introduction of Italian artists into performances at the French court. In addition, he favored Italian opera, with its emphasis on dramatic-musical content, elaborate sets, stage machinery, and costuming. With recitatives and arias designed to create an arresting theatrical impact, the Italian style contrasted markedly with the brief courtly airs of the prevailing French taste.[13]

The Fronde uprising followed the imposition of excessive taxes on the citizenry by the French government to support a production of Luigi Rossi's six-hour-long grand spectacle opera *Orfeo.* It was one of six Italian operas given (1645–1662) at the French court spearheaded by Mazarin in his attempt to strengthen the

French court's Italian faction. Premiered in the Salle des Suisses of the Tuileries palace in 1647, *Orfeo* included no French singers except for Jacquet de La Guerre's relative Anne Chabanceau de la Barre. In the ruckus following the production, members of the French court, Rossi, Mazarin himself, and some Italian singers were forced to flee Paris to avoid imprisonment.[14] As Bukofzer summed up the fracas, "Rarely in history have the relations between politics and music lain more openly on the surface than during the [era of] French absolutism."[15] However, though the Fronde crisis was over by the mid-1650s, the controversy lingered.[16]

The Jacquets

Elisabeth-Claude Jacquet de La Guerre was descended from an old, widely branched Parisian family tree of master instrument builders, singers, and instrumentalists. Yet, as artisans, they were classed lowest on the social scale in the traditional hierarchy of the French baroque musical world.[17] Both Jacquet de La Guerre's natal family and that of her husband, the La Guerres, typified those of many seventeenth- and eighteenth-century musicians who married within their own circles. In this way they established and expanded family musical dynasties of both men and women members, networks reinforced by the inclusion of powerful friends and colleagues in composing, performance, instrument building, music engraving, and publishing. Although all these pursuits were open to women, females as both soloists and ensemble musicians were largely restricted by custom to harpsichord, organ, and vocal performance up to the mid-eighteenth century, two decades past Jacquet de La Guerre's death.

Jacquet de La Guerre's remarkable family and its manifold relationships in her cultural world played critical roles in establishing her position in the Paris and Versailles orbit. Married November 24, 1655, Jacquet de La Guerre's parents were Claude Jacquet (before 1650–1702) and the widowed Anne de la Touche (d. 1698). Claude Jacquet was a much recognized organist and harpsichord builder, as well as a teacher of that instrument and organ.[18] He served as organist of the prestigious baroque church of Saint-Louis-en-l'Île from as early as 1686, although he may not have received an official title.[19]

Most scholars assume that Claude gave his daughter her first serious professional musical training. While this conviction stems only from Jacquet de La Guerre's published dedications in her music, the French baroque scholar Mary Cyr concludes that, because Jacquet de La Guerre's family was a musical one, her father's mentoring meant musical instruction as well as other support. (In addition, all three of Jacquet de La Guerre's siblings became professional musicians. After all, musical families throughout the ages—such as Thuringia's Bachs and France's Couperins—have spawned progeny who, in turn, became professional musicians themselves.) Claude Jacquet's other pupils included his grandnephew and the child prodigy Louis-Claude Daquin (1694–1772), eventually a noted composer and organist (and Jacquet de La Guerre's godchild).

In addition to Jacquet de La Guerre's many musical forebears, she also married into other leading musical dynasties of Paris. In the second half of the seventeenth century, in fact, about five hundred Parisian instrumentalists—role models to younger generations—were interrelated in these family circles, forging virtual "monopolies" through blood, marriage, and professional associations.[20] By Louis XIV's death in 1715—Jacquet de La Guerre would then have been about fifty years old—the court was employing between 150 and two hundred musicians, a number of them related to the Jacquets and La Guerres. Among the many leading professional musical families to which her family and her husband's were known to be tied were the Lorillacs, Chabanceaus, Mézangeaus, La Barres, Champaignes, and Daquins.

The harpsichordists and harpsichord builders of the Jacquet family lived in the same sections of Paris in which most other musical families, including music teachers and instrument sellers, resided.[21] These areas focused on the Île de la Cité and extended to the right bank of the Seine, where the parish of St. Eustache was located. The church is a splendid late Gothic structure built between 1532 and 1632. It was in this parish that Jacquet de La Guerre lived as a married woman and later widow.

Music making in Jacquet de La Guerre's Paris was most intensely concentrated in the cultural heart of the city, an area bordering Les Halles (the main commercial center of Paris) to the north, Saint-Gervais in the Marais quarter to the east, the Tuileries (the site of the *Concerts Spirituels* and the *Concerts Italiens*) to the west, and Saint-Séverin and the Latin Quarter to the south on the other side of the Seine. Within these boundaries were the main churches of Paris (Saint-Gervais, Notre Dame, and Sainte-Chapelle).[22]

Most shops of the *luthiers* (string instrument makers) and the builders of harpsichords and organs centered on the Rue Saint-Martin near Saint-Julien-Ménétriers. The workshops of these instrument makers and repairers served a large clientele, including both professional and amateur musicians. Because many of the most expensive musical instruments of Paris in the first half of the seventeenth century and beyond were the harpsichord and the lute,[23] the skilled artisans making these instruments were the highest paid of this time. Jacquet de La Guerre may have inherited family money from this source, and many years under Versailles patronage may explain the relatively affluent circumstances of her life, especially during her lengthy widowhood.

Nevertheless, she could not completely have escaped her class ranking. A rigid socio-musical ordering of French musicians prevailed during the *grand siècle*. The highest ranking French performers began with dancers employed in salons and on the stage of the Académie Royale de Musique; below them, lutenists, viol

players, and harpsichordists (except those in the military); and, below them, the
violinists and oboists, who—until the mid-seventeenth century—were given the
same status as hurdy-gurdy players. From c. 1660, the social-musical standing
of string players began to improve, for they were active as performers in spreading the imported Italian concerto and sonata genres—especially the music of
Arcangelo Corelli (1653–1713)—and the newer French works having Italian features. At the lowest social level was the *petite bourgeoisie,* those engaged in the
manual musical trades such as instrument makers and sellers of instruments.[24]
This ranking no doubt would have included the Jacquets. Some of Jacquet de La
Guerre's extended family, however, could easily have belonged to the Confrérie
de Saint Julien-des-Ménétriers (originally referring to minstrels), a select guild
of musicians established in 1321.

The Confrérie, a corporate association with a strict apprenticeship program,
was virtually a labor union that exercised tight control over Parisian musical
performers. But by Jacquet's earlier years—from the mid- to late seventeenth
century—many of the guild's finest instrumentalists had become increasingly
conscious of themselves as professional artists, that is, ranking high above artisan
status. Many of these musicians, in fact, were gradually shifting their professional
positions to the Royal Chamber, the Stable, and the Twenty-four Violins, and
ultimately the Confrérie lost out completely to the Royale Académie de Musique.[25]

Forebears

Jacquet de La Guerre's paternal great-grandfather Marceau Jacquet was born
in Paris in the 1580s and died before 1620.[26] Marceau, a master mason, and his
brothers lived and worked in an economically and culturally flourishing Paris
during the years when Henri IV ruled from his court at the Louvre palace. (Under
Henri, who was intent on forging an absolutist monarchy, the Louvre was expanded and a school of fine and applied arts established.)[27] Marceau's brother
Guillaume married Antoinette Lorillart (or Lorillac), her family, too, being highly
regarded as instrument builders. Marceau's brothers Sébastien and Jehan also
followed this profession; and all of these Jacquet brothers had godfathers from
the well-regarded La Barre family. Musician members of this family included
organist Loys La Barre; the noted court flutist and composer Michel La Barre
(ca. 1675–1745); court singer Anne Chabanceau de La Barre (1628–1688); court
organist Pierre Chabanceau de La Barre (1592–1656); and (probably Pierre's son)
composer Joseph Chabanceau de La Barre (1633–1678).[28]

Jacquet de La Guerre's paternal grandfather, Jehan Jacquet the Younger (c. 1575–
c. 1656–1658), the son of Marceau Jacquet, was a master mason and the father of
the organist Claude Jacquet, Jacquet de La Guerre's father. Jehan lived through
two-thirds of Louis XIII's reign (1610–1642) and into that of Louis XIV. Adding

further to the Jacquets' familial-cultural relationships, Jehan Jacquet the Elder (d. c. 1644), another son of Marceau, was a master instrument builder.[29]

Marrying Anne Daussy, Jehan Jacquet the Younger fathered four children: Claude; Marguerite (baptized March 15, 1625), who married the wood carver Thomas Daquin, the grandfather of the esteemed composer Louis-Claude Daquin; also, Charlotte (baptized September 1, 1631), who married the painter Philippe de Champaigne; and Anne (baptized October 29, 1634), whose godmother was her second cousin Marguerite Jacquet Mézangeau (baptized 1602), wife of the highly regarded lutenist René Mézangeau and mother of Geneviéve (baptized October 21, 1613), whose godfather was Loys de la Barre.

Significantly, there is scant information on Jacquet de La Guerre's mother, Anne de La Touche, and her forebears, except for a brief record of the male line.[30] As a result, we cannot trace musical ability and accomplishments on Jacquet de La Guerre's maternal side of the family, except for the information that Anne de la Touche's first husband, Claude Bourlier, had been an officer under the Duke d'Orléans (the French Regent after Louis XIV's death); and her son from this marriage, Sébastien Bourlier (therefore Jacquet de La Guerre's half-brother), was a royal sculptor at the Versailles court and later at Bordeaux.

The Claude Jacquets' second child, Elisabeth-Claude Jacquet de La Guerre, had three siblings: Pierre, Nicolas, and Anne. Unlike the traditional favoring of the first son, Jacquet de La Guerre's parents appear to have supported the intensive musical training of all four of their progeny in preparation for professional careers. Their father was probably their first music teacher, instructing them thoroughly in harpsichord and organ.

Pierre Jacquet was born in Paris c. 1666, making him only one year younger than Jacquet de La Guerre. (His death occurred there on June 28, 1739, ten years and a day after hers.) From 1695, Pierre followed his father's professions, becoming an organist, an organ and harpsichord teacher, and a composer.[31] He earned the rank of master harpsichordist, although listed as only second class. Until his father's death in 1702, Pierre was organist of Saint-Nicolas-du-Chardonnet, but soon thereafter he assumed his father's position as organist at Saint-Louis-en-l'Île, while still serving at Saint-Nicolas. Jacquet de La Guerre's brother Nicolas (1662–1707) was also born in Paris.[32] He was named organist of the cathedral of Saint-André in Bordeaux, where his half-brother Sébastien Bourlier also lived and where Nicolas probably died.[33] Like countless organists of his day, Nicolas was also a master harpsichordist and keyboard teacher.

Jacquet de La Guerre's sister, Anne (ca. 1662–?), was likewise a professional musician, serving from the age of twelve as a *femme de chambre* of Marie de Lorraine, or Mademoiselle De Guise (d. c. 1688). In this position, Anne (called Nanon or Manon) was one of fifteen musicians appointed to De Guise's small but outstanding music ensemble. It included Marc-Antoine Charpentier (1643–1704),

who composed for the ensemble and sang *haute-contre* in it; and the future music
publisher Henri de Baussen (who brought out some of Jacquet's music). De Guise's
group was established in 1670 in the Marais district of Paris, perhaps to relieve
De Guise's sense of isolation near the end of her life. Reported to be exceptionally
beautiful and acoustically vibrant, De Guise's chapel was the scene of a concert
almost every afternoon, along with occasional evening performances, mostly
consisting of sacred music.[34] Anne remained in this ensemble until 1688, the year
De Guise died and Anne turned twenty-six. On May 26, 1689, Anne married
Louis Yard (or Hiard), who had been De Guise's *valet de chambre*. The wedding
took place before royalty, including the Duke of Braunschweig-Lüneburg.[35] In
1729, Jacquet named the Yards' two sons as her heirs.[36]

The only one of the four siblings who was not an organist, Anne was also the
only instrumentalist, probably a harpsichordist, in De Guise's group. As accomplished as this ensemble was, however (it gradually expanded to include eleven
women and nine men), it ranked lower socially compared with the higher status
of the king's musicians. In De Guise's group, male musicians were officially chapel
musicians; but the women members were neither official nor salaried.

The Gilded Musical World of Versailles

In 1670, Claude Jacquet, Jacquet de La Guerre's father, presented his young daughter—her age at that time being unsubstantiated—before Louis XIV.[37] It was at
this court from 1670 to 1684 (the year she married) that she drew extraordinary
attention from the Versailles royalty for her remarkable talent as a harpsichordist, singer, and accompanist for her own singing. Above all, it was Jacquet de La
Guerre's gift for improvisation that amazed her audiences whenever she played
the harpsichord and organ (in the Chapelle Royale).[38]

The Paris monthly *Mercure gallant* had commented in July 1677 on Jacquet de
La Guerre's "extraordinary" youthful accomplishments: "She sings at sight the most
difficult music. She accompanies herself, and accompanies others who wish to sing,
at the harpsichord, which she plays in a manner that cannot be imitated. She com-
poses pieces and plays them in all the keys asked of her."[39] The journal continued:
"Mademoiselle Jacquet from her tenderest youth made known her talents and her
extraordinary disposition for music and for the art of playing the harpsichord. . . .
The King took much pleasure in hearing her play the harpsichord. . . ."[40]

As Jacquet de La Guerre matured, Louis XIV himself reportedly turned his
attention to her as a composer and sponsored performances of her works, encouraging her even after she had left the court's protection. In light of Jacquet de
La Guerre's successful debut before the king, he placed her under the protection
of his mistress Madame de Montespan, then his favorite mistress, who diligently
undertook the young musician's musical and academic education. De Montespan
herself bore several of Louis XIV's children, whose fine education (including

musical training) she closely managed. It is possible that she also extended these advantages to Louis's prodigies under her protection, such as the young Jacquet de La Guerre (and the painter François de Troy, as mentioned earlier) whom she had especially taken under her wing.[41] From 1684 to 1701, De Maintenon, De Montespan's successor earlier, organized private concerts in Louis's five-room inner apartment at Versailles. One may assume that at times Jacquet de La Guerre was in the audience. In addition, De Maintenon sponsored almost-daily performances of chamber music in her own rooms at the chateau of Meudon, a royal residence close to Versailles.

On September 23, 1684, the nineteen-year-old Jacquet de La Guerre married the organist Marin de La Guerre (1658–1704), seven years her elder, and returned to Paris from Versailles. But she continued to enjoy Louis XIV's patronage until his death in 1715.[42] Jacquet de La Guerre's marriage very likely was arranged in compliance with the customary requirements of her time and place; that is, she followed the tradition of marrying a member of the same professional circle of organist families as her own. In this way, musical family alliances could be preserved down the generations. For more than a century, from 1633 to 1739, the organist dynasty of the La Guerres and Jacquets were linked by blood, marriage, and profession with the La Barres, the Couperins, and other families. By the mid-seventeenth century, as another example, the well-trained and accomplished singer Anne Chabanceau de La Barre (another Jacquet family relative) could perform professionally at solemn services in Paris cloisters, churches, and the court, though rarely in churches outside Paris.[43]

Even after marriage, Jacquet de La Guerre's career as a harpsichord performer, composer, and keyboard teacher continued to grow—not the typical case of women musicians of her times.[44] As a rule, talented young *musiciennes* had little or no hope of continuing professional careers past marriage, leaving performance to depend mainly on young, rather than older, women.[45] Thus, although Jacquet de La Guerre's marriage brought her a permanent return to Paris, Évrard Titon du Tillet could proclaim—even as late as three years after her death—that her "merit and reputation . . . could only grow in that great City, and all the great Musicians and fine Connoisseurs went eagerly to hear her play the harpsichord; she had, above all, marvelous talent for playing preludes and fantasies on the spot. Sometimes she would follow a prelude and fantasy for an entire half hour with melodies and harmonies that were extremely varied and in excellent taste, which charmed the Listeners.[46] One could say that never did a woman have such great skills in composition and in so striking a marvelous way on the harpsichord and on the organ. . . ."[47]

Yet a number of women, even those trained to be professional musicians, were fated to become mistresses of royalty or of the lower aristocracy, that is, as long as they maintained their youthful physical attributes. On the one hand, Jacquet de La Guerre escaped such a predicament. But on the other, she, like other professionally accomplished French women of her day, typically did not obtain official court positions until the end of Philippe's regency in 1723—that is, not until the last decade of her life—when it was too late for her to fully enjoy and profit from such an honor. As a rule, women who sang in Louis XIV's chapel as soloists were not listed as part of the official court household. As we have seen, this was the case in De Guise's chapel and, no doubt, in other "satellite" courts of the French royalty.[48]

Like his wife, Marin de La Guerre had been born into an accomplished family of musicians, a family that was professionally active among the prosperous and expanding Parisian bourgeoisie. At the time of the marriage, Marin de La Guerre worked as a harpsichordist, harpsichord teacher, and organist of the church of Saint-Louis, playing there from the age of eleven. In 1688 he succeeded his older brother, Jérôme (c. 1655–after 1738), as organist of Saint-Sévérin, where their father had served, and in 1698 was appointed organist of the splendid thirteenth-century Sainte-Chapelle (du Palais), one of Paris's leading musical institutions.[49]

Ranking, like Jérôme, as an organist of the first class, Marin was also highly regarded as a composer, though no works of his have survived. The brothers' father, Michel (ca. 1605–1679), had been organist of Saint-Chapelle (on the Île de la Cité) from January 1, 1633, to November 13, 1679.[50] Michel's *Le Triomphe de l'Amour sur des bergers et bergères* was performed before Louis XIV's court at the Louvre on January 22, 1655. Probably presented there in a concert version, *Le Triomphe* consisted of a series of airs, motets, and instrumental interludes for six singers and thirteen instruments. The first known *pastorale en musique,* it was sung throughout, its bucolic setting perhaps serving as a musical foretaste of Watteau's landscapes. *Le Triomphe*'s conventionally convoluted plot centered on a mythological pair of shepherds and shepherdesses along with Cupid.[51] Cessac views this pastorale as original in that it is the first example of this genre with a structure based on a "continuous . . . series of airs.[52]

Michel's brother François (thus Jacquet de La Guerre's uncle-in-law) was organist of Saint-Sépulcre in Paris. Michel's sister Nicole (or Noelle) was married in 1643 to the master instrument builder Simon Bongard.[53] Their two younger sons succeeded Michel from 1645 to 1650 as musical colleagues of Pierre Chabanceau de La Barre, a familiar name, as we have seen, in the complex network of related Parisian musical dynasties. In 1644 Michel de La Guerre married Marguerite Trépagne,[54] with whom he had fourteen children, many of them becoming musicians and thereby expanding the conglomeration of musical families even further.

Organist of the Chapelle Royale, Pierre Chabanceau gave concerts in his Paris home with performances by outstanding professional musicians such as the organist Michel de La Guerre (Jacquet de La Guerre's father-in-law) and the brilliant singer Anne Chabanceau de La Barre (1628–1688), the first French woman musician to receive a royal contract (1661) to perform in Louis XIV's private Cabinet de Roi. Praising Anne de La Barre's beautiful voice and graceful gestures, one of her observers remarked, "In French or Italian *airs,* no one else can please him (the king) more agreeably than this lady."[55] And, likewise, Jacquet de La Guerre's talents and accomplishments continued to be proclaimed by others even after her death.

From Motherhood to Widowhood

Jacquet gave birth to her only son in 1694, notably, the same year in which her opera was premiered by the Académie Royale de Musique.[56] Her son was one of her two known students and, like her, a precocious harpsichordist. (Jacquet's other student was the later celebrated composer and organist Louis-Claude Daquin.) Du Tillet noted: "At eight years of age, [Jacquet de La Guerre's son] surprised those who heard him play . . ., whether in solo performances or in accompanying. . . ."[57] Tragically, however, the boy died in 1704 at the age of ten.[58] She lost her husband on July 16 of that same year, compounding her grief, for she lost her closest family members over a span of just six years. Her father had died in November 1702—two years before her son. Her mother had died on July 30, 1698. Jacquet de La Guerre was also predeceased by her brother Nicolas (d. October 4, 1707) and her sister, Anne (d. c. 1723–1726). Therefore, all her immediate family was gone by 1726, except for her brother Pierre (d. 1739).[59]

In 1705 the widowed Jacquet de La Guerre moved to the Rue Regrattière in the parish of St. Louis-en-l'Île; her husband had also served as organist at the local church there. But she did not isolate herself from society to the extent that Maria Bach did (chapter 4). Although no publication of her works appeared from 1694 to 1707, Jacquet de La Guerre gave concerts and taught in her home for income. Meanwhile, she was actively engaged in composition, producing sonatas and cantatas in the Italian style, which had begun to interest the French. Jacquet de La Guerre clearly exercised her talents and independence during her twenty-five years as a widow.[60] She never remarried, but fortunately she could depend on a considerable income, one derived from her teaching, private performances on the harpsichord, sales of her music, family legacies, and other financial dealings.

In 1727 she moved to the parish of Saint-Eustache on the Rue des Prouvaires. Her apartment there was large, her furnishings were elegant, and her other personal belongings included numerous precious jewels, tapestries, paintings, a library well supplied with books, and two harpsichords. Always clothed beautifully in silk and taffeta, she was truly, as Cessac says it, "a woman of taste and culture."[61]

Jacquet's Salon and the Concert Life of Paris

The success of concerts in Jacquet de La Guerre's home, for example, led to turning these events into a virtual salon for a popular private musical series. Although the frequency and specific dates of her series are unknown, we do know that her concerts drew a sizable audience of prominent professional musicians and knowledgeable connoisseurs of Paris who came to hear her playing—especially her astonishing improvisations.

Jacquet de La Guerre gave concerts in her home of works by recognized musicians—as did, for example, Marin Marais (1656–1728) and Louis Nicolas Clérambault (1676–1749). These Paris salons provided testing grounds for hearing performances of the composers' newest solo suites for lute, harpsichord, and viol; as a result of this exposure to an audience, this music would be privately engraved and circulated. From the 1660s, instrumental, then vocal compositions began to be independently distributed publically. Besides these active salons, there were several other private musical groups active in Paris during Jacquet de La Guerre's lifetime. One such establishment was maintained by a socially prominent contemporary of Jacquet, Marie-Françoise Certain (d. 1711), an outstanding professional harpsichordist whose soirées took place close to the Palais-Royal. And, as we have seen, Mlle. De Guise supported a very select musical group at her home, her private musicales serving as one of several aristocratic ensembles presenting performances that were reviewed in the *Mercure gallant*. As with similar patronage of art and literature, these musical salons were organized and sponsored privately by both aristocratic and bourgeois patrons, who were often gifted women. The groups had developed into influential forces in French cultural life, as was the case in the arts circles of other major European cultural milieus such as those in Vienna and other cities of Europe. Performances sponsored by these groups typically included a composer's latest works.[62] Such exposure could lead to publication, reviews in the musical press, and perhaps eventual public notice.

Especially after 1715 (the year Louis XIV died), the fifty-year-old Jacquet de La Guerre gradually withdrew from her professional public life, writing her last known pieces: brief airs published by Ballard from 1721 to 1724 included in the *Recueils d'airs sérieux et à boire*; those in René Trépagne's *Les Amusemens de Mgr le duc de Bretagne*[63]; and her *Te Deum à Grands Choeurs*, presented in August 1721 in the Louvre chapel, celebrating the convalescence of the future Louis XV from smallpox. The work represents her one known venture into composing liturgical music, but the score has not survived.

Jacquet de La Guerre's twilight years coincided with other pivotal developments in Parisian concert life. Though it is not known whether she had any connection to the *Concert Spirituel,* this new public institution became a major component of eighteenth-century French cultural life. It was founded in 1725 (just four years before Jacquet de La Guerre's death) by the well-known composer Anne Danican Philidor (1681–1728). His *Concert* performances were held in the Salle des Suisses at the Tuileries palace. The organization offered both grandiose French choral works and Italian instrumental music, employing the Académie Royale's finest harpsichordists, harpists, and singers, including women performers. Foreign virtuoso instrumentalists also appeared frequently at the concerts, playing their new concertos. A commercial venture that existed until 1784, the *Concert* offered a public subscription concert series (with admission fees) on religious feast days, when the Académie was closed.[64] Contemporary with the *Concert Spirituel* were the *Concert Français* (established in 1727) and the *Concert Italien* (established in 1724), both sponsoring subscription concert series. The *Concert Français* specialized in such French music fare as *divertissements* and cantatas. The *Concert Italien* performed only Italian music and employed mostly Italian musicians. In 1641, Jacques Champion de Chambonnières (1601 or 1602–1672) had established a regularly scheduled concert series with paying audiences. Generously remunerated, this seventeenth-century series' ten musicians included two women singers and a viol player, who performed twice weekly at noon at St. Eustache, Jacquet's parish church.[65]

Public concerts, as well as private musical soirées for royal and lower-ranking Parisians, were, in fact, to become permanent features of French eighteenth-century musical life. Established during Jacquet de La Guerre's lifetime or shortly thereafter, these concert organizations signaled, above all, the spreading influence of the wealthy urban bourgeoisie as music patrons in the cultural affairs of the French capital. Jacquet de La Guerre clearly played an important role in this development. Besides her training and performances in the formal court life of music at Versailles, her well-attended musicales in Paris represented an early contribution to this change.

Having been widely acclaimed as a virtuoso performer and composer, Jacquet de La Guerre fell ill in the spring of 1729, died on June 27, 1729, and was buried a day later in her Gothic parish church, Saint-Eustache. In 1726 she had willed her compositions, except for her opera and opera-ballet, to her brother Pierre Jacquet. But in 1729, only three days before her death, she had—for reasons unknown—named her two Hiard nephews as her heirs instead. (One wonders if there is a simple reason for the change: if she knew her brother was critically ill, she may have decided to pass her legacy on directly to the next generation.)

From an early age, Jacquet de La Guerre's obviously careful musical training and her performances on the harpsichord were, in one sense, typical for an era in which both aristocratic and bourgeois French women learned instruments deemed appropriately "feminine": the lute, guitar, harp, organ, harpsichord, and later the piano. Nevertheless, Jacquet de La Guerre's training was a completely private enterprise.[66] She spent most of her childhood and teenage years in a cultural setting like no other of her day. That setting, Louis XIV's court at Versailles, surrounded her with a musical life that was rich, stimulating, ordered, and, indeed, overflowing with performances.

In his *Parnasse français* of 1732, a mammoth biographical tribute to the accomplishments of outstanding French poets and musicians, Évrard Titon du Tillet (1677–1762) also paid effusive posthumous homage to Jacquet de La Guerre's achievements. Titon du Tillet distinguished five levels of accomplishment, the highest being that of Louis XIV portrayed as Apollo; for the next level, three women writers as the three Graces were listed; then followed the third level, including Corneille, Molière, Racine, La Fontaine, and Lully as the nine Muses; after that a group of male and female poets and musicians including André Campra, Michel-Richard Delalande, Marin Marais, and Jacquet de La Guerre were named; finally, a group of four female singers was selected.[67]

Originally, Titon du Tillet had planned to have a public bronze monument erected in a Paris garden honoring illustrious French writers and musicians of the Louis XIV era. Because this venture proved unsuccessful, Titon du Tillet published a description of the would-be monument in 1727. A second, expanded edition appeared in 1732—the one described here; and in 1743 and 1755, two supplemental volumes were published.

The site for Versailles' most important musical performances, the Hall of Mirrors, was not completed until 1687, and, therefore, three years after Jacquet de La Guerre had married and moved to Paris. But she remained connected to musical life at Versailles long after she had left the court for Paris. (Much of the room's dazzle was created by architectural planning to capture the sunset's rays.) But the royal chateau at Versailles had already been unofficially serving as Louis XIV's residence from 1670 on.

In 1682, when Jacquet de La Guerre was about seventeen, the Bourbon court officially moved its permanent residence to the newly expanded and decorated Versailles establishment. Until then, the court had carried on its work in a city recovering from notorious witch hunts and Black Masses. (When the court had been stationed in Paris, its operations were carried on at three locations: the Louvre, the Tuileries, and the Palais Royal.)

Before and after the king's permanent move to Versailles, court life also extended to include a number of musically active royal chateaux such as Fontainebleau, Chantilly, Chambord, Saint-Germain, Meudon, and Marly. While Paris audiences were hearing Lully's stage works, however, the royal family was sponsoring private concerts of new music by Jacquet de La Guerre and others at these chateaux—performances of dramas, comédie-ballets, and operas. At the same time, public concerts were sprouting up in Paris during the last decade of Jacquet de La Guerre's life. These were centered on contemporary music, coupled with the continuing decline of music at Versailles under Louis XV, who had returned there for his entire reign (1723–1774).[68]

Portraying himself as a divinely ordained patriarch, Louis XIV personally oversaw music at his court more closely than any other royal potentate of his time, incorporating the control of court music into an autocratically organized administrative system. Propelling all these musical displays was a rigid social protocol requiring compulsory attendance for all courtiers at the musique de cour but allowing privileged attendance at the king's musique privée, the combination applying to Louis's daily *levée* and his other personal daily rituals accompanied by music, including the royal Mass. He himself was said to be somewhat skilled on the lute and guitar.[69] The king even paid careful attention when choosing outstanding musicians to instruct his children.

Louis was in the habit of appointing his administrators from the bourgeoisie rather than from his royal household. His ministers included Jean-Baptiste Colbert, who completed the establishment of the five royal academies to govern Louis's arts and intellectual pursuits. Wielding immense power himself, Louis appointed the equally absolutist Jean-Baptiste Lully (1632–1687)—a composer, dancer, and fabled violinist—to the position of *compositeur de la musique instrumentale de roi* in 1653; *surintendant et compositeur de la musique de roi* in 1661; and *maître de la musique de la famille royale* in 1662. By 1673, Louis had given Lully control of the theater in the Palais Royal. In his position as a virtual patron saint of French music, the Italian-born Lully fit with apparent ease into Louis XIV's hyper-organized court music system. The musical forces were divided into three principal jurisdictions: Music of the Chamber, Music of the Great Stable, and Music of the Royal Chapel. Each group was also subdivided into smaller ensembles, and musicians from one smaller group could and did play in another. Appointments to these groups in effect were hereditary as legacies handed down to relatives, friends, and students.

As in other jurisdictions of court administration, court music was divided into rigid categories.[70] Music of the chamber consisted of solo singers, a choir of about forty male and female voices (male or female sopranos, countertenors, tenors, baritones, basses), and instrumentalists performing mainly secular music.[71] The most celebrated of their era, the musicians of the king's chamber included representatives of some of the most illustrious musical families of Paris and Versailles: for example, (among the singers) Delalande, Rebel, Couperin, and La Barre; (among the lutenists and theorbo players) Chabanceau de La Barre; (among the flutists) La Barre; (among the viol players) Marais; and (among the harpsichordists) Chambonnières and, again, Couperin. Jacquet de La Guerre, Marie-Françoise Certain, and François *le Grande*'s daughter Marguerite-Antoinette Couperin (1705–c. 1778) were favorite harpsichordists of Louis XIV—although they held no official position as royal musicians.[72]

Music of the Versailles Great Stable comprised ensemble instrumentalists—horsemen and predominantly brass and timpani players—for outdoor military *fêtes* (including battlefield fanfares and parades) and allegorical equestrian ballets. Music of the Chapelle Royale included the prestigious *24 Violons du Roi* (a five-part *Grande Bande,* an orchestra consisting of six violins, four each of three inner violas of various types, and six bass instruments; and the *12 Petits Violons du Roi* (the *Petite Bande).* (Orchestras in Italy and elsewhere in Europe were typically groups of soloists.[73]) These two *bandes* of Versailles became the core of the French court orchestra, often serenading Louis privately to meet his unquenchable need for self-aggrandizement.

Present at the court under De Montespan's protection, the young Jacquet de La Guerre would no doubt have at least been aware of these rigid court categories, and her everyday routine must have been affected by them. In addition, members of Jacquet de La Guerre's greater family circle had gradually won appointments as musicians of the king's chamber, holding distinguished positions. These musicians included the soprano Anne Chabanceau de La Barre, whose husband and sister were also court musicians, and her father, Pierre Chabanceau de La Barre (1628–1688), an esteemed lutenist serving regularly as court organist.

Jacquet de La Guerre's years under Louis XIV's protection, and likely later, also gave her ample opportunities to witness important, if secondary, musical events at the French court, for, powerful in their own right, the wives and mistresses of the Bourbon dynasty personally contributed to this musical activity in notable ways. Until and after the court officially moved to Versailles, this intense cultivation of music took place at various chateaus connected with the court. As described earlier, Louis XIV's mistresses De Montespan and later De Maintenon sponsored chamber music performances in the king's private quarters. Even Louis's mother, Anne of Austria, maintained her own private concerts. De Maintenon also established the Maison Royale de Saint-Louis at Saint-Cyr, a music school for young female vocal students whose salaries at graduation were relatively high.[74]

Other aristocratic women supported various musical performances, usually in their own quarters within the Versailles circle. Louis's daughter-in-law, the Duchesse de Maine, for instance, organized elaborate musical entertainments at her chateau at Sceaux, near Versailles, from c. 1700. From 1725, Maria Leszczinska, Louis XV's wife, even organized music making at Versailles itself, performing herself, in fact, in private court concerts.[75]

Louis XIV's grandson Philippe Duke of Orléans, too, sponsored private rather than public concerts, relegating a number of French sopranos to perform on these occasions to serve also as his mistresses. He had no intention, however, of supporting these women as professional singers.[76]

Elisabeth Jacquet's Music: Works for Harpsichord

In his *Parnasse* of 1732 (three years after Jacquet de La Guerre's death), Titon du Tillet pointedly affirmed her high position as a composer: "Madame de la Guerre had a very great genius for composition, and excelled in vocal Music the same as in instrumental. . . ." Jacquet de La Guerre's fame as both a performer and composer spread not only in France but outside its borders throughout the eighteenth century. Besides Titon du Tillet's *Parnasse,* Johann Gottfried Walther (1753), Friedrich Wilhelm Marpurg (1755–1761), and Sir John Hawkins (1776) included Jacquet de La Guerre in their lexicons, ranking her equal to such male composers and performers as Delalande and Marais.

Jacquet de La Guerre's eloquent and powerfully expressive music was rooted largely in her remarkable gifts for harpsichord and organ performance—notably, her virtuosity and remarkably inventive improvisations. Yet besides Jacquet de La Guerre, there were also a number of other notable French women harpsichordists of the Louis XIV era, one of the most outstanding being Marie-Françoise Certain (d. 1711).[77] (Interestingly for Jacquet's times, François Couperin declared that women were "generally better" than male performers on the instrument because "the suppleness of [their] nerves contributes more to good playing than force." At least two of his female relatives, moreover, excelled as harpsichordists.[78])

Jacquet de La Guerre's extraordinary skills won her early recognition as a brilliant performer; she had played the harpsichord regularly at Versailles, thoroughly exposing her to harpsichord literature. This experience proved invaluable to her in her compositions for harpsichord; for, the French harpsichord composers of her era counted among Europe's most celebrated. She had to "compete" with several of them, including François (sometimes referred to as Charles) Dieupart (c. 1670–c. 1740), Louis Marchand (c. 1669–1732), Jean-François Dandrieu (1682–1738), Louis-Nicolas Clérambault (1676–1749), and Jean-Philippe Rameau (1683–1764). (Their predecessors included, among others, Jacques Champion de Chambonnières (1602–1672)—generally referred to as the founder of the French school of harpsichord music; Louis Couperin (c. 1626–1661)—an uncle of François *le Grande* and a student of Chambonnières, he introduced the unmeasured prelude, combining improvisatory style with the spirit of experimentation;[79] Jean-Henri D'Anglebert (ca. 1628–1691); Jean-Nicolas Geoffroy (?–1694); Jean-Nicolas-Antoine Lebègue (1631–1702), another pupil of Chambonnières; and Marc-Antoine Charpentier (1643–1704).

French Baroque harpsichord music such as Jacquet de La Guerre's inherited both stylistic and structural features from the earliest French lute tablatures.[80] The seventeenth-century archetypal French harpsichord suite, for example, absorbed the lute suite's unmeasured prelude, its *style brisé* (chords sounded one note at a time rather than being played simultaneously), and its fixed order of dance movements, while maintaining a central tonality. Each dance movement was gradually standardized by a characteristic style, form, and a richly embellished *double* with contrapuntal textures.[81] With harpsichord music's harmonic idiom and texture, inner voices sound intact, though in reality they are shredded as if improvised—that is, continually disrupted to produce an ever-changing sonic density. The dance movements include the allemande, with its complex texture, asymmetrical phrases and counterpoint; the courante, with its rhythmically intricate texture; the sarabande—symmetrical in rhythmic and structural features; and the fast-paced gigue—generally contrapuntal in texture and cast in consistently dotted rhythms.[82]

In 1687, the year Lully died, the twenty-one-year-old Jacquet was living and working in Paris, having been married for three years. That year saw the publication of her *Premier Livre de Pièces de Clavessin*. (It is unknown exactly when she completed it.)[83] Rated by Anthony as containing her "most eloquent and original" harpsichord compositions, the *Premier Livre* is one of the rare collections of harpsichord pieces published in France in the seventeenth century. In style and construction, this set reflects other compositions of her times, but she wrote them with extraordinary inventiveness, grace, skill, and eloquence. Long thought lost, the collection (published by Henri de Baussen in Paris) was discovered in the 1980s in Venice by musicologist Carol Henry Bates.[84]

The *Premier Livre* consists of four suites, one each in D minor, G minor, A minor, and F major. The first three suites begin with a *prélude* and the fourth with a *tocade*; all four have standardized *allemandes,* two *courantes*, a *sarabande*, a *gigue* (no. 2 has two), and a *menuet*. Suites no. 1 and 3 have a *chaconne*; nos. 1 and 4 have a *cannaris*; nos. 1 and 3 have nine movements, while no. 2 has eight.

The *prélude* of Suite no. 1 (in D minor) offers much insight into Jacquet de La Guerre's stylistic approach to writing for harpsichord (fig. 10). Derived from lute and organ works, the imaginative improvisatory style of this piece firmly establishes the key of D minor. The form is threefold: two unmeasured sections and one measured.[85] The first suite displays Jacquet's signature style and structure in the dances, too: highly ornamented melodic lines in the Allemande, a pair of inventive Courantes, a Sarabande, a contrapuntal Gigue, a *Cannaris* with bold dotted rhythms and a stately Menuet in *rondeau* form. This suite also includes a *Chaconne l'Inconstante* of distinct character while Jacquet toys back and forth between D major and minor, diving into the harpsichord's lowest notes.

The remaining suites of the 1687 collection exhibit Jacquet de La Guerre's audacious, but skillful, approach in their daring harmonic interrelationships, vehement broken chords focused on a key center, rhythmic variety, profusion of melodic embellishments, and contrapuntal ingenuity. The composer was only twenty-two when these suites were published. The fluency of her writing is not surprising considering that she had played the harpsichord music of her predecessors repeatedly in her evening performances during her Versailles years, dazzling her royal audiences and learning the harpsichord repertoire thoroughly. Thus, she acquired a keen ability to compose her own works, developing, for example, a firmly set and balanced structure never attained previously, one outlined with the impression of improvisation in her writing style, especially in the opening movements of her suites.[86]

Instead of a *prélude,* Suite no. 4 opens with a *tocade* (or toccata), the only known such movement in France dating from the seventeenth century.[87] This

Figure 10. Jacquet de La Guerre, first page of the *Prélude* from the Suite no. 1 in D Minor, *Les Pièces de Clavessin/Premier Livre*, 1687. *Harpsichord Works,* Arthur Lawrence, ed., from *The Collected Works,* Vol. 1. New York: The Broude Trust, 2008. Courtesy of The Broude Trust; and the Library of Congress Music Division, Washington, D.C.

piece holds a singular position within the repertoire of French harpsichord music of Jacquet's generation—above all, for its Italianate contrapuntal play that contributes to its overall structure and for the characteristically French type of unmeasured prelude (fig. 11).[88]

Pièces de Clavecin Qui Peuvent se Joüer sur le Viollon

Published in Paris by Henri de Baussen in 1707, Jacquet de La Guerre's *Pièces de Clavecin Qui Peuvent se Joüer sur le Viollon* consist of two concisely structured

Figure 11. Jacquet de La Guerre, first page of the *Tocade* from the Suite no. 4 in F Major, *Les Pièces de Clavessin/Premier Livre*, 1687. *Harpsichord Works,* Arthur Lawrence, ed., from *The Collected Works,* Vol. 1. Courtesy of The Broude Trust and the Library of Congress Music Division.

suites: one in D minor and the second in G major. These works impressed Titon du Tillet as striking examples of melodic fluidity and rich harmony, and they were highly praised in the *Journal des Sçavans* for their "tender feeling, fire, beautiful harmony and joyful naturalness."[89] But the most outstanding new feature of the 1707 collection lies in their title, though it is unexplained: "harpsichord pieces that can be played on the violin." Cessac believes that these works were intended to be played on the harpsichord with the topmost voice doubled on the violin.[90] The instrumentation of these compositions—for harpsichord accompanied by violin—are advanced for Jacquet's day; they "anticipate" examples by Jean-Philippe Rameau, even those of Mozart and Beethoven.

In the first suite of this set, the elegant and imaginative allemande, titled *La Flamande,* is a striking character piece, one that is technically demanding. It is notable for its rich texture often consisting of three and four closely knit melodic lines proceeding simultaneously, and for its incorporation of lute idioms. Its *double* is an embellished version of the allemande itself with ornaments being spelled out in the score and/or specified by signs in the manner then current. Two other movements of this suite also include *doubles*.[91] The contrapuntal writing and sequential melodic patterns of this piece lend it a balanced, cohesive structure and a clear sense of direction. Its breadth and profuse melodic ornamentation represent a French tradition grounded in the harpsichord compositions of Chambonnières and Couperin.[92]

Les Sonates pour le Viollon et pour le Clavecin

Also dating from 1707 are *Les Sonates pour le Viollon et pour le Clavecin* (six works in D minor, D major, F major, G major, A minor, and A major). These are among ten sets of sonatas for these instruments known to have been published in France between 1704 and 1707. Fueled by the fascination of French composers for this genre, this interest has been traced back at least to 1695.[93] Fusing a characteristically French cultivation of the suite with the style and idiom of the Italian sonata, Jacquet de La Guerre's sonatas demonstrate the clarity of the Italian style, suffusing Corelli's works without abandoning, for example, such French features as rondeau form as seen predominating in the arias. This music, Cessac concludes, exemplifies "the union of French *tendresse et très-heureux naturel* [with] Italian *belle harmonie et feu.*"[94]

The *Mercure gallant* and the *Journal des Sçavans* of August 1707 give detailed descriptions of Jacquet de La Guerre's personal presentation of this music for violin and harpsichord to Louis XIV at the Marly chateau on June 13, 1707. Two musicians named only Marchand in the two journals are reported to have performed this music brilliantly. The monarch himself also praised the beauty and originality of this music, granting Jacquet de La Guerre the privilege of having the sonatas and other works published by royal command—Louis was, after all, the dedicaté.[95]

Six sonatas were published c. 1695: four trio sonatas for two violins with basso continuo and viola da gamba or cello, the latter instrument appearing in French chamber music before its use in the French opera orchestra and thus perhaps showing that in this respect Jacquet de La Guerre was at the forefront of her times; and two sonatas for violin solo and viola da gamba *obbligata* with organ or harpsichord continuo. "The solo sonatas number among the earliest of their genre in France. François Couperin *le Grande* (1668–1733) was composing his first sonatas three years before Jacquet de La Guerre wrote hers, but his were published later than hers. She herself probably played her sonatas extemporaneously; that is, improvisation accounts for the rather plain continuo part, omissions suggesting that the performer fill them in with ornamentation."[96]

Les Jeux

Since from her youth, Jacquet de La Guerre had frequently accompanied dramatic productions on the harpsichord, it is not surprising that she devoted much of her creative energy to the composition of theater works. The composer's *opéra-ballet* (or a sung ballet), *Les Jeux à l'honneur de la victoire*, was first performed probably around 1691 or 1692.[97]

Cessac cites the work as "perhaps the first example of this genre."[98] The journal *Séjour de Paris* (1727) reported that Jacquet de La Guerre had composed several works as early as 1680, including a "little opera" performed in July 1685 before Louis XIV, the Dauphin, and de Montespan. All of these have been lost except for the libretto of *Les Jeux*.[99] The text of *Les Jeux*, however, does provide some information about the work as a whole, giving the stage setting, the positioning of the dances, stage machinery, and occasionally the orchestration. The composition opens with a prologue (celebrating Louis XIV's recent military victories and hence glorifying France), three *divertissements* divided into eight scenes, an *entrée général*, the plot (a mythological allegory), choruses, solo vocal pieces, and ballets. The undated libretto also contains Jacquet de La Guerre's dedication to Louis XIV, from which the following is excerpted:

> When this play was presented to me, I was at once extremely eager to undertake it. Everything having Your Majesty's glory as its end is marvelously exciting; and when the desire to please you is added to it, what further aim could one have? It is by just such an incentive that I have always been prompted to work. From the most tender age (this memory will be eternally precious to me), presented to your illustrious court, where I have had the honor to be for several years, I learned, Sire, to consecrate to you all of my waking hours. You deigned at that time to accept the first fruits of my gifts, and it has pleased you to receive several further productions. But these particular marks of my zeal did not suffice for me, and I welcome the happy opportunity to be able to make a public [offering]. That is what led me to write this ballet for the theatre. It is not just today [but earlier] that women have written excellent pieces of poetry, which have had great success. But until now, none has tried to set a whole opera to music; and I take this advantage from my enterprise: that the more extraordinary it is, the more it is worthy of you, Sire, and the more it justified the liberty that I take in offering you this work.[100]

From her first days at the Versailles court, Jacquet de La Guerre had dedicated her compositions solely to the king. Composers of the time, such as her older contemporary the Italian-born Antonia Bembo (ca. 1643–before 1715), wrote operas only if a performance was possible. Composers, therefore, wrote only on commission, all works being directed toward specific performers and occasions. One could conclude that, in the case of *Les Jeux*, Jacquet de La Guerre's dedication to Louis XIV carried with it the probability that he would sponsor its performance. Indeed, Louis XIV was said to have liked the pastorale so much that it was given several additional performances.[101] Louis, in fact, routinely expected to be honored by formal dedications from French composers, further illustrating yet another facet of the king's rigid categorization of court music and reinforcing the centralized bias of his regime. Louis's pride was also evident in Jacquet de La Guerre's florid dedications of her music to him—but not surprisingly, for her compositions and their publication were routinely taken care of under his royal command. Yet her dedications to the *roi de soleil* also may have hinted at a certain self-confidence rising from the composer's realization that her accomplishments—precisely because they were "allowed" to be addressed to the king—were significant.

Jacquet de La Guerre's Tragédie Lyrique and Lully's Legacy

Lully's stage music had become the model for French composers of his day. In fact, before Lully, French vocal music based on a lengthy libretto that set the course of the characters' ever-evolving emotions was virtually unknown.[102] Lully's stage music comprised, above all, his *tragédies lyriques* (composed between 1672 and 1686), a genre that is generally believed he himself created. Besides his *tragédies lyriques,* Lully's other stage music included the Italianate *ballets de cour* (1653–1663). Dating from the late sixteenth century, the *ballet de cour* typically included Italian scenes (that is, sections sung and acted frequently in Italianate comic style) with coherent dramatic themes and large-scale dance *divertissements,* the king being allegorically glorified as a mythical or historical hero. Librettos of *ballets de cour* were regularly published and scrutinized by the French public very closely. (Perhaps the audience's judgment of the quality of the libretto for Jacquet's opera, *Céphale et Procris,* as being only mediocre provides a clue for its failure at its Paris premiere.)[103]

Professional dancers and singers, young nobles, and gifted commoners intermingled as performers, including Louis XIV as a dancer.[104] Even after his premature death in 1687 from a bizarre accident, Lully's works continued to monopolize the stage of the Académie Royale de Musique, especially with support of his oldest son, Louis (1664–1734), and other zealous followers of the composer, such as active performers and composers. Lully's last opera, *Acis et Galatée* (1686), was staged regularly at this theater as late as 1762.

Céphale et Procris

Published in 1694 by Ballard in Paris, Jacquet de La Guerre's five-act opera *Céphale et Procris*—the first known *tragédie lyrique* composed by a woman for the Académie Royale de Musique in Paris—was premiered there on March 17 of that year.[105] Her librettist was Joseph François, Duché de Vancy (1668–1704). He drew his text for *Céphale et Procris* from the *Metamorphoses* of the ancient Latin poet Ovid, de Vancy also adding some of his own subplots.[106] While also incorporating Jacquet de La Guerre's own particular musical features, such as the dramatic use of silences, *Céphale et Procris* was largely indebted stylistically and structurally to Lully's *tragédies lyriques* (1672–1687); in these massive works, the drama—typically based on Greek mythology centered on the theme of love opposed by powerful intervening gods—was carried mainly by recitative interspersed with lyrical *airs de cour*. (The *air de cour* genre, in fact, captured composers' imaginations throughout seventeenth-century Europe.) Lully assigned choruses—both *grand* (soprano, countertenor, tenor, bass) and *petit choeur*—an exhortatory or supplicatory role. A five-part orchestra provided overtures, preludes, *ritournelles,* dramatic symphonies, nature scenes, and dances. Judging by the stylistic temper of the times, one surmises that Jacquet's orchestra included a five-part string section, a texture particularly favored by French opera composers from the mid-seventeenth century into the 1740s. Italianate four-part scoring did not become common in French opera until the mid-eighteenth century.[107]

Jacquet de La Guerre's opera opens with a prologue glorifying Louis XIV that leads to the first of five acts, the first and last being most crucial to the tragic drama.[108] Along with stage machinery offering special effects, the opera proceeds through a series of recitatives interspersed by various airs (solos and duets), ensembles, choruses, dances, and instrumental pieces. Significantly, these are all governed by a structure based on a tonal center, giving rise to a cohesive whole.[109] This tonal organization is defined at the outset in the prologue, in reality an expansive French rondeau.[110]

All in all, Jacquet de La Guerre created a drama of imposing psychological depth, the characters' unusually lengthy airs giving vent to overwhelming human emotions. A narrative of the dramatic action, act 1 of *Céphale et Procris* establishes the plot, which presents the factor of divine intervention leading inevitably to the tragedy resolved in the final act. Providing the catastrophic resolution of these preceding events, act 2 lays out the critical theme of infidelity instigated by powerful divinities. Procris's deeply expressive air "Lieux écartez, paisible solitude," (act 2, scene 1) an Italianate da capo air (rather than a French rondeau form) expresses great suffering, challenging the singer with difficult melodic intervals and unexpected harmonies. In act 3, Céphale's air *Amour, que sous tes loix cruelles,* which is in rondeau form (ABACA'A), is skillfully balanced with a *divertissement,* ballet, other songs, and dances. Act 4 continues the theme of infidelity; Procris sings a moving lament (*Funeste mort, donnez-moi du secours*) (act 4, scene 3), followed by an all-male chorus of demons set for *hautes-contres,* tenors and basses, this in turn leading to Céphale reappearing before Procris. Cessac finds act 5 to be basically "a tragic resolution of cruelty as much as of fidelity." Procris expresses this in an impelling recitative (*Et quoyque mon coeur en murmure*), she being overcome by what she sees as Céphale's unfaithfulness, which dooms her never to be able to see him again.[111]

But, unlike Jacquet de La Guerre's earlier *Les Jeux, Céphale et Procris* enjoyed only a few additional performances. A number of reasons account for this. Some commentators conclude that the opera's brief run resulted from a limited response by the audience. But no solid evidence that this was the case has yet been discovered. Other observers agree with Cuthbert Girdlestone's opinion that the audience's reaction stemmed from the opera's dramatically weak libretto. Duché de Vancy's text even included subplots of his own creation unfolding in complicated twists and artificial effects—also his own—that interrupt the story's dramatic tension rather than intensifying it. Problems such as these in the libretto possibly failed to ignite Jacquet de La Guerre's gifts for "musical invention."[112] Second, by 1686, only two years after Jacquet de La Guerre's wedding, her musical environment was changing significantly; the elaborate *fêtes* allegorizing love and war had fallen out of favor. Third, Paris was usurping the leading role of Versailles in musical life while the court was instead directing its repertoire more toward sacred music—such as the importance given the *grand motet,* a preference reinforced by Louis XIV's mistress De Maintenon. Fourth, Louis was paying little attention to opera at Versailles, theatrical performances there gradually declining in quality. Fifth, in the 1690s, France began suffering economic problems and devastating military losses, both factors contributing to a lowered public morale. (This state of affairs may have, intentionally or unintentionally, heightened Jacquet de La Guerre's paean to the glory of Louis XIV in the prologue of the opera.) Sixth, Music of the Chapelle Royale, in fact, was being performed by choral forces, with some instrumentalists, in a sacred repertoire more heavily financed and more forward-looking than the music performed in the parish churches of Paris. Seventh, Lully's operas continued to monopolize the stage of the French capital's Académie well after his death in 1687. Finally, the Parisian public possibly harbored prejudice against a woman's work being presented on the city's opera stage.

Jacquet de La Guerre's opera found favor outside Paris, however. A composer, music theorist, lexicographer, and collector, Sébastien de Brossard (1655–1730) performed the prologue to *Céphale et Procris* at Strasbourg's Académie de la Musique (which he himself had established) between 1695 and 1698. Happily for Jacquet de La Guerre, the opera won considerable success with the Strasbourg public.[113] In 1726, Brossard left his entire music collection, including some of the composer's works, to the Bibliotèque Royale in Paris.

The Cantatas

After the failure of *Céphale et Procris* in Paris, Jacquet de La Guerre did not return to the composition of dramatic works until she wrote the first book of her *Cantates françoises,* which Ballard brought out in 1708. (The remaining sets appeared in 1711 and c. 1715, respectively.) The composer may have taken advantage of the new vogue in dramatic French vocal music that took hold around 1700: the composition of cantatas, eight hundred works of this kind being composed between 1700 and 1730, after which a decline set in.[114] Until the cantata rage, French music of the later seventeenth century had centered on the *tragédie lyrique* and the *divertissement.* Philippe d'Orléans, (an amateur musician himself) who became French regent in 1715, strongly supported the Italianate style. The controversy between advocates of French versus Italian style had continued from at least the Fronde dispute and gripped Paris into the eighteenth century. Another factor intensified the French vogue of Italian style: Lully's death gradually allowed other French composers, including Jacquet de La Guerre, the opportunity to absorb Italian music more freely.[115] Also, Louis XIV himself, together with his Bourbon relatives, had favored contemporary Italian music, as did his grandson Philippe II, Duke of Orléans, eventually Louis XV's regent and a serious composer and music patron. As regent, Philippe, in fact, even "institutionalized Italian music and theatre."[116]

In November 1713, the *Mercure gallant* reported that "a musician no longer arrives [in Paris from Italy] without a sonata or cantata in his pocket."[117] A year later, the same publication commented that the cantatas and sonatas were flooding Paris because of a shift in taste toward preferring imported Italian works, leading audiences in the French capital to grow indifferent to Lully's operas.[118]

Although the French continued to resist the importation of the newer Italian musical style and genres (and the French maintained a decided prejudice against using castrato singers), a number of Jacquet de La Guerre's works, along with those of Clérambault and François Couperin, exposed French composers to the latest Italian style of composition. However, Jacquet's cantatas were not totally Italian in their conception. Playing a critical role in the development of the early eighteenth-century French cantata, the poet Jean-Baptiste Rousseau (1671–1741) conceived his cantata texts as poems based on mythological and allegorical themes, the poems being organized into *récits* alternating with airs. Accordingly, Jacquet de La Guerre's cantatas generally followed his formal scheme, her *aires* allegorically capturing emotions, even religious feelings, with striking effect and remarkable intensity, her recitatives further heightening a sense of form.[119]

The Italianate style of Jacquet de La Guerre's cantatas included robust, inventive themes and fluid melodic lines coupled with unexpected harmonic progressions, traits marking the music of Arcangelo Corelli (1653–1713) and other Italian composers. In addition, Italian operas and cantatas were being privately performed at aristocrats' lavish *hôtels* and at the less ostentatious salons of professional performers themselves, as well as at the Palais Royal, where the audiences included royal patronesses from Versailles.

Along with her opera-ballet and opera scores, Jacquet de La Guerre's cantatas also signaled the advent of the eighteenth-century *femme-compositeur*: a French woman composer of large-scale works who typically came from bourgeois musicians' families—unlike the seventeenth century's proliferation of women composers from the nobility, who, as a rule, wrote songs only for their private use.[120] Duchess Sophie-Elisabeth proved an exception, for (as discussed in chapter 1), besides her private devotional songs, she also wrote grand *Festspiele* for public performances, albeit the audiences for these were limited to the nobility only.

Jacquet de La Guerre's cantatas appeared in three volumes: two are based on biblical subjects and one on secular themes.[121] The composer's religious works, which won popularity among the Parisian public, might again be contrasted with Duchess Sophie-Elisabeth's basically private devotional compositions, which are serious, however, rather than dramatic.

Jacquet de La Guerre's clear distinction between sacred and secular music contrasts dramatically with the characteristic practice outside Louis XIV's court, notably in Paris, where such a differentiation tended to be far less obvious. Certain cultural factors might have contributed to the composer's turn away from opera to composing cantatas, in addition to the reasons discussed earlier in this chapter. First, the composer could reasonably have been inspired—both in large-scale and more intimate dimensions—by the sensitive, beautifully wrought, and Italianate sacred compositions of the French cantata's chief exponent, Marc-Antoine Charpentier (1643–1704). Charpentier and Jacquet de La Guerre's sister, Anne Jacquet, were employed by Marie de Lorraine—Mlle. De Guise—to perform at her residence in concerts of Italianate cantatas and sonatas by French composers, including many works written by Charpentier himself on commission.[122] Isabelle d'Orléans—Mme. De Guise and also Louis XIV's cousin—also resided at this residence and employed musicians there. Jacquet de La Guerre consequently may have heard some of her sister's performances at the De Guise household.[123]

In addition, as mentioned earlier, the enormous and complex Versailles establishment itself was beginning to show a preference for sacred music.[124] For example, Jacquet de La Guerre may have been influenced by the religious fervor of De Maintenon, Louis XIV's mistress, as noted earlier, who became his wife during Jacquet's last year at Versailles. In a penetrating study of the relationship between women and the composition of mid-seventeenth-century devotional airs, Catherine Gordon-Seifert notes that at Versailles De Maintenon herself was pressured by her confessor to pay more attention to religious devotion. During Jacquet de La Guerre's childhood, devotional airs—often love songs given new sacred texts—were beginning to proliferate in Versailles and Paris. The availability of devotional airs, Gordon-Seifert concludes, was "part of a significant movement initiated by Catholic leaders to convert the laity to a life of piety."[125] French clergymen in seventeenth-century France were relying on music as a powerful force to advance their cause. François Berthod, for example, a mid-seventeenth-century French prelate and composer of devotional airs for women, instructed them to sing the passionate melodies of his works while maintaining, as he phrased it, their "modesty, piety and virtue." This priest's *airs de dévotion,* in fact, reflected "the Catholic clergy's efforts," Gordon-Seifert contends, "to wrest women of the nobility from their 'trivial and licentious life style.'"[126]

Jacquet de La Guerre was the first French woman known to have published entire books of cantatas. As mentioned earlier, two of the three volumes of them contain works based on biblical subjects, the third being based on such secular themes as moral issues. Published volume by volume in 1708, 1711, and 1715, this music stands as a sublime contribution to the early French solo cantata, the first two volumes numbering among the earliest sacred examples of this genre composed in France.[127] They also represent some of the earliest French cantatas incorporating features of the Italian cantata.[128] (Georg Friedrich Händel composed more than one hundred cantatas, all in Italian, while residing in Italy between 1707 and 1709.)

Jacquet de La Guerre's cantatas exhibit her characteristic originality. Intent on fusing musical expression and its underlying texts, she sensitively adhered to speech-rhythm rather than indulging in virtuosic bravura merely for its own sake. Her sensuous portrayal of texts in music also includes descriptive *symphonies* that speak to human emotions: for example, the chaotic noise of battle in *Le passage de la mer rouge* and the comforting promise of sleep in *Judith.*

Her preludes and interludes engage the instruments in artfully constructed contrapuntal dialogues with the voices, rather than serving only as accompaniment. In her cantatas, therefore, the composer transformed the ordinary texts of French playwright and poet Antoine Houdar de la Motte (1672–1731) into works of a highly expressive nature. Dealing with dramatic human events and experiences, her cantatas often contain precise musical depictions of subjects in the natural world as in, for example, the raging tempest in *Jonas.* Yet, for Jacquet, mimicking nature reflected more an emotional sense of the natural world rather than its strictly literal representation, suggesting parallels with Watteau's paintings.

Jacquet de La Guerre's cantatas soon attracted much public attention and favorable reviews. The *Journal des Sçavans* praised both the vocal part and the harmony in her cantatas, as well as the way she "always constructs her music according to the feeling or passion that dominate each work; the music expresses the individual words and their significance—without doing so excessively. . . ."

And in the *avertissement* of her third volume of cantatas, the composer herself confirms this assessment, explaining, " . . . I am convinced that vocal music that does not express what [the text] one sings will not be favored by . . . those whose taste and understanding go hand in hand."[129]

The first two books of Jacquet de La Guerre's *Cantates françoises sur des sujets tirez de écriture* consist of twelve works based on De La Motte's version of Old Testament subjects. Five of the twelve biblical cantatas involve women—Esther, Rachel, Susanne, Judith, and (the daughter of) Jepthé. Book 1 of the *Cantates françoises* consists of settings for solo voice, basso continuo, and *obbligato* instrumental accompaniment, this volume containing *Esther, Le passage de la mer rouge, Jacob et Rachel, Jonas, Susanne et les vieillards,* and *Judith.* The solo voices in book 2 vary between one and two. The cantatas included are *Adam, Le Temple Rebasti, Le Déluge, Joseph, Jephté,* and *Samson.*

Truly minidramas, these two sets of cantatas capture emotions, even religious feelings, with striking effect and remarkable intensity, Jacquet de La Guerre's moving recitatives further heightening the sense of drama. For instance, the composer does this by emphasizing a crucial word through an unexpected modal change, a poignant use of rests, extremes of vocal range, or continually changing the lengths of note-values. All these devices intensify emotional effects.

Perhaps designed to be staged, book 3 of the *Cantates françoises* dates from 1715, being published around or shortly after that year. Jacquet de La Guerre dedicated it to her new patron, Elector Maximilian Emanuel II of Bavaria (1662–1726), who resided in France from 1709 to 1715. Louis XIV, the composer's customary and chief *dedicaté,* had died on September 1, 1715. Book 3 contains three secular cantatas: *Sémélé, L'Île de Délos,* and *Le Sommeil d'Ulisse.* Based on mythological and allegorical subjects, they are set for solo soprano, violin, and basso continuo with additional instruments: violins and a flute in the first and third cantatas; and flute, oboe, violin, and viola da gamba in the second.[130] Set in typical French baroque air-recitative sections, these three cantatas are intentionally lengthy, as Jacquet remarked in the score, in contrast to the traditional sets of six much shorter cantatas. The three include instrumental *symphonies* dramatically imitating the sound of storms (thunder and lightning) or suggesting pastoral scenes as in much French baroque opera.

Sémélé is a tiny but potent drama drawn from Greek mythology that centers on Zeus's mistress, who is also Dionysius's mother. Marin Marais (1656–1728) composed an opera (*tragédie lyrique*) titled *Sémélé* dating from 1709. Also, the English composer John Eccles (c. 1668–1735) completed his opera *Sémélé* in 1707. The figure of Sémélé was also set as a dramatic oratorio, HWV 58, by Georg Friedrich Händel in 1744.

A moralistic tale of ultimately tragic dimensions, Jacquet de La Guerre's *Sémélé* is driven by human emotion. The cantata contains three da capo airs (that Jacquet

Figure 12. Jacquet de La Guerre, "Symphonie" from *Sémélé, Cantates françoises,* c. 1715. From *Secular Vocal Works,* Mary Cyr, ed., from *The Collected Works,* Vol. 4, 2005. Courtesy of The Broude Trust and the Library of Congress Music Division.

said could be performed independently), their size being more extensive than those in other cantatas of her day. The recitatives bear a distinctive French stamp, with their texts dictating a continually fluctuating rhythm (figs. 12 and 13).

The instruments both accompany the voice—often in dialogues—and appear in interludes between the vocal statements, these passages offering contrasted sonorities that increase the impact of the text. In addition, brazen, unexpected harmonic changes serve to underscore specific words.[131]

Figure 13. Jacquet de La Guerre, "Quel triomphe," (measures 151–62) from *Sémélé, Cantates françoises*, c. 1715. From *Secular Vocal Works*, Mary Cyr, ed., from *The Collected Works*, Vol. 4. Courtesy of The Broude Trust and the Library of Congress Music Division.

Le Raccommodement Comique de Pierrot et de Nicole

Published with Jacquet de La Guerre's secular cantatas, *Le Raccommodement Comique de Pierrot et de Nicole* is a comic duet for bass and soprano with basso continuo. The work was originally intended to be performed in Paris as part of a two-act play (*La Ceinture de Vénus*) by Alain-René Lesage. It was presented only in a shorter version without accompaniment in February 1715 at the Théâtre de Foire Saint-Germain, a popular theater customarily centered on comic productions.[132] Based on licentious subject matter, although held at the medieval abbey of St.-Germain-des-Près, the annual fair played a significant role in Parisian musical and theatrical circles, providing amusement in an essentially commercial atmosphere: one of acrobats, actors, dancers, singers, and instrumentalists appearing in witty dramatic farces in the midst of wares—including musical instruments and books—being sold by hundreds of enterprising merchants.[133]

In a comment about performing her duet, Jacquet de La Guerre emphasized a sensitive issue in French baroque vocal music. Cautioning against rearranging the vocal parts in *Le Raccommodement,* she gave explicit instructions in her *avertissement* as to the performance of her composition, emphasizing her intention "to have the piece known as I composed it. It is for a Bass and a Soprano; and it would be very difficult to execute it as a *haute-contre* without corrupting the harmony."[134]

The matter of the *haute-contre* voice in French baroque music has been addressed by a number of musicologists, including Mary Cyr, Carol Henry Bates (d. 2010), James R. Anthony, Barbara Garvey Jackson, and Laura E. DeMarco. Anthony, for example, gives a detailed listing of the choral makeup in the Versailles royal chapel, the building of which was completed c. 1710. In c. 1645, this chapel had supported eight *hautes-contres* among the male singers, including also six boy sopranos, two falsettists (*dessus mués*), eight tenors, and eight basses. By 1708 (when Jacquet de La Guerre was about forty-three years old), the chapel's male voices comprised eighteen *hautes-contres,* along with eleven sopranos (boy pages, falsettists and castratos (*dessus italiens*), twenty-three tenors, twenty-four baritones, and fourteen basses. Female singers were introduced into the chapel during Lully's reign.[135]

Laura E. DeMarco explains that, although early eighteenth-century French music highly favored the countertenor voice, the *haute-contre* in seventeenth-century French opera, unlike the case in French church music, did not signify a "countertenor" but rather a tenor voice with an extended upper range—which, however, could not reach the typical high register of the true countertenor or male alto.[136]

In baroque opera, France differed from the rest of Europe in favoring the sound quality of women's voices over those of castratos and even boys, thereby furthering the possibilities of professional employment for women singers. During the *grand siècle,* the French generally rejected the castrato voice favored by the Italians and gave soprano parts in opera to women. (There were no female alto roles in French opera until André Campra included them in 1702.) "A third of the leading roles in the operas of Lully," an early eighteenth-century observer emphasized, "are those of ordinary tenors; our women are always women; our basses sing the roles of Kings, Magicians, solemn and older Heroes; and our tenors and *hautes-contres* are the young gallant heroes and the amorous gods."[137]

The French attitude applied not only to solo roles but also to choruses. From the early 1670s, the French opera chorus had included women. As in sacred motets, French baroque operas typically included two choruses: the *grand choeur* of female sopranos, along with countertenors, tenors, and basses (plus baritones for five-part writing); and the select *petit choeur* of two sopranos (presumably female) and a *haute-contre.*[138] (Lully even saw to it that girls could train for future operatic performances in the Académie Royale de Musique.) In Paris churches, moreover, as eventually at the Versailles court, the most highly rated female singers even sang in solemn religious services, as did, for example, Anne de La Barre, a member of Jacquet de La Guerre's extended family network.[139]

David Lewin adds an additional dimension to the issue concerned with women's voices in the French baroque: "Not only, according to [Jean-Philippe] Rameau (1683–1764), are women's voices to be referred to the idealizing male voice or the fundamental bass for their musical meaning; the idealized male voice actually *engenders* the women's voices." (In other words, this is a matter of the overtones produced by a bass voice or instrument.) "The male sound," Lewin argues, " . . . gives birth to the harmonious female sound that is one of its parts, going so far as to expropriate from the female the characteristic act of parturition." (Compare Mrs. Jameson's "biological" gendering.) Such a notion, Lewin says, recalls that of the birth of Eve from Adam's rib, making it difficult "to imagine a more essential species of control."[140] This long-held explanation of Eve's creation, however, has been questioned by recent feminist scholars, who base their correction of the traditional interpretation on a revised translation of the original Hebrew in *Genesis.*

Carolyn Abbate has likewise focused on the question of vocal empowerment, but from another point of view. She asks whether in opera a female voice does or can assume male authority: "In opera, singers, as well as characters, are refigured subtly in the listener-spectator's mind as creating what they sing. Given the traditional assignments of power and creative force in our culture, this envoicing seems especially subversive when character and singers are female. Are we not, however, speaking of a masquerade, an illusion of force ended by the iron tongue of midnight, when the performance is over?" Abbate emphasizes, for example, " . . . opera's capacity to disrupt male authority" when " . . . women take over musical sound. . . . The history of [male or female] voice-types . . . for Orfeo [the role from Monteverdi's opera drawn from this myth]," Abbate believes, "gives us at least one plot that is different: how opera, with *music* [Abbate's italics] that subverts the borders we fix between the sexes, speaks for the envoicing of women."[141]

An Overview

In Paris and Versailles, the *grand siècle* marked an epoch when women musicians—even those of the lower aristocracy or with only modest financial resources—were gradually gaining more attention and respect. This reordering of French musical life continued into the eighteenth century as the *grand siècle* yielded to the age of the Enlightenment. The new socio-musical forces affecting women served principally to advance the status of the most skilled singers, harpsichordists, and composers. French sopranos won the greatest recognition, castratos, as discussed earlier, being generally out of favor in France at this time.[142] But professional musicians of both genders were becoming steadily more influential in this music-conscious society, in which an improving financial situation gradually enabled them to employ the finest music teachers, purchase instruments, support and attend a growing number of public concerts, and buy published music.[143] Yet only women born into financially stable families, such as Jacquet de La Guerre's, and those who had ample and long-term firm patronage could hope for well-paying professional opportunities as performers and teachers. In addition, some women participated professionally in building instruments, engraving, publishing, and selling music in music shops. For example, Elisabeth Ballard, the daughter of Jacquet de La Guerre's publisher Jean-Baptiste-Christophe Ballard, represented the fifth generation of her family in the music publishing business.[144]

Realistically, however, only male performers and composers could anticipate obtaining the most lucrative official positions and the most generous patronage. In addition, as mentioned throughout this book, men—not women—could obtain musical educations in organized institutions such as choir schools and conservatories. Such training, as has been observed, allowed opportunities to engage in interchanges with fellow students in performing new compositions, and to have even their large-scale works performed and criticized.

Jacquet de La Guerre was fortunate in winning considerable recognition in her lifetime for both her compositions and her keyboard virtuosity. Her extended family tree of professional musicians, her years as a Versailles protégée, and her firm social status as a member of the increasingly powerful and arts-minded Parisian bourgeoisie—which included the Jacquets and La Guerres—gave her unusual access to the musical elite. Also, she inherited a wealth of legacies in personal property, in cultural exposure to a major European capital and prestigious court at its most brilliant height, and in the musical education provided by her family. Thus the circumstances of Jacquet de La Guerre's time and place were supremely suited for nurturing her extraordinary musical talents and winning a career as a highly recognized professional artist. And in recent years her life, compositions, and notable accomplishments have been attracting increasing attention from musical scholars, while her music is being performed by an increasing number of professional early music artists.

Jacquet de La Guerre has also been credited with a number of "firsts."[145] She was the first known woman composer of harpsichord pieces; the first to have solo keyboard works and violin sonatas published; and the only French harpsichord composer to have compositions published both before and after the turn of the eighteenth century.[146] Jacquet de La Guerre is also considered to be the first French woman composer to have written sacred cantatas and have them published, for sacred compositions of considerable size were rarely published in her day. She was the first woman to compose a *tragédie en musique (tragédie lyrique)*. Her *Jeux à l'Honneur de la Victoire,* published c. 1691–1692, was among the earliest *opera ballets*. And she was the first woman to have an opera performed at the Académie Royale de Musique, the acme of performance venues in Paris.[147]

It should also be noted that the broad range of genres engaging Jacquet de La Guerre the composer clearly exemplify her remarkable adaptability and responsiveness in incorporating many of the styles and forms of her times into her own works. This alone was a notable achievement. But her prodigious keyboard gifts, which brought her much fame as a harpsichordist, also won her a degree of recognition as an organist. There is an irony here, though. At a time when the organ was the king of instruments in the performance of sacred music—not only in France, but also in German-speaking lands—Jacquet de La Guerre, as a woman, was therefore deprived of even a titled position as an organist at Versailles, the highest status to which a royal musician could aspire. But her case was not unique. Apart from those active in convents, women organists such as Jacquet de La Guerre were uncommon or at least unrecognized by historians.[148] And there are no known organ works in this composer's hand.[149]

Nevertheless, the extraordinary extent of her accomplishments as we know them today deepens our perception of the *grand siècle* even as it was fading into a new and different age. Her compositions stand among some of the most important French music written in the seventeenth and eighteenth centuries, music of increasing interest for today's musical circles.

Jacquet de La Guerre's relatively, if not consistently, stable life contrasts with that of Duchess Sophie-Elisabeth (chapter 1), who lost her dowry with the ravages of the Thirty Years' War and in her elderly years was exiled to a minor court. Likewise, Josephine Lang (chapter 3) was widowed early and compelled to support a family of six children, two of them chronically ill, by teaching. She obtained little or no income from the publication of her songs. Maria Bach (chapter 4) never married and wasted her originally handsome family legacy in legal battles with her sisters over that inheritance. As a result, she spent her late years alone and relatively impoverished. Ann Schein (chapter 5) has never stopped performing and teaching, but also has enjoyed a long and sturdy marriage and raised two children.

Works of Elisabeth-Claude Jacquet de La Guerre

(Listed here chronologically according to Catherine Cessac)

1687   *Les Pièces de Clavessin; Premier Livre* (Paris: Henri de Baussen).

c. 1691–1692 *Jeux à l'honneur de la Victoire/ Ballet* Ms.; Bibliotèque Nationale: ms. fr. 2217.

1694   *Céphale et Procris* (Paris: C. Ballard, 1694); Ms. c. 1696; Bibliotèque Nationale, Vm2, 125 (1) and Vm2. 125 (2–9).

c. 1695 *Sonates en Trio et pour violon seul et Basse Continue,* Ms.; Bibliotèque Nationale, Vm7. 1110, 1111 and 1111a-b.

1707   *Pièces de Clavecin qui Peuvent se joüer sur le Viollon* (Paris: Henri de Baussen).

1707   *Sonates pour le Viollon et pour le Clavecin* (Paris: Henri de Baussen).

1708   *Cantates Françoises, sur des Sujets Tirez de l'Écriture/ Livre Premier: Esther; Le Passage de la Mer Rouge; Jacob et Rachel; Jonas; Susanne et les Vieillards; Judith* (Paris: Christophe Ballard). Ballard (1655–1730), a royal printer, was active from the 1690s to 1702. In contrast to the rich and diverse publishing industry of France in the sixteenth century, the Ballard family alone monopolized French publication between 1600 and 1650.[150]

May 1710 Air Sérieux, "Aux vains attraits," *Recueil d'Airs Sérieux et à Boire de Différents Auteurs* (Paris: Christophe Ballard).

1711   *Cantates Françoises, sur des Sujets Tirez de l'Écriture/ Livre second: Adam; Le Temple Rebasti; Le Déluge; Joseph; Jephté; Samson* (Paris: Christophe Ballard).

1712   *Les Amusemens de Mgr le Duc de Bretagne,* par R. Trépagne de Ménerville, (4 Airs) (Paris: G. Cavelier Fils).

c. 1715 *Cantates Françoises: Sémélé; L' Île de Délos; Le Sommeil d'Ulisse; Le Raccommodement Comique de Pierrot et de Nicole* (Paris, Henri de Baussen).

1721   *La Ceinture de Vénus* par René Lesage: Dialogue de Mademoiselle de La Guerre (Paris: E. Ganeau).

May 1721 *Air Sérieux, Printemps,* "Les Rossignols, dès que le Jour Commence," *Recueil d'Airs Sérieux et à Boire . . .* (Paris: J.-B.-C. Ballard).

Jan. 1724 *Air à Boire, Parodie sur la Bourée de Céphale et Procris,* "Tant que je Verrons ce Pot," *Recueil d'airs sérieux et à Boire . . .* (Paris: J.-B.-C. Ballard).

Feb. 1724 *Air à Boire, La Provençale* "Entre nous mes chers amis," *Deuxième Air,* "Suivons nos désirs," *Recueil d'Airs Sérieux et à Boire . . .* (Paris: J.-B.-C. Ballard).

1713   *La Musette ou Les Bergers de Suresne* (Paris: Christophe Ballard). Probably not by Jacquet.

1721   *Te Deum à Grands Choeurs.* Lost.

Elisabeth-Claude Jacquet de La Guerre Selected Editions

Cyr, Mary, and Arthur Lawrence, eds. *Elizabeth-Claude Jacquet de La Guerre, Collected Works*, critical edition, 6 vols. (New York: The Broude Trust, 2005–2010).

Griffiths, Wanda R., ed. *Céphale et Procris. Recent Researches in the Music of the Baroque Era*, 88. (Madison, Wisc.: A-R Editions, 1998).

Quatre Sonates en Trio with an introduction by Catherine Cessac, facsimile edition (Courlay: Fuzeau, 2005).

There are also various other editions listed on the Internet (including facsimile and performing editions) of individual works published by the Broude Trust, Furore Verlag, and Anne Fuzeau Productions.

Elisabeth-Claude Jacquet de La Guerre Selected Recordings

Sonata for Violin, Viola da Gamba Obligata, and Organ, no. 2 in A Minor; Sonata for Violin and Continuo, no. 1 in D Minor; Sonata for Violin, Viola da Gamba Obligata, and Organ, no. 1 in A Minor; Sonata for Violin and Continuo, no. 3 in F Major; Sonata for Violin and Continuo, no. 4 in G Major La Rêveuse; Mirare (MIR 105)

Harpsichord Suites nos. 1–6 Elizabeth Farr; Naxos (8.557664-55)

Sonata no. 2 in D Major for Violin and Continuo; Prelude from the Suite in D Minor; and Allemande "La Flammande e Double" Bizzarie Armoniche; Opus 111 (OP 30341)

Complete Works for Harpsichord Karen Flint 2010; Plectra

Lisle de Délos, Jonas and Harpsichord Suite no. 3 L'Ensemble des Idées heureuses; soprano Isabelle Desrochers; harpsichordists Geneviève Soly and Isabelle Desrochers, 1993; ATMA Classique

Le Sommeil d'Ulisse Isabelle Desrochers, Christine Payeux, Les Voix Humaines; l'Oiseau Lyre

Jephté Brandywine Baroque; Plectra

Céphale et Procris Musica Fiorita, conductor Daniela Dolci; ORF Alte Edition 2008

CHAPTER THREE

Josephine Lang

*The Music of Romanticism
in South German Cultural Life*

The Lang Musical Legacy

The birth of Josephine Caroline Lang in Munich on March 14, 1815, crowned a remarkable musical dynasty with perhaps its most illustrious member. Aside from the situations of Lang's contemporaries Fanny (Caecilie) Mendelssohn-Bartholdy Hensel (1805–1847) and Clara Schumann (1819–1896)—remarkable figures now well documented for their accomplishments—it is difficult to conceive of a more advantageous confluence of extraordinary native musical gifts, favorable family circumstances, and high urban cultural surroundings in the making of a German artist in the nineteenth century. That is, Lang's life and works are defined here in terms of the particular society, time, and place that surrounded her from birth to her final years. Throughout her life, Lang enjoyed some measure of relative domestic stability, laced though it was with struggle and tragedy; and she experienced many of the advantages of her rich cultural heritage, advantages that paved her way to a professional position higher than that won by most talented German women of her day.

Family

Like the other women musicians examined in this book, Lang's parents and other male and female family members were professional, or at least serious, musicians—either composers or performers or both.[1] Lang inherited her musical gifts from both her paternal and maternal forebears. Her father, Theobald Lang (1783–1839), principal waldhornist of the Munich court orchestra and eventually its *Kapellmeister* (court director of music), had been a member himself of a musically accomplished Lang family in Mannheim, the Bavarian Palatinate court. (Munich was the chief Bavarian court residence.) Theobald Lang's own father had likewise been a waldhorn virtuoso in the famed Mannheim court orchestra, along with several other Langs, leading wind players of their day. In 1778 Prince-Elector Carl Theodor (who reigned at Mannheim from 1742 to 1778) transferred his Mannheim court to Munich. At that time Mannheim was one of Europe's most brilliant musical centers, chiefly because of its celebrated orchestra. (Mozart's music was unquestionably influenced by the Mannheim style, which particularly impressed him during a visit to the Mannheim court in 1777–1778.) Consequently, the merger of the two court orchestral forces of Mannheim and Munich substantially enriched the already excellent court music establishment of Bavaria's capital.

Josephine Lang's maternal grandmother, Sabina Renk-Hitzelberger, enjoyed a highly successful professional career as a coloratura soprano. She was born on November 12, 1755, in Randersacker, near Würzburg, a Bavarian court residence northwest of Munich, where she died sometime after 1807. All four of Josephine Lang's grandparents, in fact, were professional musicians. As a ten-year-old soloist, Renk-Hitzelberger debuted publicly in local church choirs. Her extraordinary three-octave vocal range, remarkable span of vocal timbres, and persuasive interpretive powers soon captivated Würzburg's prince-bishop. As head of all city affairs, he awarded Sabina Renk the financial support needed to pursue vocal and other musical studies with the court's leading vocal pedagogue, Domenico Steffani.[2]

A princely nod also gained Sabina Renk easy entry into the professional corps of Würzburg court musicians, her voice winning immediate public acclaim there, and her fame soon spreading beyond Germany to France. In addition, she won a handsome financial award from Elector Maximilian of Cologne. At twenty-one Sabina Renk appeared in Paris at the Concerts Spirituals, one of the earliest organizations of its kind in Europe to sponsor musical performances open to the general public.[3] In 1776, on command of the French king and queen, Louis XVI and Marie Antoinette, Sabina Renk sang at Versailles, where even the ultra-discriminating French music critics succumbed to her astounding vocal feats, awarding her lavish praise. After her marriage in 1777 to the brilliant Würzburg court flutist Franz Ludwig Joseph Hitzelberger, Sabina Renk-Hitzelberg declined offers of prestigious appointments, including several from Paris and the electoral court at Mainz.[4] She chose instead to return to her native Würzburg, where her spellbinding performances drew generous public acclaim and a host of young students. But, after the birth of four daughters, Hitzelberger confined her teaching exclusively to her children: Regina and her three sisters, who would eventually be, respectively, Josephine Lang's mother and maternal aunts.

It comes as no surprise that all Sabina Hitzelberger's daughters were gifted singers. Two died prematurely in the same year, 1795: the eighteen-year-old Catharina Elisabeth, reportedly a fine contralto and pianist; and Kunigunde, a year younger, who was said to be a promising soprano whose voice was "harmonious and full of tenderness."[5] (Whether both might have fallen victim to a local epidemic is unknown.) Sabina's two younger daughters, however, survived childhood, married, and established successful careers as professional singers. Johanna, a contralto, was born in 1783, marrying Joseph Bamberger, a French hornist in Würzburg's court orchestra. Bamberger soon won a position at the Munich court, where Johanna herself was named a chamber singer. Her voice was immediately acclaimed for its resonance and expressive nuances—to a striking degree in her lowest register. Ultimately the couple returned to Würzburg, following Joseph's reassignment to the court orchestra there. Presumably for domestic reasons, Johanna never resumed her own career.

Sabina Renk-Hitzelberger's youngest daughter, Regina Hitzelberger (February 15, 1788–May 1827), grew to maturity in Würzburg, the Bavarian provincial capital. From Regina's earliest years, her mother, Sabina Hitzelberger, was her chief musical tutor—and a superb one at that. In 1804 Sabina launched her daughter's stunning Würzburg career as a sixteen-year-old virtuoso coloratura. The birth of Sabina's daughter Regina had coincided with an important transitional period in Würzburg's thriving musical life—one result of the city's administrative "secularization" of 1802. This process ended the Bavarian residence's exclusive rule by a single prince-bishop, ushering in the complete separation of church and state. Würzburg's flourishing and court-sponsored chamber music was consequently transferred to a rising citizen force that assumed control over the arts. Accordingly, concerts now were financed principally through admission fees, significantly increasing general public access to Würzburg's musical events.[6]

By 1804 the sixteen-year-old Regina had already debuted professionally at Würzburg's brand-new civic opera. That same year also saw the completion of the city's music conservatory, the first German state institution of its kind. The opening of both the opera and conservatory finally established full citizen authority over music in Würzburg. At the same time, the governmental secularization also severely reduced the city's sacred music establishment, ending its brilliant court chapel performances and its central role in German organ building. By 1814 Europe's post-Napoleonic turmoil had toppled Würzburg's entire court establishment, including its own musical organizations, along with their then-fashionable importation of Viennese waltzes and Venetian opera productions.

After her marriage to Theobald Lang in 1805, the seventeen-year-old Regina resettled in Munich and quickly established her role there as both a leading soprano and the youngest member of the Bavarian court theater. (Her husband had moved with the Mannheim court to Munich in 1778.) Her dazzling voice was further honed by three of the court's distinguished *Kapellmeisters*: Peter (von) Winter, Georg Joseph Vogler, and Carl Cannabich.[7]

It is one of history's ironies that in 1805, during the French occupation of Munich (and much of Europe), Napoleon himself appeared at one of Regina's court performances. Enraptured by her beautiful voice, he named her one of France's prestigious chamber singers, her new title winning her the customary generous financial remuneration. The young soprano continued to win accolades from such musical luminaries as Carl Maria von Weber (fig. 14). It is noteworthy to

Figure 14. Regina
Hitzelberger-Lang,
Josephine Lang's mother
and a professional singer.
Charcoal drawing,
undated, unidentified
artist. Courtesy of the
Theater Museum, Munich.

observe here that Lang and her maternal forebears appeared in the public sphere
solely as singers, not as instrumentalists, as was the case on her paternal side.

In 1806, one year after Regina Hitzelberger's marriage and move to Munich,
Bavaria won kingdom status, Munich remaining the capital. The city had enjoyed a long period of vigorous sacred and secular music making sponsored by
the powerful court electors Maximilian III Joseph (reigned 1745–1777) and Carl
Theodor (reigned 1777–1799). Though still at the fledgling stage of development,
public performance organizations were further intensifying Munich's musical
scene. As part of it, a significant proportion of both the music (operas above all)
heard in Munich and the musicians who conducted and performed it were Italian, for Munich had long enjoyed Catholic and other cultural connections with
Italy itself.[8] Munich's cultural prosperity gave Regina Hitzelberger-Lang fertile
soil for the blossoming of her career.

A skilled instrumentalist and composer himself, and a powerful arts patron,
Bavaria's elector Maximilian III Joseph championed Italian opera performers
and *Kapellmeisters*. (Yet he also commissioned new operas by several German
composers, including several by his sister Maria Antonia Walpurgis, Electress of

Saxony [1724–1780].)[9] Maximilian commissioned Mozart's *La finta giardiniera,*
K.196, an *opera buffa,* the Munich premiere of which Josephine Lang's grandmother Sabina could possibly have heard in 1775. Maximilian's cousin Duke Clemens of Bavaria (d. 1770) likewise was an ardent music patron who kept several
German composers in his employ.

After Regina's glowing success in the premiere of Étienne-Nicolas Méhul's
comic opera *Joseph* in 1807, Napoleon, who had heard her perform two years
earlier, is said to have remarked again that the singer's artistry had profoundly
moved him. But he tempered his admiration with suspicious gender bias, describing her "as an amiable phenomenon" possessed with "child-like charm." In 1811,
after six years (she was married in 1805) of brilliant stardom at the Munich court
opera, Regina Lang followed the example of her mother, retiring from the public
stage. She had defied society's expectations for a newly married German woman
of her times for a half-dozen years—surely something of a record. Sadly, she died
in 1827 at only thirty-nine, leaving her daughter Josephine Lang a motherless
twelve-year-old.[10]

Munich

In her position as a professional musician, housewife, and mother, Regina Hitzelberger-Lang was witness to and part of vast socioeconomic changes affecting
Munich and most of Germany. Music in her native city had become mainly a
public concern and responsibility, as mentioned earlier, owing significantly to
major demographic changes elevating the middle classes to an important new
social status. An immense population explosion rattled Europe from 1750 to 1850,
disrupting the very foundations of European society. Germany tripled its population. Coupled with the fast expansion of urbanization and industrialization, this
demographic phenomenon contributed to a gradual reordering of Europe's old
social structure. The system of local, rural subsistence agriculture—the very financial basis of the landed aristocracy—was giving way to a developing capitalistic
and centralized market economy within burgeoning cities as rural populations
migrated to their fast-growing urban industries. A nouveau riche society, with
its market economy, emerged, creating a new upper layer of the middle classes
that assumed support of German cultural life and formed a new concert public
to replace a dwindling aristocracy. As the court system lost command over the
arts, now sponsored by civic authorities in an increasingly commercialized cultural situation, musicians were thrust into the role of independent entrepreneurs.

Yet music in Munich continued to thrive, as the growing bourgeois public
took over the governmental reins of the city. This dramatic transition to civic
leadership resulted in the creation of the city's Musical Academy (1811–1832),
public subscription concerts, and private societies sponsoring performances by
celebrated virtuosos. Munich also became home to dozens of newly established
male choirs from 1826 on.[11] As for Munich's other opportunities for institutional-

ized music education, in 1830 (the year Josephine Lang turned fifteen) a Central Singing School was established, becoming municipal in 1845. It trained musically gifted children from eight to fourteen years and eventually older students, thereby spawning even more Munich choral societies from the citizenry. Founded in 1846, when Lang was a new mother in Tübingen, Munich's Royal Music School became the Royal Academy of Music in 1892.

Though there is no evidence that Josephine Lang studied full-time in any public, institutional setting, this was the Munich that Lang knew—a world, for a composer at least—in which she had to carve out her own professional niche and be recognized as a "commodity" valued by a general public. By the nineteenth century, the publication and reviews of her music in professional musical journals had become necessary generally as part of composers' and performers' success in obtaining recognition. (This situation was much the same as that faced earlier by Elisabeth-Claude Jacquet de La Guerre in France and later by Maria Bach in Vienna.) Yet to earn a living wage, these artists—like many of their male colleagues—were compelled to teach private students. As a young widow, Lang would ultimately come to depend on income gained in the private milieu of vocal and instrumental teaching, while her role as hostess-entrepreneur in her Tübingen "salon" at home established and reinforced professional contacts and offered musical stimulation. Both these occupations coincided with the new age of commercial opportunism.[12]

Childhood and Adolescence

Josephine Lang was born into the culturally intense city of Munich, the chief Bavarian court, in 1815, the year in which the Congress of Vienna finalized Europe's victory over Napoleon (fig. 15). Indications of Lang's prodigious musical talent had already emerged by the age of three, from her first piano lessons with her mother, who also encouraged her vocal gifts and initiated her into the song repertoire. (Compare this situation with that of pianist Ann Schein in chapter 5.) Lang later recalled, "I had to sing when we had guests. At times when I was not observed, I took the footstool to the piano, climbed on top so that I could reach the keyboard, and then sought my own accompaniments and playfully invented new melodies."[13] At the age of five, Lang undertook her first efforts at composing. At eleven, she made her public debut at the keyboard. Like the model courtier "of culture," delineated in the sixteenth century by Castiglione's *The Courtier,* in nineteenth-century European society, many citizens—particularly mothers—of the emerging upper middle classes envisioned the ideal daughter as one who had attained even modest skill at the piano with a repertoire dazzling in effect. Such an achievement, it was hoped, would assure the young maiden—and, in fact, her entire family—a firm position in the upper-middle-class stratum of society.[14] We do not know if this motive played a part in Lang's training as a pianist; yet her talent became obvious at a very young age, making it virtually expected that her mother would become her first music teacher. One commentator, however, expressed a more positive aspect of women's domestic role. Referring to the French natural scientist Baron Georges von Cuvier (1769–1832), he remarked, "France has still wondered how Cuvier came to be so great a man; the secret was, he was schooled upon his mother's lap."[15] Today perhaps, this comment sounds outdated, but the women discussed in this book owed much to the early support given by either their mothers or other close maternal figures.

But tragedy struck Lang on the verge of puberty with the death of her mother on May 10, 1827. This sad event left the twelve-year-old without the devoted maternal guidance, comfort, and professional mentoring that she had known. Unfortunately, the loss of Lang's mother must have immediately become even more painful, for, while still only twelve, this remarkable youngster was compelled to begin teaching piano several hours daily to supplement family income, her father's earnings reportedly being insufficient. This situation leaves one to wonder whether the Lang family had also largely depended earlier on the mother's income as a music teacher.

In fact, Lang herself had been a keyboard prodigy. Though her first piano teacher had been her mother, she may have had subsequent instructors, the most important being a Frau Berlinghof-Wagner. As reported by Lang's son H.

Figure 15. Josephine Lang, pencil drawing by Carl Müller, c. 1842. Heinrich Adolf Köstlin, *Josefine Lang* (Leipzig, 1881). Courtesy of the Württembergische Landesbibliothek, Stuttgart.

A. Köstlin, Lang recalled that Berlinghof-Wagner "opened the heavens" for her, Köstlin himself commenting that "the strict discipline of a good method and conscientious direction" did wonders for Lang's keyboard technique. Although while only eleven she had performed publicly at the local Museum Society, her repertoire consisted chiefly of trivial virtuoso display pieces by such popular composers as Henri Herz.[16]

Lang undertook serious composition at thirteen, although we lack any samples of her first works; and from early childhood she also enjoyed another source of musical stimulation, for she frequently visited her godfather, the Munich court artist Karl Joseph Stieler (1781–1858).[17] Famed for his paintings of Goethe and other important figures of his day, Stieler had long hosted a popular salon of distinguished cultural figures in his home, his young goddaughter also attending.[18] It was at Stieler's soirées that Lang eventually met Felix Mendelssohn (1809–1847) in addition to Mendelssohn's close colleague and friend, the composer Ferdinand Hiller (1811–1885), and other luminaries in the arts.[19] In line with her maternal forebears, Josephine Lang taught voice and piano in Munich until her marriage and, again following in her mother's and maternal aunt Johanna's footsteps, she was appointed—at the age of twenty—a Munich Court opera singer in 1835.[20] Her court appointment continued for five years.

From the age of fifteen, Lang enjoyed several brief opportunities to develop her composition skills in serious study with Felix Mendelssohn in 1830 and 1831 and later perhaps received some advice from the composer and virtuoso pianist Stephen Heller. This occasional coaching extended through most of the 1830s, the decade of Lang's most intense and prolific period of composition. Yet, aside from Lang's mother, Mendelssohn and, some believe, Heller were the young composer's only professional mentors. (Nancy Reich believes that Lang "was almost entirely self-taught in composition.")[21]

Mendelssohn was to become Lang's teacher (see below) and a staunch supporter of her music throughout his life. At one time, like Stieler, he attempted to arrange for her to go to Berlin and engage in an intense study of composition with Carl Friedrich Zelter (1758–1832) and piano with his sister Fanny. But Lang's father objected, owing in no small part to the family financial situation.[22] Recalling his favorable impression of Lang's vocal and keyboard gifts from an earlier visit to Stieler's Munich salon, Mendelssohn gave the young teenager lessons in double counterpoint, four-part writing, and other aspects of music theory to improve her technical skills in composition during two stays in Munich: for several weeks each in 1830 (early June to October) and 1831 (September 10 to November 5).[23] In a letter of October 6, 1831, written from Munich to his sisters, Rebecca and Fanny, Mendelssohn lavished glowing praise on Lang in her midteens, citing her prodigious talent and accomplishments: "Every day at twelve o'clock I give little Mademoiselle L. an hour's instruction in double counterpoint, and four-part composition, etc."[24] (Professional musicians, Heinrich Schütz, for example, noted that Duchess Sophie-Elisabeth needed more skill in writing counterpoint. For centuries, we have noted, the choir schools open to boys for studying counterpoint and composition from an early age were not available to girls.) Describing Lang as a "sweet," "delicate-looking, pale girl, with noble, if not pretty, features," Mendelssohn wrote, "Her every gesture and word are full of talent. She has the gift for composing songs, and singing them in a way I never heard before, causing me the most unalloyed musical delight I ever experienced." When Lang played and sang her own songs, Mendelssohn praised her keyboard gifts and voiced admiration for the singular tone-quality of her voice: "The music floats strangely to and fro, and every note expresses the most profound and delicate feeling," deeply moving the listener, while "her voice [is] so innocent, so unconsciously lovely." Referring to Lang's lessons with him the previous summer, Mendelssohn recalled enthusiastically that every song she had written by that time had shown "a bright flash of talent." He had convinced even his discerning longtime friend, the composer and virtuoso pianist Ignaz Moscheles (1794–1870), of the girl's extraordinary and "natural" musical gifts, adding that Lang had advanced "remarkably" since that encounter.

Mendelssohn also expressed some concerns about Lang's particular situation as a composer: "She has no one to understand or to guide her . . . in honing her ability to discriminate between 'good music and bad,' he noted, adding, "in fact, except for her own pieces, she thinks everything is wonderfully fine. If she were to become satisfied with herself, it would all be over for her," he cautioned.[25] Virtually from infancy, Lang's musical training remained private, even piecemeal—that is, without the opportunities for any institutionalized training. But males in her era probably also were taught privately in such subjects as solo instruments, theory, and composition. As said in previous chapters, when males did have institutional musical education—in a conservatory or a church choir school—they could experience the competition and criticism of colleagues, enabling them to develop their full potential. Lang and other women musicians of her day—in fact, German women in general—had no opportunity for institutional study at the secondary level until the outbreak of World War I. "The general disposition of bourgeois society in the nineteenth century," notes Gordon Craig, "was [to be] hostile toward any extension of civil rights to women." In addition, when nineteenth-century women in Germany married, Craig believes, they "were imprisoned in a contract that guaranteed them no [civil] rights. . . ."[26]

Lang had copied out several of her songs for Mendelssohn in appreciation for his encouragement of her compositional talent, "guiding," as he phrased it, "her a little way towards good and solid music."[27] Mendelssohn's fervent admiration for the young teenager's musical accomplishments, coupled with his own lofty reputation as a leading German composer, probably contributed to Lang's ultimately commanding position as one of Munich's most celebrated singers, composers, teachers, and promising fledgling composers. On the one hand, with Lang's voice and piano training given only privately rather than through an institution, she lacked the credentials and privileges of talented males, who could become faculty members of conservatories or universities. On the other, her teaching proved highly lucrative as a supplement to her annual salary of two hundred florins received in her employ by the Munich Court Opera.

During brief periods in Augsburg during the summers of 1835 and 1838, Lang came to know Stephen Heller (1813–1888), perhaps obtaining help from him in composition, although it is not clear whether she actually studied with him.[28] In 1830 the brilliant young Hungarian-born pianist and composer had settled in Augsburg for a lengthy "sabbatical" from exhausting concert tours as a much-sought-after piano virtuoso.[29] While Lang resided in Augsburg, its thriving musical life—led by its well-established bourgeoisie—centered on popular contemporary oratorios and cantatas performed by skilled amateurs from the local symphony orchestra and male choral societies. Heller enjoyed financial support from such wealthy bourgeois dynasties and arts patrons as the Fuggers. This family had gained its immense fortune from Augsburg's flourishing banking and commerce industry. The Fuggers extended their arts patronage principally to promising young composers, while some individual family members were also serious collectors of priceless musical manuscripts.

The celebrated composer-critic Robert Schumann (1810–1856) named Heller a corresponding critic in Augsburg for Schumann's pathbreaking musical journal, *Die neue Zeitschrift für Musik*. It was, therefore, not surprising that Heller introduced Lang to Schumann's music, leading to her undertaking a serious study of Schumann's works in light of the outstanding composer's evolving concept of writing music in his self-proclaimed "new direction." Heller was one of the composers whom Robert Schumann named a member of his select group of *Davidsbündler* (David's League).[30] For Schumann, in fact, ranked Heller—along with Chopin, Ferdinand Hiller, Mendelssohn, and several others—as one of the most promising younger composers of truly "romantic" music.

As a result of Heller's suggestions, Schumann gave some of Josephine Lang's newly published songs a stunning positive appraisal in a review of 1838 for his journal. The high score he assigned some of Lang's finest songs retains value even today, especially given Schumann's aesthetic views on the contemporary scene with its deluge of newly composed songs, "the more trivial," Schumann complained, "far outnumbering the worthwhile."[31]

Tübingen: A Picturesque University Town and its Musical Legacy

While taking a spa cure at Bad Kreuth in 1840, Lang met her future husband, the poet and law professor Christian Reinhold Köstlin (1813–1856). Ultimately she set fifty or more of his published poems, providing music for forty-one of them between July and August of that same year, coincidently Schumann's own prolific "Song Year."

But with Lang's marriage to Köstlin in 1842 and as the age-old tradition for women "dictated," she relinquished her position as court singer—and stardom—in her native Munich, moving to Tübingen, where Köstlin was a university faculty member, an influential scholar, prolific author, and teacher. (He obtained tenure in 1849.) His many fields included theology, philosophy, German literature, and aesthetics (including music).[32] Already professionally recognized for her musical art, this gifted woman thus entered the domain of a new family life with all the age-old responsibilities of wife and—not long afterward—mother of six. With Lang's marriage, Ferdinand Hiller once remarked, "Music had to give way to cooking."[33] And in a letter of December 15, 1841, to Lang's future husband, Mendelssohn himself wrote, "For heaven's sake, keep her composing diligently. Truly it is your responsibility towards us all, seeking and thirsting as we constantly are for what is good and new." Lang's marriage greatly restricted her musical pursuits. As was typical of his time, Mendelssohn failed to rank Lang's responsibilities as a wife, mother, hostess to an important salon, and a composer—even if no longer a prodigious one—as modes of creativity. (During the 1840s decade—when Lang was in her twenties—George W. Bethune wrote, "what were man's labour worth, if he had no home where woman reigned in her realm of affection? Yet within that home are trials, cares, duties and difficulties, to which only woman's tact, conscience and endurance are equal.")[34] Yet, as described later in more detail, it is true that bearing, raising, and financially supporting six children—with the added burdens of nurturing one paralyzed, one ailing, and one mentally disabled—Lang would have had little time for composition, her chief mode of artistic creativity, one that never again blossomed to the extent it had in her younger years.

Tübingen, Lang's new home, was a modestly sized university town of fifteenth-century half-timbered houses and shops situated on a picturesque site poised on the sloping banks of the placid Neckar River.[35] Friedrich Hölderlin (1770–1843), one of Germany's finest lyric poets, was imprisoned in Tübingen—in a tower overlooking the Neckar—from 1802 until his death, for he had been diagnosed as suffering from a severe mental disability. Josephine Lang moved there one year before Hölderlin's death.

Even by the late renaissance, music in Tübingen was still anchored in the sacred repertoire. By the late baroque, however, an inevitable succession of political and cultural events shifted the focus to secular music for instruments. Tübingen audiences heard performances of symphonies and overtures by leading early classical composers fresh from Italy, as well as from Mannheim, where Lang's father had been a member of its court orchestra, an ensemble praised by Wolfgang Amadeus Mozart. With the turn of the eighteenth century, Tübingen's musical affairs had passed, as elsewhere in Europe, to an affluent, expanding bourgeoisie.

When Josephine Lang, newly Frau Köstlin, moved to Tübingen in 1841, the town had already been drawn into the intoxicating, fundamentally middle-class and amateur vogue of choral music making that had taken Germans everywhere by storm, spawning preponderantly male over female and mixed choruses. In 1817 the important Swabian song composer Friedrich Silcher (1789–1860) had been appointed Tübingen University's first music director. He soon established the city's first mixed (male and female) oratorio society, which he conducted until 1860, and its first student orchestra, inaugurating a new public concert series. This was Tübingen's musical *Zeitgeist* during the last four decades of Josephine Lang's life.[36]

Lang's Tübingen Salon

With marriage, Lang created—perhaps as compensation—a new "career" in the arts markedly different from her previous activities. As hostess of soirées for prominent figures in the arts, she turned her new home in Tübingen—a town long known to be visually beautiful and intellectually stimulating—into a focal point of Swabia's intelligentsia.[37] Lang's salon would have been a stimulating literary and musical affair, for her guests included a number of celebrated German lyric poets—the Swabians Eduard Mörike (1804–1875), Ludwig Uhland (1787–1862), and Silcher. The list also included Friedrich Rückert (1788–1866).[38] Those invited to Lang's soirées also included other well-known musical figures, along with the esteemed Danish sculptor Bertel Thorwaldsen (1770–1844).

Widowhood

Lang's economic situation took on a new urgency when her husband's lingering illness, beginning in the early 1850s, led to his premature death at forty-three in 1856. Bearing some physical ailments herself and in desperate need of additional income, Lang nevertheless intensified her teaching schedule and resumed the composition of songs and solo piano pieces with hopes of lucrative publication.[39]

But Lang's ultimately quarter-century of widowhood and the immediate need to support her entire family brought her even more tragedy. For, at her husband's death, all her six children were still dependent, ranging in age from about four to thirteen years. (The earliest was born c. 1843 and the youngest c. 1852.) In addition, three of her six children (Pauline, Maria, Felix, Theobald, Eugen, and Heinrich Adolf [1846–1907], her biographer), were chronically and critically ill and destined to die prematurely. Her son Felix—named for his godfather, the composer Mendelssohn—had to be committed to a mental hospital in nearby Winnental, where he tragically perished in a fire in 1868. Her son Theobald, a lifelong paralytic, died only five years later. An unknown illness felled Lang's third son, Eugen, in 1880. Of the males, only Lang's biographer, Heinrich Adolf

Köstlin (1846–1907), survived her, becoming a church choral director, theologian, and pastor. His biography of his mother, however, is now considered somewhat unreliable.[40] Lang's two daughters, to whom she dedicated some of her music, had married in their twenties and moved away.

"These exceptional women managed home and professional responsibilities and were often the sole support of their families," Nancy Reich comments.[41] Like their male contemporaries, many women pursuing professional careers as both composers and concert virtuosos wrote their music to exhibit their instrumental prowess and, conversely, often performed their own works in public performances. In the nineteenth century, these women included Lang, along with others of her day such as Clara Schumann (1819–1896) and Pauline (Garcia) Viardot (1821–1910).[42]

In 1880, the last year of her life, Lang visited her daughter Maria (1849–1925) in Vienna and met Johannes Brahms. As prominent members of Vienna's commercial and cultural elite bourgeoisie, Maria Köstlin-Fellinger and her husband, Richard Fellinger (1848–1903), numbered among Johannes Brahms's (1833–1897) closest and most faithful friends throughout his final years. Shortly after Josephine Lang's death on December 2, 1880, Brahms set poems by her husband published under his nom de plume, "Christian Reinhold."[43]

Support from such musical luminaries as the virtuoso pianist and composer Clara Schumann (she, too, was widowed in 1856) and her husband's close colleague Ferdinand Hiller won Lang publication of several of her lieder sets. Not until 1882 did Breitkopf & Härtel publish even forty of her songs, many for the first time.[44] None of these efforts eased her economic circumstances significantly, yet the appearance of Hiller's biography of Lang in 1868 sparked new public recognition, edging close to the level the composer had enjoyed early in her career.[45]

Josephine Lang's Music

Lang was one of the earlier nineteenth-century women composers recognized as professional in the sense that, as Reich puts it, "their music was published and performed, and they received money for their work."[46] In Lang's Germany, the socially circumscribed domestic status of women composers charged with the responsibilities of marriage and children typically spelled the confinement of their creative efforts to the lied, solo piano pieces, and other small-scale musical genres. Women composers responsible for dependent children had few, if any, opportunities for professional exchanges to allow, for example, trial performances of new works to test the effectiveness of large-scale compositions such as symphonies and operas and to identify technical procedures suggested by colleagues for "improving" a piece.

Lang's compositions number around one thousand works. Of these, the majority are songs set chiefly for solo voice and piano. Because the composer assigned the piano such a prominent, independent role in her songs—with preludes, interludes, and postludes not only supporting the voice but reinforcing the poem's meaning—it comes as no surprise that she composed numerous pieces for this instrument alone. Supremely voicing nineteenth-century Austro-German sentiments, Lang favored waltzes above all, these written in fluid style cast perfectly in the idiomatic language of the piano. Other typical nineteenth-century genres that Lang composed include gallops, barcarolles, mazurkas, marches—some for specific German patriotic causes and commemorations—minuets, songs without words, and an assortment of various other styles. She also composed several works for piano with violin: for example, a piano sonata with *obligato* accompaniment for violin, a "Sonata avec Violon," and another piano piece with *violino obligato.* Four years before her death, she wrote an "Elegie" for violin and piano entitled "Nachruf in's Jenseits." Lang composed several sacred choral works, among them: some "Cyries" (Kyries), the movements opening a Mass, for chorus with piano and an "Ave Maria" in two versions, one each for four-part men's and women's chorus.

The German Romantic Song:
The Piano and German Lyric Poetry

Lang's lifetime coincided with the Saturnian age of German song composition. One cannot imagine the nineteenth century without the vast store of German solo songs with piano accompaniment that were composed and published in those one hundred years. The song was one of the most profound musical means of expressing the heart, mind, and soul of the German romantic era. Lang, in fact, was born only a year after Franz Schubert wrote his pivotal setting of Goethe's poem "Gretchen am Spinnrade" (1814), one of the Viennese composer's hundreds of songs that launched a century in which the German song, the development of the piano, and the blossoming of German lyric poetry miraculously coincided. Some of the nineteenth century's most prominent (as well as those in the second and third tiers regarding quality) composers devoted much of their talents to lied composition. These include Felix Mendelssohn, Robert Schumann, Carl Löwe, Robert Franz, Peter Cornelius, Johannes Brahms, Franz Liszt, Richard Wagner, Hugo Wolf, and Richard Strauss. Apart from the songs of Schumann's wife, Clara, and Mendelssohn's sister, Fanny Mendelssohn Hensel, however, those of many other professional women composers of German romanticism have only begun to be closely examined relatively recently.

Among the factors contributing to the flowering of the German romantic song were the escalating role of the piano in captivating composers, performers, and the public at large and the part played by the outpouring of German romantic lyric poetry. After the Italian harpsichord maker Bartolomeo Cristofori (1655–1731) designed and built the first-known functioning piano, German technical craftsmen set out to expand the expressive dimensions of the new instrument, their work leading to the production of easily affordable, accessible pianos adaptable to a variety of performance situations. Like those of Europe as a whole, the German middle classes cultivated music making at home— a perfect setting for intimate, small-scale performances of songs with piano accompaniment and solo piano works. The steady technical modification of the piano in turn boosted the place of public concerts in displaying virtuoso keyboard artists.[47]

By 1830, while the fifteen-year-old Josephine Lang was singing and playing her own compositions for Mendelssohn, piano makers were continuing to enlarge and refine the instrument's spectrum of expressive sonorities in pitch, dynamic levels, touch, timbral scope, harmony, and texture. Technical improvements soon made the piano a new voice accommodating the German romantic aesthetic, centered as it was on the expression of nature's imagined anthropomorphic feelings, as well as on deep human emotion. Significantly, these subjects also formed dominant themes in the burgeoning of nineteenth-century landscape painting. The piano, moreover, was increasingly acceptable as "proper" for a female musician in Lang's day, female string or wind players not yet having been given that status.

Lang's Texts

The flowering of German romantic lyric poetry served the same expressive ends as the piano. In their lyric poems, Johann Wolfgang von Goethe, Matthias Claudius, Heinrich Heine, Eduard Mörike, Friedrich Hölderlin, Ludwig Uhland, Ludwig Heinrich Christoph Hölty, Joseph von Eichendorff, Clemens Brentano, Friedrich Klopstock, Friedrich Rückert, Ludwig Tieck, Wilhelm Müller, and others probed humanity's innermost emotional being and its place in the natural world.[48] Composers of this era set lyric poems expressing various shades of *Weltschmerz, Wandern* (wayfaring, roaming), *Sehnsucht* (longing—for the unattainable), and *Werden* (becoming, or seeking), all these themes sharing the notion of literal or symbolic change such as a journey or a loss—that is, movement, meaning a kinetic outlook on life as a quest that drives humankind's inner self.[49]

Like her much-discussed contemporaries the composers Fanny Hensel and Clara Schumann, Lang favored texts of romantic passion, at times mercilessly unrequited. Often focusing on kinetic themes regarding a mill (water in perpetual movement) and *Wandern,* Lang also favored texts addressing the many-faceted beauties of nature. Reich emphasizes that " . . . unlike their male counterparts, women generally avoided poetry extolling heroism or war."[50] Several of Lang's songs nevertheless offer exceptions, these being outright patriotic settings.

For her songs, Lang set the verses of many important German lyric poets favored by the most imposing nineteenth-century composers. For example, she set several songs to poems by Wilhelm Müller, the poet of Schubert's cycle

Die schöne Müllerin; and she set numerous poems by Johann Wolfgang von Goethe, Friedrich Rückert, Heinrich Heine, Clemens Brentano, Ludwig Uhland, Johann Heinrich Voss, Jean Paul, Wilhelm Müller, Friedrich Schiller, Ludwig Hölty, Matthias Claudius, and Johann Gottfried Herder. Among Lang's many Müller settings are several, for example, focused on kinetic imagery: themes such as *Wandern* (not the aimless wandering implied by the English "wander"), brooks, and mills. Many of these appeared in Schubert's song cycles. Lang also set, though less often, poems by Friedrich Mathisson, Graf von August Platen, Viktor von Scheffel, George Gordon Lord Byron, Max von Schenkendorf, Max Schneckenburg, Christian Fürchtegott Gellert, Robert Reinick, Theodor Körner, Robert Prutz, Justinus Kerner, Nikolaus Lenau, and Christoph August Tiedge. (She also set several Rhine poems at the time when more than four hundred Rhine songs during the 1840s decade were composed or published, even sparking a contest for the best one.)[51] In addition, Lang set poems by members of her own family and by friends. Above all were her many settings of poems by her husband C. Reinhold Köstlin composed between 1838 (that is, four years before her marriage) and 1878 (two years before her death). Most of Lang's settings of her daughter Maria's poems were composed during the last two decades of the composer's life. Lang also set one of her own poems (undated). In the 1860s and 1870s she set poems by three members of the Stieler family: Ottilie, Carl, and Josephine. (As mentioned earlier, Lang's godfather was the artist Joseph Stieler.)

Lang's Works: Publication and Reviews

Several collections of Lang's songs encompass more than thirty opus numbers. Over 150 of her songs were published in her lifetime. Ironically, the prestigious firm of Breitkopf & Härtel did not bring out a two-volume collection of her songs until two years after her death in 1880. At least thirty-one solo songs covering six opus numbers and one male chorus setting were published by the period January 1844, through December 1851—that is, through the years when her husband was still alive—as recorded in Adolph Hofmeister's celebrated *Handbuch der musikalischen Literatur.*[52]

Many of Lang's compositions were extolled by critics, for the most part professional musicians themselves. In Robert Schumann's prestigious *Neue Zeitschrift für Musik* and in *Die allgemeine musikalische Zeitung,* most reviews of her songs expressed great admiration for their richly textured (some even say "Schumannesque") lyricism and musical sensitivity in each poem. Schumann's founding of his bold new professional music journal in 1834 coincides tellingly with Josephine Lang's most prolific decade of composition. With Schumann's establishment of the *Neue Zeitschriftt,* which he served both as editor and writer, he created a revolutionary style of music criticism: one encompassing the need for a critical perspective in judging new music based on a broad chronological continuum, the most promising of which should have roots in the past and function in the present to herald a poetic future—that is, a new historical point of view.[53] Schumann set out in 1834 to wage war against the deluge of "Philistine" composers of music created solely, he believed, to display technical wizardry. In creating his imaginary and symbolic *Davidsbündler,* Schumann looked to a new age led only by truly gifted composers.[54] Schumann's review of Lang's song "Traumbild" in the November 1838 edition of his *Neue Zeitschrift* (the actual music was printed in the journal supplement) appeared in the autumn after her second summer stay (under Stephen Heller's mentorship) in Augsburg. Schumann's positive opinion must have buoyed Lang's confidence and zeal to continue composing. "[This] lied of Josephine Lang," Schumann wrote, "is a delicate, extremely tender growth that we recommend for the reader's keener consideration; its inwardness is totally pleasing . . . ; also, the whole is declaimed with great expression. It shows the merits that one will meet, in even greater numbers, in a song collection published recently by Haslinger; the same collection also contains a setting of the prize-winning poem written for the Mannheim Music Society, [a setting] that, among all those that have likewise come to my attention, appears to me as the deepest and most original that she has composed. [And she is] still very young. . . ."[55]

Assessing some of Lang's songs, the critic Oswald Lorenz noted that "in several aspects, these are the very opposite of [Lang's] earlier songs. Everything in them is feeling [*Empfindung*], momentary features: a warm, lively grasp of details, dedication, openness; there is form and a rounding off of the whole as if [these songs were] written instinctively in creating and structuring them; therefore, [there is] much unevenness in the more important relationships, but a considerable and fortunate overall grasp of the appropriate and beautiful in details, grace, and feeling [*Empfindung*]." "A feminine spirit," Lorenz continues—with no apology for his gender prejudice—"obviously prevails—as in the predominance of feeling [*Gefühl*]; in giving way light-heartedly to swinging back and forth in a stream of emotions; in the inclination and sensitivity towards ornamenting and dressing up even of subordinate elements; [and] in technique, above all, in agreeably fashioning harmony and voice-leading." Lorenz's sexist attitude is also more than evident in his next remark: "[but] there are, in addition, many uncertainties, much lack of direction, many mistakes—as well as, once again—many a delicate turn, [and] occasionally a certain comically naïve stealth in bypassing an awkward conflict—evidence of a woman's hand, more tender than firm. In content as in external shaping and skill in writing, the songs generally are not equal in worth, [yet] none of them [is] completely without content or interest—except the last one in Op. 9 and, all the more, the third ("Nach dem Abschied," [Reinhold]), the setting of Blumauer, and . . . the second of the same volume.")[56] Lorenz never defines "a feminine spirit" as he used it.

Yet Lorenz goes on to "recommend" only three songs for alto out of more than four dozen chosen for review: "'Abschied' (E. Schulze); 'Scheideblick,' (Lenau);

and 'Im Frühling' (an unnamed poet). Mignon's 'Nur wer die Sehnsucht kennt' (Goethe) is realized with so much visible affection, industry, and warmth that we especially fear doing injury to the composer if we call this very song unfortunate in conception and too fastidious in its entire effect; this is, nevertheless our honest opinion."[57] Similarly in May 1847, the unnamed critic of some songs by Lang's contemporary Fanny Mendelssohn-Hensel resorts to condescending and formulaic patriarchal descriptions as "a harmless, deeply feeling female spirit [*weibliches Gemüth*]," cautioning reviewers to avoid "apply[ing] the scalpel of analytical criticism to these gifts of charming feminine feeling...."[58] Later reviews of Lang's songs Op. 14 and 15 appeared in the *Neü Zeitschrift* in 1848.[59] One is reminded here of Mahler's use of Goethe's *das ewig Weibliche* (the eternal female) in his Symphony no. 8. In other words, the critics attribute the stylistic features of Lang's songs to her "female spirit," this quality encompassing delicacy, excessive melodic ornamentation, intimacy, fragility, inward expressivity, feeling (both the German terms *Gefühl* and *Empfindung*), harmlessness, and charming ambiance.

Little evidence remains of Lang's earliest songs, those of the late 1820s (her adolescent period). A few composed from the later 1840s into the 1850s (that is, after her marriage) have survived; and only a sprinkling of songs date from her widowhood (these composed from the 1860s to her death in 1880).[60] Lang's autographs supplied with dates, therefore, tell us that her most intense and prolific years of composition—when her level of creativity and skill in the musical expression of emotions were at their highest—extend through the 1830s decade to her marriage in 1842. Never again did her focus on song composition equal that of these twelve years. Yet we could not comprehend Lang's achievements in those twelve years if we had listened to Lorenz's biased intimations that Josephine Lang's music could not be the subject of serious criticism, or Charles Rosen's negative assumptions that the "attempt to review the works of those few women composers who remained almost completely repressed during . . . [the romantic era] would be in vain."[61]

Lang resorted to a number of musical styles in her vocal compositions, not least her songs. At times they reflect a sense of *Volkstümlichkeit*—the consciously folklike—that was coursing through the lieder and choral music of her times.[62] Many of her settings of lyric poems, for example, are tinted with only gentle pastel intimations of Swabia's folksong style. Especially in their fluid vocal and piano writing, Lang's songs partially reflect the stylistic traditions of southwestern German song composers such as Konradin Kreutzer (1780–1849) and Friedrich Silcher (1789–1860).[63] Reinhold Sietz, however, overstates the influence of folklike Swabianisms in Lang's songs.

Even from the tender age of fifteen, Lang was composing songs that surpassed conventional lieder and piano compositions of her day. The harmonic fluidity and essentially diatonic basis of her music are edged at times with sudden, turbulent dissonance and audacious chromatic elements in both the voice and piano parts, these often erupting in brazen modulations to a key far from the central, established key of the composition. Many of Lang's finest and most original examples are marked by equally wrenching melodic and harmonic passages. Also, the vocal line in her songs often makes dramatic shifts of register (pitch level) over broad intervals while the piano, in true romantic fashion, frequently is assigned an independent prelude, interlude, or postlude, or all three. These reinforce the imagery and emotions of the song—that is, the piano is not mere accompaniment. And Lang often toyed with a given rhythmic pattern, tempo, or dynamic range, creating effects intended to move the listener with their abruptness. At the very least, she tempers these jarring effects to accommodate both specific and overall expression of a given poem, often doing so in original, individual ways.

In their detailed discussion of "hypermeter" in Lang's songs, Harald and Sharon Krebs address one of the telling characteristics of Lang's rhythmic style, referring generally to metrical expansion and irregularity. In contrast to Lang's songs set in the regular phrase rhythm of folk style, Harald Krebs singles out others to which he attributes such expressive devices as "irregular phrase rhythm" to the text structure of a poem (for example, extra syllables in a line that extend a particular phrase); or, more often, to the emotional cast of a text (for example, a specific feeling that Lang expresses through prolonged dissonance).[64]

Many of the stylistic features of Lang's piano works and solo songs with piano accompaniment were already current in her day, showing the skill and idiomatic sensitivity of professional composers in treating both voice and piano. Not surprisingly, Lang's compositions reflect a certain melodic liquidity and melancholy akin to the style of her mentors Mendelssohn and Heller. The *cantabile* style of her writing and representation of nature in character pieces particularly suggest characteristics of Mendelssohn's style. And occasionally one detects the more stabbing melancholy central to Schubert's songs.

Proceeding from decade to decade, the following examples of Josephine Lang's songs illumine some of the more extraordinary beauties of her creative mind.[65]

The 1830s

Josephine Lang's song "Frühzeitiger Frühling" ("Tage der Wonne, Kommt Ihr so bald?"), Op. 6, no. 3 (Goethe), is one of her most cited songs, the date of composition usually given as 1830. But Krebs's database, when this author last saw it, gives the date as still unknown. It is possible that Mendelssohn heard it in Munich during his stay there that year. In this setting for mezzo or contralto voice, Lang underlines the emotional import of salient words with abrupt chromaticism, unexpected leaps in register, and brazen changes in the density of the texture. Accordingly the piano engages in sweeping arpeggiated figures and a steady triplet (three-note) motif balancing the voice's irregular phrases. This triplet motion, coupled with a separate prelude and postlude, gives the piano striking independence from the vocal line.[66]

Lang's song "Mignons Klage" ("Nur wer die Sehnsucht kennt"), Op. 10, no. 2 (1832 or 1835), is a setting of a well-known Goethe poem also set by many other composers, including the poet's colleague Carl Friedrich Zelter (two); Beethoven (four); Schubert (at least five); and Tchaikovsky (one). The voice (measure two) sprints dramatically higher (a major sixth) on the critical words *kennt* (acquainted with) and *weiss* (knows), offering a striking example of Lang's sensitivity to the text; for the German reads "Only one who is acquainted [*kennt*] with longing knows [*weiss*]," each expressing two very distinct levels of meaning but both covered by the single English "know." As in "Frühzeitiger Frühling," Lang characteristically heightens poetic meaning with unexpected harmonic turns through passing chords and intimations of keys veering far from the home key of B minor, including a daring cadence modulating to a very "foreign" C major.[67]

Josephine Lang's song, "Mailied," ("Wie herrlich leuchtet mir die Natur"), Op. 40, no. 2 (1833), is another setting of a famous Goethe poem. The music unfolds over a moderately wide expanse of pitch levels intensified by sudden changes in vocal range; also, chromatic elements pervade the piano writing (which includes a prelude), as in the brazen modulation from the central key of B-flat major to a distant but unmistakable G-flat major. The exhilaration of the poem also fuels the racing tempo of broken chords in the accompaniment.[68]

Harald and Sharon Krebs single out the setting of "Auf de Reise," a poem by Ludwig Bechstein, for its "effective hypermetric expansions at cadences and a telling use of mode mixture. . . ."[69] But in a review of October 12, 1855, the *Neue Zeitschrift für Musik* condemned this song as too feminine in what the critic considered the work of an unimaginative "dilettante" (fig. 16).[70]

In delineating the image of a fluttering butterfly (in "Schmetterling"), Lang resorts—mainly in the piano part—to such stylistic devices as lofty trills, abrupt rhythmic changes, and fleeting triplets, the keyboard ever driving onward to show insensitivity to the grief expressed by the voice. These musical elements underline the poetic image of a lover's inconstancy (fig. 17).[71]

Additional songs from the 1830s similarly illustrate Lang's skillful treatment of the piano to highlight poetic meaning through changes in range and pace, salient harmonic twists, and independent keyboard preludes and postludes.[72]

The 1840s and 1850s

The 1840s decade covers the period of Lang's engagement, marriage, and most of her child-bearing years. In 1840, for example, Lang made two impassioned settings of her future husband's poem "Am Morgen," Op. 9, no. 4. Dating from 1841, "Traumleben," Op. 27, no. 1 ("Noch kaum erwacht von Träumen") generally displays more orthodox harmonies, yet the composer continues to assign both the voice and piano distinct roles. Lang's songs from the 1850s are marked by equally staid musical settings, as in "An einer Quelle," Op. 27, no. 2 ("Wenn das Herz dir ist bekommen") from 1853.

Figure 16. Josephine Lang, "Auf der Reise" ("So viel am Himmelskreise"), Op. 22, 1837. Autograph. Courtesy of the Württembergische Landesbibliothek, Stuttgart.

Figure 17. Josephine Lang, "Schmetterling" ("Frühlingsbothe! Schmetterling"), Op. 8, no. 1, 1832; published score, 1838. Courtesy of the Württembergische Landesbibliothek, Stuttgart.

The 1860s, 1870s, and 1880s

The "Lied des jungen Werner," Op. 45, no. 2 ("Am Ufer blies ich ein lustig Stück")
J. V. von Scheffel, a lied from *Der Trompeter von Säckingen,* dates from 1860. Strikingly in the second measure, the vocal line bounds abruptly down a tenth at the chief word, *Trompete!,* and is otherwise etched in vivid chromaticism. By this time, the pace of Lang's composing had slowed dramatically. On November 23, 1878, she finished the "Danse Infernale" and on February 4, 1879, the "Walze Infernale," Op. 46—both for piano. Not published in Lang's lifetime, the lied "Du bist mir lieb" (a setting of Julius von der Traun's poem) dates from February 14, 1879. The fourteenth of May 1879 brought "Dem blauen Augen" and September 1880 "Wiegenlied" (a setting of Therese von Niemeyer's poem). Dedicated "to the little Prince Ulrich."

Lang's Patriotic Choral Settings

Lang's patriotic choral settings typically give communal expression to national or ethnic sentiments—in contrast to the focus of her solo songs, which typically voice the intimate emotions of a single individual. The gentler side of these feelings for Lang were encapsulated in music by the term *volkstümlich* (see p. 95), an unpretentious compositional style allowing a song to be singable by anyone. Lang herself composed three of the more than four hundred mostly patriotic song settings associated with the image of the Rhine River and written and/or published during the 1840s. Lang's song "Sie sollen ihn nicht haben, den freien deutschen Rhein" ("They [the French] shall not have it, the free German Rhine"), a setting for solo voice and piano of Nikolaus Becker's outrageously popular poem of July 1840, was composed and published by Challier in Berlin that same year.[73] Even Schumann commented on Lang's setting, but then he, too, set the Becker poem, along with the composers Konradin Kreutzer, Carl Löwe, Heinrich Marschner, and Peter Cornelius. Mendelssohn, however, refused to set Becker's poem.

Lang's setting of Becker's poem fits perfectly into the Germans' volatile post-Napoleonic period, with its intensifying socioeconomic struggles toward a united German state, the turbulent unease of the *Vormärz* (literally, pre-March) years ultimately erupting with the Revolution of 1848.[74] Lang's patriotic songs of the 1840s clearly reflect the nationalistic currents of that *Vormärz* decade that many other German composers voiced in song. In one special case, there was one contemporary of Lang whose life strangely paralleled hers. Despite the differences in the lives of Lang and her German contemporary Johanna Kinkel (Matthieux; née Mockel) (1810–1858), the resemblances are striking. Like Lang's husband, Kinkel's was a theologian, an amateur poet, and later a historian of the arts. Kinkel married at thirty-three and bore four children during her first six years of marriage.[75]

Lang's second *Rheinlied* was "Ich Muss zum Rhein" ("Es braust ein Ruf,' wie Donnerhall"), Op. 53a–55b. ("Die Wacht am Rhein" is a poem by Max Schneckenburger.). A solo rather than a choral song, it was set to music on June 12, 1841, for bass or tenor and piano. Here Lang combines her *volkstümlich* atmosphere with a military-patriotic style marked by martial rhythm, a chordal role for the piano, a simple texture, and bland harmony—everything in her typical 1840s style (fig. 18).

During the following year, Lang set a third *Rheinlied,* "Vögelein," to a poem by Lang's husband, "written," Reinhold noted, "on a Rhine journey." The Krebs described in detail how the melodic structure and hypermetric design of the music contribute to the poem's avian imagery (fig. 19).[76]

The following songs likewise express Lang's heartfelt patriotic emotions late in her life as Germans were nearing the formation of a single homeland. On November 10, 1859, Lang, now forty-four, composed the regal "Apollo-Marsch" for piano solo as part of a centenary commemoration of the poet Friedrich Schiller's birth. Curiously, this memorial march for solo piano honoring a great poet is stylistically ordinary, a setting markedly regal: "patriotic" with martial rhythms and expansive forte chords outlining conventional nineteenth-century harmony. But the march section is followed by an oddly contrasting trio in a dance mode.

Other patriotic songs composed in Lang's last years include "Neues Deutsches Lied" ("Wer Sprenget auf dem stolzen Ross") (Max Schenkendorf), composed after 1870, published as "Dem Königs-Sohn," and dedicated to the German Em-

Figure 18. Josephine Lang, "Ich muss zum Rhein" ("Es braust ein Ruf"). Text by Max Schneckenburger, "Die Wacht am Rhein." Incomplete autograph, 1841. Courtesy of the Württembergische Landesbibliothek, Stuttgart.

Figure 19. Josephine Lang, "Vögelein" ("Ein Vögelein fliegt übern Rhein"), Op. 14, no. 5, 1842. Autograph. Courtesy of the Württembergische Landesbibliothek, Stuttgart.

press Auguste; "Deutscher Sieges-Marsch," Op. 48 (1870), set for piano; "Heil dir, Heil, mein Vaterland" ("Deutsche Völker allesammt") (Müller von der Werra), composed c. 1870. (This song is also known as "Ein deutsches Bundeslied," dedicated "to all German hearts by a German Lady on the Neckar.)"

Other Genres

Lang also wrote several sacred choral works, including Mass sections such as her unpublished and undated "*Cyrie*" *(*Kyrie) movements for chorus with piano and an "Ave Maria," ("Ave Maria! Ave Maria! Maria, sey gegrüsst"), (poet unknown), with versions for men's or women's chorus. In addition, the composer wrote a number of instrumental works, especially piano compositions—above all, waltzes—along with some pieces for violin and piano. "Nachruf in's Jenseits: Elegie" for violin and piano was composed March 26, 1876, and dedicated to her chronically ill son Eugen, who died in 1880, immediately prior to her own death that same year. Her numerous waltzes for the piano include "Valzer," Op. 31, written in 1828—when she was only thirteen years old.

Conclusion

The course of Josephine Lang's life led from her childhood (left motherless at twelve) as a prodigy in piano and composition to a professional career as a celebrated singer and ultimately as a cultural patroness. Lang's accomplishments paralleled the professional path taken by her mother, maternal grandmother, and aunts. But she exceeded even their attainments.[77] This was so despite the hierarchical structure of Lang's nineteenth-century German world with its accepted and clear-cut division of roles—for example, determining that, after Lang's youth, her domestic roles as wife and mother should become a woman's, even a gifted one's, chief "task," artistic pursuits being relegated to a lower order of importance.[78] Yet, in a decidedly creative move, Lang turned her otherwise confining residence into a salon (by no means a minor achievement) providing a stimulating professional outlet for this *echt* German *Hausfrau*. Otherwise, unlike her husband's professional situation, Lang's was constricted. Throughout her youth, she had been privately educated. Consequently she lacked a significant array of fellow students and colleagues available that male musicians in academia traditionally enjoyed: continuing access to stimulating critical, intellectual, and artistic interchange that provided help in honing the compositional skills necessary for fledgling composers' creative work. In addition to this situation, there was little or no societal expectation of women in the German nineteenth-century world—and elsewhere at that time—to compose large-scale works; women were limited to composing solo songs and keyboard pieces. (One cannot, however, disregard the fact that, after all, the nineteenth century marked the apex of song composition and the first flowering of piano literature.) These two chamber-music-sized genres, in fact, typically engaged women composers of many eras. Duchess Sophie-Elisabeth and Elisabeth de La Guerre (chapters 1 and 2, respectively) proved to be exceptions, however, both composing large-scale works, as did Clara Schumann during Lang's lifetime, for example.

At the same time, Lang's marriage and birthing of children coincided with the tense, tumultuous decade of Germany's *Vormärz*, a time of social and political turmoil that penetrated her life as did, in different circumstances, the Thirty Years' War in Duchess Sophie-Elisabeth's years. Yet they pursued active musical lives. Of course, the lives of such extraordinary male composers as Richard Wagner, too, were considerably affected by the political chaos of this period, but in other ways.

There are further issues involved in assessing Lang's and other women's professional achievements before and after her lifetime. Today's societal standards and ideals affecting women's "successes," Marian Wilson Kimber argues, apply only to the present. Our traditions and hence expectations lie far from those of the German bourgeoisie of Lang's day. Kimber's assessment of Fanny Mendelssohn Hensel's professional obstacles applies generally to Josephine Lang's. "It would have taken the entire transformation of the culture," Kimber says, "not merely the encouragement of her younger brother [Felix], to have enabled Fanny [Mendelssohn] Hensel to have a successful professional career."[79] The adoption of current male or feminine models for a nineteenth-century female composer's biography, Kimber argues, centers on a woman's failure to achieve public success. Such a comparison, she notes, "does more to undermine the 'recovery' of historical women composers than it does to critique the patriarchal conditions in which they lived."[80]

Adding to these considerations, Charles Rosen believes that a truly critical assessment of nineteenth-century women's compositions would obscure "the real tragedy of the creative female musician" at that time in history and would be unrealistic and naive; for women composers, even those of promise, either failed to gain recognition for their works or—more devastating to contemplate—they never were offered the opportunity to develop and thereby gain well-deserved pride in their accomplishments because their music was never heard and thus unheard of in records of the past.[81]

Lang's domestic and professional life can fairly be compared with that of her two most discussed and exceptionally gifted contemporaries—Clara Schumann and Fanny Mendelssohn Hensel. Like Lang, both these women composed and were gifted, even brilliant, pianists; both married, bore children, and developed a prodigious talent nurtured in various ways by professional families active in the very midst of the highest realms of German music. Unlike Clara Schumann and Lang, however, Hensel enjoyed great wealth and prestige in Berlin, a city well on its way in her day ultimately to assume a central place in European cultural and intellectual life. Yet, unlike Clara Schumann and Lang, Hensel died early, at forty-two, leaving her husband widowed and her children motherless. Lang was widowed at forty-one and left with six underage children to raise on her meager income alone.[82] Clara Schumann had eight children in thirteen years; four of them predeceased her, and one was permanently institutionalized. Between and soon after their births, moreover, every Schumann child was cared for by a hired wet nurse for its first six months and was then even boarded with family members scattered through Germany. In addition, Schumann's husband, Robert, suffered from a severely disturbing mental condition and died when she was only thirty-seven. Yet, through all these tragedies, she continued performing—even internationally—also composing, teaching, and supporting her children and grandchildren.[83]

List of Works

Songs (See the listing in H. and S. Krebs, *Josephine Lang,* 295 and following, and their database.)

PIANO COMPOSITIONS

Published:
Elegie auf den Tod Ludwig Uhlands, Op. 31; *Zwei Charakterstücke,* Op. 32 [33]; *[Zwei]*
Lieder ohne Worte, Op. 35 [37]; *Hochzeits-Marsch,* Op. 42; *Gruss in die Ferne,* Op. 44;
Danse infernale, Op. 46; *Deutscher Siegesmarsch,* Op. 48; *Zwei Mazurkas,* Op. 49; *In*
der Dämmerung, Impromptu, Op. 50; *Apollo-Marsch,* WoO; *Arabeske; Der trauernde*
Humor; Drei Klavierstücke, WoO; and *Heimweh.*

Unpublished:
Lied [Song without Words]; *Nocturno* [fragment]; and *Sonata for Pianoforte and Violin,*
first movement.

Josephine Lang: Selected Discography and Editions

CDS

Thirty Songs: appendix to H. Krebs and S. Krebs, *Josephine Lang: Her Life and Songs* (Ox-
ford University Press, 2007). Sharon Krebs (soprano), Harald Krebs (piano), Pamela
Highbaugh-Aloni (cello)
A Selection of Josephine Lang's Goethe, Heine and Uhland Lieder: appendix to Aisling
Kenny, dissertation, *Josephine Lang's Goethe, Heine and Uhland Lieder: Contextualizing*
her Contribution to Nineteenth-Century German Song (2010). Aisling Kenny (soprano),
Judith Gannon (piano)
Feenreigen. Audite Musikproduktion (2002). Heike Hallaschka (soprano), Heidi Kom-
merell (piano)
Lullabies for Samantha. Private publication (KS-102). Sharon Krebs (soprano), Patricia
Kostek (clarinet), Harald Krebs (piano)
Münchner Komponistinnen der Klassik und Romantik. Musica Bavarica (MB 902) (1997),
Christel Krömer (soprano), Werner Grobholz (violin), Sylvia Hewig-Tröscher (piano),
Monica von Saalfeld (piano), Jutta Vornehm (piano)
Neue Liebe, Neues Leben. Lieder von Josephine Lang und Fanny Hensel. Private publica-
tion (TSO 01305) (2001). Christine Cerletti (soprano), Andrzej Pikul (soprano)
Zwanzig Lieder: appendix to *Literatur in Bayern* (München; 72 (June 2003). Sharon Krebs
(soprano), Harald Krebs (piano)

EDITIONS

Lang, Josephine. *Lieder for Voice and Piano.* Harald Krebs, ed., vols. 1 and 2. (Bryn Mawr,
Pa.: Hildegard Publishing, 2006).
———. *Lieder nach Texten von Reinhold Köstlin,* Harald Krebs and Sharon Krebs, eds. Den-
kmäler der Musik in Baden-Württemberg, Band 20. (München: Strube Verlag, 2008).
———. *Selected Songs,* Judith Tick, ed. (New York: Da Capo Press, 1982). Women Com-
posers Series. New edition of the *Collection of 40 Lieder* (Breitkopf & Härtel, 1982) with
twelve additional lieder.
New Historical Anthology of Music by Women, James R. Briscoe, ed. (Bloomington: Indiana
University Press, 2004).

CHAPTER FOUR

Maria Bach

Vienna from Imperial Splendor to the Second Republic

On February 19, 1930, after a performance of music by the Viennese composer Maria Bach (1896–1978), an unidentified critic for the *Neue Freie Presse* slung demeaning arrows: " . . . This young woman is decidedly gifted. Certainly, she glows and storms. But knows not where she is going! Ability and childlikeness coexist. All said, the music turns into an enchanting jumble! And she does this with talent. How much little Maria imagines herself to be Stravinsky . . . ; genius or philistine, holy or devilish, she could become anything—perhaps even a completely useful composer!"[1]

And on March 23 of the same year, a critic identified only as "ber" wrote in the *Neuigkeits-Welt-Blatt* after the premiere of Viennese composer Johanna Müller-Hermann's "Lied der Erinnerung" at the fourth Gesellschaft der Musikfreunde Concert: "The row of female composers of rank has been sown very sparsely. In all types of art women have, by chance, reached a certain equality of rights as opposed to a man; but music, as a productive factor of art, has remained noticeably closed to them. With a few exceptions. And Johanna Müller-Hermann numbers among them. Her lyrical cantata *Lied der Erinnerung* for Solo [vocal] Quartet, Orchestra and Organ, which took up the evening shows, besides an imposing ability and knowledge in the technical details of orchestration, a surprisingly blossoming fantasy and invention, power in the forming of . . . pictorially graphic clarity and richly flowing melody." (The text was based on a Walt Whitman poem on Abraham Lincoln's death.)[2]

These comments by Viennese critics encapsulate Maria Bach's promising professional future and yet portend her lifelong struggle to attract renown and respect as a "serious" woman composer. Born into Austria's late-nineteenth-century privileged "aristocracy"—the affluent upper middle class—Baroness Maria Bach, Viennese composer and pianist, prided herself on her intellectual and artistic heritage. (The family name had been entitled early in Emperor Franz Josef's lifetime.) For her birth in 1896 set her solidly within the imperial capital's golden age, that brilliant constellation of the arts known as Viennese modernism. From the last decade of the nineteenth century to World War I, fin-de-siècle Vienna was a cultural mecca unequaled anywhere else in central Europe. Its now-affluent *haute bourgeoisie* had gained social prominence and entrepreneurial optimism, creating both motive and means to further the arts—with an intensity matching the splendor of the newly constructed Ringstrasse encircling the city.

Genealogical Convolutions

Maria Bach inherited a legacy of cultural achievements over many generations of ancestors. Her parents claimed descent from Catholic ancestors linked, though distantly, to the composer Johann Sebastian Bach (1685–1750) and his Thuringian branch of the Bach family. Although no hard evidence has surfaced, the belief passed down through generations of Maria Bach's forebears was that Catholic ancestors of the Bachs had emigrated early in the Reformation period from Thuringia in Germany to Grafenberg in Lower Austria, establishing there a vineyard and winery.

Among the progeny of these emigré Austrian Bachs was a Sebastian Bach, mayor of Grafenberg, where his sons Johann Baptist Bach (1779–1847) and Michael Bach (dates unknown) grew to adulthood. Both the maternal and paternal sides of Maria Bach's family descended from Michael Bach, whose sons Alexander Bach (1813–1893)—a high official in the Austrian Interior Ministry—Eduard (1814–1884), and Heinrich Josef (1835–1915) were ennobled court officials under Emperor Franz Josef. Heinrich Josef was also a composer and painter. Both Heinrich and a fourth brother, Otto Johann Baptist (1833–1893), were Maria Bach's grandfathers, consequently making her parents first cousins. In 1860 Heinrich married Maria Theresia Kolisko (1837–1922), the daughter of a respected Viennese family of physicians and attorneys. Heinrich's son Robert fathered Maria Bach. Her grandfather Otto, another Austrian Bach composer, was music director of the Salzburg Mozarteum for twelve years. Maria Bach claimed that his appointment to this position had rested on the recommendation of the celebrated Austrian composer Anton Bruckner. From 1880 Otto was a church *Kapellmeister* in Vienna, where he married Therese Katharina Jander (1825–1884), the widow of the well-known German opera composer Heinrich Marschner. Therese Katharina, an accomplished singer and pianist, was a member of the Vienna Conservatory voice faculty for seven years. Her daughter Eleonore was Maria Bach's mother.[3]

Maria Bach's father, Robert Bonaventura Michael Wenzel Freiherr von Bach (1864–1927), an attorney and imperial court official in Vienna, later moved to an estate inherited from a wealthy uncle in Leesdorf near Baden. (A famous spa town not far south of Vienna, Baden remained the center of Maria Bach's youth and was one of her homes in later life.)[4] Maria Bach rated her father "a very good violinist with excellent technique and an expansive tone." And, interestingly, he, like her mother, was also a painter. (Maria Bach's own artworks are discussed later in this chapter.) As a youth, he had played chamber music with Vienna Philharmonic musicians. Using family wealth, he had acquired both Amati and Guarnieri violins. Robert Bach enjoyed wielding his power even over professional musicians of the highest rank; for, as his daughter Maria recounted in her memoirs, "Father often played Beethoven's *Kreutzer Sonata* and on one occasion even yelled up to a violinist giving a recital in the Grosser Musikvereinsaal"—the most important concert hall in Vienna—"forcing him to play the *Kreutzer* instead of an announced change in the program."[5]

But Maria Bach seems to have inherited her talent for art from both sides of the family. In February 1890, Robert married the Salzburg baroness Eleonore Josepha Maria Auguste Theresia Bach (1869–1939), a professional singer esteemed in Austria and Germany. She was also a composer and honorary member of Vienna's Gesellschaft der Musikfreunde. This honor was explained by Maria: "Our mother, because of her beautiful singing, [was] an honorary member of the Gesellschaft der Musikfreunde in Vienna and was often invited to sing the soprano part in the festive oratorio performances there in the Grosser Musikvereinsaal. Great singers sang with her under the direction of such famous conductors as Arthur Nikisch (1855–1922), Gustav Mahler (1860–1911), Johannes Brahms (1833–1897) and Hugo Wolf (1860–1903)."[6] Maria also recalled, "Often our mother told us how beautifully the celebrated composer Hugo Wolf accompanied her on the piano." For her it was an experience ten times over to sing his "Lied vom Wind" for him. "Also," she continued, "there was a frequently cited remark [according to Maria's parents] made by the . . . composer [Johannes] Brahms, who made music with my parents and was entertained with wine. On one occasion Brahms suddenly said, 'This wine makes no impression on me.'"[7]

One of Eleonore Bach's landscape paintings was accepted for exhibition at the Vienna Secession and sold, Maria reported, "likewise the second painting [sold from the Secession] was then hung in the Hotel Sacher."[8] Eleonore's painting provides one of the myriad factors linking her marriage with Robert Bach as an integral part of Viennese cultural life at its apogee.

But this cultural utopia rested on a foundation of increasing political and socioeconomic upheavals that were soon to shatter both the empire and dynasty of the Habsburgs. And this was the world that Maria Bach's parents bequeathed to their four daughters, Maria being the third. Therese (1891–1987), the eldest, married a count, inheriting some valuable real estate. But the war years 1941–1945 brought death to her husband as well as to her two sons and also destruction to the family castle. Therese found solace in writing poetry (published posthumously), some of which Maria set to music. Therese died at the age of ninety-six, outliving Maria by nine years, having wasted away in total seclusion through the last four decades of her life.

Maria's second sister, Katharina (1892–1954), had made some attempts at composition. She married into a highly educated aristocratic family whose older members had known Goethe. After her two daughters died at a young age, she spent the rest of her life, like Therese, in isolated rejection of society.

Until World War II, Henriette, the youngest sister (1903–1980), led an active career as a solo cellist in both Austria and Germany and successfully premiered several of Maria's works. She never married, but eventually was the administrator for several of the Bach family possessions near Vienna.[9]

Vienna: Cultural Modernism (1890–1918) and Music

The Bach sisters grew up for the most part in the palatial family villa in Leesdorf. Theirs was a family whose Sunday musical soirées were close to the cutting-edge of mainline Vienna's cultural scene. But, ironically, even as an active professional composer and pianist, Maria Bach herself never participated significantly in the social life of the city's musical mainstream.

And what a mainstream that was. Aside from the hedonistic glitter of operettas, waltzes, and polkas engulfing Vienna's café culture, the composer-conductor Gustav Mahler began and ended his turbulent reign over Vienna's Court Opera and Philharmonic. It is impossible here, of course, to name all the major musical figures of Vienna in this astounding era. Mentored by Alexander Zemlinsky (who also taught composition to Alma Mahler, Gustav's wife), composer Arnold Schönberg launched the so-called Second Viennese School. Together with pupils Alban Berg and Anton Webern, Schönberg set music on the brave new course of atonality with a psycho-pathological intent akin to contemporary expressionist art: the dissolution of traditionally imposed boundaries and a baring of the irrational, private realm of human experience.

One of Vienna's leading music critics at that time was Josef David Bach (1847–1947), an Austrian music critic for Vienna's *Arbeiter Zeitung* (a voice of the Social Democratic movement); a musicologist; a founder in 1905 of the Vienna Workers Symphony Orchestra Concerts; a close friend of Schönberg and Webern; a great admirer of Mahler; and a Vienna city councilor.[10]

Concurrent with Vienna's avant-garde were the lives of the influential composer Joseph Marx, a leading faculty member of the Vienna State Music Academy (and Maria Bach's only composition teacher) and the composer Erich Wolfgang Korngold, the young son of the influential and feared Viennese music critic Julius Korngold. As composers, Marx and the younger Korngold sought to extend harmonic and other dimensions of nineteenth-century romanticism.

Several aspects of Vienna's musical world foreshadowed the eventual course of Maria Bach's professional future. Her family's Sunday musicales thoroughly exposed her to the classical repertoire of chamber music composed during the eighteenth and nineteenth centuries. Among the influential musical figures invited to these affairs were composers (with their families) whose works, to a greater or lesser degree, extended the romantic aesthetic. Besides Brahms, these important figures included Joseph Marx, Erich Wolfgang Korngold, Gustav and Alma Mahler, Siegfried Ochs, Arthur Nikisch, and Paul Grümmer. Other Bach guests were several members of the Vienna Philharmonic Orchestra, and the painters Gustav Klimt, Oskar Kokoschka, and Ferdinand Hodler. And it was the memory of these celebrities and the legacy of the romantic style that pervaded Maria Bach's music intensely all her life. Contrary to Vienna's acknowledged vein of anti-Semitism, moreover, the Bachs' invitation lists for these occasions, Maria specifically noted, never excluded Jewish guests.

When the Bach sisters "came of age" in their instrumental skills, Maria on the piano and the younger Henriette on the cello, they were allowed to participate in these soirées. On one of these occasions, Maria made the acquaintance of the younger Korngold (1897–1957), a prodigy in composition and on the piano. He was already dazzling the Viennese musical world with his compositions, one already premiered. From his Vienna youth to his emigré years as a Hollywood film composer, Korngold's music remained anchored in traditionalism, the harmonic, melodic, and other stylistic features forming the bedrock of Joseph Marx's teaching aesthetic—and hence the only formal composition instruction that Maria Bach ever received.

Visual and Literary Arts

The winds of Cultural Modernism swept over fin-de-siècle Vienna and wafted in a new *Gefühlskultur* (cultural sensibility).[11] This "culture of the senses" toppled the half-century reign of classical realism with its rigid code of historicism—as in the Ringstrasse's trophy architecture, edifices resurrecting styles from Europe's past. Parallel with the emphasis Sigmund Freud (1856–1939) placed on recognizing the power of individual subjectivity, the secessionist artists, led by Gustav Klimt (1862–1918), ushered in the *Jugendstil,* a provocative new aesthetic: the expression of human psychological truth. Like the secessionists, the radical *Jung Wien* writers probed man's instinctual being with bold erotic depictions.

The secessionists' art nouveau images had conveyed sexual messages of psychological truth, sanctifying beauty as good. But by 1910 (Maria Bach was fourteen) they were challenged by expressionist painters such as Oskar Kokoschka (1886–1980) and Egon Schiele (1890–1918), whose geometrical symbols revealed their human subjects' inner psyches. These artists envisioned their art in a solely decorative role that encompassed even the ugly.

Among architects in Vienna at this time, however, Adolf Loos (1870–1933) saw function (rather than merely the decorative espoused by the expressionists) as the purpose of his creative works. The pivotal architect Otto Wagner (1841–1918), too, championed the designing of urban landscapes to accord—that is, to function—with edifices already present.[12] Similar views were held by the architect Josef Hoffmann (1870–1956), the painter-designer Koloman Moser (1868–1918), and Alfred Roller (1864–1935), Mahler's stage designer at the Court Opera. In yet another voice amid the sometimes conflicting, sometimes coinciding currents of Viennese modernism, the adherents of the *Wiener Werkstätte* placed arts and crafts on equal footing with painting and sculpture.

Nihilism, absurdity, hedonism, and hopelessness, which voiced the wrenching sentiments of the imperial capital's looming demise, pervaded fin-de-siècle Vienna's dense network of salons and cafés—and also the lives of the Bach sisters. A highly charged intellectual exchange was dominated by a singularly Viennese vein of cultural pessimism among the literati of *Jung Wien*. This doomsday mentality even overshadowed their probe—paralleling that of their fellow cultural luminaries in other fields—of essential sociological and psychological truth free of moralistic nineteenth-century sanctions. *Jung Wien* circles included the works of philosopher Ludwig Wittgenstein (1889–1951), the absurdly hopeless stories of Franz Kafka (1883–1924), the doom-filled dramas of Arthur Schnitzler (1862–1931), the tales of Hugo von Hofmannsthal (1874–1929), the vicious social critiques of Karl Kraus (1874–1936), and the writings of Peter Altenberg (1859–1919).[13]

Maria Bach's Younger Years

Maria Emilie Bach was born in Vienna on March 11, 1896. One year later the Bachs moved to the family castle in Leesdorf (fig. 20).

In her memoirs, Maria reflected on her early years in the "seigneurial castle, entrusted to a French governess, cook, laundress, gardener, chauffeur, and personal servant."[14] As children, she and her sisters enjoyed the carefully landscaped, expansive castle grounds as a playground, where they could run among the gardens or collect nuts and strawberries. They also pedaled bicycles there and swam in the castle pool, for their parents wanted to surround them with nature.

According to the strictures of Vienna's social caste system, the Bach sisters lived the life of the privileged class, the children being totally enclosed within the family's inner intellectual and artistic circle. This stimulating, purely inbred social environment, however, ruled out a healthy balance of psychological factors that more exposure to the outside world might have provided, along with a wider perspective by which to assess one's own place in society—and in the musical world—more accurately. For Maria Bach, her parents' stranglehold on her childhood forbade playtimes with their gardener's daughter and taking dancing lessons with the "ordinary" children of Baden, where she took piano lessons.[15] In her memoirs, Bach reveals a similar sense of being excluded in the sense of being overprotected, noting that frequently, "when my parents were away or when my mother was on a concert tour in Germany, we remained alone with our governess while the dog howled and bellowed because of my parents' absence" (fig. 21).[16]

Figure 20. Schloss Leesdorf, near Vienna. Maria Bach spent most of her child-hood here. Courtesy of the Archiv Elena Ostleitner and Alexander Ostleitner.

Early Music Education

Maria and her sisters spent their childhood more under the supervision of hired caregivers—whose ideals they no doubt absorbed—than with their parents. In this controlled environment imposed by their parents, education was the responsibility of private tutors in the children's quarters of the Bach household. Accordingly, the daughters never had access to the peer relationships experienced by students in institutional systems.

Like her siblings, Maria Bach began private piano and violin lessons at the age of five and practiced daily on the family's magnificent Bösendorfer, the pride of Austrian craftsmanship. (The Bachs also owned a piano made by Germany's noted Blüthner firm.) Maria studied the piano with a faculty member at the private Grimm Music School in Baden, where she was recognized and given awards for her musical skills. A critic for the *Badener Zeitung* of January 21, 1906, reviewed her first public concert, given at the age of ten. He remarked that the young baroness had mastered her music, but doing so with an affecting "naive, childlike" performance.[17]

Maria and her sister Henriette also studied the violin, eventually attaining sufficient skill to play before such distinguished guests at their parents' musicales as the celebrated violinist Arnold Rosé (1863–1946). Founder of one of the leading string quartets of his day, Rosé was the longtime concertmaster of the Vienna Court Opera (now the Vienna State Opera) and the Vienna Philharmonic from

Figure 21. The Bach sisters at Leesdorf, in the family's elegant garden park. From left, Henriette, Maria, Käthe, Therese. Courtesy of Madeleine Delarue.

1881 to 1938, when he emigrated from Austria to London after the Nazi *Anschluss* of Austria.

The numerous interrelationships, as described earlier, concerning those variously tied to Maria Bach's family include those among the Mahlers, Rosés, Zemlinskys, Korngolds, and Kolisches. For example, Rosé's wife, Justine, was Gustav Mahler's sister, and Rose's daughter, Alma, was the namesake of Mahler's wife, Alma.[18] (Alma Rosé eventually married a Czech violinist, but, for some reason, never fled the Nazi regime like her brother and father. She was sent, alone, to Auschwitz, where she directed a women's orchestra but ultimately perished, although attempts were made to save her, including efforts by Sergey Koussevitzky, famed conductor of the Boston Symphony Orchestra.)[19] On Gustav Mahler's recommendation, the composer Erich Wolfgang Korngold studied composition (as did Arnold Schoenberg) with Alexander von Zemlinsky, whose sister, Mathilde, was Schönberg's first wife. His second wife, Gertrud, was the sister of Rudolf Kolisch, another Austrian virtuoso violinist and string quartet founder. Kolisch had taught violinist Otakar Sevcik, the teacher of Alma Rosé as well as of Maria and Henriette Bach.

Maria Bach had much to say in her memoir about these soirées. For example, she wrote, "My mother frequently received many guests, and artists of high station and also important personalities would come to these invited musical occasions in the great hall at Leesdorf." She also noted that the family continued these musicales "in Baden in the large music room of their Braiten castle—where Beethoven had once lived. Julius Korngold and his wife often visited the Sunday events. . . . The young Erich's piano playing [he was only one year younger than Maria] inspired me to compose and from then on I tried to compose several things." At one time, Bach added, Korngold played one of her pieces and praised it.

Elsewhere Bach adds, "In this charming music salon, the piano was covered with a beautiful multi-colored silk cloth. . . . And there I wrote, without help, my first fugue for our mother to sing. . . . Yes, we will never forget how my parents' playing—my father on the violin and my mother on the piano—inducted us into true art."[20]

Recalling an occasion when Maria and Henriette had performed a Spohr duet for Rosé during one of her family's Sunday musicales, Maria Bach reminisced— with uncharacteristic humor—that he had enjoyed the freshness of their youthful approach and had praised them, as young student musicians, for "keeping together on the beat, playing totally in tune, and, above all, ending [the duet] together. . . ."[21]

As for private music lessons, Bach remarked, "Arnold Rosé referred me and my sister Henriette to Professor Jaroslav Suchy from the Vienna Opera, who for many years came to us weekly at Baden and gave us violin lessons."[22] Suchy himself had studied with the famous Czech violinist Otakar Sevcik (1852–1934).[23] Although Maria disliked the intensive practicing that Suchy demanded, as well as his strict teaching method, both sisters learned much of the major eighteenth- and nineteenth-century violin repertoire. They were additionally prodded by their father, who valued "a beautiful sound," which, Maria said, was his foremost musical goal. Robert, in fact, founded an in-house string ensemble in which Maria took turns playing second violin or viola and Henriette the cello, joined by Joseph Marx or Paul de Conne on the piano and by other prominent Viennese musicians.

Joseph Marx (1882–1964) was an outstanding composer, music critic, and teacher of theory and composition at the Vienna Academy of Music (1914–1952). After World War I, Maria Bach began composition studies with him. But even at an earlier age she had fallen under his influence in associating chamber music with nature and the Vienna woods, this association remaining with her all her life. She began piano lessons with the famed teacher Paul de Conne in 1912, the year the Bachs moved again, this time to the family castle estate at Mauerbach. Both Marx and de Conne thoroughly acquainted Maria and Henriette with the classical and romantic repertoire. Whenever de Conne played the family Blüthner, he usually took on the taxing demands of Anton Rubinstein's (1829–1894) etudes and Franz Liszt's (1811–1886) transcriptions, Maria noted, "with the greatest strength of his fists." On one such occasion his prowess provoked her father's admonition that "he would not buy another piano. . . ."[24] The two daughters lived at home until their father's death in 1927, after which their widowed mother moved to a luxurious apartment in Vienna. By 1936, however, severe financial losses—no doubt owing at least partially to the worldwide depression of that era—compelled Eleonore Bach to sell her furniture and move to the family hotel, Tulbinger Kogel, in Mauerbach. She died in December 1939.

Austria: World War I and Its Aftermath

In the decade and a half preceding the outbreak of World War I—as Maria Bach proceeded through her formative teenage years—Austrian imperial pride had fallen victim to an uneasy presentiment of approaching loss, a sense of tragedy that spawned "resignation, cynicism, and the frantic plunge into the pleasures of the moment."[25] One could well imagine such an environment affecting the mood of Vienna. Maria Bach grew to adulthood in this atmosphere. The assassination of Austria's imperial heir-apparent in June 1914 by a Serbian fanatic, in fact, sealed the fate of empire and dynasty alike, igniting World War I—that "real Armageddon" predicted only days before its outbreak by Britain's prime minister.[26] The conflagration was ultimately to destroy the vast Austro-Hungarian, British, and Ottoman empires.

Many historians today believe that a sizable number of Austrians hoped that the outbreak of World War I would alleviate their weakening political and economic situation. But assassination only compounded the interlocking forces already enmeshed in the Balkan lands' long-simmering state of unrest. After two years of war and the death of Emperor Franz Josef in 1916, however, the Austrians' joyful expectations yielded to bitter sorrow and ultimately to the pain of defeat.

With its cutting harmony closely expressing a darkly tinted text, Maria Bach's lied "Tief ist der Abgrund," (Deep Is the Abyss), composed in November 1918, was timely, coinciding with the month in which the World War I armistice was signed and imperial Austria vanished forever. Similarly, Bach's song "Draussen im weiten Krieg" (Outside in the Wide World) reflected sadly on Austria's losses in 1918. This song dates, however, from 1929. In early November 1918, the Slavs of the Austro-Hungarian Empire declared their independence. Austria, now permanently deprived of both its ancient dynasty and hegemony over an enormous empire—that had boasted a population of thirty million and covered an area of 180,000 square miles—shrank in 1918 to a national state of only six-and-a-half million people and 50,000 square miles.[27]

The defeat of 1918 (Maria Bach was twenty-two) brought to Austria and Germany political chaos, mass starvation, and runaway inflation followed by the Great Depression, which engulfed the entire world into the 1930s. Amid the turmoil of their loss, Austrians locked horns over questions of national identity—a conflict remembered by many people in central Europe still today. After World War I, this issue drove an ever-widening gap between those considering themselves "Germans" by reason of their Teutonic history and language or "Austrians" by virtue of their common imperial past. As focused in Vienna, the hierarchical social ranking so deeply embedded in its *Geist* never quite disappeared altogether in the aristocratic pretensions of Maria Bach's world.[28] Even in the massive bombardments of Vienna in the later years of World War II, the crème de la crème of society remained safe and relatively affluent, lunching at the elite Bristol, Imperial, and Sacher hotels and residing in their villas, as did Maria Bach in a more modest home located safely outside the center of the city.[29]

Despite Austria's defeat in World War I and its loss of both dynasty and empire, the Bachs seemed to have felt themselves unscathed—at least in their outward circumstances—by the chaos and devastation around them. On the contrary, the family continued to engage in the cultural lifestyle of their affluent prewar years, still quite comfortable in their privileged state of relative wealth. Or was it that the Bachs simply were unaccustomed to admitting their painful family rifts at this time?

Growing Up

The Bach sisters grew to adulthood in a family that demanded from them consistent individual practicing and private performances as a matter of course. "As young people," Maria Bach recalled, "we experienced the most beautiful musical hours and marvelous impressions through our parents. . . ."[30] (During their earliest years, however, Maria and her siblings had been confined upstairs to their rooms under a governess's watchful eye while their parents engaged in their Sunday musicales over a period of many years.)

Later, after a considerable period of formal music study, Maria and her sister Henriette themselves had opportunities to display their talents at these concerts. Maria at one time played, for example, a challenging Liszt concerto. Some of her early compositions were even aired before Vienna's most feared critic of the day, Julius Korngold, who often visited the Bachs accompanied by his wife and son. Maria relates, in fact, that it was the captivating piano playing of the young Korngold that "inspired me to compose and from then on I tried to write something." Korngold even sight-read some of her compositions on the piano and praised her keyboard performances.[31]

It was through these hours-long music-reading sessions, which often continued through dinner time, that the Bach sisters—Maria on violin or piano and Henriette on violin or cello—learned much of the principal literature of the classical and romantic chamber music repertoire. At times the Bach family chamber ensemble barely survived challenges to their technical skills. Maria noted with amusement that the group struggled to keep the beat together because her father "was always a bit ahead, my sister, Henriette, correctly held back on the cello, and I, poor church mouse, fiddled the violin in between. . . ."[32]

The Bach family musicales continued over many years as established events in the household routine, the guests arriving from Vienna by horse and carriage. As Maria related, "Much music was made on the Blüthner piano and when guests came, I had to play the piano, or my mother, accompanying herself on the piano, for example, sang Schubert's 'The Erl King' and 'The Nun' or 'The Moon Night' of Schumann, and many other treasures that today I still keep in my ears exactly." "Sometimes," she added, "playing with members of the Vienna Philharmonic, my father often also played sonatas by Caesar Franck, Brahms, or Rubinstein, also the 'Kreutzer' Sonata of Beethoven. How often did we hear Brahms' Violin Concerto!"[33] Often, Bach observed, each parent accompanied the other and at times collaborated in playing chamber music masterpieces with some of the guests, such as Hugo Wolf, Brahms, and Joseph Marx (later Maria's composition teacher). Inattentive to Vienna's long-entrenched anti-Semitic persuasion, the Bachs' invitees included prominent Jewish figures in the cultural life of the imperial capital. The long hours of music making took place in a magnificent room, its walls covered in elegant silk tapestries imported from China. Elaborate feasts capped the evenings. The musicales continued when the family moved in 1907 to the Braiten Castle at Baden.

Viennese Women Composers

The Bachs' Sunday gatherings formed an integral part of social life in fin-se-siècle Vienna, its cultural ferment centered in the imperial capital's network of cafés and salons hosted by such influential women such as Bertha Zuckerkandl (1864–1945) and Alma Mahler (1879–1964). Maria Bach's mother, in fact, played a similar role as hostess of the family's Sunday musicales. Indeed, the pivotal position these women occupied in the city's era of cultural modernism gave one clear indication of Vienna's roiling social unrest provoked, among other factors, by the changing status of women. In the decades immediately preceding World War I, women were demanding a greater political role, more control over the domestic and professional course of their lives, and, perhaps the sine qua non, more exposure to institutional education. In Vienna, as elsewhere, the prevailing misogynistic attitude confined women to housework and motherhood or—in cultural life—little or no participation other than as hostesses in the fashionable cultural world of the salons and cafés. Women writers found publishers only if they had husbands of prominent social rank. Lacking this asset, women involved in literary pursuits and other areas of the arts simply faced anonymity. Vienna's modernist artists, notably Gustav Klimt, reinforced this mindset, portraying female subjects as unapproachable and unfathomable and confining them to three character types: the beautiful high-ranking socialite, the erotic femme fatale, or the innocent young girl.[34]

As far as we know, Maria Bach left no personal reference to, or opinion on, the status of women in Vienna, not even that of her own (mostly female) colleagues, or on the growing unrest concerning women's rights. But the archival records of performances given at Vienna's Gesellschaft der Musikfreunde indicate more than merely an incidental number of works composed by women, including works by Bach and other Austrians—such as Mathilde von Kralik, Johanna Müller-Hermann, Frida Kern, Grete von Zieritz—during the years between 1929 and 1945.[35]

The review cited at the beginning of this chapter reveals only a guarded admission that even a sprinkling of women composers could be ranked with their male counterparts: high praise in the gender-ridden press of Maria Bach's Vienna, which clung to its image of gifted females whose right to both domestic and artistic success ran counter to the structures of a patriarchal society.[36] But in Vienna during the Nazi era, Maria Bach fared well as both a woman and as a composer of "non-threatening" music. The Reichsmusikkammer approved twelve Austrian women composers who could remain active professionally in this city during that period. (Bach herself registered with this department in early 1940.) Bach, Johanna Müller-Hermann, Mathilde von Kralik, Johanna Müller-Hermann, Frida Kern, and Grete von Zieritz were five of those twelve. Strikingly, Maria Bach's account of her life mentions none of them, not even herself. Nevertheless, the record of performances given at Vienna's prestigious Gesellschaft der Musikfreunde in the Musikverein's large, gilded concert hall and adjacent chamber music room between 1929 and 1945 indicate a surprising number of compositions by these select women performed there, in addition to Bach's.[37]

The oldest of these Maria Bach contemporaries, Mathilde von Kralik (1857–1944), was active in Vienna as both a composer and pianist. A onetime private counterpoint student of the influential composer Anton Bruckner, she then went on to study at the Vienna Conservatory. She belonged to the Austrian Composers' Union and the Vienna Bach Society and was president of the Vienna Women's Choral Society, for which she additionally composed. Kralik's compositions include an opera, melodramas, sacred choral works, an orchestral overture, and several chamber works. She cited the music of J. S. Bach and Liszt as her favored models. Mathilde von Kralik's brother Richard was a poet and cultural critic; his son, her nephew Heinrich, was a music critic.

The music of Johanna Müller-Hermann (1878–1941) was widely praised during her lifetime as "progressive."[38] She had studied composition with the Austrian conductor and composer Alexander von Zemlinsky (1872–1942), Schönberg's and Alma Mahler's only composition teacher.[39] Müller-Hermann was appointed a professor at Vienna's New Conservatory and gained public notice for several of her orchestral and chamber works for their inventive harmony and instrumentation.

Unlike Maria Bach, who never obtained a degree, Frida Kern (1891–1988), the first woman to graduate in composition and conducting from Vienna's Music Academy (1923–1927), wrote symphonies, string quartets, other instrumental chamber works, lieder, and choral settings. She remained professionally active even during the Nazi era, perhaps enjoying the Reich's favor because of her music's conservative tendencies in adherence to Bruckner, whose works were high on the regime's list of approved compositions. She even gained a faculty position at the University of Vienna in 1943, which she held until 1945. More than a few commentators have strongly suggested that her leave-taking from the university reflected retribution for her earlier complicity, or at least sympathy with, Austria's Nazi regime. She had, for example, composed vocal works for Nazi publications. This music displays an extremely obvious simplicity of style that accorded with Nazi principles. That is, her music contrasts remarkably with that style condemned by the Nazis as *entartete Musik* (degenerate music). Yet her compositions pre-dating the Nazi *Anschluss* show radical harmonic modulations, dissonance, and chromaticism, as in, for example, her *"Russian" Piano Sonata* (1925) and *Sonata for Cello and Piano,* Op. 10 (1931). Nevertheless, in 1960 she was awarded an honorary professorship by the Austrian president.

The Austrian composer and pianist Grete von Zieritz (1899–2001) attended the Graz Conservatory. In 1917 she moved to Berlin, where she studied with the Austrian composer and Schönberg ally Franz Schreker at Berlin's Hoch-schule für Musik. Like Maria Bach and Frida Kern, von Zieritz was granted an honorary professorship in 1958 by the Austrian president—the first woman to be so honored. Again, for example, like Maria Bach and Frida Kern (as in Kern's *Afrikanische Stimmungsbilder*), Zieritz explored exotic, non-Western subjects in her compositions, such as her "Japanische Lieder," which brought her considerable public recognition. Although she was most prolific in com-positions for chamber ensembles, she also wrote vocal and orchestral works. Like Maria Bach, she also favored musical depictions of nature images. And as with Bach and Kern, Zieritz's conservative adherence to tonal harmony and classical structures allowed her to pursue her career freely during the era of National Socialist cultural politics; but the very same stylistic features excluded her from the avant-garde direction of much composition in Europe, the United States, and elsewhere after 1945.[40] Her music was far outdated and, therefore, rarely recognized after the war ended.

Wartime

By 1914, the opening year of World War I, the eighteen-year-old Maria Bach was composing in earnest, her style at this time noticeably influenced by that of the Russian composer Alexander Scriabin (1872–1915) (fig. 22). Maria's habit of composing at the piano, she noted, annoyed her father at work in his study on the floor above—the top floor of the old castle tower in Leesdorf near Baden. Yet every Christmas she composed a piece especially for him, rolling up her composition in a red ribbon and placing it proudly on his desk—"the greatest joy for him."[41] Practically all of these early works were published c. 1930 by the famous music house of Ludwig Doblinger.

As World War I became a reality, Maria's compositional drive caught fire, shifting her professional focus from the career of a concert pianist to that of a composer soon after the death of Emperor Franz Josef in 1916. The war years (1914–1918) saw Bach's first serious composition of music, for example, her piano piece "Flohtanz" (Flea Dance) (fig. 23).

The work's musically graphic depictions of the insect, encapsulated in the piano's fleeting repeated figures, show her fondness for grotesquerie. Inspired by the beauty of her mother's voice, Bach also composed lieder at this time to poems by Rückert, Dehmel, Morgenstern, Falke, and Ricarda Huch.

Almost without exception, Bach left no written reference to her life in Vienna during World War I or its aftermath, despite such economic catastrophies as the depreciation of Austrian currency in the early 1920s. Yet her lied "Tief ist der Abgrund," composed in November 1918, was a timely setting coinciding with the signing of the World War I armistice dealing the final, mortal blow to imperial Austria. The music's cutting harmony closely expresses its darkly tinted text.

Rampant in postwar Austria, economic and political chaos spilled over into every corner of Vienna's arts scene, forcing, for example, the onset of massive

Figure 22. The eighteen-year-old Maria Bach in 1914. In this professional photograph, the composer is attired in elegant dress, reflecting her high social standing. She is posed formally, although she appears to show a tiny trace of a smile. Courtesy of Madeleine Delarue.

Figure 23. Maria Bach, "Flohtanz," for solo piano, 1917. Vienna and Leipzig:
Ludwig Doblinger (Bernhard Hermansky), 1931. Courtesy of the Archiv
Elena Ostleitner.

emigration by composers and other musical figures, extending from the 1920s
through the Nazi years. Despite the situation, however, the theater genius Max
Reinhardt established the Salzburg Festival, which opened in August 1920.[42]

Vienna: Composition with Joseph Marx

Maria Bach's period of study at the Vienna Academy of Music consisted only of
private composition lessons, beginning in 1919, with Joseph Marx. Marx had been
recommended to Bach by family friend Julius Korngold, who in 1902 succeeded

the fabled Eduard Hanslick as chief music critic of Vienna's powerful daily *Die Neue Freie Presse*.[43]

Bach passed the entrance examination for composition students with flying colors, performing her own four-part fugue on the piano for academy faculty members Marx and Franz Schmidt.[44] Known from 1970 as Vienna's University of Music and the Performing Arts, the Academy of Music had previously been a private conservatory under the aegis of the Gesellschaft der Musikfreunde until 1909, when it became the Academy of Music and Performing Arts under state control. That same year another private music school was put under local government administration (later renamed the New Conservatory of the City of Vienna), directed by Josef Reitler, one of Maria Bach's future reviewers as Julius Korngold's associate music critic on *Die Neue Freie Presse*. Important male composers contemporary to Maria Bach who attended the Vienna Conservatory include Gustav Mahler (1875–1878), Franz Schreker (1892–1900), and Alexander Zemlinsky (1887–1892).

As a composition teacher, Marx carefully honed his students' creative freedom while also demanding their acquisition of solid technique and improvisatory skill.[45] When Maria Bach studied with Marx at the Vienna Academy, he reined in her tendency to revel in Lisztian grandiosity, confining her compositions to the centuries-old technique of strict four-part fugues; and he restricted her to small forms—brief pieces for piano or voice with piano accompaniment (fig. 24).

Figure 24. Maria Bach's caricature drawing of herself and Joseph Marx, 1942. The drawing shows Bach's deprecating view of herself compared with her composition teacher, Joseph Marx. Courtesy of Madeleine Delarue and the Wienbibliothek im Rathaus, Musiksammlung.

Marx assigned to Bach for analysis works by Chopin, Debussy, Scriabin, Mussorgsky, and Stravinsky. When he judged Bach to have acquired a sufficiently disciplined technical foundation, he then allowed her to explore the effects of varying sonorities, rhythms, and other compositional means to define her personal musical style. The virtuosic technical demands that Bach's music frequently poses for pianists reflect, above all, the high level of her own keyboard ability and her lifelong absorption in the keyboard's expressive resources (fig. 25).

Toward the late 1920s, Bach's career continued to take visible wing.[46] Despite such gender-specific slurs as that in the review cited at the beginning of this chapter, Edition Vienna published several of her lieder and solo piano pieces in 1928, although information on any further publications of her music—or anyone else's—by this firm was destroyed in World War II. Yet, spurred by Marx's initiative, the prestigious Vienna music publisher Doblinger had already brought out much of her music by the early 1930s.

On January 15, 1928, an anonymous critic from *Die Mannheimer Volksstimme* favorably reviewed the premiere of Maria Bach's cello sonata, composed in 1924 and played by Paul Grümmer. The critic referred to the cellist as "excellent" and praised the "captivating" and "thematically charming" *Rondo Capriccio,* which the audience, too, had warmly received. Henriette Bach's cello teacher and a close family friend, Grümmer (1879–1965) was an influential virtuoso in earlier twentieth-century Vienna and Berlin. He repeatedly performed Maria Bach's compositions and followed the careers of the two sisters over many years, reportedly having more than professional interest in Henriette.[47]

One of Bach's few surviving works from the 1920s, the cyclic "Vier Narrenlieder" (Four Fool's Songs) (1921) for tenor and piano was premiered in 1924 in a program of student works at Vienna's renowned Konzerthaus. Julius Korngold, praising an orchestrated version of these lieder made in 1929, remarked, "Maria Bach shows talent. The male guild beware!"[48] Thus Korngold, one of Vienna's most powerful critics at that time, made a sly reference to the city's gender prejudice with a touch of wit.

Side by side with Bach's professional life, her personal relationships intensified during the late 1920s when she met the ambitious young Russian composer-conductor Ivan Boutnikoff. Soon becoming her mentor in conducting and orchestration, he had at one time been a student of the renowned conductor Arthur Nikisch (1855–1922), one of the guests entertained at the Bach family's Sunday chamber music soirées. Boutnikoff was drawing a steadily mounting collection of press accolades. For example, *Das Neue Wiener Extrablatt* of March 11, 1931, reported that, as a conductor, "Boutnikoff [was] . . . unusually gifted . . ., far exceed[ing] the ordinary in raising public interest." And, as a composer, his works won high praise from the discriminating Julius Korngold, who commended Boutnikoff's symphonic suite "To Pan" for its merger "of Lisztian and Wagnerian" features—"focused tonality" and "a pleasing orchestral sonority"—that had

Figure 25. Maria Bach, "Geh' nicht," for soprano and piano, 1919. (Text by Gustav Falke.) Autograph. The bitterness of a farewell is mirrored in the highly dissonant chromatic harmony and restless, fragmented vocal line. Courtesy of Madeleine Delarue and the Wienbibliothek im Rathaus, Musiksammlung.

heralded "New German" romanticism, along with Slavic modal tendencies and touches of Debussy and Tchaikovsky.[49]

Bach's family exerted every effort to conceal what developed into Maria's intimate relationship with Boutnikoff. But to no avail. In the winter of 1932–1933, she accompanied him to Paris, where she met the prominent composer Roger Ducasse (1873–1954), then director of the Paris Conservatory. In February 1933, Ducasse coached some of his students in a performance of Bach's "Wolgaquintett," following up with a letter of both encouragement and suggestions for improvement: " . . . The first movement begins in a very agreeable poetic atmosphere. I am a little sorry that you have chosen for the following movements a familiar theme that in structure somewhat lacks musical vigor. But the whole is perfectly written and pays homage to your natural gifts and to your culture. Do your work courageously; you are well on your way."[50]

Yet, when Bach returned to Vienna from the French capital, she apparently could not resist becoming ensnarled in family money matters, eroding rather than furthering her creative work. The substantial real estate holdings of the Bach sisters' father proved to be their undoing. Their internecine troubles had only begun when Robert Bach died in 1927, forcing Maria, Henriette, and their mother to relinquish their home. Robert Bach bequeathed his property to his daughters in four relatively equal shares. The first blow rained down when Katharina, the second oldest Bach sister—married but already long estranged from her natal family—commandeered her own full inheritance immediately after the funeral. Therese, the other married daughter (and the oldest sister), took similar action. The speed with which this happened was devastating to the incomes of her younger sisters.

Enflaming the situation further, Robert Bach had willed the major share of his properties to his two youngest, unmarried daughters. Maria, for example inherited estates at Königsstetten, Weinwartshof, Zeislmauer-Muckendorf, and Hintersdorf, along with several houses south of Vienna. Henriette received a comparable share of the Bach fortune.[51]

The substantial number of properties Maria Bach inherited should have provided her sufficient financial security to devote herself to composition to the end of her days. Though well educated in the arts, Maria Bach—so secluded in her youth—tragically lacked any knowledge of financial matters. (As with so many Viennese women in this era, Bach received only a private, rather than institutional, education by tutors who came to her home. It seems unlikely, therefore, that financial affairs would have been a subject that she learned under these circumstances.) Consequently she left the management of her new estates to untrustworthy caretakers and sought counsel with ill-advised attorneys. To make matters worse, Maria's endless feuds with Therese and Henriette over their sizable inheritance—even clothing and minor household items—led to a series of bitter lawsuits among the three that continued to entangle them long after World War II and drained the family inheritance even more.

Several other factors contributed to this sad state of affairs: astronomical managerial expenses accumulated because of the ceaseless litigation, financial troubles of an elderly aunt, Maria's sheer generosity (she had aided Boutnikoff and a number of friends and acquaintances), a disastrous real estate venture, and a lifestyle that far exceeded her financial assets. In one typical case, she undertook the renovation of a major property in the Vienna Woods, turning it into a hotel, partly designed by a member of the Vienna secession. But the venture failed and a bank repossessed the building. Interestingly, however, the

Nazi government absolved her debt in 1940 but relegated the property to the Hitler Youth, confining her to two top-floor rooms. This was her only home until 1953, when she moved to an apartment in Vienna on Kupferschmiedgasse 2, in the Third District, then to the Kärntnerstrasse 12, in the First.[52]

Austria's Political Fortunes: 1938–1945

While Bach was pursuing her career and was enmeshed in these financial problems, her homeland was entering one of its most tragic historical eras. The *Anschluss* of 1938 ushered in Austria's seven years of Nazi domination, accompanied by the devastation and hardships inflicted by the country's complicity with Germany in World War II. Throughout the Nazi era, *entartete* (degenerate) *Musik*—that is, music by Jewish composers; by other composers—even Aryans—considered too "modern" (including those employing jazz elements) for ears accustomed only to traditional style; or by composers and other musicians who harbored anti-Nazi or pro–Weimar Republic political and cultural sympathies. The proscription covered works by Mahler, Mendelssohn, Korngold, Schönberg, Berg, Webern, Stravinsky, Weill, Hindemith, Krenek, Bartók, Eisler, Toch, and many others, including numerous Austrians who immigrated to the United States in the 1930s. As a result of Austria's role in the Nazi era, postwar it had to face the loss of its political independence, its empire, and vast physical devastation. And it suffered a massive brain-drain in losing untold numbers of artists in many fields through slaughtering them and emigration.

Voicing an opinion held by many historians, Erik Levi remarks, "The Germans could not have accomplished these changes in such a short period without the active and enthusiastic support of the Austrian Nazis. While anti-Semitism and pan-Germanic feeling had already been a strong component in the Austrian musical tradition from the middle of the nineteenth century, it was the Nazis who emerged as the most effective political force in exploiting such sentiments during the 1930s."[53]

Between 1933 and 1937 there had been some resistance among Austrian government circles to the Nazis' musical prohibitions. But the scale of pro-Nazi activity had grown so strong by 1937, only a year before the *Anschluss*, that the Fascist government allowed only the Viennese orchestral repertoire to be performed; for the music of Mozart, Haydn, Beethoven, Brahms, Wagner, Bruckner, Pfitzner, and Richard Strauss suited the Nazis' love of the classical tradition to the exclusion of the "modernist" *entartete* composers.[54] Andreas Giger points out the Austrians' double-faced, even ironic, version of patriotism: though they were pan-German politically, favoring the *Anschluss* with Germany, they were Austrian—that is, Viennese—in their musical taste.[55] And thus the works of Maria Bach and her eleven women "colleagues" remained acceptable to the Nazis' musical outlook, one generally conservative in style and technique.

Yet without hesitation, Eiselmair believes that "neither the National Socialist takeover nor the outbreak of war in 1939 influenced [Bach's] artistic work." Perhaps Eiselmair refers to Bach's focus during the Nazi years on song compositions, largely based on nature themes, and also to the composer's professed neutral political outlook. Bach's Aryan descent, after all, did allow her to remain active as a composer—albeit one whose music shattered no traditions—even after the Annexation of 1938. The Reichsmusikkammer, in fact, registered her at the outset of the 1940s as one of a dozen women composers legally allowed to remain resident in Vienna. (At that time it also listed five approved women composers in Munich and twelve in Berlin.)[56]

As if to reinforce Bach's self-portrait as a disinterested citizen, the composer pictures herself between 1939 and 1945 as devoted to "a true life of Nature with cats, dogs, and chickens. I was very happy . . . cultivating tobacco, vegetables and yellow carnations. . . ." (In all its domesticity, her life at this time sounded ironically—at least in Bach's eyes—like that of a typical German hausfrau.) Her lifestyle in her modest country house in Mauerbach was truly a "Vienna Woods idyll."[57] Yet Bach admitted that on some occasions during the war she was nagged by thoughts of terror and death, feelings, partly patriotic ones, that prompted her to mend clothes and handkerchiefs for "the brave [Austrian] soldiers." She delivered all of these items every week on her bicycle, even pedaling on an icy mountain road in winter to the village inn. In her *Blitzlichter,* Bach recalls, "I spent the war years [World War II] in my tiny little house in the heart of the Vienna Woods, spending this time with great feelings of anxiety, but also in touch with the beauty of nature." "But I had," she muses, "to use saccharin in cooking." Then she notes, "During this time I worked on composing my opera and the beginnings of my piano concerto." She also commented that nearby was one of the villas where she grew up, but now it was "the empty and vacated Hotel Tulbinger Kogel."[58] In other words, even while escaping most of the immediate realities of living in a "war zone," Bach was disconsolate and melancholic.

In addition, Bach's household employees attested that, urged on by her sister Henriette, Maria Bach aligned herself with other former members of the Lower Austrian landed nobility in such "innocuous" actions as flag-waving at parades by the Heimwehr (Austrian Fascist Party). In fact, she dedicated her lied "Stratosfera" (composed in the period 1939–1940, while the Nazi forces devastated Czechoslovakia, Poland, and the rest of Europe) specifically to Austrian military pilots, "our heroes in the stratosphere," as she phrased it. Similarly, her lied "Draussen im weiten Krieg" had clearly reflected her personal sympathies during World War I. One might also note that Bach's "Drei Hebräische Gesänge" were composed in 1932, shortly before her homeland would be heading to the Nazi *Anschluss.* Likewise, one wonders whether Bach's composition of the orchestral lied "Japanischer Frühling" in 1930 and at least four performances of the work on three different continents over the next twelve years might reflect

Austrian leanings toward the Nazis' Pacific ally in World War II.[59] (Several of her female contemporaries were also composing works at this time culling up pleasant visions of Japan.)

Now devoted to composition and the wartime struggle for food and survival, Bach's personal life also took a new turn. In 1940 she met the Italian painter Arturo Ciacelli, who became her life partner until his death in July 1966. An art teacher at the Italian School in Vienna between 1939 and 1941, he became a permanent resident in Bach's cottage in Mauerbach from 1942, having passed the peak of his career at the age of nearly sixty.

Bach's home also provided Ciacelli with an atelier, his own having been lost under Nazi auspices, together with most of his paintings and writings on art theory. His paintings had been specifically targeted in 1937 as *entartete Kunst* (degenerate art) and therefore prohibited from public exhibition in Vienna. As a result of these measures, the Italian artist derived income only as an art teacher.

Ciacelli soon became the overriding influence on Bach's personal and professional life. Born near Rome, his painting style evolved from futurism and the abstract into that of the *novecento italiano* style (that Eiselmair calls "Italian fascist romantic-neoclassical"). He had also established connections in Paris with Pablo Picasso, Maurice Utrillo, Amedeo Modigliani, and Charles Le Corbusier, among others.

From 1941, early in the quarter century she spent with Ciacelli, Bach continued composing steadfastly. She also wrote lyric poems concentrated on nature themes cast in impressionist musical language. In 1942 she began work on a piano concerto, left unfinished at her death. The early 1940s also produced Bach's initial sketches for *Glaukus,* an opera based on a drama of Luigi Morselli.[60]

By the first week in April 1945, the Battle of Vienna had ended—that is, only days before the Nazi surrender to the Allies. At her return to the city, Bach faced dismal conditions. After fifty-two aerial bombardments of the city, the roof of St. Stephen's Cathedral, its colorful tiles a city landmark, collapsed, adding to the gruesome tale of devastating infernos. The State Opera, the city's pride, lay in ruins. The charred frame of a streetcar sat paralyzed on the Ring, the chief traffic artery in the central district of Vienna.[61] Destruction so massive would require untold restoration undertakings in Vienna, as in Europe as a whole. On April 27, 1945, the Vienna Philharmonic gave its first postwar concert; one day later, the Austrian national radio network resumed operation and five streetcars transported passengers along city rails; and on April 30, the Burgtheater company, despite its burned-out home, again offered a production.[62]

In her secluded cottage outside Vienna during the war years, Bach faced little threat of an air attack by Allied forces. In fact, even in the heart of Vienna's First District, members of the city's upper social ranks continued—through the harrowing final bombardments in March in 1945—to indulge frequently in such recreational activities as lunch dates at the Sacher, Imperial, and Bristol hotels, situated immediately adjacent to the ruins of the State Opera, burned to the ground. In addition, the Vienna Philharmonic played every day despite the heavy bombing.[63]

Nestled in her haven amid the Vienna Woods, Bach's own personal version of suffering, as recorded in her *Blitzlichter,* seems minor compared with the exceedingly brutal reality of war unfolding outside her private domain.

In her memoirs, she noted hearing Russian prisoners of war returning from their work in the fields, "beautifully singing old four-part Russian choruses that deeply gripped me." Yet the war did influence her composing, as evident in the unhappy feelings of that time injected into some of her sacred vocal works. Her lied "Maria und der Schiffer" is a mournful, stylistically simple a cappella chorus, a brooding lament of the Virgin Mary that dates from February 1944, when Austria's defeat was approaching. Many of Bach's lieder on religious themes written in the war years reflected her nostalgia for a past, envisioned only in her imagination and devoid of devastating conflicts. Nevertheless, contemporary German and Austrian music critics were quick to point out that, despite the war, Bach managed somehow to have her music aired publicly, the composer herself often performing in the concerts as pianist (fig. 26).

Figure 26. Maria Bach at the piano in her later years. Courtesy of Madeleine Delarue.

Bach's inner feelings expressed at this and every stage of her life strikingly accord with an elemental factor in Vienna's cultural sphere. In a review of Allen Shawn's *Arnold Schönberg's Journey,* published in 2001, *New York Times* music critic Anthony Tommasini wrote that Shawn successfully defined Viennese culture (at least at a time contemporary with Maria Bach) through contrasting it with that of Berlin: "the progressive artistic climate in Berlin seemed to foster social satire and political commentary. But in Vienna, the city of Freud, Shawn writes, 'artists tended to pursue expression that was removed from a political and social context,' and 'art turned inward to the aesthetic, spiritual and psychological realms.'"[64]

In the years immediately following the end of World War II, the Austrians, like other Europeans, endured severe economic deprivations. And they faced a decade of military occupation. In addition, the tiny Austrian republic had to confront not only the mammoth economic and political turmoil of defeat but, in addition, its new crisis-ridden status: for it was irretrievably blocked off from the rest of central Europe, once the mainstay of the Austro-Hungarian Empire, with the onset of the cold war. Yet Austria had cause to celebrate with the advent of 1955, marking both the launching of the Second Republic and the reopening of the Vienna State Opera, once demolished.[65] Yet, even with the hardships to be endured by both the winners and losers in the postwar era, Maria Bach continued to compose, being limited chiefly, however, to solo piano music.

By the end of World War II, Maria Bach had become even more isolated from Vienna's musical mainstream than ever, performances of her music made possible only through the efforts of dedicated friends and colleagues. And she herself often participated as pianist in these concerts. She continued to compose, but in the same stylistic vein to which she had long adhered: romanticizing a contrived folklike simplicity, indulging in subjective anthropomorphic depictions of nature; resorting to imagined non-Western melody, harmony, and rhythm; and clinging to impressionist tendencies from decades long past.

Even in the years leading to World War I, Bach had never set foot into the avant-garde ranks of the Second Viennese School, "headed" by Arnold Schönberg (1874–1951) and his pupils Anton Webern (1883–1945) and, less so, Alban Berg (1885–1935). Immersed from early childhood in the traditional musical language inherited from nineteenth-century romanticism, Maria Bach held no place among her radical contemporaries: those composers who had abandoned the old ideal of a discernible tonal focus based on the structural principle of tension-release, or time-span oriented structure. Instead, Schönberg turned to a compositional method, as he summed it up, "with twelve tones related only to one another." With various composers in as many different ways, the new atonal reordering of pitches was also extended to explorations in nontraditional procedures for organizing rhythmic elements of a composition as well as spatial dimensions, hence in structural concepts.

Although at times Maria Bach ventured far from conventional harmonic practice, her basic adherence to the harmonic sense of key parallels her clinging to the class-oriented codes of Vienna's old social order. Though oversimplifying the subject, Schorske makes an interesting comparison in this matter: At the turn of the nineteenth to the twentieth century, he noted, "tonality in music belonged to the same socio-cultural system as the science of perspective in art—with its centralized focus—the baroque status system in society and legal absolutism in politics."[66]

To an even greater degree, Bach could not compete with the experimental directions being taken in Europe and the United States by her younger, postwar colleagues probing new areas of musical style and sound production: the extension of twelve-tone composition, aleatoric techniques, and explorations into yet untried resources of taped recording and electronic sound production.

On the one hand, the new postwar Viennese public simply lacked all interest in the outmoded ways of Bach's music. Her music no longer had a significant market even in her native city. Bach won performances of her music in Vienna, in fact, only through the women's musical organizations to which she belonged. On the other, Ciacelli's influence also gained her at least some performances of her musical works in Italy and opened up other channels for her creativity. For example, besides composing poetry, some of which provided texts for new compositions, she turned in earnest—like her parents—to painting landscapes, hers depicting southern Europe, especially Italy. This was, of course, hardly surprising in view of the artistic achievements of her mother and earlier forebears. Her Italian journeys from 1951 on with Ciacelli, she said, "inspired me as much to paint as to write poetry."[67] The Ciacelli years also gave rise to Bach's prolific succession of collages.

Bach's Italian period bore fruit of yet another kind. After attending an African dance performance in 1950 at Milan's Teatro Piccolo, she described the instrumental accompaniment to the dancers: "curious musical inserts, partly from a recording, partly on new [for Bach] kinds of instruments [and] plucked harp sounds, played very fluently, and [there was] also loud and rather shrill Negro singing." "We heard," Bach noted, "the trampling of wild orgiastic beasts and man-eaters and a thunder roll of three drums; [we] were therefore truly far from our much played Mozart. . . . One [dancer] wore a long bright blue gown, the others, on the contrary, white or dazzling red pants with naked upper bodies."[68] Bach's excitement sparked by the event resulted in her collage cycle entitled "Negro Spiritual, Collage di Maria Bach" and her lieder cycle "Drei Negro Spirituals," both dating from 1950.

By the end of the 1950s, in fact, Bach had completed more than one hundred vividly colored collages, many with African dancers as the theme. As early as February 1951, her collages had already been exhibited in a Milan gallery side by side with futurist art works. Exhibitions of Bach's collages in Vienna, Graz, Hamburg,

Milan, Rome, and even the United States between 1954 and 1963 won—as Bach recorded it and therefore unconfirmed—some favorable reviews in the press.

Always having viewed herself primarily as a composer, Bach once reflected in her *Blitzlichter* with some irony that exhibits of her collages "in Vienna and in foreign countries confirm the spontaneous success with the public and press, which with music takes much longer until one is recognized." And, seizing on the opportunity she saw with the success of her artwork, Bach soon attempted to attract interest in her music. On October 12, 1956, she informed her sister Therese of her successful collage exhibit at Milan's Galleria Schettini: "Yesterday," Maria Bach recalled, "I had to say several words on the radio about my collages, and today a short broadcast was aired half in German and half in Italian. Perhaps a broadcast with a recording [of my music] will even follow. . . . Perhaps I can obtain a proper radio broadcast here, which can never be done with a recording in Vienna, where it would rest for a year in the archives, awaiting better times."[69]

Bach's collages also showed her fondness for mixtures, this inclination also leading her, during her Ciacelli years, to the creation of some experimental stage works—1950s versions of multimedia art. (One thinks of the composer Alexander Scriabin's [1872–1915] "synaesthesia." At an earlier time, Bach had played a number of Scriabin's works.)

Beginning in 1953, when they established permanent residence together in Vienna, Bach and Ciacelli together evolved their concept of *Teatro Sintetico,* a fusion of music, song, dance, pantomime, melodrama, and light. As Bach's contributions to these joint undertakings, she turned to her large orchestral works, which she adapted to stage presentation.[70] For the visual aspects of these productions, Bach used her collage techniques in designing scenery and costumes. Ciacelli was responsible for the libretto and choreography. Colored lighting effects and the freedom granted the dancers to improvise heightened the impact on audiences.[71]

Yet only three Teatro Sintetico works reached the stage. The ballet *Bengele* was performed in New York in 1940 by the renowned Ballet Russe de Monte Carlo, its production conducted by Bach's longtime friend Ivan Boutnikoff; *Japanischer Frühling* was given in 1942 at the Kobé Theater, Japan; and *Silhouetten* was heard in Paris. (The date of the Paris performance is unknown.)

Ciacelli's death in July 1966, however, deprived Bach of her most intimate companion and staunchest advocate of her music and artwork. The loss of her partner dealt her creative incentives a massive blow, her compositional impulses already ebbing with the deteriorating financial and family situation, along with the inevitable effects of the aging process.

Adding to this miserable state of affairs, Bach's relationships with her sisters grew even more acrimonious over financial matters and even spread to artistic rivalry, the saddest being that between Maria and Henriette, who had become a professional cellist. Bach died without any reconciliation with this younger sister. Until the composer's last decades, Henriette had been her only close family member and musical partner. Contemporaries of the two sisters, in fact, described them as uncommunicative, unapproachable, and somewhat arrogant—a bearing ironically belied by the sisters' appearance in public in shabby, outmoded attire.[72]

Despite her aristocratic pretensions, Bach nevertheless continued to promote performances of her music—above all, her songs, accompanying them herself on the piano until her last year of life. Her concerts in Viennese salons, private homes, and Wiener Frauenclub recitals, moreover, were often recorded. In addition, Bach's colleagues in the Frauenclub and other longtime associates continued giving her a generous measure of support in both composing and writing poetry. Her already established friendship with the coloratura soprano Berty Staar, for example, grew even closer and her longtime colleague and friend Ivan Boutnikoff faithfully maintained correspondence with her.

When Austrian President Rudolf Kirchschläger awarded Bach an honorary professorship in February 1976, her joy was tinged with regret as expressed in her self-deprecating poem "Ehrendekret" (honorary degree), written the following June, dismissing such honors as meaningless documents doomed ultimately to rot away in secondhand shops. In light of this award, Austrian Radio (ORF) attempted unsuccessfully to produce a television documentary on Bach. (With questionable significance, Bach was listed in *The International Who's Who in Music 1976*.)[73]

After a one-year hiatus in composing following Ciacelli's death, Bach produced no more than one or two works per year—mostly songs or solo piano pieces. By early 1977 she had stopped composing altogether. Her sudden death at the age of eighty-two on February 26, 1978, was ascribed to a gas leakage from a defective oven in her Vienna apartment. Ironically, her estranged sister Henriette inherited her property. But by this time, again ironically, her estate was—because of all the litigation over it—a mere remnant of the Bach family's onetime fortune. Maria had inherited chiefly the musical estate of the German opera composer Heinrich Marschner, a legacy that her grandmother had given her.

The Music of Maria Bach

But what of Maria Bach's music itself? As of this writing, it lies in seven dusty cardboard cartons stacked in a corner of the reading room in the Wiener Stadt- und Landesbibliothek (Stadtbibliothek im Rathaus). One thousand pages stored there are in massive disarrangement covering her music (autographs and published copies), handwritten and typed records pertaining to performances, scattered professional information, sketches for future drawings, and related memorabilia.[74]

The scrambled condition of this collection graphically illustrates the state of virtual total oblivion into which Bach's musical legacy has fallen.[75] Yet her compositions, along with those of other women composers of her times, tell a pivotal, scarcely known story of Vienna's musical life from the fin-de-siècle reign of central Europe as the city's dazzling cultural hub to its overthrow by inevitable forces decaying within the Habsburg Empire itself. There followed the onslaught of two world wars and economic ruin of an international scope, along with the political realignments turning the map of Europe upside down as the Second Republic of Austria struggled to find its place after gaining independence from military occupation in 1955.

Bach's Musical Genres

Almost 70 percent (248) of Bach's compositions consists of songs for solo voice and piano, while close to an additional 5 percent (17) is made up of large-scale vocal settings with orchestral accompaniment. The other areas of vocal composition in which she engaged are the a-cappella chorus (29), and a single opera under 1 percent. (This opera and a piano concerto written in the Vienna Woods during World War II remained unfinished.) All totaled, her vocal works considered together amount to more than 80 percent (295) of her compositions as a whole.

Her piano compositions make up almost 11 percent (39) of her purely instrumental music. The remaining twenty-three works consist of chamber music for two or more instruments (11); compositions for orchestra alone (7); works for a solo instrument and piano (4); and one work for a solo instrument and orchestra. Bach's orchestral compositions—that is, all of her works requiring an orchestra—amount to about sixteen.

Bach's music, however, centers by far on small-scale works, their limited number of performers offering greater, primarily because less expensive, chances for performance than compositions for massed forces. As in the traditional situation of women composers until the later nineteenth century, Bach's concentration on small-scale works can also be attributed to her lack of institutional musical training. She consequently lacked experience in writing extended compositions for large groups of performers at least partly because she lacked significant exposure to critical assessments of her compositions by "fellow" students and professional composers. This theme threads many times through this book.

Bach's sixty-three years of composing indicate that songs consistently remained the central focus of her creative powers. "I grew up in the country; it was always my wish to reproduce moods in music," she once remarked. "My inclination towards the song was perhaps encouraged by the fact that my mother numbered in her time among the first-rank oratorio singers of Vienna."[76] That is, though her mother was often absent, she was an early role model, a stimulus, for Bach as a composer. The first musical idea—emotion and form—for a song came to her, she said, immediately after reading a poem or hearing "a single tone on the piano." Immediately afterward, she composed the song.[77]

Works for piano appeared consistently in every decade. Instrumental chamber pieces occupied her chiefly between 1914 and the 1950s—that is, through World Wars I and II. She added large orchestral compositions to her work list from the 1930s to the 1970s. (For example, "Japanische Frühling," from 1930, was set for tenor or soprano and a massive orchestra, the instruments often divided within an individual section into four or even six independent parts producing an extremely dense and overpowering texture.) Bach's composition of choral works extended from the 1930s into the 1960s.

Between 1950 and 1977, Bach did compose some large-scale orchestral compositions, all of them vocal settings except for one work for orchestra alone. Perhaps it was the central position occupied by the song genre in Bach's works that explains how and why she solved the structural challenges of her large-scale works by resorting to such late romantic techniques as thematic repetition—often by varied instrumental timbres—rather than advanced contrapuntally based melodic development or complex thematic transformation. Also striking in this period was Bach's composition of twenty pieces for chorus a cappella.

By and large the music of her later years often expressed nostalgia for Italy, the homeland of her longtime companion Ciacelli, and for a Vienna long past. Italy and imperial Vienna, in other words, represented symbols far distant from her present situation—again, that old theme of isolation that ran through Maria's and her sisters' entire lives. These later works, moreover, were based on outdated moralistic texts coupled with harmonic clichés and trite textures looking more to the nineteenth rather than the mid-twentieth century.

Musical Style

Bach reached perhaps her deepest creative recesses in her imaginative explorations into late romantic sonority and harmony—reflecting the music of Liszt, Wagner, Mahler, Richard Strauss, Korngold, Debussy, and early Schönberg. This attraction held true in both orchestral and chamber compositions. A pianist herself, Bach indulged in her instrument's seemingly limitless capacity for striking harmonic effects. These gain even greater emphasis because of the piano's dense sonorities and dominant role in enriching the expression of the text. Bach's songs clearly reflect those not only of Hugo Wolf but also the manner of Schubert and Schumann much earlier in the nineteenth century.

Some of Bach's earliest songs, however, (written soon after her student pieces submitted to Marx as standard exercises in classical contrapuntal technique) already reveal her obvious efforts at stretching the boundaries of traditional tonality with its system of central keys. As time went on, she expanded her stylistic horizons with chromaticism (covering all possible notes in a scale by including all half- as well as whole-steps), pentatonic melodies (based on a five-note scale), polytonality (two or more keys used simultaneously), harmonic ambiguity created, for example, through nonfunctional parallel chords in the mode of French impressionism (resulting from Bach's longtime attraction to the music of De-bussy), complex chord progressions, and cutting dissonances. Into the 1940s, Bach continued to experiment with harmonic and timbre possibilities as well as melodic gestures suggesting ancient modes.

Maria Bach's fascination, one might even say obsession, with non-Western themes led her to "re-create" the musical idioms of a number of non-Austrian cultures according to her personal conceptions of styles foreign to her homeland. (This turn of direction was also followed by such Viennese contemporaries of Maria Bach as Johanna Müller-Hermann and Frida Kern, most notably in musical styles inspired by Japan—a close German-Austrian ally in World War II—and by personally conceived African styles.) These sorties into "exotic" effects extended to her use of parallel "empty" intervals: open fourths, fifths, and octaves in her attempts at re-creating an imagined "Middle Eastern" ambiance (as in "Drei He-bräische Gesänge"), or intimating "Asian" delicacy in a reflection of her admiration for Puccini's own eastern-influenced operas—through fine textures produced by divided sections of the orchestra. "Japanische Frühling," for example, requires a massive instrumental force often divided—within a single section, each player becoming a soloist, producing four or even six independent parts.

At times, Bach structured a composition through changes of specific instru-mental color rather than through elaborate thematic development or divided or-chestral sections. Her captivation with the musical language of other cultures—as she herself conceived them—also led her to attempt reproducing the flavor of, for example, Arabian and Persian music (for example, "Arabische Nächte," 1931, and "Vier Hafislieder," 1941, respectively); also Italian and Native American styles and idioms ("Giacona und Tanz [Ayacucho-Perou])," 1941. She characterized her pentatonic settings as "Indian" and "African" (the ballet suite "Bengele," for orchestra, 1937; and "Negroid," subtitled "Cake-Walk," a dance for piano solo, in which she sadly managed a pitifully awkward imitation of Joplinesque ragtime style.) Bach's numerous attempts at exotic styles again reveal a way of distancing, hence isolating, herself from expected norms.

Her imaginative use of open harmonic intervals, however, also suggested the then-current fashion of conscious primitivism as, for example, in the percussive and oppressive driving rhythms of Carl Orff's bombastic *Carmina Burana* (1937). But her turn to such imagined primeval techniques seems merely pasted into her scores. They cannot compare with the skill in which a throbbing elemental pulse was deeply incorporated into works of her contemporaries Stravinsky or Bartók.

Bach's descriptive powers led to numerous works "picturing" landscapes, individual elements of the natural world, and fleeting human emotions, such as a nostalgic feeling for old Vienna—with folksong overtones—or her per-sonal fascination with all things Italian. This "personal" element of inspiration, however, often weakened the quality of her later works through consciously simplistic settings bordering on the trite. Her pictorial images at times even shifted into the more grotesque side of nature, as in other character pieces such as humoresques.

Venturing into both the secular and sacred realms, Bach's choice of texts centered on the verses written by both well-known and more obscure poets such as those of Rainer Maria Rilke, Ricarda Huch, Gustav Falke, Friedrich Nietzsche, Christian Morgenstern, Hermann Hesse, Wladimir von Hartlieb, Grete Urbanitzky, Otto Julius Bierbaum, Franz Theodor Csokor, Edmund Schwab, Anna Laube, Maria Zwinz-Breyer, and Hedy Peitlschmied. In addition, she set poems by her sister Therese Lanjus-Wellenburg (despite the family's legal harangues), and those by her colleagues and friends from the numerous cultural groups in Vienna to which she belonged: Felix Braun, Grete Körber, Martha Hoffmann, Hilde Strauss-Guttmann, Maria Klar, Karl Wache, and others less well known.

Performances, Reception, and Concert Sites

Bach's listing of 127 performances of her music show that, decade by decade, the largest number of concerts (31) took place in the 1940s—while Vienna was being heavily bombed—followed closely by those (29) in the 1970s; next in line were the concerts (24) of the 1930s, those (22) of the 1950s, and those (16) of the 1960s. Bach's records also make evident that in the years from 1932 to 1943, her performances consisted chiefly of song recitals given in German-speaking cities—more accessible perhaps because she was one of the women composers who had been accepted by the Nazi regime.

From the 1930s through the 1970s, Vienna predominated as the chief concert locale for performances, the most prestigious being the Musikverein and the Konzerthaus. Tying for second place in frequency were other Austrian locations: Baden, Mödling, Braunau (Adolf Hitler's birthplace), and Salzburg. Concerts of Bach's music took place in nine German cities: Mannheim, Altenburg, Regensburg, Berlin, Leipzig, Munich, Frankfurt, Dresden, and Saarbrücken-Eschberg; then Italy, in Rome, Milan, and Genoa; Kobé, Japan; the United States, in Hollywood, California, and New York City; and Paris.

After World War II, however, Bach's compositions were performed exclusively in Vienna in the city's most prestigious concert house, the Musikverein, in the concert hall of the Gesellschaft für Musikfreunde, and also at the important Konzerthaus. By and large, these performances were given by women's chamber music organizations such as the Wiener Frauenclub, the Wiener Musikerinnen, the Verein für Schriftstellerinnen und Künstlerinnen, and the Verband der geistig Schaffenden.

In concerts sponsored by these groups Bach herself regularly participated as a pianist, sometimes even accompanying her own songs. These were the twilight years of her life, the composer having no other access to the dominant all-male Viennese organizations devoted to the creation and performance of contemporary music. Paul de Conne, however, her onetime piano instructor, often included her works in his own recitals.

During the final two decades of the composer's life (c. 1958–1978), Bach's music won relatively fewer performances and hence press reviews than it had in her earlier years. The performances that did materialize in these years were almost totally confined to her own private circles of female musicians, such as the Wiener Frauenclub, the Club der Wiener Musikerinnen, and the Wiener Mozartgemeinde. Yet Joseph Marx (1882–1964), her former composition teacher and director of that eponymous society, arranged several performances of her works by the Vereinigung Beta Sigma Phi, the Österreichische Gesellschaft für zeitgenössische Musik, the Österreichischer Lyceumclub, and the Verband der geistig Schaffenden Österreichs. Bach's performance circles conspicuously did not include the male-dominated Vereinigung Schaffender Tonkuenstler, founded in 1904 in Vienna by Arnold Schönberg and Alexander Zemlinsky to foster their new music.

Bach had to work almost exclusively with amateur or semiprofessional singers. With these limited performing resources, she could not gain the degree of recognition by the Vienna public that she wished—despite the efforts of de Conne and Marx, who performed a few of her compositions and gave her moral support. In a letter of March 1, 1949, de Conne praised Bach's "Der Tanz," a piano composition that she had recently played. Noting that it had engrossed the audience, he added, "Your playing, too, was highly artistic. . . . I would like also to study your piece . . . because it has a stimulating effect on me." He regretted, however, that he did "not know where it could be published."[78] In a review of that same concert appearing in the *Wiener Zeitung* of February 27, 1949, Marx praised her compositions but offered a somewhat gender-specific comment: "Maria Bach is not exactly the frequent example of a woman who is creatively active in the musical arena." He then lamented that a performance he had just heard of Bach's "Narrenlieder" ("Fools' Songs") revealed "a personal tone that one, however, hears better when she, an accomplished pianist, accompanies herself. . . ." Marx concluded with a tribute to her talent for impressionistic tone-painting and for preserving the artistic integrity of a poet's texts in her songs.

Performances of Bach's compositions were further hampered by her inability to secure sufficient financial resources for concerts of her large-scale works. Ironically, by this time she had virtually drained her once-substantial personal legacy to pay for the years of litigation with her sisters. Even for moderately sized concerts of her music, she had been forced to draw on her own meager funds to pay copyists, concert hall rentals, and other basic expenses for such events. She was consequently reduced to sponsoring private house concerts—in her Mauerbach residence or Vienna—financed on her own, by friends, or by her sister Henriette, while the two were still on relatively cordial terms. She also eliminated the expense of hiring a piano accompanist by assuming the role herself. And, despite a humbling aspect, she was at times aided in small private concerts by Henriette on the cello and Therese as reciter of her poems. Young singers who participated in her house musicales were reimbursed with merely wine or candy.

Bach even acted as her own marketing agent, an unflagging one, routinely supplying impresarios and conductors with her catalogue of compositions, supplemented with press reviews of her works and invitations to her house concerts. Rejections never deterred her from continuing her promotional efforts, and there were successes. In 1962 her first String Quartet ("Variationen über ein griechisches Klagelied," ["Greek Song of Mourning"], composed in 1935, received one of eight gold medals awarded at the International Competition of Women Composers, held in Buenos Aires and, interestingly, sponsored no less by the American cosmetics firm Helena Rubinstein. The award included publication of Bach's quartet in Argentina and its promotion throughout Latin America.[79]

Maria Bach and the Viennese Press

Fin-de-siècle Vienna's nouveau riche, realizing the futility of their attempts to play a role in the city administration, now found their place in its cultural life. Among the many areas of the arts in which the *haute bourgeoisie* could directly participate was that of cultural journalism, a field not immune to inroads of the then-current forces of psychoanalytic thought, especially in Freud's Vienna. Buoyed also by glints of freedom granted the press in the wake of the revolutionary year 1848, Vienna's music critics from then on tended to weight their judgments in favor of their own subjective response to the music being discussed.

With the Vienna critics' newly spawned writing style, "adjectives engulfed the nouns," resulting in reviews colored by a "personal tone [that] virtually obliterated the contours of the object of discourse."[80] Favoring a sensual musical style over the austere, respected Austrian critics valued compositions that were Viennese in temperament—having the folklike simplicity of waltzes and other dances, spontaneity rather than ponderous symbolism, and spare signs, if any, of academically tinted counterpoint.[81]

Despite his flowery language, however, Eduard Hanslick (1825–1904), the most prominent Viennese music critic in the second half of the nineteenth century, had given musical journalism new respectability and prestige through his discriminating commentary. Hanslick was the reigning music critic of the *Presse* from 1855 on and for the *Neue Freie Presse* and had contributed reviews to the *Wiener Zeitung* from 1848. His postulate—that compositions should be judged purely in genuine musical terms—locked horns with the then-current extremes in Viennese musical journalism in discussing music's emotional effects. The highly influential critic and Bach family friend Julius Korngold (1860–1945) followed Hanslick as chief music critic of the *Neue Freie Presse,* basing his judgments of music according to the quality of both librettos and piano scores.

By the decades immediately preceding the outbreak of World War I, music critics had gained the chief authority in Vienna's musical life. Their opinions mattered.[82] Through his periodical, *Die Fackel,* the pivotal Viennese satirist and social critic Karl Kraus (1874–1936) attacked local journalists, even some of Vienna's music critics such as Max Kalbeck (1850–1921), whom he characterized as typical of "the vacuity and pretentiousness of Viennese cultural journalism."[83]

A composer in his own right, Joseph Marx was also a critic for the *Neue Wiener Journal* (1931–1938) and the *Wiener Zeitung* (1945–1955). He cautioned his fellow journalists to keep technical considerations of music foremost, to admit the strength of personal opinion in their reviews, and to place humility before arrogance, showing respect for both performers and composers being cited.[84] These are challenging standards to follow for any music critic anywhere and at any time.

The Vienna critics' appraisals of Bach's music covered four aspects of a composition: the technical skill of the writing process; the structure of a composition; certain subjective elements (for example, talent and inspiration); and style, the latter two typically intermingling in a review:[85]

(1) Concerning compositional skill, the reviewers cited her "inventive," "idiomatic," and "technically difficult" piano part, her understanding "the secrets of the human voice," "finely wrought accompaniment" in her lieder, polished orchestral writing, and solidly structured counterpoint.

(2) As for the form of her compositions, praise included "historicism in form," "charming" thematic structure, and "a sense of broad melodic structure."

(3) The matter of style was approached from many different directions: decidedly "impressionistic," "wonderful humor and wit," "strict rhythm," "genial and dashing," "radiant impressionistic polytonality," "personal," "exoticism," "folk-like expressivity," "striking sense of mood," "exoticism," "harmony in some cases reminiscent of Puccini and H. Wolf," "expressivity," "playful tone-colors," "talent for exotic foreign-sound-combinations," "folkloristic style," "gift for tone-painting," "clear rhythms," "wildly, stormy cascades of sound," "dramatic mood-images," "harmonic turns of charming tone-painting," "limitless fantasy of a dreamy world of sound," "grotesque musical undertones," and "talent in characterization and local color."

(4) The comments verging closely on subjective viewpoints also included the following: "inspired," "brutality," "joyful piano part," "ecstatically heightened vocal part," "stormy inspiration," and "orchestral writing that goes to the heart."

Bach's own typewritten list of eighty selected reviews of her music performed publicly from 1928 to 1960 lies randomly sandwiched between her music manuscripts in the Wiener Stadt-und Landes Bibliothek collection. A comparison of Bach's excerpted examples (forty-five of which are cited unchanged in Eiselmair) with the original newspaper versions, however, reveals that Bach was more than once prone to distortion and outright falsification (or omission) of critics' full statements. As sifted through Bach-Eiselmair, critics' comments are sometimes slightly rephrased or negative remarks reversed to present Bach's music in a more favorable light than as originally published. Here and there words are omitted and critics' views on performances of music by other composers uniformly bypassed. And rarely in Bach-Eiselmair do we read of the influences on Bach's music of other composers' music, her works consequently appearing "fully hers." In short, never do Bach-Eiselmair include negative assessments of Bach's compositions, leaving one to wonder if Eiselmair thoroughly examined original reviews instead of accepting Bach's versions prima facie.

On the days when reviews of Maria Bach's music appeared in the Vienna daily press, these critiques are also embedded in accounts and photographs of news about Vienna and Austria in general. Highly biased and sensationalist reports during World War II, for example, are splattered in large boldface type across front pages each day. Needless to say, the articles and photographs (in, for example, the *Neues Wiener Tagblatt,* in which Fritz Skorzeny's music reviews appeared) favor Nazi military forces against the "aggressive" allies, who are said to have continually bombed nonmilitary targets in Europe without cause. There is, for example, a sizable photograph of Franz Lehar (a composer most known today for his operetta *The Merry Widow*) proceeding down an aisle of Vienna's Konzerthaus with a leading Nazi official, Baldur von Schirach. This proud procession preceded Lehar's conducting a *Wehrmacht-Grosskonzert*—as reported on December 23, 1943, in the *Voelkischer Beobachter: Kampfblatt der nationalsozialistischen Bewegung Grossdeutschlands.* A review of Maria Bach's music by Otto Repp appeared that day in this paper. There is also a report (no critic is named) in the *Völkischer Beobachter* of December 7, 1940, on the famed German conductor Wilhelm Furtwängler, who was to play—as a pianist—his own Violin Sonata, no. 2, in Vienna's Musikverein, the city's most prestigious concert hall. During the Great Depression in the early 1930s, reviews of Bach's music can be found alongside reports on the critical unemployment of countless musicians. In January 1930, the *Neue freie Presse* reported that "over one-third of Austria's trained professional musicians have been unemployed now on an average of two years."

On April 13, 1945, Vienna surrendered to Russian forces. Taken from St. Stephan's Cathedral, roofless and open to the sky, photographs captured the extensive wreckage strewn about the surrounding Stephansplatz. The scene of devastation spreads outward to the charred remains of the Vienna State Opera, where a half-century earlier Gustav Mahler had shattered traditions. But, amid the cleanup and reconstruction of the city, the public's reception of Maria Bach's music—although never overabundant—had stalled for good, as had any further chance of significant support from professional colleagues. Even Bach's most skillfully wrought compositions sounded timeworn compared with those of younger composers in Austria and other countries. Both the serialism and atonality rooted in early twentieth-century Vienna and Europe's midcentury exploration of nontraditional modes of sound production were beyond Bach's ken. She was never attracted to composing by means of tape and synthesizer—altering, augmenting, electronically generating music, even totally replacing "live" performers and "real" musical instruments.

The unfortunate fate that Maria Bach's music experienced also befell that of many previously *entartete* composers, whose creative powers had been stifled during their years of youthful blossoming. Like many of his fellow émigrés from Vienna, Erich Korngold had won success writing film music in Hollywood. But, also like other *entartete* composers, the end of the war left his music stylistically stranded, even his later instrumental works being debunked as outmoded. A definition of what "modern" meant in Bach's world, however, is not so easy to pin down, for this word has many shades of meaning that often overlap. Walter Frisch, for example, recently has taken readers through some of this entangled etymological territory in *German Modernism: Music and the Arts*.[86]

Meanwhile, the status of women, perhaps even more so of women composers, in Maria Bach's Vienna had not visibly improved. That circumstance, along with the composer's own dysfunctional family situation with its outlook of gloom, created overwhelming odds against any increase in the public reception of her music. Perhaps most of all, the morose mindset of her family, rather than merely the decaying world of imperial Vienna, distinguishes Bach from the musically gifted women mentioned elsewhere in this book. This distinction holds despite their commonality in sharing with her the support of affluent and artistically informed, culturally sophisticated parents. Some of Maria Bach's intimate friends, in fact, ascribed her limited success as a composer to that very stance of social-class-conscious elitism that her parents had maintained in the midst of a socialist Vienna. This outlook limited the potential of her professional career by isolating her from Vienna's musical mainstream. (Class rank and gender, Bach's contemporaries say, had probably cost her, for example, the most prestigious awards that composers of her day could hope for.)[87]

In addition, Bach never enjoyed the pride of holding a professional title or official position in Vienna's musical hierarchy. Some of her Viennese contemporaries did not suffer her fate, however. The composer Marianne Gary-Schaffhauser (born July 19, 1903), for example, was a professor of German and history in Vienna until 1948, when she retired from the University of Vienna to devote herself to composing, the defeat of Nazi rule no doubt playing a large part in this move.[88]

Conclusion

Because Maria Bach never held an official professional position in music, remaining a freelance artist with membership only in women's musical circles, she consequently would have had few prospects of composing music for costly large-scale forces. Producing such small-scale works, moreover, gave her a more realistic chance for eventual performance. Her chamber music, however—forming the major proportion of her works—depended almost solely on women's musical organizations to perform it.

Yet the affluence, dedication, and musical expertise of Maria Bach's parents provided her with a childhood of first-rate, though all private, musical education and extraordinary early exposure to leading musical figures in Vienna. In an interview published in the *Wiener Wochenschau* in 1976, the composer commented, "One . . . should harbor no illusions, for [in my life] . . . I remained spared from many a disappointment."[89] When all is said and done, Maria Bach did manage to forge a professional career worthy of notice in a musically glorious city through the first half of the twentieth century and two World Wars.

Maria Bach's life and career tell a story of plusses and minuses. Her musically accomplished parents had won renown for their musical soirées, their Sunday musicales welcoming some of Vienna's most famous composers, performers, artists and literati of the city's elite cultural establishment. Maria Bach's upbringing thus assured her an environment devoted to music, as well as ample exposure to other arts of Vienna's cultural world. Her family's active participation in the city's intellectual life as a whole almost guaranteed her a degree of acceptance and a measure of success, especially in a musical career.

No matter the century or society, it is almost a universal phenomenon that no small percentage of performers and composers—professionals and amateurs alike—earn a substantial amount of their income through teaching. Yet, strikingly, Bach apparently never engaged in this profession. Despite the extensive legal battles waged with her sisters and greatly diminished financial resources, Bach still had enough income to devote her working hours to composition and piano performance.[90]

Yet, from her childhood even through her professional lifetime, the elitism of the *nouveau riche* brought rigidly monitored social exclusion, hence isolation from all but the loftiest echelon of Viennese society. The Bach daughters were ensnared by their parents' overprotection in a fatal web from which they never escaped. As described earlier, Maria's later years were plagued by escalating dissension among the sisters over the onetime considerable legacy left to them by their father, an inheritance ironically, as discussed earlier, whittled away by their long years of litigation. This situation, together with the death of Maria's longtime companion, brought her almost complete professional withdrawal from society. Her recognized talent and busy career as a composer and performer never fulfilled its promise. And, as her supportive teachers and early patrons passed away, her compositions were overshadowed by new forms of music, hers being played and heard only by a few friends.

Maria Bach's long and steady descent into total obscurity paralleled in microcosm the sense of impending doom that enveloped the Austrian psyche during her lifetime. As she entered her professional years, escalating unrest in the Balkan lands of the Habsburg Empire propelled the cultural paradise of fin-de-siècle Vienna toward catastrophe. Austro-Hungary, a multinational confluence of five major religions and a dozen languages, was reduced by defeat in 1918 to a tiny republic. Subsequent worldwide inflation and depression, the Austrians' obliging the Nazi *Anschluss* of 1938, the defeat in World War II, and the decade-long postwar Soviet occupation took their toll.

Yet, in her day, Bach earned some degree of success and recognition as a fully professional pianist and composer. Many of her works were performed by important musicians in some of Europe's best known concert halls. She maintained a steady schedule of performances and composition until the end of World War II. Devoted to the art of music, she made a discernible, if modest, contribution to Viennese cultural life through the first two-thirds of the twentieth century.

Appendix: Reviews of Maria Bach's Music in the Viennese Press [91]

From my position as a newspaper critic, I include the following reviews of Maria Bach's music as a rich source of information giving insight into her personal view of herself as a composer and artist performer as well as a unique, if partial, glimpse into her intriguing cultural/historical world, that of the arts in the Austrian capital in its passage from imperial glory to a modest European state.

JANUARY 20, 1930, JOSEF REITLER, *NEUE FREIE PRESSE*

Original: "Richard Krotschak, the congenial blond solo cellist of the Vienna Symphony Orchestra offered, together with Otto Schulhof, a sensitive evening revealing outstanding chamber music qualities. The success of this concert was also due to a tender gleam of light that fell on a Cello Sonata by the young Maria Bach, obviously influenced powerfully by Josef Marx."[92] (In commenting on this concert, Bach omits the performer's name and ascribes the success of the evening solely to her cello sonata, although Reitler's review referred to the entire concert. In addition, the composer omits the remark that her piece was "obviously influenced powerfully by her teacher.")

MAY 13, 1931 "J-H-R" [JOSEF REITLER?], *DAS KLEINE VOLKSBLATT*

Original: "The participants, Henriette, cello, and Maria Bach, piano, performed an excellent Sonata for Cello and Piano by Bach, a work deserving our full attention."[93] (Bach accurately reports the critic's brief accolade for her cello sonata, but, curiously, fails to mention the performers and even herself as the composer.)[94]

APRIL 7, 1940, LEOPOLD SCHMIDT, *NEUIGKEITS-WELTBLATT*

Original: (Liederabend by Emy von Pichler) "[Hugo]Wolf, Josef Marx and his student Maria Bach made up this program, at the center of which stood the new lieder of the familiar composer M. Bach. Marx's school is recognizable everywhere in all that Bach's rich, well-known creative talent favorably has shown, including her own strong personality before the public, especially in these new lieder. Emy von Pichler, accompanied by the composer, knew how to transmit the lieder, making a splendid effect with beautiful vocal means and good understanding."[95] Bach's version: "Maria Bach's rich, well-known creative talent produces her strong personality before the public, especially in these new lieder."[96] Note Bach's omission, which skips reference to the other composers, the importance of her teacher, and the description of von Pichler's performance.

DECEMBER 6, 1940, FRITZ SKORZENY, *NEUES WIENER TAGBLATT*[97]

Original: "Maria Bach is no longer an unfamiliar name among Viennese composers. How often has she also joined with the singer Emy von Pichler at her very warmly received Composition Evenings in the Schubertsaal. She used her resonant soprano and warm reading in a long series of lieder. In all this unlocked and melodious female lyricism, this richly knowledgeable musician expresses herself with a penetrating sense of mood in her choice of texts: Trakl, much Rilke ('Portuguese Sonnets') and ancient Japanese; while, among the numerous premieres, the finely spun textures correspond especially to Karl Wache's 'Sehnsucht' or the Lanjus settings."[98] (Bach omits "Vienna's" in the first sentence above, an omission that could imply that her reputation extended beyond this city.)

Besides Skorzeny's review, one can see above it a much larger article concerning Franz Lehar, the still-celebrated Viennese operetta composer, conducting the Third Wehrmacht-Grosskonzert. A well-displayed article was placed side-by-side with the Maria Bach review, leaving food for thought for the readers of this book. The piece was headlined "Lehar dirigiert für das Kriegs- Wehrmacht Grosskonzert." Describing the event taking place in Vienna's important Konzerthaus, the unidentified reporter wrote that on this occasion, "the walls were richly adorned with national flags . . ."; and that "Reichsleiter, Reichsstatthalter Baldur von Schirach and his wife . . . were escorted to the special box seats [reserved for the highest National Socialist state officials], where they were greeted by Meister [Franz] Lehar." The featured program was described as a "Lanner-Strauss-Ziehrer-Lehar Evening." On the first page of this newspaper, Lehar and Schirach were photographed striding together down the main aisle of the Konzerthaus.

DECEMBER 7, 1940, OTTO REPP, *VÖLKISCHER BEOBACHTER*

Original: "In a large number of lieder that Emy von Pichler sang with all attention to feeling and with musical fidelity to the work, the composer Maria Bach handles the accompaniment in equally rhythmic chords of captivating harmony, while the often ecstatically intensified vocal part movingly fits the inflection of very polished speech. Japanese and Portuguese lieder are winners, besides local color, in that one definitely feels reminded, with the last occasionally, of Puccini, in some cases also a bit of Hugo Wolf."[99] (As Bach records this review: "Maria Bach's ecstatically intense vocal part successfully [renders] local color and harmony. [It] occasionally recalls Puccini and Hugo Wolf.")

DECEMBER 11, 1940, LEOPOLD SCHMID, *NEUIGKEITS-WELT-BLATT*

Original: "Because we are considering Liederabende of Maria Bach, the charming composer of melodic, beautifully sensitive lieder, has prepared hearty joy for us with an evening of various groups of her numerous creations. Lieder on Rilke and ancient Japanese poems especially show the highly gifted woman, again in the process of her noble endeavor, which friends of music already have long followed. Among them are lieder that also deserved to be sung elsewhere. Emy v. Pichler, who sticks in my mind since her Liederabend last year, has given the composer, who provided the piano accompaniment herself, a beautiful success with her singing."[100] (Although Schmid goes to some length in praising Bach's lieder, Bach mysteriously cites only one of his compliments.)

Original: "Of quite special peculiarity was the Composition Evening of Maria Bach, who incorporated Japanese, ancient Greek, Portuguese and Persian music into her own style, with a great gift of understanding, in captivating lieder and instrumental works showing her own personal stamp. The Graz soprano Emmy von Pichler, the Graz Michl Quartet and the cellist Wilhelm Knajasevsky were her splendid assistants with great success."[101] (Bach omits everything except to note that "the Composition Evening with captivating lieder of Maria Bach was of a quite special character." Also she again fails to mention the performers and their role.)

Original: "Manifold elements are brought together in Maria Bach's works: a dose of exoticism, a return to a clear sound-image more nearly approaching the folk-like in dances, already premiered, from the ballet *Bengele* and lieder of a more recent date for piano and cello—everything constructed in a forward-looking style of composing that harmonically is often rich and captivating—that is, inspired mood-music. Already the composer has repeatedly demonstrated that she has mastered her craft and is also an excellent pianist, so also at her concert last night, which Luise Brabbée's resonant soprano, Esta Mara's mature dancing, the expressive baritone of Viktor P. Sedely and the sensitive cellist Elisabeth Rössler helped make a heartfelt success." (Here Bach refers to herself as a "superior," rather than just excellent, pianist and mentions that there was great applause and many encores—information missing from the critic's review.)[102]

Original: "The Weissgärber Quartet premiered Maria Bach's Second String Quartet, an ensemble that is interested in new music. Again the composer's repeatedly worthy talent for exoticism is evident in these five movements following each other in the style of a dance suite; in her talent for a sensitivity to foreign sound-complexes, and in connecting these with the style of her own musical language."[103] (Bach omits the writer's specific reference to her "sensitivity to foreign sound-complexes" and Skorzeny's praise for the Weissgärber Quartet for its championing of new music.)

Original: "The Weissgärber Quartet offered, in the Brahms-Saal, an unusual arrangement of performances, which placed the premiere of a String Quartet by Maria Bach between a Boccherini Quartet and an Octet by Svendsen, an arrangement which, in this work, also again makes evident her preference for foreign rhythm, melody and harmony."[104] (Bach does not list the other compositions performed.)

* W. Pichler was possibly related to the singer Emma (Emy) von Pichler. The latter's husband and her frequent piano accompanist was Karl von Pichler.

DECEMBER 22, 1943, BRUNO PROHASKA, *DAS KLEINE BLATT WIEN*[105]

Original: "Between the charming three-movement String Quartet, Op. 6, of Boccherini and the effective, sonorously beautiful Octet, Op. 3, of J.S. Svendsen,[106] one heard a world premiere, namely, a string quartet by the composer Maria Bach, at the second Chamber Music Evening by the proven Weissgärber-Quartett. Maria Bach again took up the basic timbres of romantic, chiefly Spanish and Rumanian music and executed the chosen themes very delicately. The musicians joining in with Max Weissgärber were splendid interpreters of these works."[107] (Bach omits mention of the Boccherini and Svendsen compositions, while also changing "romantic" to (neo-Latin) "Romanic" and altering Prohaska's remark to say simply that Bach herself had *composed* "finely . . . selected themes.")

DECEMBER 22, 1943, FRIEDRICH MATZENAUER *WIENER NEUESTE NACHRICHTEN*

Original: "A new String Quartet by Maria Bach was heard [in which the] joy of the composer in the exotic and folkloristic again had an interesting and stimulating effect. Before that came a Boccherini—always desirable, supremely suitable as a concert introduction, and delicately played; as something new, Svendsen's Octet followed played by Vienna Philharmonic musicians."[108] (In recording yet another review of this concert, Bach again fails to include the critic's comments on music other than hers.)

DECEMBER 23, 1943, OTTO REPP, *VÖLKISCHER BEOBACHTER*

Original: "The Weissgärber Quartet performed Op. 6 of Boccherini, rendered in its totally soaring rococo grace, and Svendsen's Octet, Op. 3, which resounded in intense early nationalistic romanticism; in the performance, four outstanding string players performed consistently and with blended sonority. And, in her Second String Quartet, Maria Bach showed astounding empathy for the peculiarities of Rumanian and Spanish music, which also appear mixed here and there. The composer Bach—here as much in content as in form—attempts to pour new blood into sonata form, without thereby, however, going beyond the forms of dance and lied, that is as far as improvisations are concerned."[109] (Besides omitting mention of the other composers represented at this concert, Bach omits "attempts," thus making her accomplishment appear totally successful; and she reverses "without, however" to success in "content as in form" and omits the reference to "dance and lied" and "improvisations.")

MARCH 27, 1944, KARL DAUMER, *NEUES WIENER TAGBLATT*

"After a long pause, Paul Marion, remembered as a former member of the Vienna Opera, was heard here once again; this time in the Concert Hall. His powerfully room-filling, blossoming tenor makes Italian influences evident in every sense, namely in a well-behaved *messa di voce* that, raised to full volume, makes his tone wonderfully elastic, and that always has a pleasant effect. In arias and songs, among them captivating ones of Maria Bach and in other pieces heard, the artist, splendidly stormy, gave a good account of these fine qualities."[110] (Bach omits "former" and all references to the other works and to the performers.)

Locations of Documents

The Stadtbibliothek im Rathaus in Vienna (formerly the Wiener Stadt- und Landes Bibliothek) is the library that holds the main body of Maria Bach's music manuscripts and published editions, as well as the Vienna newspapers from which the author excerpted reviews of her music.

The Nationalbibliothek in Vienna holds her self-published personal journal *Blitzlichter aus meinem Leben.*

The Archiv der Gesellschaft der Musikfreunde in Vienna holds a collection of her letters and music.

The Bayerische Staatsbibliothek in Munich holds secondary literature concerning the composer.

Selected Editions

1928 Edition Vienna "Idylle" for piano
1928 Edition Vienna "Capriccio" for piano
1929 Edition Vienna "Gustav Falke Lieder" (includes "Geh' nicht")
1930 Doblinger "Narrenlieder" for tenor and 9 winds (3 flutes, 3 oboes, 3 clarinets)
1930 Doblinger "Wolgaquintett" ("Klavierquintett")
1930 Doblinger "Draussen im weiten Krieg" soprano and piano (also for piano solo and four-part chorus, both unpublished)
1930 Doblinger "Japanische Frühling" cycle for tenor or soprano and orchestra
1931 Doblinger "Drei Orchesterlieder" for tenor and orchestra
1931 Doblinger "Flohtanz" for piano
1932 Doblinger "Klagegebet" for cello and piano
1932 Doblinger "Negroid (Cake-walk)" (also "Tanz") for piano
1947 A-Tempo-Verlag "Sechs Altdeutsche Marienlieder" cycle for soprano and piano or orchestra
1951 Self-published "Drei Lieder nach Texten von F. Nietzsche" cycle for baritone and piano
1955 Self-published "Drei Negro Spirituals" cycle for baritone or bass and piano
1958 Self-published "Heimkehr" eight-part male chorus
1964 Self-published "Altdeutsche Marienlieder" cycle for baritone and piano
1964 Frauentöne "Silhouetten" Symphonic Suite (also ballet)

Vienna Press Publications Consulted

Das kleine Blatt
Das Neue Wiener Extrablatt
Das Neue Wiener Tagblatt
Das Neuigkeits-Welt-Blatt
Der Völkische Beobachter
Die Neue Freie Presse
Die Neuigkeits-Welt-Erinnerung
Wiener Neueste Nachrichten

CHAPTER FIVE

Ann Schein

An American Concert Pianist in Today's World

"Oh, do I have piano stories to tell."

This author has been hearing Ann Schein play since we were both about junior high school age. In fact, a prodigy first recognized when she climbed up on the piano bench at the age of three, she has never stopped playing. And her parents, Ernest and Betty Schein, gave her unceasing encouragement and expertise gained from their own intense musical pasts. What was it about Schein that has always drawn me and countless others to her playing? From the first time I heard her, I was entranced by the tonal beauty she could draw from the piano (by no means always a superb instrument). Her sensitive phrasing, deep emotional experience in performing, and her brilliant technique all reveal her total immersion in the music at hand. In short, she takes unmistakable delight in interpreting a score with the result that the audience, too, can comprehend, relive, and revel in what a composer is expressing. And since those early days, she has never lost any of these aspects of her artistry, meanwhile gaining the experience and depth that only the years can provide. But the road has by no means been strewn with roses. She herself once remarked that "being a musician is the building of character. But music is a brutal, competitive world full of managers, boards, egos, ambitions, and 'career elbows,' and you have to learn to deal with it."[1] (And this "brutal, competitive world" is made all the more apparent when one surveys the critiques of the press, upon which today's performing artists—and at least back to those of the nineteenth century—realistically depend to succeed in their profession. Samples of such reviews, therefore, are included in both the Schein and Maria Bach chapters.

Why Schein?

Until several years ago, I had heard and read about Schein only from a distance. I did not come to know her personally until I set out to interview her for this book. And I found a gold mine. As I worked with her, I was struck that here was a musical artist who could express feelings, subjective opinions that I could record instantly and as accurately as possible. I did not need to rely solely on second- or even third-hand quotes taken from written sources in historical annals. Also, I wanted to include someone whose story would strike a balance with those of the other women I discuss, but offer some contrast. First, as a critic of music today, I wanted a living subject currently engaged in music making now and therefore immediately accessible for first-hand study. Second, I wanted someone who belonged to the same Western society as the earlier women, therefore maintaining a historical continuum with the others—but a woman representing a different corner of Western society, the New World set against the Old Europe of the other artists. Third, I wanted someone who has pursued a career first and foremost as a performer. The musical roles of Duchess Sophie-Elisabeth, Elisabeth-Claude Jacquet de la Guerre, Josephine Lang, and Maria Bach encompassed performance as only one—not necessarily foremost—of several musical undertakings.

Schein continues to pursue a decades-long distinguished career as a performer in more than fifty countries, as well as having taught hundreds of students, lectured, and presided as an adjudicator at internationally renowned musical competitions. She has appeared with such notable conductors as George Szell, James Levine, Seiji Ozawa, James DePriest, David Zinman, Stanislaw Skrowacewski, and Sir Colin Davis—all leading the world's most famous orchestras, such as the Vienna Philharmonic Orchestra, the New York Philharmonic, the Philadelphia Orchestra, the Cleveland Orchestra, the Los Angeles Philharmonic, the Baltimore Symphony Orchestra, the National Symphony Orchestra, the London Philharmonic, the London Symphony, and the BBC Symphony Orchestra. Schein also has played at the White House during the Kennedy years and before royalty, as well as other distinguished audiences.

Today her schedule continues to overflow with solo recitals, chamber music concerts, and solo concerto appearances with major symphony orchestras—ranging widely throughout the United States, Europe, Asia, and Latin America. Schein is one of an exclusive roster of pianists chosen to present piano recitals in new venues in American cities and communities under the auspices of the Adams Foundation Piano Recital Series. By the end of the 2007 season, the series had sponsored 103 recitals in twenty-five communities in nineteen states. Besides teaching at the Peabody Conservatory for over two decades, she has also served as an artist-faculty member at the Aspen Music Festival and School in Colorado since 1984 and was appointed visiting professor of piano at the University of Indiana in 2008.

Born on November 10, 1939, in White Plains, New York, Schein has performed virtually everywhere in the world, doing so under many different circumstances. When, for example, at the age of twenty-five she debuted at the Hollywood Bowl with the Los Angeles Philharmonic, she had to contend with a twenty-foot-high spotlight shining in her eyes and a piano bench with a wobbly swivel device, enduring both while playing Tchaikovsky's Piano Concerto in B-flat Minor, Op.

23, no. 1, very near a gargantuan moat of water between the stage and 20,000 people. (But, of course, performers at every level of accomplishment have their own versions of such hazardous experiences.)

As accompanist to the celebrated singer Jessye Norman on a tour in Brazil, Schein was compelled to play in countless concert halls at more than one hundred degrees Fahrenheit because Norman will not perform anywhere with an air conditioning system in operation. When Schein was performing and giving master classes at the University of Maryland Piano Festival, the chief pedal of the piano at hand had fallen off the instrument. Then there was the concierge at a hotel in Kennebunkport, Maine, who asked her to leave the premises because her practicing on the establishment's piano was, he claimed, "disturbing the other guests." "Thank heaven for Ann Schein . . . what a relief it is to hear a pianist who, with no muss or fuss, simply reaches right into the heart of whatever she is playing—and creates music so powerful you cannot tear yourself away."[2]

Author's Note

The research for this chapter is drawn largely from the author's interviews with Schein between 2005 and 2009. (And, apart from her consistently serious observations and memories, she was on several occasions a witty, insightful raconteur.) Taken into account, too, have been her recordings, press reviews (including one of my own), my personal recollections of her performances since our teenage years, and conversations with members of her family and others connected with her personal and professional life. I have also aimed to verify and round out my source material through the informative and perceptive genealogy of her biological and adoptive father's family written by Schein's sister Linda Schein Greenebaum, *Elizer's Troupe: Scheins in America, 1890–1999*.[3] Finally, in compiling all this information, I have sought to reveal the artist's own perception of her life and career, as well as the events and situations she has experienced in her particular segment of society, time, and place. Interviews can capture a sense of immediacy not obtainable in treating the other women presented in this book. Thus the present examination of Schein's life, both private and professional, offers a type of evidence that can shed unique light not only on the past, but also on the present by way of an American artist still intensely active.

A Family Adoption; Early Childhood (1939–1945)

"I would never have been in music," pianist and New York Yankees fan Schein has said repeatedly, "if my parents (Ernest and Betty Cain Schein) hadn't lifted me out of a wretched and unhealthy situation." As with all the other women artists discussed in this book, Schein's family has played a central role in the shaping of her musical artistry.

As Schein remembers Betty's explanation, "my biological parents—George Schein and Kathleen Janney Lynch—had been heavy drinkers, leaving them unable to give me a healthy and secure family upbringing.[4] Both my adoptive parents, devout Christian Scientists, gave me a stable family and therefore greater promise for my future career."

With a touch of humor, Schein is very forthcoming about her adoption in early 1942 at the age of two years. (She has a November birthday.) At the age of fourteen, she was studying the piano in Mexico City with her dedicated Polish teacher Mieczyslaw Munz. At that time, she relates with a smile, her adoptive mother, Betty, an avid bridge player, "was trying unsuccessfully—as she had many times—to teach me a game in which I had no interest." On one such occasion, Schein adds, "Betty felt she had found the perfect moment to disclose the identity of my biological parents." But, in Schein's words, "My mother also told me that Ernie, my adoptive father (brother of George, my biological father), did not ever want to talk with me about the adoption." Therefore, Schein notes, "this part of my family history was never again discussed." All Schein's family—including half-siblings and friends—were sworn to keep her adoption secret, as Ernie wanted it, though he approved Betty's disclosure to Schein. Not learning about her adoption until she was old enough to understand this chapter of family history protected her, Schein believes, from an emotional shock.[5]

With her adoption, Schein grew up as a Christian Scientist, not aware of the Jewish side of her family. She remembers that in 1956 a Jewish boy refused to show affectionate advances to her because he understood that her family was not Jewish. But his questions, Schein remarks, led to her first confrontation with her own Jewish heritage.[6]

The Scheins

> "Schein was a child smiled on by the gods."[7]

Even today, the list of Scheins variously involved in music is endless. One day many years ago, Schein and her sister Linda walked into a well-known Chicago music store, Lyon and Healy, their last name on a check drawing instant recognition by an elderly employee.[8] This is not surprising when you survey the American Scheins' family history, beginning with Jewish immigrant musicians from Austro-Hungarian Galicia (the first was Elizer Schein) who settled in Chicago in the early 1890s. From those years into the present, a number of Scheins have become noted professional musicians.

The first generation of Chicago Scheins did ensemble playing, relying at times on the brilliant eleven-year-old cimbalom player Fanny Amsterdam, whose musical performances must have added a "selling" factor to the Scheins' concerts at functions held with the families of suburban Chicago society. (Part of Ann

Schein's extended family, the Amsterdam branch of the Scheins also included the cellist Maurice Amsterdam and comedian Maury Amsterdam.) A family member has explained that "the cimbalom was then [in the late nineteenth century] an essential feature of the hussar-costumed ensembles presenting Hungarian atmosphere for fashionable social functions" in the Illinois city.[9] Amazingly, the cast of characters in this drama—family members extending at present even to the sixth generation—has, above all, continued to nurture the art and practice of music. This phenomenon, even the name "Schein," has survived and flourished regardless of the Scheins' marriages to "non-Schein" spouses of widely contrasting abilities and ethnic-religious heritages.

Ann Schein's great-grandfather Elizer Schein (1840–1909), the progenitor of the American Scheins, was married to Esther Loeffer (1840–1910) and had five children, including Ann Schein's grandfather Louis Schein (1858–1931), born before Elizer's family immigrated to the United States and settled in Chicago. The Scheins' emigration from Europe was prompted by the encroaching anti-Semitic pogroms in their homelands. America offered them a safe haven in which to continue as musicians.

Louis's immediate family and a number of other Schein relatives had already settled in Chicago before Elizer arrived in 1899.[10] Louis Schein was a founding member of the Chicago Musicians' Union, and several Scheins became actively involved in union politics.[11] A number of Scheins and their in-laws worked long hours performing in Chicago's music theaters, even playing in pit orchestras and for silent films and thus earning a living as freelance musicians.

Louis, his brothers, and in-laws made up a professional music ensemble that performed regularly, playing in 1893, for example, at the Chicago Columbian Exposition. Louis married Frieda Langer (1862–1939), the couple bearing eight children—some born in Europe before arriving in the United States—who were to have twenty-six first cousins, including Ann Schein's biological father, George Langer Schein (1888–1942), and his younger brother Ernest (Ernie) Isador Schein (1898 or 1899–1967), who was to be her adoptive parent.

According to Greenebaum, George Schein was "very dapper like his father, Louis, and brother Ernie" and, like Ernie, continually quoted poetry.[12] In fact, George, who held a high-profile position in criminal law, cultivated many interests, including legions of friends in the arts. No strangers to Al Capone and other Chicago Mafia celebrities of the 1920s, George and Ernie developed a significant group of Chicago clients in their law practice, as well as colorful, wealthy, and influential figures in politics and journalism. Their firm, for example, helped establish the still well-known meat-packing plant of Oscar Mayer in Madison, Wisconsin.[13] George's first wife, Louise Emily Mayer (1891–1927), was a Protestant and the mother of his three oldest children, the family living in a grand home on Astor Street near Lake Michigan. "A young society matron," Louise died of cancer at thirty-six in 1927. George—constantly traveling to other cities, most often, Washington, D.C.—resettled his family in Scarsdale, New York, marrying his client Kathleen Janney Lynch, who died in her thirties in 1947. (By then, Ann would have been about seven or eight years old. This death remained unknown to Schein until her adoptive mother's revelation in 1953.) Now widowed, George meanwhile had turned to nannies to care for his children. (Elsa was Schein's personal German nanny in Scarsdale; she was still in charge of Ann when Ernie brought his newly adopted two-year-old daughter home to Evanston.) Inspired by Franklin Roosevelt's presidency, George and Kathleen Lynch had moved to Washington, D.C., to be near the White House and its political connections. They resettled in a large home on Kalorama Road in an upscale Washington neighborhood, their biological daughter "Sharon" having been born in November 1939.[14] Renamed "Ann" (after an earlier Schein family member), the child was adopted by the Ernie Scheins when George died at fifty-four in 1942 from cirrhosis of the liver resulting from the ravages of alcohol. As a tragic consequence, one could conclude that George and Kathleen would never feel the joy and pride of knowing their prodigiously talented daughter and her considerable professional achievements.

George Schein and his first wife, Louise Emily Mayer, daughter of Oscar Mayer, had three children, Ann Schein's biological half-siblings: George Langer Schein, who changed his last name to "Shields," (1919–1999), Louise Elizabeth Schein McDougall (1921-), and Bette Denver Schein MacDonald (1923-).[15]

A graduate of the University of Chicago and Harvard Law School, Ernie Schein served prominent clients, including the Chicago Musicians' Union and the Chicago Musical College, where he eventually met Schein's future adoptive mother, a violinist and student at the college. Besides his professional clients, however, Ernie was still a family man, who "embodied the essence of old-world paternal authority," Schein recalls. An irrepressible punster in addition, he exuded, she adds, a "warmth and cheerfulness" that, along with his talents as a comic, pervaded the whole family. Broadening his activities even further, Ernie even ran for Congress in 1929 as a "progressive" Republican—a maverick among his Democratic brothers. And though he was an avid anti-Prohibitionist, he became a tee-totaling advocate after he married Betty only a year later. It was a remarkably unsettled time for America—the years of Prohibition and the Great Depression. As a consequence of his conversion to a Christian denomination, Ernie never discussed his own Jewish background, confessing once that "George and I intuited that being Jewish was something to be left far behind."[16]

Schein describes her mother, Betty Schein, as "a stoic of truly epic proportions and a natural leader with unflinching integrity," adding proudly that she was "also an accomplished violinist." During the family's Evanston years, in fact, Betty was concertmaster of a local orchestra and, as a soloist, performed at times in public concerts. In addition, Schein's mother played the violin in chamber music sessions at home and elsewhere. But, in the age-old tradition, she had given up her idea of a professional career when she married.

In great contrast to the Scheins, Betty Schein's forebears were farmers and bankers who had emigrated from Britain's Isle of Man to Kansas before the American Civil War (in which some of them participated), Schein adding that Betty's "family had what we might call today solid midwestern values." Born in Kansas City, Missouri, Betty entered the University of Kansas in Lawrence at sixteen and, as a freshman violinist, won a prize as "the most gifted instrumentalist" there. After two years, she transferred to the Chicago Musical College (where she first met her future husband), studying with the renowned French violinist Jacques Gordon, who, Schein relates, "passed on to her a life-long love of chamber music, leading her on to play in orchestral and chamber ensembles in Chicago, and later in Washington, D.C." Betty's musical accomplishments, therefore, formed one of the primary reasons why, as Schein grew up, "music filled our Evanston home," and "where, at the age of three, I climbed onto a piano bench for the first time!" Schein had heard the "Marines' Hymn" on the radio and played it note-for-note. (Patriotic songs flooded American airwaves during World War II.)

With Schein's adoption, Ernest Schein and his wife Elizabeth (Betty) Grindrod Cain (1907–1967) now had four children. As a result, Ann Schein "acquired" as siblings her new parents' three oldest offspring, who thus were already her biological cousins: Robert Louis Schein (1932-), Linda Schein Greenebaum (1935-), and Paula Leslie Schein (1936–1947). Ann became the youngest child in Ernest Schein's family. Like many other Scheins, her brother Robert has worn several hats (among them, that of a pilot and electronics engineer), moving his family to Turkey and the Middle East and Southeast Asia. He ultimately settled down in the United States as a successful computer programmer. Despite the presence of three talented sisters, Robert nevertheless claims that he enjoyed a "conventional middle-class male childhood of the 1940s and 1950s."[17] Schein's sister Linda Schein Greenebaum has degrees from Radcliffe and Smith colleges. A Fulbright scholar, professional violinist, teacher, and mother of four daughters, Greenebaum sometimes engages in chamber music concerts at her home. Many times Ann Schein joins in these events. Schein's other sister, Paula, even as a young child, was already a "very talented pianist radiating a remarkably mature serenity," the family remembers.[18] She and Ann studied with the same piano teachers in Evanston and Washington.

But fortune was not kind to Paula. In 1947, with Betty and her daughters still in Washington, Ernest took an assignment as chief examiner of the War Damage Commission in Manila, the Philippines. After he left for the Philippine city, however, ten-year-old Paula had become critically ill with nephritis, although her mother referred to it as "a condition," according to her Christian Scientist faith. Sadly, Paula did not survive her illness, Betty bravely enduring the burial in Chicago.[19] Nevertheless, Betty, Linda, and Ann stalwartly journeyed on to Manila even in the immediate wake of the tragedy, their travel further anguished by a violent storm-tossed voyage of two weeks across the Pacific on a less-than-luxurious freighter. Yet the Schein family persevered courageously for a year and a half in Manila, Betty even finding the seven-year-old Schein an excellent piano teacher, Julio Esteban, a well-known Spanish virtuoso in his own right. Schein studied with Esteban from 1947 to 1949. The girls attended the American School in Manila, the postwar city, Schein recalls, "being a scene of complete devastation."

Earlier, in Evanston, Schein's parents—fueled by her musical gifts—had overridden the initial reluctance of a prominent pianist, Agnes Conover, who taught privately once a week in the Scheins' Evanston neighborhood, Schein learning how to read music. This arrangement continued until the family's move to Washington. With these first piano lessons—from 1942 to 1945—Ann Schein's career preparation was already off and running. In March 1945, the dean of Northwestern University (in Evanston) wrote to Schein's adoptive parents: "Yesterday, and again today, I had the happy privilege of seeing and hearing your midget daughter perform at the Orrington School. . . . In forty years of teaching—all of that time to some extent associated with children—I have never seen the equal of your child. . . . [She] shows signs of being in the genius class. . . ."

(Because of Betty's ongoing personal experience with Schein, other parents often sought Betty's guidance in directing the lives of their own gifted offspring. And Betty gladly responded to them. At this early stage, Schein's mother was already exhibiting that fortitude and sensitivity needed for her difficult job in guiding and supporting a prodigy along the obstacle-filled path toward a career as an artist in the front ranks.)

Music in Washington, D.C.: A City at War

In the late summer of 1945, the Schein family moved from Evanston, Illinois, to Washington, D.C., the capital city of a United States still actively engaged in a global conflict like none before. In April of the same year—while America was yet at war on two fronts—President Franklin Delano Roosevelt had died suddenly in Warm Springs, Georgia, giving the United States a new president, Harry S. Truman. One must, therefore, keep in mind that Washington was and is first and foremost a federal city—a factor to remember when assessing the city's cultural scene.

Consequently, with the move to Washington, the Schein family faced a vastly different lifestyle than they had known in Chicago. In its own singular way, however, the city was enjoying a thriving and expanding arts scene. Ever-increasing crowds of federal workers poured into Washington (to an unprecedented degree because of the war), a city still undergoing air-raid drills, with all-city blackouts under a sky routinely illuminated with searchlights. There was also food and gas rationing and all the other restrictions that applied across the country during World War II. But, because of Washington's proximity to the East Coast, it was also experiencing an air of underlying anxiety. (Schein's half-brother, George, was a navy flyer and sank a German ship off this coast.) German U-boats, after all, were lined up all along the entire coast while actively involved in sinking merchant vessels. Arriving in Washington in the wake of the war, the five-year-old Schein nevertheless continued to develop her uncommon musical gifts.

But talent needs support from beyond the family circle. For many years, Washington impresario Patrick "Pat" Hayes (1909–1998) fulfilled some of that function as a font of information and support for Schein and her family.[20] In fact, Schein says, "My father and Hayes had forged a bond unshaken through all the years that the Scheins lived in Washington." (In the early 1960s, Ernest Schein, Mieczyslaw Munz [her teacher at the Peabody], and Hayes met once a month to help plan and make decisions about her career direction that led, for example, to studying with the renowned virtuoso pianist Arthur Rubinstein and winning a contract with the fabled contract manager Sol Hurok.) As one of the last major American impresarios, Hayes was virtually the only commercial entrepreneur engaged in presenting performing artists in Washington, D.C., before the opening of the Kennedy Center in 1971. Manager of the National Symphony Orchestra in the early 1940s, he directed his highly successful familiar Hayes Concert Bureau from 1947 until 1966. In that year, with Ernest Schein's ten years of legal guidance, Hayes turned the bureau into a long-envisioned nonprofit agency, the Washington Performing Arts Society (WPAS), which Hayes headed until 1982. Among the endless number of world-renowned instrumentalists, singers, and dancers Hayes brought to the nation's capital were Marian Anderson, Arturo Toscanini, Van Cliburn, Vladimir Horowitz, Jascha Heifetz, Leontyne Price, and Louis Armstrong—to name only several. Among the arts companies that he attracted to Washington—besides leading American symphony orchestras—were the Metropolitan Opera, the Martha Graham Dance Company, the Bolshoi Ballet, and the Ballets Russes de Monte Carlo.

Of course, Hayes knew a countless number of leading American and international artists, especially those who performed in Washington and New York musical circles—with all their global connections. In addition, his second wife, Evelyn Swarthout Hayes, was a well-known local concert pianist and a faculty member at Washington's American University. (She had studied with the eminent piano pedagogue Tobias Matthay.) Hayes and Swarthout seemed to be present at every concert ever given in the capital city, and they were the Scheins' close personal friends from the time Ann Schein was nine or ten.

Swarthout, in fact, first heard Schein play in a local radio station's competition in which Mrs. Hayes was a judge. Playing Ravel's "Alborada del Gracioso" (originally for orchestra), Schein took first place. When Swarthout later asked Bessie Gunn why she had given Schein such a difficult work, Gunn replied, "I didn't tell Ann it was difficult," Schein recollects.

Besides the musical activities of organizations such as Hayes's, Washington in many other aspects was by no means "a cultural wasteland"—as uninformed commentators on the city's past decades still say today. Washington is a government city, not an urban center like New York, for example, a city with a long history of private cultural funding bequeathed by generations of wealthy financial, industrial, or commercial donors. In short, the level of music and the other arts in Washington when the Schein family settled here—and even earlier—was not comparable to that of New York, Chicago, or any other major American metropolis.

Counting music alone, Washington's public musical scene thrived in its own way. The Library of Congress's Coolidge Auditorium, Carter Barron Amphitheater, and numerous important art galleries such as the National Gallery of Art and the Phillips and Corcoran galleries, as well as other performance sponsors, maintained active concert schedules. The sound of music resonated throughout Washington, all these venues drawing in not only Washingtonians but also audiences from the close-lying suburbs, enclaves formed by residents of Northern Virginia and Maryland who lived immediately adjacent to the city's official boundaries. But today, in great contrast to the mid-twentieth century, large segments of the Washington metropolitan region now support extensive musical establishments of their own.

Dominating the musical scene when the Scheins moved to Washington was the historic Constitution Hall, a stately edifice housing the national headquarters of the Daughters of the American Revolution. For decades, the hall served as Washington's main classical music center, continually hosting the world's most celebrated performers and drawing its audiences from everywhere. In 1971, Constitution Hall was replaced (for most concerts and other types of performances) by the new Kennedy Center for the Performing Arts as Washington's main concert space, offering a number of sizable halls, one each for major symphony orchestras and soloists, opera, and drama; smaller recital halls, such as the Center's Terrace Theater, have been accommodating chamber ensembles and other modestly sized performing groups; and there are other smaller Kennedy Center places where additional performances of various kinds take place.

Washington's National Symphony was established in 1930 by its first conductor, Hans Kindler (1892–1949), also a highly respected cellist. (Schein played with the NSO's Youth Symphony as a seventeen-year-old.) Over the years, a number of additional symphony orchestras have made their marks in Washington, depending on economic conditions. Other sites have hosted symphony orchestras, such as the Pan American Union (now the Organization of American States).

In addition, one cannot overlook Washington's unique supply of fine military bands. These organizations represent all the branches of service and have continually provided countless excellent concerts all year—first and foremost for all important official occasions, such as White House visits by foreign heads of state and for similar events at the Capitol and Lincoln Memorial. But Washington's general public, too, enjoys the bands' music making, especially in the summer, when these groups can perform outdoors on the wide-open Mall stretching from the Capitol to the Lincoln Memorial, a monumental edifice edging on the Potomac River. Many of the service bands have long histories; for example, the United States Marine Band, called "The President's Own," dates back to 1798. And these young conservatory-trained musicians in the bands also perform individually in nonmilitary concerts.

Still very active, Washington's Friday Morning Music Club has sponsored local concerts since the mid-1880s, continuing to make valuable contributions to Washington's musical scene both on a professional level and in supporting budding young musical performers. Founded as an exclusively women's organization, the FMMC gave men full membership in 1967. From its beginning, the club has presented weekly concerts, while gradually gaining increasing support from countless musical artists, philanthropists, businessmen, political leaders, and other visionary individuals of the city—besides Patrick Hayes and arts patron David Lloyd Kreeger, a skilled amateur violinist.

At the age of seven, Schein presented her first formal solo recital, which took place at the YWCA's Barker Hall, another concert space in downtown Washington and one not far from the White House. Reportedly, Schein's audience raved, the young pianist even remembering wearing a yellow-dotted Swiss dress and receiving beautiful yellow roses presented to her by her father. Besides regular performances by local musicians Emerson Myers, Charles Crowder, Richard Bales, and Margaret Tolson, for example, at Barker Hall and those sponsored by the FMMC, concerts by voices and instruments resounded from the city center's churches in presentations of major choral works by Bach, Mozart, Haydn, Schubert, Beethoven, Brahms, and other celebrated composers. The music departments of Catholic, Howard, and American universities also sponsored concerts.

Nor can we exclude another Washington institution: the numerous summer concerts of symphonic fare, operas, operettas, and musicals given for decades at the Watergate, the longtime popular floating stage on the Potomac (the audience sat on riverside steps). Because of the increasing din of jets overhead, racing along the river to and from nearby National Airport, the Watergate succumbed to replacement by the Kennedy Center and apartment buildings, including the elite but now-infamous Watergate development.

This was the Washington, D.C., that welcomed the young Schein, her family soon setting in motion a serious plan for her piano study. Arranging the five-year-old Schein's musical training, in fact, would continue to absorb her parents for many years.[21] After all, Betty and Ernie knew what challenges artists face in the professional musical world because of their own involvement in it during their Chicago days. Using their broad musical experience and knowledge of musical performers, the Scheins accordingly contacted Glenn and Bessie Gunn in Washington, whom they had known in Chicago. (Both had studied with the well-

Figure 27. Ann Schein at ten performing for NBC television for a public broadcast at the network's studio WNBW, Washington, D.C. Courtesy of Schein, 1950.

known pianist Arthur Friedheim, who had been a pupil of Franz Liszt.) Glenn Dillard Gunn was the chief music critic of Washington's *Times Herald* and also a conductor.[22] He and his wife, Bessie Bracken ("B.B.") Gunn, were both highly respected pianists and teachers in the capital. Bessie Gunn immediately accepted Schein as a pupil, the years of study stretching from 1945 to 1947 and from 1949 to 1953. In addition to the lessons, Schein recalls that "the Gunns brought a whole world of culture into my experience, which nurtured my musical development for years to come," continuing, "and they knew legions of great musical artists personally," information that Schein eagerly absorbed.[23] By 1946 (after only a year of study with Bessie Gunn), Schein not only had given her first formal recital, but she was also practicing Beethoven's Concerto no. 1 in C Major, Op. 15, her first full-length concerto and one that remains in her repertoire (fig. 27).

Broadening Horizons

About halfway through Schein's years with Mrs. Gunn, Hendrick Essers, conductor of the Washington Civic Symphony Orchestra and music director of Woodrow Wilson High School, had come into the Scheins' musical circles. Essers was Linda's violin teacher, both Linda and Betty also playing in his orchestra. In 1950 (at the age of ten), Ann Schein made her orchestral premier as a soloist playing (with the Civic Symphony) the opening movement of Beethoven's Piano Concerto no. 1, Op. 15, with Essers's ensemble. Essers, moreover, led the bands and orchestras of Alice Deal Junior High School (attended by Schein and Linda) and Woodrow Wilson Senior High School (attended by Linda). Essers even convinced Schein to study the cello and play, as a seventh-grader, in Deal's orchestra, presenting her with a school cello and saying, "Try this—you'll like it." She took to it instantly with Essers as her teacher. Although Schein was not to pursue cello study with eyes on a career, she says, "I loved the cello, and I played it, together with studying the piano, for quite a few years." In addition, both sisters—Schein on both cello and piano—studied at the well-known Interlochen National Music Camp in Michigan. Essers was also a faculty member there during the summers of 1951 and 1953. (Schein was, respectively, eleven and thirteen in those years.)

In the summer of 1953, the thirteen-year-old Schein won Interlochen's Concerto Competition, playing Edward MacDowell's Concerto in D Minor, no. 2, Op. 23. She was the youngest winner in the camp's history. Her next and last competition experience was in 1956 as a contestant in the Marjorie Merriweather Post Competition, in which she performed Sergei Rachmaninoff's Concerto no. 3 (fig. 28). Schein did not place in this competition—nor did James Levine, at this writing director of the Metropolitan Opera and the Boston Symphony Orchestra.[24] "While Mrs. Post," Schein remembers, "told me later that my performance reminded her of Rachmaninoff's own," Ann also notes, "Munz, with whom I was now studying, was devastated by my losing and forbade me ever entering another competition. And I never did."

As a result of Schein's Interlochen triumph in 1953, her parents undertook an active search for a world-class pianist/teacher who would continue to contribute to the blossoming of her pianistic skills and sheer musicianship. (By now, the Gunns were in their eighties.) After several auditions with faculty members at leading East Coast music schools—including Eduard Steuerman at New York's Juilliard School of Music and Mieczyslaw Horszowski at the Curtis Institute in Philadelphia—Schein's parents decided on Miecsylaw Munz at Baltimore's Peabody Conservatory.[25] In September 1953, he heard Schein play only once, immediately accepted her into his advanced class—with two-hour lessons twice weekly—and devised a "five-year plan" of study with him (1953–1958) that he believed would solidify her technique, expand her repertoire with increasingly demanding works, and thereby help launch her future as a pianist. Schein recalls, "I had missed some of these areas in my otherwise musically inspired early instruction." But only one year after beginning study with Munz, Schein—at age fifteen—played the first movement of Chopin's Piano Concerto no. 2 in F Minor with the National Symphony Orchestra at Washington's Constitution Hall.[26]

Figure 28. Schein, 1956, playing Sergei Rachmaninoff's Piano Concerto no. 3 in D Minor, Op. 30, with the National Symphony Orchestra conducted by Howard Mitchell at the Merriweather Post Competition, Washington, D.C. Courtesy of Schein.

Munz and the Émigrés

Most striking and horrendous of all the world events coinciding with Schein's youth was World War II and the Nazis' overtaking most of Europe, turning Munz's life upside down, as it did to millions of others. This event ravaged and consumed European life in its many dimensions—politically, economically, socially, and culturally through the 1930s until the war's end in 1945, and beyond. As in the arts and many other professional fields, persecution, emigration, and death in concentration camps brought about a vast "brain drain" from Nazi Europe. Leading composers, artist performers, and musical scholars flooded into the United States and other safe havens—not the least being Arnold Schoenberg, Eric Korngold, and countless others. But, ironically, this consequence of the war enriched American musical life and overall culture, perhaps most visibly in Los Angeles, with its university faculties and the Hollywood film industry. Here European composers flocked in great numbers. Two of the Jewish émigré Poles who made an indelible mark on the course of Schein's career were the pianists Munz and Arthur Rubinstein (1887–1982), both of them world-renowned artists.[27]

When Schein began her studies according to Munz's visionary five-year schedule, he propelled it immediately into action. "My family agreed and fully complied with his plan," Schein emphasizes. Eventually the young pianist's talent and achievements with Munz prompted him to contact European managers whom he knew firsthand through his own career—"a rare thing [for him] to do," Schein says, adding that "he planned meticulously for the beginnings of my performing career." Munz possibly may have conceived his vision unknowingly as compensation for the massive losses he had endured as a result of the Nazi takeover of Europe: he suffered, for example, from being cut off from his homeland and by the death of twenty-two family members, including his parents and brother. He also lost his wife, Nela Mlynarski (see endnote 27), to Arthur Rubinstein, who was himself to teach Schein in the future. These catastrophic circumstances, Schein recalls, "left him emotionally and socially bereft." Munz's tragedies may partially explain his later and bitter remark that Earl "took" Schein from him by marrying her. He lashed out, Schein reports, referring to "all that work [that he had done as her teacher and she had accomplished as his student]."

Munz suffered from guilt, Schein believes, because he was the only member of his family to escape the Holocaust; he had left Poland on an American concert tour before his relatives perished. As if these painful experiences were not enough for one person to bear, Schein remembers that on one occasion, "Munz's right hand failed him in the middle of a concert, ending his performing career." And even after all these losses," Schein continues, "Munz also found himself destitute in New York City, for he had gambled all his money away. He was in a terrible, pitiful state." As Schein believes, "Reginald Stewart, then director of the Peabody Conservatory in Baltimore, encountered Munz by sheer chance on a New York street. Having previously conducted Munz as a soloist with an orchestra more than twenty times in Toronto, Stewart then offered Munz an opportunity to join the Peabody faculty, which Munz accepted. Munz was now in place for Schein's entrance as a student onto the Baltimore scene.

The Friday Morning Music Club

Schein joined the FMMC as a student member in 1953, the year that she began study with Munz. Betty Schein had joined the Friday Morning Music Club as a performing member shortly after the family's relocation to Washington in 1945 and participated actively in the organization for more than twenty years. In fact, Schein's parents had both become deeply involved in the growing influence of the FMMC. "The tangible results of this relationship," Schein remarks, "are still evident today in every aspect of the vibrant cultural life of Washington." Schein's mother, for example, helped establish the FMMC's foundation in 1948 and the

Washington International Competition in 1957, both designed to support young pianists, other instrumentalists, singers, and composers in developing professional careers.

In addition, Thomas Mastroianni led the Friday Morning Music Club in endowing a permanent prize in the name of Betty and Ann Schein, the award being launched by a piano recital that Schein gave in the autumn of 2005. On that occasion (which this writer attended), Schein said, "It is my deepest joy and honor to be joined together with my mother" in an award to be given to the winners of the Washington International Piano Competition.

The Baltimore Commute:
Balancing Piano Lessons and Schoolwork

Wise in the ways of raising a child in the professional music world and especially concerned with her daughter's daily commitments, Schein's mother began the family's Washington years by making special arrangements with school principals so that Schein could attend academic classes while still having ample time for an intense schedule of private lessons and practicing. (Schein's later colleague Elisabeth Adkins, associate concertmaster of the National Symphony Orchestra, remarked to me in 2007 that "unlike pianists [who must, for the most part practice in isolation, except in ensemble work], most other instrumentalists have many opportunities to practice while playing with other musicians in chamber music and orchestral organizations.")

From an early age, Schein practiced every morning from eight o'clock to ten, then walked to her local public elementary school. Following those years, Schein emphasizes, "Going to Alice Deal [a public junior high that she attended from the seventh through the ninth grades] was just one of my parents' wise decisions to keep a healthy 'normalcy' in my life." By this time, Schein's lessons in Baltimore had also begun, and she was now practicing up to four and five hours daily with two-hour-long lessons.

After graduating from Deal, Schein entered the private Holton-Arms School, for girls from the tenth through the twelfth grades, and graduated at seventeen.[28] She then took courses at George Washington and American universities. In these years of 1953 to 1958 as a student at Deal and Holton, Schein relates, "My mother drove me twice a week for five years to Baltimore (about forty miles northeast of Washington) for my piano lessons at the Peabody, where I had been admitted as a special student of Munz—besides managing what were considered college-level courses at Holton. It was at this point that my parents began their long-term commitment to fulfill my teacher's far-reaching goals for my future as a musician. My parents never wavered from every effort to realize this goal from that time on."

Besides commuting to Baltimore during the school year, Schein also devoted whole summers (1954 and 1955) to daily lessons and grinding daily practice in

Mexico City, where Munz spent his yearly vacation. Munz oversaw her practicing (six to eight hours a day) diligently, but patiently, hour after hour, Schein adds.[29] "And between him and my mother, there was no escape," she says, continuing, "It was in these summers that I truly learned how to practice with iron discipline and how to work at another level beyond anything I had experienced up to that time."

Because of her practice and lesson schedule, Schein did not arrive at Holton until 1 P.M. in her senior year. But she made lifelong friends at Holton; and there were other "special" students there—for example, Olympic-minded swimmers and an inspiring ballet student (who later was admitted to the New York City Ballet). In Schein's final year at Holton, she was graciously invited to lead the school's graduation procession and carry the school's traditional red roses. At that time, she had not yet earned a diploma. But, in the following year, she completed courses in advanced French and Spanish at Washington's Georgetown University and art history at American University. With credits for these classes, along with two more for her music study, she graduated officially from Holton, having finished courses specifically designed to advance an international performance career. (In the 1970s, Holton honored her with a distinguished alumnae award, Schein explains, "as part of its dedication to the visionary guidance of women in their lives and careers.")

In January 1956, when Schein was sixteen and still justifiably considered a "child prodigy," she played her first performance—which received a ten-minute ovation—of Rachmaninoff's monumental Third Concerto with the Peabody Conservatory's student orchestra under conductor and Peabody faculty member Guillermo Espinosa (also music director of the Pan American Union in Washington, D.C.). Schein had rehearsed five times with the orchestra. Munz passed on a tape of this concert to the record producer Alan Silver of (Richard) Kapp Records. Schein's performance convinced Silver, Munz's Peabody associate, that Schein should be one of four classical pianists sought by Kapp for his upcoming recording (Schein's first) featuring popular musical artists, also including Roger Williams. The recording received extraordinary press reviews about her playing, with references such as "incredible," "not to be believed," "the surprise sensation of the year." The noted harpsichordist and critic Igor Kipnis wrote a review entitled "Who Is Ann Schein?" Schein recalls him remarking, "She took the piano world by surprise except perhaps for Munz." "Schein's legend will endure; from her recordings alone, she will be remembered as a real artist."[30]

Schein's Memories of Dedicated Parents

Schein warmly recalls her parents as providing an extraordinary foundation and inspiration for building her coming life as a concert pianist. Describing Betty Schein as "always a devoted mother," Schein adds, "She was always present at my piano lessons, after which she would review Munz's comments with me so that no significant points would be missed." Her mother's guidance, Schein remembers, "gave me a strict schedule for time spent at the piano that was a key factor in my musical progress."

"My mother's close watch over me with a stern sense of discipline for my practicing and schoolwork," Schein says, "was often unappreciated by me in my teenage years!" "Even my school classmates," she adds, "confessed to having difficulty getting past 'Mrs. Schein' in their attempt to engage me in more pleasurable activities than just one practicing!" Schein adds that "in the early days of my career—between the ages of seventeen and twenty-two (from ca. 1958 to 1962) my mother always accompanied me on my early concert tours. This kind of dedication was invaluable as I began performing and traveling to different countries around the world." In 1958 alone, Schein gave debut recitals in England, Iceland, Norway, Sweden, Denmark, Poland, Germany, Switzerland, and Greece. In the 1960–1961 season, she took Europe by storm, positive reviews flooding the newspapers. The Hamburg critic for Germany's *Die Welt* wrote in 1960, "Without a doubt, the 21-year-old pianist is already now as far in musical talent, musicianship, and technique as are many of the well-known artists of today." Schein toured with the BBC Symphony under Rudolf Schwarz; one English reviewer remarked that "in Rachmaninoff's Third Piano Concerto, Schein gave a marvelously alert, controlled, unaffected performance, showing little strain and a lot of sympathy for the music." On that same tour, after Schein had performed in Moscow and two other Russian cities, the Moscow Bureau of the *Baltimore Sun* reported that she was "the first American woman pianist to perform in the Soviet Union."

On these tours, Ann also remembers, "My mother, however, was also a wonderful companion, giving me musical feedback and encouragement, conveying unshakeable confidence in my ability to meet every challenge." After that time, Betty receded into the background, telling Schein, "It's time I lose my job." She became "a co-cheerleader with my father," she remembers, continuing, "together they allowed me to pursue my own life and career from then on."

"My parents' joy was my entire reward," Schein recalls. "They didn't want me to be, as they put it, 'bitter and disillusioned' by the professional musical world," the pianist emphasizes—as in the case of many musicians they had known. Yet Betty and Ernie Schein, Schein emphasizes, "never allowed me to slip for a second or get away with any laziness, whether I liked it or not."[31]

A Personal Note

Schein's life in her Washington-Baltimore years strangely intersected with some of this author's own musical experiences. Perhaps an accounting of these coincidences sheds some personal light on Schein's life and career that not all biographers can be privy to. In 1952, Washington's long-established Hamilton National Bank sponsored a competition for young instrumentalists among local junior and senior high students—including myself. I will never forget Schein's beautiful playing, which won first prize. Also coincidently, Schein and I both recall hearing a fine oboist in the competition, Michael Senturia, who later conducted the Harvard-Radcliffe Orchestra, in which I also played the flute. In addition, Schein and I may have unknowingly met on the stairs of Washington's historic Avalon Theatre on Connecticut Avenue in Chevy Chase, again in the early 1950s.[32]

In the fall of 1955, Schein's path again crossed with mine, this time at the Peabody Conservatory, where I, too, studied the piano with Munz. In his repertoire classes, I still remember Schein's playing at that time: her sensitive touch, ebullient lyricism, lucid handling of textures, and the structural acumen of her phrasing— in addition to all those mysterious qualities that make up sheer musicality.

Schein's Early Public Career

In August 1961, Schein made a spectacular New York "pre-debut" (as she calls it) at the city's Lewisohn Stadium, playing Rachmaninoff's Third Piano Concerto in D Minor with the New York Philharmonic Orchestra under the celebrated Chicago-born conductor Alfred Wallenstein (1898–1983). (He had led the Los Angeles Philharmonic from 1943 to 1956, a period including his directorship of the Hollywood Bowl [1952–1956], where Schein played in 1965 with this orchestra under Maurice Abramavel.) Actually, Wallenstein objected to her playing the Rachmaninoff for this Lewisohn appearance, Schein admits, "But Munz's will prevailed."

The concert took place outdoors in August on a very hot night with 90 percent humidity, the weather rendering the piano keys, Ann recollects, "as slippery as ice." But "most of the critics," Ann recollects, "were highly enthusiastic." Only Alan Rich in the *New York Times,* Schein says, "reported unfavorably, writing, 'fate has brought a young girl who came a cropper.'"[33]

However, as a result of Schein's performance, the well-known classical music manager Anne Colbert and her husband sought to enlist Schein in their ranks. There were other offers to manage her, too, such as that of Fritz Steinway (the large Steinway family being best known to us as the makers of supreme pianos). The well-known publicist Alix Williamson was extremely enthusiastic, too, as was the Columbia Artists agency. But Schein's father turned down all of them, insisting that his daughter was too young to accept such offers. Later, manager Sol Hurok's important office played a major role in Schein's career.

Schein's Musical World

As a teenager, Schein stepped into a musical scene of international scope, one touched on by convoluted cold war politics that had sharply divided East and West, until the late 1950s brought an easing of relations between the Soviet Union and the United States—a *glasnost* most visible in the arts, which thrived on improved economic resources. In 1961, Schein made her first concert tour in Russia, which was in reality a tryout for possible management by Hurok.[34] The pianist's mother accompanied her.

Like that of other brilliant pianists, Schein's young and prodigious artistry, however, had arrived on the world stage of cutthroat competition, the heights of which Schein's teachers knew as concert pianists themselves. The reign of the pianist as superhero—celebrated men far outnumbering celebrated women—was dramatically intensifying in the years when Schein was growing up and preparing for building a professional career. Referring to this period, the longtime *New York Times* critic Harold Schonberg recalls, "[American] concert halls were swamped [by] very able young pianists, . . . unfortunately, apparently with no place to go."[35] Among those whom Schonberg singles out are, besides Van Cliburn (b. 1934), Artur Schnabel (1882–1951); Arthur Rubinstein (1887–1982); Vladimir Horowitz (1903–1989); Robert Casadesus (1899–1972); Rudolf Serkin (1903–1991); José Iturbi (1895–1980); Jorge Bolet (1914–1990); Sviatoslav Richter (1915-); Emil Gilels (1916–1985); Eugene Istomin (1925-); Leon Fleisher (1928-); Vladimir Ashkenazy (1937-); Gary Graffman (1928-); and Daniel Barenboim (1942-). Many of the younger pianists—those born in the 1920s (Leon Fleisher and Gary Graffman) and 1930s (Theodore Lettvin, Ivan Davis, Ralph Votapek, Malcolm Frager, and John Browning) were winning major national and international competitions by the 1950s and 1960s.

Nevertheless, the times were right for the idolization of promising young or already "proven" pianists. And along came the twenty-four-year-old American virtuoso Harvey Lavan "Van" Cliburn, whose public career (most prominently from 1958 to 1970) coincided with the critical stage of Schein's own career-building years. In 1958, Van Cliburn won Russia's prestigious Tchaikovsky Piano Competition, held in Moscow, "crowning" him prince of the keyboard. His immediate rise to fame, moreover, attracted the most influential managers and media coverage. His victory enabled him to slip into stardom on both sides of the iron curtain and to gain Sol Hurok (d. 1974) as perhaps the most powerful concert manager in America at the time. The winning of both the contest and Hurok (aided, some say, by Van Cliburn's handsome features and personal charisma) provided him with two key factors for success in winning a "great" career. In this era of music history, success hinged most closely on the power of managers to persuade the public and to fill a performance schedule on the world's most sought-after stages, including both solo recitals and appearances with leading orchestras.[36]

When Van Cliburn won the Tchaikovsky contest, Schein was an upward-bound eighteen-year-old: she had already entered the international professional scene, debuting in Mexico City in August 1957, playing the third Rachmaninoff one week, the first Tchaikovsky concerto the second week, and giving a solo recital the third week. And by the late 1950s (debuting in 1958 at the Pan American Union), she had chalked up a number of other public performances throughout Europe, having finished her studies according to Munz's schedule for her (at the onset of which he had tragically already stopped performing himself) by the time of Van Cliburn's stunning Moscow success.[37]

Schein's Place in the Piano World; Women Contemporaries

Schonberg's list of "great" pianists whose careers reached far into the twentieth century and—therefore into Schein's lifetime—is incomplete. Some important women pianists are missing. The following list includes many important women pianists not mentioned by Schonberg.

Older Stars of the "Big Time"

Schein's older contemporaries (listed chronologically) include Wanda Landowska (1877–1959), Rosina Lhevinne (1880–1976), Ania Dorfmann (1890–1982), Myra Hess (1890–1965), Clara Haskil (1895–1960), Guiomar Novaes (1895–1979), Amparo Iturbi (1898–1969), Gaby Casadesus (1901–1999), Lili Kraus (1903–1986), Sari Biro (1912–1990), Gina Bachauer (1913–1976), Rosalyn Tureck (1914–2003), Moura Lympany (1916–2005), and Alicia de Larrocha (1923–2009). Among Schein's younger contemporaries are (in alphabetical order) Martha Argerich, Lydia Artymiw, Jean M. Barr, Angela Cheng, Monique Duphil, Lidia (Lydia) Frumkin, Judith Gordon, Anne Koscielny, Katia and Marielle Labeque, Ruth Laredo (1937–2005), Anne-Marie McDermott, Barbara Nissman, Marilyn Neeley, Ursula Oppens, Rebecca Penneys, Navah Perlman, Karen Taylor, Frances Walker-Slocum, Diane Walsh, Janice Weber, and Juana Zayas. And there are others. Argerich, Laredo, and the two Labeques have won some attention by the press. The others are active now, at least in the United States, but, like Schein, deserve more serious attention.

When Schein's career and sociocultural surroundings are compared with those of other professionally accomplished women pianists of today, her place in this world ranks high. Though each woman's career path, of course, varies, some of the basic factors remain similar. All or most of them—like their male colleagues—began formal piano study in early childhood, many beginning under a mother's watchful eye. After the earliest stage, they moved on to pursue more advanced instruction by outstanding teachers in conservatories or university music schools, some eventually winning degrees at various levels. A number of them placed high in piano competitions, even winning other impressive honors and awards and becoming jurors themselves in adulthood. Many serve on university or conservatory faculties. All those in the "younger" group listed above remain active performers in solo appearances with first- or second-tier symphony orchestras, as solo recitalists, or members of chamber music groups. Repertoires among them vary widely, some concentrating on older, classical staples by tried-and-true "master" composers, some venturing into older or more recent contemporary fare, some focusing on music by three or four composers, and some presenting works from all of these areas. Interestingly, few or none of these pianists are recognized composers.

Schein belongs firmly in this world as both a performing artist and distinguished teacher. Like the other chapters in this book, this one, however, aims to inform the reader about her life—her family and the culture in its broadest sense—that she represents to allow a deeper understanding of her as an artist. Partly because of my observations as a critic and writer of program notes, this inquiry seeks to remedy the lack of biographical information published in historical and biographical accounts, program notes, press releases, and Internet biographies. These provide copious lists, for example, of the orchestras (and conductors) with which a performer has played, celebrated teachers, and (long) citations of recordings, competitions won, awards presented, and similar accounts. But where is even a little hint about their personal lives, that is, what factors affected their careers? Did these artists grow up in a family of professional musicians or in some sociocultural environment totally different from music? What kind of domestic scene surrounds them now—spouses, children? Do they have any other serious avocations, such as painting, mountain climbing? After all, even in program notes for a performance, the writer could throw in at least a smattering of such information; program notes often tend to be longwinded anyway. These factors could liven up otherwise standard historical annals by contributing to the whole picture of a musical artist, and perhaps show a difference from male pianists' careers even into the present. Have women musical artists typically set aside professional performance careers with continuous concert tours to teach at home and raise children?

Sari Biro and Martha Argerich

With the preceding perspective on key issues in mind, here are capsule summaries, but more detailed accounts, of two women pianists, one older and one younger contemporary of Schein: Sari Biro (1912–1990) and Martha Argerich (b. 1941). Both are foreign-born and made their mark largely in New York.

The Hungarian-born concert pianist Sari Biro is little remembered today, except by connoisseurs. Appearing as an orchestral soloist at an early age under conductor and renowned composer Ernst von Dohnanyi (1877–1960), she graduated with highest honors from Budapest's Franz Liszt Academy and played with many major European orchestras, such as the Berlin and Vienna philharmonics and the Orchestre nationale in Paris. Like composer Béla Bartók a year later, Biro left Nazi-dominated Europe in 1939, moving to New York. Pursuing her career there for eighteen years, she played on local television in the late 1940s, gave several Carnegie Hall recitals in the early 1950s, and debuted at Town Hall in 1940. At that time the *New York Herald Tribune* reported that she was "indubitably one of the most gifted pianists *of her sex*" (italics are the author's); a *New York Times* critic wrote, "Sari Biro must be reckoned among the foremost *women* (italics are the author's) exponents of the keyboard of the time." Maria Watts concludes that "seldom does a pianist elicit the unanimous acclaim that greeted this debut, which launched her career in America." (Biro's last New York recital took place in 1972 at Lincoln Center's Alice Tully Hall.) In 1947 Biro also gave a series of thirteen live half-hour recitals on a New York radio station, her programs ranging from Rameau and Scarlatti to Bartók, "who," Watts says, "particularly praised her interpretation of his works." In addition, Biro appeared with noted American orchestras, including the Chicago Symphony and the Philadelphia Orchestra. Becoming an American citizen in 1949, she gave the New York premieres of Milhaud's Concerto No. 2 and GianCarlo Menotti's Concerto. In that same year, Watts notes that Biro "became the only *woman* (italics are the author's) to perform nine piano concertos in a series of three concerts at Carnegie Hall. Every concert presented a piece from the classical era, introduced a 20th-century work, and concluded with a work from the Romantic repertoire."

(In the following comments, the italics are again the author's.)

From the mid-1950s, Biro lived in San Francisco and made frequent appearances up and down the West Coast. The press continued to praise her artistry, but typically did so in stereotypical gender-directed terms: for example, the *San Francisco Examiner* wrote, "One reason why the Menotti [Concerto] proved delightful was the *blonde* [italics mine] Miss Biro played it magnificently. . . ."; a Hartford daily remarked, "As much as it must irk Miss Biro to have it said of her, her technique is *man*-sized, as she amply demonstrated in ploughing up a fine Lisztian spray all over the keyboard last night. . . ."; and the *Burlington Free Press* colorfully commented that "her playing proved a surprise to a large part of the audience, which still held to the popular fallacy that there is no comparison between the playing of a *woman* and such *men* [italics mine] as Rubinstein. . . . This illusion was effectively and completely dispelled by the quality of Miss Biro's playing, . . . [for] she is capable of lifting the audience out of themselves and transporting them with her to the realm of pure music."[38]

Like Biro, Argentina-born pianist Martha Argerich is known more or less by only a limited segment of the general public—but for a different reason despite her active performance schedule today: she is known for her aversion to the press and other forms of publicity and is thus less prominent among general audiences.

Perhaps the *New Yorker* music critic Alex Ross has summed this up most tellingly: "Argerich reigns supreme over the feudalistic world of virtuoso pianists . . .," and she "brings to bear qualities that are seldom contained in one person: she is a pianist of brain-teasing technical agility; she is a charismatic woman with an enigmatic reputation; she is an unaffected interpreter whose native language is music. This last may be the quality that sets her apart. A lot of pianists play huge double octaves; a lot of pianists photograph well. But few have the unerring naturalness of phrasing that allows them to embody the music rather than interpret it."[39]

"Even in the few hours I [Ross] was with her, I caught a glimpse of her child-like temper . . . ; it flared . . . that is, she is notoriously difficult to pin down. She cancels concerts, even entire tours, at the last minute, changes programs at will, and generally drives the programming people crazy. She has become a substantial presence in New York in recent years, but only because her stardom has given her unprecedented latitude to schedule events on short notice. Some administrators attribute her antics to self-indulgent eccentricity." "These days [as of 2001]," Ross continues, "performers are expected to commit to 11 A.M. rehearsals in the year 2006. The result is a lockstep concert world in which New York debuts feel like the ratification of deals made years ago and celebrity initiatives have the momentum of continental drift. Argerich is driving a wedge into the system, as Sviatoslav Richter did before her, with his spur-of-the-moment piano happenings in towns scattered between the South of France and Siberia."

Argerich debuted at eight in Buenos Aires, playing Beethoven's Piano Concerto no. 1 in C Major; at nine, she performed Mozart's Concerto no. 20 in D Minor. K. 466. She began winning European competitions at sixteen. In Vienna, where her parents were Argentinian diplomats, she studied with teachers such as the renowned Austrian pianist and composer Friedrich Gulda. (But Argerich's personal life has not always gone smoothly. She has a daughter by each of her three husbands, the last being conductor Charles Dutoit. And melanoma that spread to her lungs forced her to stop smoking.)

One notes, however, that Argerich's public career continued to flourish in the same 1960s decade when Schein was building her career and when Van Cliburn and all the other stars of the piano world vied for the public's attention. In 1965, for example, the twenty-four-year-old Argerich won the seventh International Frederik Chopin Piano Competition in Warsaw, some of the press coupling praise for her brilliant playing, including her formidable technique, and her physical beauty. Gender bias, that is, had not yet been visibly challenged. At nineteen, she made her first recording—of Prokofiev and Liszt. Also a first was her initial recording of Chopin's works in 1966. Much more Chopin followed, and, in addition, her recordings won two Grammys. At twenty-five, she gave her first American performance at Lincoln Center, in New York.

After 1980, she presented few solo recitals and focused instead on performing concertos, chamber music, and accompanying instruments. She has also been directing an annual music festival in Japan and one in Italy, a yearly chamber music series in which old and untried works are presented.

Schein and Arthur Rubinstein (1887–1982)

After hearing Schein's solo recording of the third Rachmaninov concerto for Kapp records, the fabled pianist Arthur Rubinstein summoned her—accompanied by her parents—to New York to play for him. Consequently, in the following summer of 1961, she studied with the great pianist in Paris. In summer 1962, Rubinstein again invited her to study with him in the French capital and then in Lucerne, Switzerland, during his family vacation. During the Lucerne weeks, Rubinstein arranged with the local piano dealer for her practicing needs. And he often visited her at those times to encourage her. She remembers her small pension there and took two lessons a week. Between those two summers, Schein spent Christmas and New Year's Eve, 1961, recording Rachmaninoff's Third Piano Concerto and Chopin's Piano Concerto no. 2 in F Minor, Op. 21, with Eugene Goossens conducting the Vienna Philharmonic Orchestra in the Austrian capital's historic, spectacularly gilded Musikverein.

As a result of the 1961 successful Vienna recording (Kapp) of the Rachmaninoff, Patrick Hayes, who had already presented Schein himself in important concerts in Washington's burgeoning cultural scene, introduced her to the powerful and influential Russian-born American impresario Sol Hurok (1888–1974). Hurok soon became Schein's manager.[40]

Also during the early 1960s, the State Department in Washington—with Hayes's recommendation—chose Schein to participate as an American artist in a cultural exchange. (Hurok's office disapproved of this assignment.) But Schein consequently played overseas concerts in more than fifty-five countries from 1964 to 1975, recalling recently that she "gained a tremendous education from this experience in the international arts world." "For my first State Department tour in Asia," Schein continues, "my airline ticket was inches thick because it was to cover six weeks and many destinations."

The year 1962 was an especially exciting one for Schein. Her second summer of study with Rubinstein included lessons in both Paris and Lucerne. Although his wife, Nela, had anticipated that summer would be strictly a family occasion when her husband had some unscheduled time, Schein reflects, "Nela cooperated and proved to be a great friend, accompanying Rubinstein to my Carnegie Hall appearance." The summer of 1962 in Lucerne was an extraordinary one for expanding Schein's repertoire. She also enjoyed such experiences as turning pages for a trio made up of violinist Isaac Stern, pianist Eugene Istomin, and cellist Leonard Rose—all of them renowned virtuosos. (They referred to Rubinstein, Schein relates with a smile, as "the old man.")

During this second summer with Rubinstein, Schein worked on Franz Schubert's profound late Piano Sonata in B-flat Major, D. 960. As she notes, "My study of this music had begun when Rubinstein said to me, 'bring the score of the

Schubert sonata, and we'll go through it together.' He himself was very affected by this piece."[41]

In 1962, Schein made her Carnegie Hall debut, her performance being presented by Hurok.[42] "Ann Schein could take her place among the leading woman pianists in an amazingly short time." (Miles Kastendieck, the *New York Journal-American,* in a review of Schein's Carnegie Hall debut in March 1962.) On March 29, 1962, *New York Times* critic Ross Parmenter wrote a balanced account of this recital, carefully weighing the plusses and minuses in a commendably constructive way for the twenty-two-year-old pianist, prefacing his observations with "word of her talents had spread [judging by her] large audience." In her playing of Beethoven's "Les Adieux" Sonata, no. 26, Op. 81a, Parmenter noted, "There was no question of her poetic sensibility," although "some of her *fortes* sounded punched and the articulation was not always perfect where both speed and volume were required." Parmenter summed up his reaction to Schein's performance of Robert Schumann's *Davidsbündlertänze,* in which, he said, "she did her finest playing in her most demanding selection," Parmenter adding that "within her admirable technical framework, there was much that was imaginative, beautiful and expressive." Of Dimtri Kabalevsky's Sonata no. 3, the critic praised her "fluency" but then commented that in this work "she sometimes appeared to be playing through something she knew like a streak, rather than performing something she was deeply engaged in." He concluded, "But she is certainly gifted, and it will be interesting to watch her development."

Even into 1963, Schein's American career seemed to proceed splendidly. Conductors and other foremost musical artists, as well as audiences, were astounded almost unanimously by her virtuosity. Listeners were moved especially by her deeply introspective approach, a quality remaining distinctly hers.

Schein appeared with the BBC Orchestra and the London Philharmonic at the famous Proms concerts for the three traditional "Last Nights" events; and she performed with orchestras in Holland, Sweden, and Norway every year. In 1963, Schein also debuted in Akron, Ohio, with the Cleveland Symphony Orchestra in Chopin's Concerto no. 2, led by conductor George Szell's young assistant, James Levine. Levine also conducted Schein's Cleveland concerts in 2003. Schein recalls that playing those concerts was an "exciting experience," adding that, besides Levine's brilliance (he had been a student of the famous piano pedagogue Rosina Lhevinne), he was "cute and funny." Both performances received good reviews; and, for the 1964–1965 concert season, Hurok's publicity brochure listed Schein among his leading roster of pianists, including Arthur Rubinstein, Sviatoslav Richter, Emil Gilels, Van Cliburn, Gina Bachauer, Byron Janis, John Ogdon, Eugene Istomin, Daniel Barenboim, Ralph Votapek, and the duo Luboshutz and Nemenoff.

But Schein's professional life did not always go smoothly. She remembers particularly that the second half of her Carnegie Hall recital in 1963 got "terrible reviews." Here, she recalls, "I was feeling worn out with my repertoire and concerned that my career was beginning to lag, for the Hurok agency was not booking enough concerts for me." The year 1963 was also clouded for a different reason. On one Sunday afternoon, Schein gave a recital in Plymouth, England, afterward asking her hosts, "to see the storied English moors." For many people, a request such as this one conjures up visions of dark, stormy nights in scenes of desolation, as English mystery novels typically depict them. Her wish was granted, the pianist being treated to dinner on a nearby moor. "But afterwards," she discloses, "my ride back to my hotel proved quite misfortunate, because the driver had consumed too much ale, the car crashing into a ditch in that coal-black landscape." As a result, Schein broke her left wrist. Back in the States, both her parents told her to "locate the best London surgeon." Despite her wrist being encased in a cast for the next six weeks—though her fingers could move—she proceeded as originally scheduled, giving three major performances. The first one, under Hurok's management (which was unaware of her wrist mishap), took place at the Ravinia Music Festival, the summer home of the Chicago Symphony Orchestra. With Seiji Ozawa conducting, Schein played Beethoven's Concerto no. 1, Op. 15, followed by Tchaikovsky's Piano Concerto in B-flat, Op. 23, no. 1 at the Hollywood Bowl with the Los Angeles Philharmonic under Maurice Abravanel (1903–1993). She played Schumann's Concerto in A Minor, Op. 54, at the Dell, the summer residence of the Philadelphia Orchestra. Schein's conductor was Joseph Rosenstock (1895–1985). Yet, Schein remembers, "between 1963 and 1967, I had few other American concerts. But I enjoyed them despite the modest performance spaces I had to play in."

As noted earlier in this chapter, no small factor operating at this time was the formidable competition that Schein faced from a host of other virtuoso concert pianists under Hurok and other agencies. Even today, Schein feels, "this was the beginning of the end of my career development in the United States, though it was still flourishing in England, South America, and Asia, where I had lots of successful concerts," she notes. And, she added, "The United States State Department was still supporting my international tours." Schein, that is, was one of a number of American pianists who were relatively little recognized or promoted in their homeland, but much acclaimed internationally.[43]

In post–World War II America, there were other reasons for Schein's situation. A burgeoning host of American pianists, Schonberg notes, typically had "studied with foreign-born teachers with their nineteenth-century repertoire." But some American performers had begun to refocus their repertoire to include contemporary fare, hoping in this way to attract added attention from managers and audiences.[44] In this era, Schein remarks, "My repertoire [like Munz's] was focused on earlier music."

Enter Earl Carlyss

"At the lowest point in my American career," Schein recounts, "Earl Carlyss, my beloved husband-to-be, best friend, and profound artist, entered my life."[45] On October 13, 1966, while Schein was preparing for the rigors of a second six-week Russian tour, she first met her future spouse "out of the blue," she relates. Schein had attended a concert by the Juilliard Quartet, the longtime resident ensemble at the Library of Congress. Schein's friend, pianist William Masselos (b. 1920), especially admired for his championing of contemporary music, had invited her to the performance. (Schein notes with amusement that he watched the musicians through his binoculars.) After the concert, Masselos took her to a post-concert reception for the quartet at a private home, where she met and talked with Carlyss, the group's new second violinist, for the first time. After that time, the two kept in communication by letters and phone calls.

Providence continued to shape their romance. In the spring of 1966, Carlyss had embarked with the Juilliard group on his first tour with the quartet, an extensive one including a series of concerts throughout the Far East. (When he had joined the Juilliard group earlier that year, Carlyss had had to learn forty quartets in a very short time.) By sheer chance, in May 1966, Schein arrived in Hong Kong just two weeks after Earl had played there. In her six-week tour of Asia, Schein also gave recitals in many of the places where the Juilliard musicians had just played. As Schein relates, concert manager Maple Quon, who made the arrangements for every visiting artist's concerts in Hong Kong, always brought each performer to her home. After Schein's recital in the city, Quon treated her to "a wonderful dinner at the host's luxurious house." By the end of that evening, Quon, whom Schein calls "a fortuitous matchmaker," confidently proclaimed to the young pianist, "I have found your husband-to-be, who will be the love of your life." As Schein's future proved, Quon had shown amazingly keen foresight.

The late 1960s brought Schein both momentous personal losses and unbounded, if unexpected, joys. In June 1967, her father died of cancer at Washington's George Washington University Hospital. At her father's death, Schein's mother sold the family home on Bancroft Place, resettling in an apartment nearby on Massachusetts Avenue. She made the move, however, while very ill, "although," Schein sadly recalls, "we knew not what malady was consuming her body." For Betty Schein, whom Schein characterizes as a "brave stoic, who never consulted a doctor," staunchly adhered to her Christian Science belief to the end of her life.

In December 1968, after Schein had given a concert in Los Alamos, New Mexico, her sister Linda called with the message that their mother had died, at age fifty-seven, in a Christian Science nursing home in New England without any medical help. Schein recollects that "no one at this facility told me the cause of her illness and death." Thus, at the age of twenty-eight, Schein had lost in quick succession both parents—her loving protectors and artistic supporters. In addition, she was, she says, "unceremoniously dismissed by Hurok," his agent Walter Prude having told her, "You have the wrong personality" for an artist whom Hurok would sponsor.

At this crucial personal and professional stage in her life, Schein now was without her vital longtime role model—her mother, who had supported and encouraged her in her career to the extent no other person ever could. And this loss had followed the death of her father only a year and a half earlier. Numerous studies done over the last few years have emphasized the impact of role models in women's—like men's—careers to develop women's own positive self-image as professionally successful. Perhaps most true in musical composition, women's self-image has fallen far short of men's largely because relatively few women composers in the historical past had their music recognized and published. Even their names are largely unlisted in written records, forcing historians to discover their existence from "asides" in secondary sources. In short, there has been little or no preserved record of their professional success to take pride in and, therefore, relatively few role models to impel new careers. But Schein's parents had been aware and experienced in the ways, including the hazards, of the professional musical world. They chose the course of study she should follow, adapted her growing-up years to fit that kind of training, and found the best teachers to advance her position as a concert pianist in the most important professional musical circuits of the mid-twentieth century.

In the summer of 1968, Schein played her third Proms Concert in England— this one with an orchestra under the baton of the famed English conductor Colin Davis (b. 1927). And, for the first time, Earl was able to come to London and hear her play publicly. Also in 1968, Schein and Polish violinist Wanda Wilkonirsha were recording two violin sonatas of Sergei Prokofiev for producer Alan Silver's Connoisseur Society. Earl worked on this music with her. "Both of us," Schein remembers, "felt another force at play. It was our first teamwork" (fig. 29).

At Easter in 1969, Schein recalls, "I spent a couple of days with Earl's parents, who coincidently lived in White Plains, where I was born." After that, she remembers, "we saw each other a lot." And, with a smile, Schein added, "Earl wasn't one to hesitate—especially in view of his Juilliard Quartet schedule and the coming Aspen summer. We were married at the First Baptist Church at my birthplace, White Plains, New York, on May 24, 1969—a beautiful morning." Carlyss's father presided over the couple's wedding service.

To accommodate a large number of widely scattered family members and friends invited for the wedding, the couple arranged two receptions: the first in White Plains, followed by a second at the Cosmos Club in Washington, D.C., the city being Schein's home for over two decades. Her longtime friend and acclaimed soprano Jessye Norman, with whom Schein would collaborate on

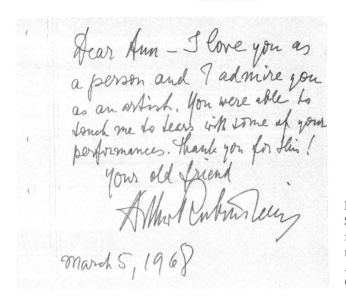

Dear Ann — I love you as a person and I admire you as an artist. You were able to touch me to tears with some of your performances. Thank you for this!

Your old friend

Arthur Rubinstein

March 5, 1968

Figure 29. Note to Schein, March 5, 1968, from her former teacher, pianist Arthur Rubinstein. Courtesy of Schein.

international concert tours three decades later, sang Robert Schumann's profoundly intimate song cycle *Frauen Liebe und Leben,* but she omitted the final heart-wrenching song (as inappropriate for such a joyous occasion). In addition, the Juilliard Quartet surprised Carlyss (the violist's wife substituting for him), playing the slow movement of a quartet by Felix Mendelssohn.

Along with her sheer happiness at marrying Earl, this life-changing rite of passage coupled her professional with her personal life. While, on the one hand, she felt that "this was a low time in my career," as she puts it, she quickly adds, "I firmly believe that when we married, Earl, with his joyous outlook on life and music and his irrepressible wit, had arrived in my life at just the right moment." Nevertheless, much uncertainty lay ahead of her in pursuing the profession of a concert pianist without an official manager—and without her devoted parents. Schein reflects, however, that Munz, who had meticulously carried out his "five-year plan" for her, reacted bitterly to her marriage, his resentment extending over several years. Understandably, Schein's Peabody teacher had placed his hopes and dreams on Schein's achieving a concert career by the later 1960s. Perhaps he even felt that, with Schein's marriage, he had again "failed." Yet, even with marriage and raising two children, Schein always emphasizes, "I have never stopped playing." In fact, she adds, "Munz's inexhaustible energy has prevailed in my professional outlook." And her husband has continued to support her career and encouraged her to believe in her musical strengths.

Earl Carlyss (b. 1939)

"Surely, the same angelic being who placed me in the safety of that Schein family in Evanston, Illinois," Schein firmly believes, "also saw to it that I was given an equally miraculous husband—violin and all."[46] With her marriage to Carlyss, Schein had won the heart of a virtuoso violinist, a prodigious musical artist in his own right. She also won the talents of an extraordinary raconteur (like herself), for Earl can describe the professional world and life itself with an uncanny mixture of enlightening perceptions and sardonic humor. But, up to his wedding day, this violinist's life had followed a course somewhat different from Schein's, though ultimately their union proved a perfect fit. Earl's life and career became an integral part of Schein's "story."[47]

At the time of this writing, besides his twenty years with the Juilliard String Quartet, Carlyss directs the freshman string quartet survey course at the Juilliard School, while also heading the Aspen Center for Advanced Quartet Studies since 1984.[48] In addition, he frequently performs with Schein and appears as well in numerous chamber music concerts.

Earl Carlyss was born in Chicago on October 27, 1939—only a few days before Schein's birth. Equally coincidentally, both Carlysses can trace some of their early past to Chicago roots. Because Earl's Swedish-born father, Simon Paul Carlyss (his name having been changed from Karlson), had dedicated his pastorate to strengthening a succession of church congregations spread across the country, Earl grew up in a series of different homes, moving more than twenty times to different cities. The moves had a positive effect on Earl's later life, for, as he once told this author, "I have always done things on the fly." And this was someone who, as a member of the Juilliard Quartet, in fact, would one day be constantly on the move following challenging concert tour schedules, some concert seasons totaling as many as 120 performances.

Earl's strongly religious parents, like Schein's, nevertheless managed to provide a stable and supportive home environment in a family of three sons, "even though," Earl remarks, "we lived on a shoestring. But I didn't know that. I just went along with it." In fact, Earl's mother, Evelyn Daniels Carlyss, whom he describes as being "full of adrenaline," made all the family's clothes, having relinquished—in the age-old tradition—hopes for a career as a concert pianist in favor of her family responsibilities. (She had studied with Julie Rivé King, who herself had studied with Franz Liszt in Weimar.) At the same time, as Schein describes her, "she was a phenomenal pianist, even further gifted as a virtuosic improviser."[49]

Contrasting his childhood with Schein's, Earl relates that he did not begin violin lessons until he was ten. In fact, as Earl remarks, "I had a relatively casual start in preparation for a professional career. One day, when we were living in Pasadena, California, my father offhandedly suggested to me, then ten years old, that I study the violin." "My mother," Carlyss remarks, "then placed me first with Abram Goldfarb for violin lessons. She accompanied me from the beginning of my studies, and her sense of discipline was a good thing." Carlyss recalls Goldfarb warmly, remembering his mentor as "a free spirit and a teacher who inspired me." And, only ten months after starting lessons, Carlyss won a "Search for Talent," an important local competition for young musicians. By the age of twelve or thirteen, he was studying in Pasadena with the noted violinist Vera Barstaw, whose mentoring included a solid technical grounding.

At sixteen, Earl skipped his senior year in high school, crossing the Atlantic to study violin with Roland Charmy and chamber music with Jacques Février at the Paris Conservatoire for two years. (At that time, the Carlysses had moved to Europe also, establishing themselves in his father's Swedish birthplace.) The celebrated Conservatoire and the intense cultural life of the French capital itself opened Earl's eyes to a vast new world. Because only French was spoken at the school, Carlyss says, "I had to learn a lot of French fast, and in addition the Conservatoire brought me my first encounter with advanced solfège." (This is an ancient method of musical ear training, cultivated fastidiously by the French, teachers using the syllables *do-re-mi-fa-sol-la-ti-do.*) Earl recounts, "I was compelled to solfège everything and worked hard to keep up with the precocious students there." But, he admits, "by the time I entered Juilliard, my ear training was in great shape."

"I had a hard lifestyle as a student in Paris," Earl admits. "More than once, I had food poisoning, and, in January and February 1956, Paris had its coldest winter in a century." In the first year, he shared a tiny apartment with his mother and younger brother, a tympani student at the American School in Paris. "But by the next year," Carlyss relates, "my family had left the city, and I lived in Paris alone there, while the strenuous amount of work assigned me by my Conservatoire classes almost took its toll on my health." Nevertheless, Carlyss won the Conservatoire's Premier Prix in his first year at the school.

Paris also offered Carlyss wonderful musical opportunities. Discounted student tickets were typically available to him as to other students, gaining him easy entrance to countless concerts with outstanding performers. "My drinking up the intense, even crazy, musical life of Paris," Earl continues, "brought my musical awakening." Time after time, in the city's concert season, as Carlyss puts it, "I had to choose between as many as five concerts to attend in a given day, and I heard fabulous artists, such as the violinists Jascha Heifetz and Zino Francescatti."

After his two years at the Conservatoire, Earl gained admission to the equally prestigious Juilliard School of Music at a time that he calls "the school's golden years." There he studied with the renowned violinist and teacher Ivan Galamian (1903–1981) and took classes with such important American composers as William Schuman (1910–1992) and Vincent Persichetti (1915–1987).[50] Carlyss also won the Juilliard's Epstein Prize, and graduated in 1964 with two degrees earned simultaneously: both a bachelor's and master's degree in music. He was appointed concertmaster of the New York City Ballet in December 1964. Only one year later, Rafael Hillyer, the Juilliard Quartet's violist, invited Carlyss to rehearse with them. A week after the audition, Hillyer called Earl to rehearse with the group. "At a rehearsal only two weeks later in 1966," Earl recalls, "I was offered and easily accepted the position of second violinist. I was stunned by this sudden turn of events."

Soon after this, he took his first Juilliard tour, playing sixty concerts of forty different works in the United States alone. Earl's intensive preparation served him well. His capacity to assume new responsibilities at a lightning-quick pace (as he phrases it, "on the fly") would prove inestimably valuable in his new Juilliard position and also for such future hurdles as balancing family and professional commitments, as countless musical artists know well.

Two Artists Merge

With her marriage, Schein smiles, "I became a 'quartet wife,' and I loved every minute of it."[51] "During our first year together," she continues, "I easily dropped the piano, even traveling with the Juilliard on tour in Europe." For the couple's first summer together (in 1969), Ann again joined Earl, this time at Colorado's noted Aspen Music Festival and School, where the Juilliard Quartet was in residence, performing and teaching. The couple has spent almost every summer since then—for a while with their two infant daughters. ("During these early Aspen summers," Schein notes, "I did not perform or teach there, but traveled abroad from there to play concerts." In 1984 she was appointed an Aspen artist-faculty member, while Carlyss was offered the directorship of the advanced quartet program.)

Motherhood

In 1970, Schein received two messages: the first was an invitation "out of the blue" to give concerts in Russia, she remembers, followed by a second invitation to perform at two important English festivals at Bath and Cheltenham. The English summons based its acceptance on the daunting condition that she play nine Beethoven sonatas—with a deadline of six months until the performances. Up to that time, she had performed only one of the Beethovens: the "Appassionata." "It was truly a challenging time," she admits, recalling having to learn the other eight sonatas with such a close deadline. She was consequently preparing a telegram to decline the invitation to England. But as Schein relates, Carlyss intervened, saying "of course you will learn this music. We'll do it together." "After all," Schein continues, "Earl had been playing whole cycles of Beethoven quartets with the Juilliard." With that assurance, she cabled back to England her acceptance of the offer. "And then," she notes, "Earl and I had a wonderful time. I had begun to tire of my repertoire—almost with a sense of boredom. But, after working on the Beethoven sonatas, I knew I would never have another boring period in my life." As for her Beethoven performances in the decades since 1971, Joe Banno, a contributing critic for the *Washington Post,* once told this author, "No one can play Beethoven to equal Schein."

After sending her acceptance to perform in England, Schein proceeded to Bath and Cheltenham. But, by the time she had played one concert, Schein recalls, "I realized I was pregnant—thrilling news." Yet, in Schein's words, "the concerts went okay, considering that performing at this festival (in a program including eight Beethoven sonatas) was a brand-new thing for me."

Due, nevertheless, to signs of a possible miscarriage, Schein continues, "The doctor told me to go to bed and not perform." Citing "professional commitment," however, Schein—in spite of the doctor's order—went on to perform nine Beethoven sonatas, including the "Appassionata." "Only three days later," she relates, "I played the Rachmaninoff's Concerto, no. 3, with Charles Groves—a great conductor."[52]

Yet Carlyss reacted differently to the situation, Schein explains. "Earl was shattered at the risk involved since I was pregnant," Schein notes, adding, "so I canceled two weeks of upcoming performances in Yugoslavia, remaining in England and in bed for several weeks." In January 1971, Schein gave birth in White Plains, New York, to Linnea Elizabeth Carlyss, a healthy newborn.[53] "But," Schein notes with a touch of regret, "the birth took place while Earl was in San Francisco on tour with the Juilliard, although he did come home two days after Linnea was born." Carlyss also had to miss the birth of Pauline, the Carlysses' second daughter. Things smoothed out, however, for with Linnea's birth, Schein remembers, "Earl and I were living in New York City in a top-floor apartment with a baby and a piano, and that was fine since I wasn't playing all that much."

Thus in the space of only four years, from 1967 to 1971, Schein had endured the loss of both parents, had married, and had given birth to her first child—dramatic changes in her personal life. And the following two years brought further challenges. In 1972, Schein and Carlyss moved from their New York apartment to a house in White Plains directly across the street from the home of Earl's parents. As noted earlier, it was by chance at White Plains that Schein had been born, had married, and had given birth to their first daughter—in the same hospital where she had been born. In April 1973, Schein gave birth to Pauline without sedation. "I had been in the final stages of labor with Pauline," Schein relates, "while the Juilliard Quartet was giving a live broadcast (one of many over the decades) in Washington at the Library of Congress. But the quartet quickly reversed the order of the program so that Earl had to play only in the first half of the concert, arriving in time to see our one-hour-old Pauline."

The first years of motherhood for Schein were far from easy. The Juilliard Quartet's many concert tours often kept Carlyss away from home for lengthy periods, "leaving me," Schein remembers, "feeling that I had been left, as a 'single parent,' in an impossible situation caring for an infant and toddler. Earl's parents, though, willingly helped me during these years."

"Since Earl was so frequently away on tour with the quartet," Schein admits, "I also felt that my role as a musician could not be continued as before." But, she remembers that Carlyss encouraged her to keep on performing. And she did to some degree, including Elliot Carter's complex piano sonata in her programs.

As we have seen in many cases cited in the earlier chapters of this book, gifted women musical artists for generations have traded their professional careers for the responsibilities and demands of marriage and motherhood. Chief *Washington Post* music critic Tim Page offered telling insight in an interview with this author in 2007. Referring generally to women in music working to build a professional career at the same time they are faced with family roles such as motherhood, Page remarked, "It's tough for women to have a career and family—more than for men, though that's changing now."

By 1975, the Carlyss family had sold their White Plains house and moved with the two children to Scarsdale, New York. "At that point," Schein happily reflects, "we began a golden era for both of us. There was a good public school there, so we passed some idyllic years until 1986, when we moved to Baltimore. I was totally into being my daughters' 'school mom.' I did car pools, play dates, music lessons, and I loved it."

"Even while Earl was playing with the Juilliard Quartet," Schein further relates, "Earl was a wonderful parent when he was at home," she says, adding that "at such times, he did car pools, too, and attended our children's school concerts. And he called us every day while on concert tours." "Deep down," Schein emphasizes, "he was a true homebody dad. And I was more the gypsy—I think I loved traveling more than Earl." In Schein's opinion, "the girls worship their father and are proud of him."

One Era Yields to Another

In 1975, Munz had a heart attack, and he died the following year. While he had been recuperating, however, Schein and Carlyss brought their children along to visit him every day at a rehabilitation center in White Plains. Schein recalls those times with a touch of sadness, remembering, "He was sweet to both of us because he had finally realized how important my family was in my life." "His reconciliation with Earl," she says, "was especially welcome, for it contrasted dramatically with his previous years of bitterness over our marriage." "At one time in the past," Schein confesses, "Munz had even rebuked Earl directly, charging him, 'How dare you take Ann away from me.'" "And he had made a dramatic exit from his teaching studio whenever Earl would pop in to say hello, for Earl understood and nevertheless continued his visits." Munz's behavior was just a telling sign of his intense attachment to his onetime star student, Schein firmly believes. However, Munz still harbored deep down a feeling of despondency because, at the time of her marriage, Schein had not been as fortunate in her public musical career in the way Munz had carefully planned many years before.

Ironically, during that same year, Schein notes, "Earl and I decided that I would again play at Carnegie Hall as my return to a major New York concert hall." Schein's program included compositions by Chopin, Beethoven, Gottschalk, von Weber, and Elliott Carter. But, disappointingly, Schein says, "the recital got only a fair reception." The *New York Times* critic Donal Henahan, Schein recalls, "was not ebullient. He said that I was okay, but not great, and he characterized my selection of works as 'bland and a too eclectic mix.'" Schein also remembers that "the *New York Times* continued to be difficult, hindering my further career push at that time."

Alix Williamson Steps In (1978–1981)

> "Schein is beyond the everyday great."
> (*Die Welt*, Berlin)

Enter Alix Williamson, whom Schein rates as "New York's premier publicist of her day, . . . and, in fact, the most important figure in public relations for musicians for forty years." (The following story has a personal history, too.) She had long been encouraging Schein professionally, following her career from the pianist's early years. Williamson and her husband had come to the Lewisohn concert, after which, Schein remembers, "she had asked to be my personal representative"—although Schein's father had said that she was "too young" to have a manager, as noted earlier. By 1978—only two years after Schein's return to Carnegie Hall—Williamson suggested presenting Schein in a Chopin cycle at Alice Tully Hall in New York's Lincoln Center arts complex for an entire concert year.[54] The event would be the first cycle of Chopin's piano music to be given in New York in thirty-five years.

But Schein had to think things through, for up to this time she had felt indecisive about her professional future, realizing regretfully, she said, that "Earl had been bearing the burden of supporting me in the difficult times and aspects of my career. Also, we would have to borrow the money to finance such a gigantic project." With these thoughts in mind, Schein admitted spending two years vacillating about doing the cycle at all. But, no doubt with a touch of exasperation, Alix ultimately "demanded a response from me. So I finally agreed to do it. I had now become convinced that her determination would rekindle my career and give it a vital new sense of direction by bringing me to the attention of New York's limitless audiences and attracting a new manager." To accomplish this, Williamson then proceeded to schedule the Chopin cycle officially at Tully, arranging for one recital a month throughout the 1980–1981 season. "Williamson's exuberance, personal warmth, and confidence in my artistry," Schein relates, "had given me a vision, hope, and, with that, a renewed self-image."

"Alix took over everything to do with the Chopin cycle," Schein recalls, "even telling me what I should wear for the performances." "She further insisted," Schein continues, "that I perform all twenty-four of Chopin's etudes—I had never played eight of them—as the last of the six concerts, and that I was to offer other works besides those for piano solo." Carlyss and Schein accordingly decided to program chamber music, songs, and concertos.

Schein then spent two years preparing specifically for the cycle and giving trial concerts. But Schein adds, "I was still unsure about playing this music on such a scale in New York." "At the same time," she adds, "getting ready for the cycle was a deep artistic experience and I had constant support—plus a final burst of encouragement from Rubinstein in preparing for it." "Strangely," she muses, "I felt that I was actually living with Chopin." And she told Joel Krosnick, the celebrated longtime cellist of the Juilliard Quartet and one of her collaborators in the Chopin cycle, that she "felt alive doing this cycle." Krosnick responded, "We have to keep you that way." Schein also reflects that she is certain that "doing that cycle (which played to a sold-out house for all six concerts) deepened all my musical senses." All and all, she views this era in her life "as a life-embracing artistic period" (fig. 30).

"Even our neighbors on our Scarsdale street," Schein adds, "were supportive of me. And both our young daughters came to all of the Tully Hall concerts equipped

Figure 30. Schein. Press release for her six-concert Chopin cycle, New York, Tully Hall, Lincoln Center, 1980–1981. Courtesy of Schein.

ANN SCHEIN
Pianist

with books and crayons. When Linnea saw me walk onto the stage for the first recital, Earl said she said lovingly to him, 'We have to help Mommy.'" In fact, at one of the solo Chopin recitals, the Carlyss daughters (Linnea would have been around nine and Pauline about seven years old) were seen happily by this author skipping along during intermission with Earl and wearing long pastel dresses.

Among the critics' raves that Schein received was that of a young New York critic, Tim Page, who told this writer that he "first heard Schein play in her Chopin cycle in New York City in 1980–81." "I went to a lot of concerts in this series, and I never forgot Schein's playing." But critic Donal Henahan wrote in the *New York Times* that, in the Chopin cycle, Schein played "a tedious recital of all one composer's music, and it [her performance] lacked character." Despite this response, however, Schein remained undaunted, commenting, "After I read Henahan's review the next morning, I was confident that he was wrong, because all the other reviews were 100 percent positive."[55] Reflecting further, Schein adds, "in fact, this series began a whole new era for me as a pianist" (fig. 31).

New Horizons: Joining the Peabody Faculty (1980–2001)

"I have to teach, or my breath is taken away."[56]

Meanwhile, even as the Chopin cycle was underway, the Peabody Conservatory of the Johns Hopkins University in Baltimore appointed Schein to its piano faculty as an artist teacher. She was filled with sentiment as she returned to her alma

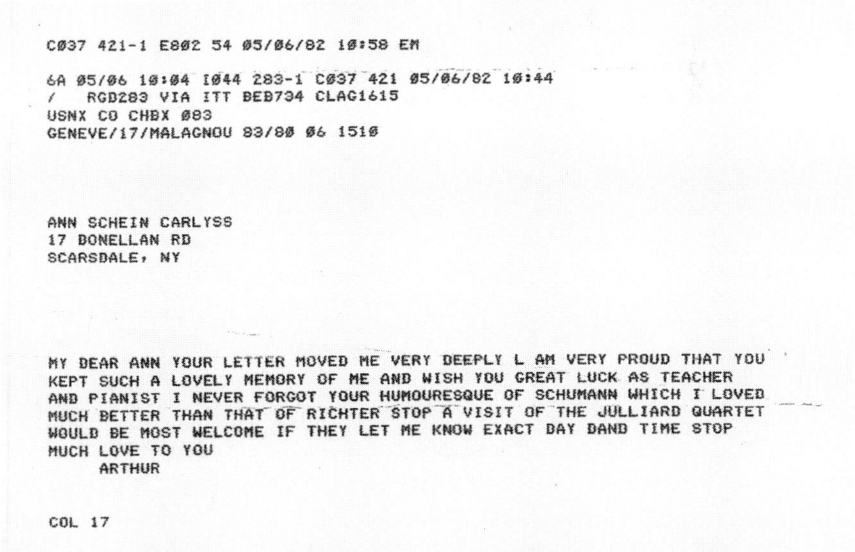

```
C037 421-1 E802 54 05/06/82 10:58 EM

6A 05/06 10:04 I044 283-1 C037 421 05/06/82 10:44
/    RGD283 VIA ITT BEB734 CLAG1615
USNX C8 CHBX 083
GENEVE/17/MALAGNOU 83/80 06 1510



ANN SCHEIN CARLYSS
17 DONELLAN RD
SCARSDALE, NY



MY DEAR ANN YOUR LETTER MOVED ME VERY DEEPLY L AM VERY PROUD THAT YOU
KEPT SUCH A LOVELY MEMORY OF ME AND WISH YOU GREAT LUCK AS TEACHER
AND PIANIST I NEVER FORGOT YOUR HUMOURESQUE OF SCHUMANN WHICH I LOVED
MUCH BETTER THAN THAT OF RICHTER STOP A VISIT OF THE JULLIARD QUARTET
WOULD BE MOST WELCOME IF THEY LET ME KNOW EXACT DAY DAND TIME STOP
MUCH LOVE TO YOU
        ARTHUR


COL 17
```

Figure 31. Telegram to Schein, June 5, 1982, from Rubinstein. Courtesy of Schein.

mater, where, only two decades earlier, she had studied with Munz. With this new opportunity in Baltimore, moreover, came an outpouring of more requests for Schein to give concerts.

The steps by which Schein adjusted herself and her family life to teaching at Peabody is a story in itself. Her involvement with the school and her students began rather modestly, teaching only part-time. Recalling her first year as a faculty member at Peabody, Schein notes, "In 1980, I began going to Baltimore and returning home the same day." "But," she says, "Peabody turned out to be another turning-point in my life. It took only teaching one student for me to explode with excitement, for each student was a different challenge."

"At first, I left Pauline in pajamas in the morning to go to Baltimore, returning the same day. But the next year was more difficult, for by then I had ten students, each for an hour, so I had to begin staying overnight, a situation hard for Pauline. When the number rose to nineteen students for the third year of teaching, I had to stay in Baltimore even longer. Yet, in those early years at Peabody, I was pretty much with my girls, aside from the teaching."

As time went on, the course of the Carlysses' lives continued to change, both musicians adapting to new circumstances but always taking account of their family's personal needs—even in the face of intense professional pressures. In 1986, Carlyss made the momentous decision to retire from the Juilliard Quartet, although he was at the height of his career with this ensemble. His two decades with the prestigious ensemble had brought a rigorous schedule of performances. The quartet's national and international tours, as noted previously, often took the players away from their families for extended periods. At the time of his retirement from the quartet, moreover, Earl told this author that he wanted more time with his family than he had had in his years with the Juilliard, noting regretfully that "I was never with Ann at the birth of my two daughters."

More professional advancements further tightened family cohesion. In 1986, the year of his retirement from the Juilliard, Carlyss was appointed to the Peabody Conservatory artist faculty, holding the school's first Sidney Friedberg Chair in Chamber Music. Because Schein had already been teaching at the Peabody since 1980, Carlyss's faculty appointment there dictated that the family would move to a new home in Stevenson, Maryland, in the Baltimore area. Also, the Carlyss daughters were growing up. "They were great teenagers," Schein notes, "in fact, by Linnea's junior high years, she had already won awards in piano, violin, and oboe. And Pauline was playing the flute and piccolo. At Friends School in Baltimore, Linnea also sang high soprano (with perfect pitch) and won lead roles in many musicales such as *Babes in Arms* and *The Music Man*. After a year at the University of Indiana, Linnea transferred to the University of Maryland and studied voice with noted singer Linda Mabbs."

Pauline, the Carlysses' younger daughter, "has much musical talent, too," Schein says proudly. Pauline graduated from Johnson and Wales University in

Providence, Rhode Island, where she was a Golden Quill Society honoree. Her work involves the travel industry—appropriate, given her parents' careers and concert tours.

Aspen

Along with her position at Peabody, Schein's Aspen summers took a new turn in 1984 when she was appointed as an artist-faculty member of the Aspen Music Festival and School. From 2007 to 2009, she held the prestigious Victoria and Ronald Simms Chair, awarded for teaching. Carlyss's appointment to the directorship of Aspen's quartet program intensified the Carlysses' professional scene. As head of the quartet program, Carlyss auditions and awards Aspen fellowships to an average of three young quartets each summer. "These are exceptionally promising young string players. Many of them have eventually formed such ensembles as the Shanghai and Calder string quartets." Schein adds, "Music for these ensembles has been written by a number of distinguished composers such as Shulamit Ran, Christopher Rouse, John Harbison, and John Corigliano." Schein concludes, "The Aspen chapter of both Earl's life and now mine—in both performing and teaching there—has been great."

During the 1980s, Schein also performed and taught students at the University of Maryland's celebrated annual International Piano Festival, held on the school's campus in College Park, a close-in Maryland suburb of Washington, D.C. The roster of other distinguished pianists participating in the festival has included Jorge Bolet, Stewart Gordon, and Alicia da Larrocha.

As one of her "piano stories," Schein vividly recalls that "to prepare for a festival performance by Da Larrocha, I was asked to choose the piano to be played. But the Steinway provided for the festival that year proved to be in terrible shape—to the extent that the pedals had fallen off!" So Schein and the festival staff called in the highly skilled piano technician Percy Aycock. Even for him, repairing the instrument was a difficult challenge. Despite his repairs, however, Da Larrocha was still displeased with the Steinway's condition. As a star soloist at this distinguished Maryland event, Schein did not shy away from programming such daunting works as an Elliott Carter sonata. On the day following a performance at the festival, she gave master classes—at times a complicated assignment. And, as Schein sadly concludes, "Most of the students who attended the classes didn't know what they could do, or what they felt they could do." Schein believes firmly in, as she words it, "fostering a student's independence."

Schein's own recital at the festival amazed the usually tough *Washington Post* critic Alan "Mike" Kriegsman, who said that this performance set a "standard high enough to put Schein beyond comparisons" with the other artists that year. His praise came with only one exception: her playing of Schubert's "Little" A Major Sonata, Op. 120, was too "grandiose, heavy and lethargically soulful in a manner that might have been thoroughly appropriate to some of Liszt." Otherwise, he noted, "Everything thereafter was so dazzlingly played, so musically right that all one could do was sit back in gasping admiration." In particular, Kriegsman continued, "If [Elliott] Carter's early (1946) Piano Sonata is going to be played at all, . . . it would be hard to imagine a more highly charged or persuasive way of doing it. . . . Her playing made difficulties vanish, complex matters clear and abstruse relationships obvious. It had power and logic and conviction. What composer could ask for more?" (Schein's success with the challenges of this piece, as with much of Carter's music, is even more admirable when one sees the score with Schein's myriad analytical markings.)

Colleagues: The American Chamber Players (1981–1986)

In 1981, the same year as the Chopin cycle, Schein accepted an invitation to join the American Chamber Players, an ensemble in the Washington-Baltimore area made up of seasoned musicians of the highest caliber. The group had been founded by its director, violist Miles Hoffman (a onetime member of Washington's National Symphony Orchestra).

In Washington, D.C., the Players have held a residency at the Library of Congress and performed at the Kennedy Center Terrace Theater, the Kreeger Museum, and other important concert halls. The ensemble has also played throughout much of the United States and internationally. In Paris, as Schein recalls, the group played for two "intense and exciting" weeks at the Opéra nationale de Paris. And at the Bibliothèque nationale, where the ensemble performed Aaron Copland's *Appalachian Spring* (starring the celebrated dancer Martha Graham), Schein remembers that "we had to play in the library's extremely dark space on the first floor of its five-storey reading room (with books shelved all the way up to the ceiling adding to the murky visibility)." "Elisabeth Adkins, associate concertmaster of the National Symphony Orchestra—a wonderful musician and person—conducted with her bow." Schein played with the ACP for five years (1981–1986), performing more than fifty works with this ensemble. Working with the ACP, Schein has said, "made me feel more confident in the chamber music repertoire."

A distinguished violinist and Texas native, Adkins has been an important colleague in Schein's career. Adkins, for instance, recalls a past that has been parallel with Schein's in some ways: the violinist, for example, relates that "I grew up in Austin amid music—especially since I had strong support from musical parents." Both Adkins's parents are still active performers themselves and hold university teaching positions. This author's interview with Adkins (in 2007 at Washington's Kennedy Center) provided valuable insight into Schein's professional world, specifically that of women musical artists.

Similar to the families of Jacquet de La Guerre, Josephine Lang, and Maria Bach, all but one of Adkins's seven siblings are professional string players.[57] Having begun violin lessons at age four, Adkins recalls her youth spent as one of daily hours of practicing while attending public schools. Entering the University of North Texas at fifteen, she earned a bachelor's degree, followed by a master's, after which she obtained a doctorate from the Yale University School of Music in Princeton, New Jersey.

As Schein's professional collaborator, Adkins describes the pianist's music making in superlatives, remarking that Schein "is totally committed to and absorbed in the music she plays." Adkins adds that "Schein treasures everything in the service of music, making her playing exciting to watch—without the distracting flashiness of some younger performers today." "Schein," the violinist continues, "immerses herself in the individual style of each composer, concentrating on the narrative, the flow, of the music she plays." "It is interesting," Adkins continues, "how she puts the music she plays across, for she takes music as poetry and gesture, as feeling; and she takes the audience into the story." And Adkins voices amazement that everywhere the ensemble played, "Schein was welcomed by close friends," Adkins adding that "she is one of those people who is on everybody's radar screen." "It is magical and inspiring to play with Schein," Adkins emphasizes. "When she's playing, it's almost maniacal: she's in a trance-like state, strong. And she is demanding to rehearse with. When she is unhappy about some aspect of a piece, she works even further with the group, prompting everyone to think about it some more."

From 1982 to 1985, Schein toured as accompanist for the celebrated American soprano Jessye Norman (b. 1945). The pianist called this chapter of her career "an extraordinarily inspiring and life-changing experience. I consider Norman's voice," she adds, "as one of the greatest of any singer in the second half of the twentieth century." Schein had first met Norman—a true dramatic soprano known for her magisterial stage presence—in 1965 at a convention in Minneapolis when the eighteen-year-old singer, Schein recalls, "was a joyful and loquacious student at Washington's Howard University."

"When Norman was on the stage," Schein relates, "she could do anything— she was spontaneous, creative in phrasing with breath that seemingly went on forever." Besides Norman's huge repertoire, Schein recalls how much she "felt at home with Norman's voice—that sound." Schein says, "She could sing the most ravishing pianissimos even while lying down, as I remember she did at her Metropolitan Opera debut. And, when Norman improvised spontaneously in performances, I followed, giving me a sense of elevation, for working with her was a whole saga." Schein and Norman performed together over three seasons in the 1980s. On Schein's two-week-long Brazilian tour with Norman, the pianist remembers, "The heat was excessive, and Jessye allowed no air conditioning—we had to sponge ourselves off with water continually." Nevertheless, "Jessye electrified the audience." Schein adds, "In Brazil, as always, on arriving at each concert hall, Norman first checked out the acoustics of the particular concert space and the positioning of the piano for maximum tonal projection and beauty." "This was

Figure 32. Schein
with soprano Jessye
Norman, 2001,
recording early
Alban Berg songs
for Sony Classical at
Concordia College,
Bronxville, N.Y.
Courtesy of Schein.

very enlightening for me," Schein concludes, providing an aside: "I always wore
a black dress on stage. In fact, I had several little black dresses for accompanying
Norman, who always wore gloriously colorful dresses" (fig. 32).[58]

On April 12, 1995, *Washington Post* critic Tim Page reviewed a performance
of Norman and Schein in the capital, describing the singer as "robed in billows
of purple and black" while also commenting that Schein as accompanist was
"strong of mind, ear and hand, a glittering partner and pianist." Several years later
(on January 28, 2002), Page wrote, "Schein was joined by violinist Earl Carlyss,
violist Michael Stepniak, cellist Thomas Kraines and contrabassist Paul Johnson
for Schubert's 'Trout' Quintet. The performance was one of driving momentum,
at once ruminative, tempestuous and elegiac. Solos alternated seamlessly with
duets, and the ensemble was as coordinated as if the musicians were a single
instrument. Embassy Series director Jerome Barry introduced the quintet with
Schubert's song 'The Trout,' the subject of the work's variations."

In recent years, Schein has performed in the Embassy Series concerts in Washington, D.C., as both a recital soloist and chamber group member. A privately
sponsored musical organization founded over two decades ago by its director,

baritone Jerome Barry, the series presents accomplished performers—both young musicians and acclaimed veteran artists—in a multitude of Washington's foreign embassies, with a particular focus on performers and composers from the country that each embassy represents. The important musical events sponsored by Barry's organization contribute significantly to advancing the United States' role in international cultural relations.

Barry told this author in 2007 that he had first become acquainted with Schein at the Polish embassy, when she and Carlyss had performed as part of his Embassy Series. (She has also appeared in the series at the Austrian, Hungarian, and the German embassies, among others.) In 1997, Barry recounts, "Schein accompanied me in a wonderful Brahms and Liszt concert that included the series' later resident ensemble, the Mendelssohn Trio." "I have the highest opinion of Schein and her intense professional commitment," Barry concludes, "and also of Carlyss, who has frequently played in the series concerts."

The author's *Washington Post* reviews of Schein performing at an Embassy Series concert given on March 26, 1999, reflect long-held impressions of Schein's playing: "From the moment that pianist Schein began two of Schubert's Impromptus, D. 899, it was clear that her concert Friday at the Austrian Embassy would be an absorbing one. Schein penetrated the realm of elusive emotions that roil beneath the surface of Schubert's music and the culture of Biedermeier Vienna. She turned scurrying passages of arpeggios and tremolos into shimmering textures through which the melody and its intimately connected harmonic structure emerged. Intimations of dark melancholy alternated with dreamy wistfulness, neither fully revealed."

More Adventures

Schein is frequently invited to lecture on various musical topics, often as pre-concert commentaries to programs by major American ensembles such as the Philadelphia Orchestra. ("I speak," she says, "to people who genuinely want to learn more about music.") She has spoken on Chopin and many other composers, lecturing as well on her teachers Arthur Rubinstein and Myra Hess (1890–1965). Hess's mentors included the often-cited piano pedagogue Tobias Matthay (1858–1945). Although winning international acclaim in her day, Hess was a particular favorite with American audiences, her playing—which Schein heard for many years in Washington—being best known for its poetic intimacy coupled with warmth and sensitivity. It is perhaps this aspect of Hess's stylistic legacy that Schein inherited from the storied pianist. But Schein made it her own.

Both Carlysses retired from Peabody in 2002, after two decades of teaching there. Schein notes that "since then, my focus has become the summer faculty position at Aspen." (After their retirement from Peabody, Schein and Carlyss moved to Westchester County, New York. As of this writing, they live in Westport,

Connecticut.) "It is exciting to be in Aspen with its educational tradition," Schein says, noting that she teaches students "from everywhere in the world, exchanging ideas and enjoying working with my colleagues. It has been good for Earl and me."

During the summer of 2005, Schein opened the first concert of an Aspen series covering all of Beethoven's piano sonatas, performed by faculty members. That summer, Schein also performed Brahms's G Minor Piano Quartet with Carlyss, Darrett Atkins, and Sabina Thatcher. She also played John Corigliano's violin and piano sonata with Herbert Greenberg.

The Critics

Schein continues to make a significant mark on American music history. Over the years numerous critics, such as those in the *New York Times,* the *Washington Post,* and the *Baltimore Sun* have praised her "controlled passion" and her "absolute technical command." They have called her playing "dazzling," worthy even of "gasping admiration" and "powerful grandeur." Things have changed, however, since the early days of Schein's public career, as the following references to her gender demonstrate:

1. Irving Lowens, April 22, 1963, for Washington's *Evening Star*: "Miss Schein's Chopin (the Concerto in F Minor with the Hague Philharmonic conducted by Willem van Otterloo) is, in many ways, an astonishing thing. Her interpretations strike me as completely feminine—but not at all effeminate. There is no lack of strength or fire in her playing; the power is there, but it is veiled by the silkiest of touches, by the daintiest and most exquisite of phrasings. Indeed, Miss Schein's Chopin was as lovely to hear as she was lovely to see. Here is a 23-year-old virtuoso who is blessed with grace and beauty as well as magnificent artistry and a solidly dependable technique."

2. Around 1965 Lowens again emphasized Schein's gender: "It was interesting to compare [Gary Graffman's] recital, the epitome of masculinity, with Ann Schein's equally sensational recital . . . two weeks earlier, the epitome of femininity."

3. Paul Hume, February 6, 1966, the *Washington Post*: Referring to Schein's performance of Mozart's Sonata in F Major, K. 332, Hume wrote: "For a time the playing sounded more unmistakably feminine than any I had heard for a long time. Looking at Miss Schein, it is easy to see how this might be the case, but in music gender is not always so much to the fore. The Mozart was more shapely than usual, a bit more pliant. Beautifully molded, it was somehow softer, especially in the opening movement, than that first theme really implies."

4. Lowens, reviewing the same concert, on February 6, 1966, for the *Evening Star*: "Once again as in the past, I was deeply impressed by the unique com-

bination of delicacy and strength that seems to be so characteristic of Miss Schein's playing. It is not only that it is so precise, so exquisitely proportioned, so feathery light: even more, it is that it is shot through with sunlight and shade, that it is blessed with maturity and youth and femininity."

The gender-oriented reviews of Schein, however, have generally disappeared with the passage of time. *Washington Post* critic Tim Page, in an interview with this author in March 2007, for example, defined "the great artist" in a very distinctive way, paying Schein the highest compliment one can pay a performer: "Schein is one of those few outstanding artists who has no sense of using ruthlessness to advance her career. What makes a great career? Greats are not unknown to knock down everybody in order to have their careers." "I have known," Page continued, "something of Schein's personality over the last nine years. She doesn't have that kind of all-consuming characteristic to advance her career. She is a wonderful artist completely without that kind of negative reputation, although being in music is a terrible business. Schein has—and this is very important—sheer musicianship radiating from her playing." Page adds that "Schein is open-hearted, and I just love her work. Over time, her recordings will be cherished because of her musicianship."

Continuing on the theme of celebrated artists, Page noted that "careers are built on playing and personality." "Harold Schonberg, [longtime *New York Times* critic] flipped over Alicia da Larrocha. He loved her playing, which wasn't flashy. And Schein's playing is not blasting away. She is never flashy, but she has a fine technique. Schein's playing is not 'ultra'; it's not a sporting event; instead she has taste and lyricism—qualities I like."

"Never Flashy"

With only the two words "never flashy," Page paid Schein perhaps the highest compliment any critic can pay an artist, capturing in a micro-second the essence of her playing and revealing his own keen perceptivity in doing so. It would be a useful exercise in understanding the nature of Schein's playing, moreover, if we briefly surveyed some of the ways other critics have expressed a view similar to Page's. Therefore, excerpts from their reviews of both her live performances and recordings follow below. These comments are generally grouped composer by composer and echo Page's remark with additional detail.

Conclusion

Having performed in almost every state in America, Schein looks back over her career, summing things up: "In addition to my family life, my performing years recently have been some of my best. My musical life continues to blossom and

fill my days. In fact, I have played more concerts than earlier in my life." "Now,"
she says, "I am totally free to go wherever I am asked to perform."

Schein began as a prodigy who, with perfect pitch, could play tunes by ear
from the age of three, tunes that she heard all around her, "like a little monkey,"
Schein's mother would say with a smile. After those Chicago years, the family
moved to Washington, where Schein's parents immediately entered some of the
capital's most vital cultural circles, such as that of the city's impresario and family
friend Patrick Hayes. "My parents," Ann adds, "also enjoyed legions of friends in
many places, such as our church and community and my father's law practice."
As in her Evanston childhood, then her Washington "era," Schein enjoyed the encouragement and opportunities to develop that came with this dedicated support
network, followed by her years of intensive piano studies, particularly with Munz
and Rubinstein. And Schein's musical advancement prospered, Washington's daily
press—especially in her youthful years—even claiming her as "the city's own."

As the years passed, Schein was faced with the early deaths of her parents and
her own questions about her professional standing. At this time, however, Carlyss
entered Schein's life, bringing her both renewed confidence in her musical artistry
and a gratifying family life, to which she devoted many years. Alix Williamson,
her "fairy godmother," unexpectedly stepped into the scene at another critical
point in Schein's life, endowing her with Williamson's own brand of New York–
honed managerial expertise and personal warmth. In targeting the challenging
notion that Schein would give a Chopin cycle for New York's 1980–1981 concert
season, Williamson jump-started a new phase of the pianist's American professional life. From that encouraging Lincoln Center venture onward, professional
honors and concert engagements have poured in. In the last two decades, Schein
has performed in more than forty states, playing, she notes, "as opportunities
present themselves." In addition, she won the Peabody appointment, the Aspen
position, the invitation to join the piano faculty at the University of Indiana as a
visiting professor for the 2008–2009 season, and her appointment to the Adams
Foundation, an organization dedicated to the reopening of a major piano recital
series across the United States.

Appendix: Reviews of Schein: Live Performances

CHOPIN

A reviewer from classical music radio station WGMS wrote of a Dumbarton Concert
Series performance in Washington, D.C., "What modern pianist is usually associated
with Chopin—Pollini, Perahia, Ashkenazy? . . . For several hundreds of people who
attended the Dumbarton Concert Series over the weekend, that pianist is Ann Schein."
The critic compared her with her teacher Rubinstein, accordingly praising her playing
above all for its "poetic quality" and "beautiful tone."

A Portland, Oregon, critic called Schein "the perfect Chopin pianist—elegant and aristocratic," complimenting her "smooth cantabile phrasing spun as fine a filigree as anyone's" and adding that she is "a self-effacing performer," comfortable with "the 19th-century language of poetic melancholy." The reviewer, William Thomas Walker (after a recital at Elon University), noted that in Schein's performance of Chopin's 24 Preludes, Op. 28: "Each gem was presented with unaffected simplicity."

In Chopin's Sonata no. 3 in B Minor, Op. 58, "Schein's tone, touch and interpretation were exhilarating," said Nora Beck, adding that Schein's playing "was a cross between the precision of Maurizio Pollini and the creativity of Rubinstein." (Nora Beck, *The Oregonian,* December 6, 1999)

RAVEL AND DEBUSSY

For a performance of works by Ravel and Debussy, Schein's playing was "luminous"—in perfect line for impressionist music. As for the "Olympian demands" of a Liszt work, a critic noted, "Schein handled them with aplomb, as if they had been no problem at all. . . ." (Peter Jacobi, *Herald-Tribune,* Bloomington, Indiana, June 22, 2007)

PROKOVFIEV

One critic summed up Schein's performance of Prokofiev's Sonata no. 3, noting, "Schein tackled the craggy score with an abandon that rested on careful analysis and superb control." (Jennifer Weiniger, *Telegram and Gazette,* November 16, 1991)

SCHUMANN

Another writer commented that, after Schein's performance of Robert Schumann works, "Her readings tend to be straightforward and without exaggeration, but sensitive and subtly nuanced." (*Fanfare Magazine*)

Reviews of Schein: Recordings (as of 2009)

In Schumann, a critic noted that of Schein's playing, "most remarkable . . . is the flawless ability to manage the emotional and expressive mood shifts so quickly and with such telling effect in this mercurial music—really an interpretive tour de force more than a technical one." (Mulbury, *The American Record Guide,* May/June 2001)

Schein's Schumann disc, one reviewer notes, "shows great perception, . . . imagination, poetic beauty, and intimacy. . . ." (Walden Hughes, *Clavier,* January 2002)

A CD purchaser in Freeport (Long Island), New York, writes that Schein's playing of Schumann shows "an attractive romantic impetuosity, though never at the expense of lyricism or nuance, and obviously she eschews flamboyance for its own sake," emphasizing that she is "more introspective than most pianists." (Melvyn M. Sobel)

CARTER

In an English publication, a critic notes, " . . . She does not consistently emphasize Carter's [in his piano sonata] frequent *espressivo* markings or deliver his *molto legato* directives with the specificity of Charles Rosen and Ursula Oppens, nor match the younger Winston Choi's feathery suppleness in rapid passages. Yet her wide dynamic range, contrapuntal awareness and sense of harmonic tension and release never fail to hold attention." (Jed Distler, *Gramophone,* September 2009)

COPLAND

Distler also praises "the energetic and impeccably dovetailed ensemble work that [Schein] and her husband, violinist Earl Carlyss, achieve in [Copland's] 1943 Violin Sonata." (Jed Distler, *Gramophone,* September 2009)

A critic reviewing Schein in Carter's piano sonata and Schein and Carlyss in Copland's violin sonata writes, they "brought an easy confidence to modern works . . ., none of which call for (or could stand any) kind of theatricality."(Cook, *The American Record Guide,* September/October 2009)

Schein's recording of Copland's *Piano Variations* is described by one commentator as "pungent" and "striking in its unvarnished emotion, frenetic dissonance and poetic interludes." And Schein's performance "balances dissonance with vision." (Robert Moon, *Audophile Audition,* 2009)

Ann Schein Selected Recordings

Kapp Records. (1957, but the vinyl LP is still available) Frederick Chopin: Scherzos in B Minor, Op. 20; B-flat Minor, Op. 31; C-sharp Minor, Op. 39; and E Major, Op. 54.

Koch International Classics. (1990) W. A. Mozart Trio in F; M. Bruch, Pieces, Op. 83, nos. 1–8

Koch International Classics. (1991) I. Stravinsky, L'oiseau de feu, no. 2; Duo Concertante

Phoenix USA. (1991) N. Rorem, Day Music; Night Music

Sony. (1995) Jessye Norman Sings Alban Berg

Phoenix USA. (1997) Charles Ives, Sonata no. 4 for Violin (Jaime Laredo) and Piano; Aaron Copland, Sonata for Violin (J. Laredo) and Piano; includes additional works played by other performers

Ivory Classics. (2000) Robert Schumann: Davidsbündlertänze, Op. 6; Arabeske, Op. 18; Humoreske, Op. 20

Ivory Classics. (2002) W. A. Mozart, Sonata in C Major, K. 545; includes additional works played by other pianists

MSR Classics. (2004) Frederick Chopin, Sonata no. 3 in B Minor, Op. 58; 24 Preludes, Op. 28

MSR Classics. (2007) Elliott Carter, Piano Sonata; Aaron Copland, Piano Variations; Copland, Sonata for Violin and Piano (Earl Carlyss, violin); John Patitucci, Lakes

Delos Records. (2008) W. Walton, Sonata for Violin and Piano (violinist Herbert Greenberg)

MSR Classics. (2008) E. Carter, Piano Sonata (1945–1946); A. Copland, Piano Variations and Sonata for Violin and Piano (violinist Earl Carlyss)

NOTES

Preface

1. Mrs. Jameson, *Characteristics of Women: Moral, Political, and Historical* (Boston and London: William D. Ticknor, 1846), 35.

2. Among the many valuable contributions to the field of women in music, I have found the following scholars especially helpful, even if not directly cited. In compiling this list, I became aware that one cannot fully distinguish between musicologists in feminist theory and those involved in historical-biographical accounts of women. But my bibliographies of individual chapters list works in more detail. These scholars include (in alphabetical order) Carolyn Abbate, Robert Adelson, Carol Henry Bates, Adrienne Fried Block, Edith Borroff, Jane Bowers, Catherine Cessac, Marcia J. Citron, Susan C. Cook, Suzanne G. Cusick, Mary Cyr, Leslie C. Dunn, Barbara Engh, Karl Wilhelm Geck, Barbara Garvey Jackson, Nancy A. Jones, Gabriele Knapp, Harald Krebs, Sharon Krebs, Ellen Koskoff, Jacqueline Letzter, Renee Cox Lorraine, Susan McClary, Carol Neuls-Bates, Elena Ostleitner, Karin Pendle, Jennifer C. Post, Nancy B. Reich, Danielle Roster, Ruth A. Solie, Judith Tick, and Judy S. Tsou.

Introduction

1. While I worked on this book in Washington, D.C., an hours-long march for "Women's Equality Day" was assembling in front of the White House to mark the ninetieth anniversary of the Nineteenth Amendment to the Constitution, granting American women the right to vote, thus bringing women more into a public space from their sequestered sphere of the private home. Indeed, the independence of women in both the public and private arenas has been a key theme underlying feminist movements.

2. "What distinguishes a woman is not her biology, but the way society categorizes her and treats her *because* [italics the author's] of her biology." See Christine Battersby, *Gender and Genius: Towards a Feminist Aesthetics* (1989), cited by Ruth A. Solie, ed., *Introduction to Musicology and Difference: Gender and Sexuality in Music Scholarship* (Berkeley and Los Angeles: University of California Press, 1993), 9. Solie adds, "To put the same idea another way, sexual difference is constitutive of one's sense [of the] possibilities of existence." See Solie's citation from The Milan Women's Bookstore Collective, *Sexual Difference: A Theory of Social-Symbolic Practice* (1990) in *Musicology and Difference,* n. 28, 9.

3. Even today, traces of Mrs. Jameson's view on the nature of womankind linger still, as in the following sarcastic comment mocking her antiquated, biologically slanted bias offered by a female character in a British spy novel from 2002: "Before [World War II], no woman ever rose above the level of secretary-assistant in MI6 (a British intelligence

agency). We didn't have analytical minds, you see. We were more suited to homemaking and child-rearing. But since the war broke out, women's brains have undergone a remarkable change, and we have become capable of work that previously could only be accomplished by the masculine mentality." See Ken Follett, *Hornet Flight* (London and New York: Dutton, 2002), 31.

4. One might think of British author Virginia Woolf (1882–1941), who grew up in a financially stable family steeped in literature. Specifically, she is remembered for her oft-quoted dictum that "a woman must have money and a room of her own if she is to write fiction" (from her essay "A Room of One's Own," 1929). That is, said more generally, women (and men) need "space"—which includes time in the larger sense—to create a work of art. A woman artist's need for this kind of space as described by Woolf and her personal family situation amid affluence and eminent literary circles also underlines major themes considered for all five women treated in this book. Also, during a time of active British feminist leanings, Woolf studied classical languages and history—some subjects at the degree level—at the Ladies' Department of King's College London. Education is another principal consideration throughout these chapters.

5. This is the chief concern in my earlier book, *The Rhine as Musical Metaphor: Cultural Identity in German Romantic Music* (Boston: Northeastern University Press, 1996).

6. A striking and relatively recent case in point is the Vietnam Veterans' Memorial (1982) in Washington, D.C. A work created by the American artist, architect, and sculptor Maya Lin (1959–), it concisely voices this notion that the arts—to some extent—exemplify society's appraisal of itself, in this instance, as sculpture expressing America's conflicted views on a violently controversial chapter of its history. In another visual art, German artist Käthe Kollwitz (1867–1945) focused exclusively on printmaking media centered on then-radical subjects running counter to her sociocultural environment—humanitarian ideals paired with graphic realism.

7. The types and scale of artworks by women (not excluding men) in numerous other "creative" fields result, at least partially, from multiple intersecting and interacting cultural factors, critical among them being an era's societal traditions and prejudices. Whitney Chadwick sums it up nicely for the visual arts: "History continues to privilege prodigious output and monumental scale, or conception over the selective and intimate." One thinks immediately of two themes: first, the relatively extensive production of lieder by the composers Josephine Lang and Maria Bach, as well as the modest private devotional songs of Duchess Sophie-Elisabeth; and second, the narrow social—that is domestic—circumstances of Lang's married life, Bach's sequestered childhood, and perhaps the duchess's enclosed lifestyle within the powerful German baroque court system. In these cases, does scale owe in part or primarily to these composers' societal situation? Examples of genre scale and type or style abound equally in other arts. The American poet Emily Dickinson (1830–1886) devoted virtually all of her adult life to caring at home for her ailing mother. Sequestered in this type of domestic setting, she composed poems prodigiously though in condensed miniature scope. And the question remains: Was isolation a determinant factor in Dickinson's extraordinarily unconventional writing style—in capitalization, punctuation, vocabulary, imagery, and even meter? While probing the social environment of Dickinson's work, one could also think of her contemporaries the painter Mary Cassat (1844–1926) and the novelist Louisa May Alcott (1832–1888), both of whom spent time in Paris as part of a group of closely knit female student painters and writers. In some of her writings, Alcott pondered the relationship of artworks by her many contemporaries

with political forces and spinsterhood. (See Chadwick, 230.) It would be interesting to consider two of Cassat's paintings in this respect: women's consignment to domestic roles in *Mother and Child* (c. 1905) and *A Cup of Tea* (c. 1880). More than one cultural historian considers domestic entrenchment as the sanctification of women in the arts.

8. Chadwick also notes that we must "examine how art history is written and the assumptions that underlie its hierarchies, especially if the numerous cases of attributions to male artists of works by women are to be reviewed" (11). This includes searching through male pseudonyms fueling the long reign of the *masters* outlook and practice in writing histories of the arts. It also includes such centuries-long situations and actions as the following. Marietta Robusti, the talented daughter of the celebrated Venetian artist Tintoretto's (Jacopo Robusti, 1518 or 1519–1594), grew up in his workshop and became an artist in her own right. As his culture's tradition dictated, Tintoretto, however, forbade her to accept a professional position at the Viennese imperial court, forcing her to marry and remain in her native Venice. She died during childbirth at the age of thirty. Robusti's fate is but one striking instance of "cultural amnesia" to the extreme.

9. Charles Rosen, *The Romantic Generation* (Cambridge, Mass.: Harvard University Press, 1995), xi.

10. Besides star performers who fled to New York, many émigré composers also relocated elsewhere in the United States, moving to Los Angeles, for example, where some joined the Hollywood film industry—principally to earn a living.

11. See Cecelia H. Porter, book review of Wolf Gruner, *Das Frauenorchester in Auschwitz: Musikalische Zwangsarbeit als Element der Verfolgung, 1938–1943*, *Holocaust and Genocide Studies* 13, no. 3 (Winter 1999): 467–69.

12. A younger contemporary of Jacquet de La Guerre, Venetian painter Rosalba Carriera (1675–1757), worked in a sociopolitical environment quite similar to that of this composer, shedding more light on the arts in Paris at that time. (Strikingly, Jacquet de La Guerre was as successful in her urban surroundings in Paris as in the court environment of Versailles.) In 1720 Carriera had been summoned as a professional artist to join Louis XV's court, which, along with much of the nobility, was returning to Paris from Versailles and its subsidiary royal establishments. This new public—the urban intellectual aristocracy—favored paintings in a decorative style focused on capturing the pleasures of the senses. In addition, Carriera was taken under the patronage of the wealthy financier and art collector Pierre Crozat, whose circle included the painter Jean-Antoine Watteau (see chapter 2).

13. Harald Krebs and Sharon Krebs, *Josephine Lang, Her Life and Songs* (Oxford and New York: Oxford University Press, 2007), 10–15.

Chapter 1. Duchess Sophie-Elisabeth

1. This list is taken from the eulogy given Sophie-Elisabeth at her funeral in Brandanus Daetrius, Königes Davids Hertzens-Lust und Liebe zum steten Lobe Gottes: Als Der Weylandt Durchläuchtigsten Fürstinnen und Frauen/Frauen Sophien Elisabeth/Veriwittibter Herzoginen zu Braunschweig und Lüneburg, Geborner Hertzoginnen zu Mecklenburg/ Fürstinnen der Wenden/ zu Schwerin und Ratzeburg/ auch Gräffinnen zu Schwerin/der Lande Rostock und Stargart, Fraün/ Unserer gewesenen hochpreisslicher Landes-Mutter hohes Herstammen/ glückselige Geburt/ Christlicher Lebens-Lauff und hochseliger Abschied. Verblichener Fürstlicher Leichnam, Den VI. Octobris nechst verflossenen 1676sten

Jahres beygesetzet worden. Niedersächsisches Landesbibliothek; Hannover: C 15782; also published in Braunschweig (Christoff-Friederich Zilligern, 1676). By permission of the Stadtbibliothek, Braunschweig.

2. See Yvonne Demoskoff, "Yvonne's Royalty Home Page," www.mypageuniserve.com/canada, 2006.

3. Considering that Margareta died at thirty-two, the date suggests death at the birth of her second daughter, Christine Margareta; Johann Albrecht died at forty-six during the Thirty Years' War conflagration.

4. See Karl Pagel, *Mecklenburg: eine Biographie eines Deutschen Landes* (Vanderhöck & Ruprecht, 1969), 92–104. Sophie-Elisabeth's great-grandfather Duke Albrecht of Prussia had been a respected poet. Reportedly her grandfather Christoph von Mecklenburg had shown strong musical inclinations and interests.

5. See Karl Wilhelm Geck, *Sophie Elisabeth, Herzogin zu Braunschweig und Lüneburg (1613–1676) als Musikerin* (Saarbrücker Studien zur Musikwissenschaft 6; Neue Folge; Saarbrücken: Saarbrücker Druckerei und Verlag, 1992), 23–30.

6. Gina Spagnoli, "Dresden at the Time of Heinrich Schütz," in *The Early Baroque Era: From the Late 16th Century to the 1660s,* ed. Curtis Price (Music and Society) (Englewood Cliffs, N.J.: Prentice Hall, 1994), 165.

7. Duchess Elisabeth played an influential role in Stanley's obtaining the lutenist position in the flourishing musical milieu of her uncle's court in Kassel. See Geck, 24–26.

8. Geck, 27.

9. George J. Bülow, "Protestant North Germany," in Price, *Early Baroque Era,* 185–86.

10. As Duke of Mecklenburg, von Wallenstein allowed the state to remain Lutheran, but cruelly ordered its Calvinist population to convert to Catholicism. See Geck, 28–29.

11. The landgrave increased the number and salaries of the court chapel musicians and appointed as *Kapellmeister* the well-known English organist-composer John Stanley, with whom Sophie-Elisabeth and her sister at one time studied. See Geck, 31–32.

12. See John Butt, *Music Education and the Art of Performance in the German Baroque* (Cambridge and New York: Cambridge University Press, 2005), 39–41, who comments that Praetorius, whose treatise Syntagma musicum (1614–1620) represents the first important attempt to use the new style developed in Italy, was organist, then *Kapellmeister,* at the Wolfenbüttel court and in absentia at Dresden.

13. See Hans Joachim Moser, *Heinrich Schütz: His Life and Work,* trans. and ed. (2nd ed.) Carl F. Pfatteicher (St. Louis: Concordia Publishing House, 1959), 147 and 165; also Geck, 31–34.

14. Geck, 31–34.

15. Geck, 36 and 39–40.

16. Literally, "one who can get on in life," "one with her own free will," and "the liberating one," respectively.

17. Geck, 47; also 66–69.

18. Considerably north of Wolfenbüttel, Lüneburg (referred to in the duchess's title after marriage) enjoyed wealth and magnificent arts patronage during the seventeenth century as its legacy from Hansa membership. Several prominent Lüneburg musicians had ties with J. S. Bach's native Thuringia, such as the famous Lüneburg organist-composer Georg Böhm (1661–1733), and the Wolfenbüttel organist-opera composer Johann Jakob Löwe (1628–1703), who was there when Bach studied at the Michaelschule (1700–1703). Celle was a residence of the Duchy of Braunschweig-Lüneburg from 1378 to 1705. After the end

of the Thirty Years' War, the court became home to a brilliant orchestra, including ten trumpeters. Some believe Johann Sebastian Bach (1685–1750) played the violin in that ensemble when he visited the court.

19. See Hans Wiswe, "Handel und Wandel in Wolfenbüttel vor dem Dreissigjährigen Kriegs," in *Beiträge zur Geschichte der Stadt Wolfenbüttel* (Wolfenbüttel: Stadt Wolfenbüttel, 1970), 21.

20. Geck, nn. 467, 468, and 71.

21. By the thirteenth century, Wolfenbüttel/Braunschweig, again like other Hansa centers, had become an active focus for German culture—principally literary and musical—not only for north Germany but also for central Europe generally. By the fifteenth century, music education had advanced so far that the curriculum of the two city Latin schools included music theory, and there was a well-established boys' choir, which performed for city church festivals. See Geck, 40; and Alfred Keilitz, *Die Wirkungen des Dreissigjährigen Krieges in den Wittumsämtern des Herzogtums Braunschweig-Wolfenbüttel* (Wolfenbüttel: n.p., 1938).

22. Moser, 174.

23. Hanseatic cities, Buelow notes, cultivated "a culture based on the tastes and wealth of the merchant class, and while individual cities had individual characters, there was an overall similarity related to the structure and purpose of the Hanseatic League." See Buelow, 186.

24. Spagnoli, 166.

25. See Arnfried Edler, "Organ Music within the Social Structure of North German Cities in the Seventeenth Century," in Paul Walker, ed. *Church, Stage, and Studio: Music and its Contexts in Seventeenth-Century Germany* (Ann Arbor and London: UMI Research Press, 1990), 23–24; also Philippe Dollinger, *The German Hansa*, trans. and ed. D. S. Ault and S. H. Steinberg (London and Stanford: Macmillan, 1970), 114 and following pages; and Johannes Schildhauer, *The Hansa: History and Culture*, trans. Katherine Vanovitch (Leipzig: Edition Leipzig, 1985), 224–26.

26. Wolfenbüttel was established in 1150 as both a city and the chief court residence of the Guelph Duchy Braunschweig-Lüneburg. By the thirteenth century, Wolfenbüttel had developed into a cultural center in literature and music notable not only for north Germany but also for central Europe generally. See Wiswe, 21.

27. Paul Zimmermann, "Zur Biographie des Kapellmeisters Michäl Praetorius," *Jahrbuch des Braunschweigischen Geschichtsvereins*, 2. Folge/3 (Wolfenbüttel: Braunschweigischer Geschichtverein, 1930), 91–97. During this duke's reign, in fact, Wolfenbüttel was one of Europe's great tourist attractions, chiefly for its planned physical layout, which had been initiated by Julius in May, 1585. The town's large-scale unified fortification system surrounding the castle and city drew many admirers. See Joseph König, ed., *Wolfenbüttel: Wappen und Stadtgeschichte: Eine Ausstellung des Niedersächsischen Staatsarchivs in Wolfenbüttel* (Göttingen: Vandenhöck & Ruprecht, 1970), 14; also Wiswe, 16–17 and 24; and Robert Bohlman, "Die Zeichen oder Monogramme des Herzogs Julius von Braunschweig," in *Festschrift für Paul Zimmerman* (Wolfenbüttel: Bohlman, 1914), 256–62.

28. Geck, 40.

29. Moser, 165–66.

30. Spagnoli, 165.

31. Geck, 63.

32. Daetrius, 7; also, Geck, 61–64.

33. Geck, 61–63; also n. 402.

34. Letter from Sophie-Elisabeth to her husband, October 11, 1641. Niedersächsisches Staatsarchiv, Wolfenbüttel, 1 Alt 23, Nr. 247, Bl. 53.

35. According to Schütz's letters to Sophie-Elisabeth written on October 22, 1644, and March 17, 1645, one can see clearly that Duke August did transfer the reorganization of court music to Sophie-Elisabeth, although he still maintained control over most of the court's administration. See Geck, 63.

36. August had hired Körner in 1637. In that year, August had decreed that a new *Kapellmeister* "should, above all, see to it that he engage exemplary musicians who are especially experienced in the science of art, who are beyond suspicion in doctrine, life, and conduct, and who are not given to drink or other misconduct." See Geck, 41, and Moser, 165 and 208.

37. Ibid., 147.

38. Schütz (1585–1672) was at the center of Dresden's musical life. At the Lutheran court of Saxony's capital, he was responsible for special musical events for royal and aristocratic visitors to display longtime Elector Johann Georg I's (reigned 1611–1656) "honor and glory" (Schütz's words in 1645). See Spagnoli, 164.

39. Schütz officially became chief *Kapellmeister* at Dresden at least by 1619. In addition, the Saxon elector, Johann Georg, fell into arrears in paying Schütz's salary by the autumn of 1631. The additional expenses assumed by Saxony on its entry that year into the Thirty Years' War, moreover, had affected not only the composer himself but also the Dresden chapel as a whole. Within a year, the size of Schütz's musical forces at the Saxon court had diminished drastically, and music making had been reduced to nearly nothing.

40. Moser, 175.

41. Ibid., 177.

42. Ibid., 208.

43. Löwe was succeeded as Wolfenbüttel's *Kapellmeister* by Martin Colerus (c. 1620–1703) and then Johann Rosenmüller (c. 1619–1684). Löwe's important and innovative Sinfonie, or instrumental suites, reveal his exposure to musical styles that he had absorbed at the Italian-dominated Viennese court: that of the canzona, or chamber sonata, with its freely flowing series of contrasting sections. Italian elements also appear in Löwe's aria-like lieder, structurally unified through the thematically repeated technique of the ritornello. See Geck, 80–82 and 87.

44. For the duke's birthday on April 10, 1661, Schütz sent copies of his newly published Becker Psalter to the duke and his Pietist wife. (Duke August did not pay the composer again until May 1663.) Electoral Saxony had been the most important Protestant state in the sixteenth century. But, similarly, in a letter of Schütz to Sophie-Elisabeth back as far as November 27, 1655, the composer complained that the duke had not yet paid him.

45. Moser, 206.

46. Ibid., 207.

47. John Butt defines the critical baroque notion of rhetoric as a function—"the art of persuasion, a system of devices" that can move the listener's *Affekt,* or mood; rhetoric also referred to a system of embellishing a melody. See Butt, *Music Education,* 41.

48. Moser, 175. It is not known what composition Schütz referred to.

49. Idem.

50. See Joshua Rifkin, "Heinrich Schütz," *The New Grove Dictionary of Music and Musicians* (London and New York: Macmillan, 1980), 11.

51. Moser, 174–75.

52. Rifkin, 11; also 15, citing Schütz's letter of July 24, 1655.

53. Her earlier Arien (dating from 1642 to 1647 and hence composed before Lütkemann's arrival) already showed her deep involvement in sacred music, though these songs expose her limited contrapuntal skill.

54. His main work, *Der Vorschmack göttlicher Güte* (The Foretaste of Divine Goodness), from 1653, had become a highly popular book of Pietist edification, along with his prodigious number of sacred poems. Lütkemann was one of the "Rostock Reform theologians," who, although grounded in Lutheran Orthodoxy, shared much with Reformed believers drawn to the ideas of Pietist Philipp Jakob Spener (1635–1705). See Geck, 69–74, 483, and 484.

55. Hajo Holborn, *A History of Modern Germany: 1648–1840* (New York: Alfred A. Knopf, 1971), 124, 136–37, and 139.

56. Daetrius, 43.

57. See Butt, 28–29 and 43.

58. For a general picture of this matter, still valid, this author thinks, is Manfred F. Bukofzer's classic *Music in the Baroque Era from Monteverdi to Bach* (New York: W.W. Norton, 1947), 79.

59. Geck, 61–64 and 74–76.

60. See Robert L. Kendrick, "Devotion, piety and commemoration: sacred songs and oratorios," in *The Cambridge History of Seventeenth-Century Music,* eds. Tim Carter and John Butt (Cambridge and New York: Cambridge University Press, 2005), 337–39.

61. Ibid.

62. Holborn, 140.

63. Buelow, 197.

64. Kendrick, 337–39.

65. Geck, 74–75: "Kurtze stossgebehtlein auf ein jedess Capitel durch die gantze biebel in allerhandt not undt anligen zu gebrauchen, undt zu meiner undt aller fromen Christen erbauung erfunden und aufgezeichnet, alhir zu Wolfenbüttel. . . ." Herzog August Bibliothek: Cod. Guelf 53 Noviss.2* Bl. 181r-182v.

66. Besides the translations, all made by this author, the verses are given here in the original German to preserve the rhyme and rhythm of her poem. Sophie-Elisabeth's journals also indicate that, besides her Calvinist-Pietistic persuasion, her religious poems—apparently translations of French verse—also evidenced her involvement in what today we call "consciousness-raising" for women. See Geck, 77.

67. Herzog August Bibliothek: Cod. Guelf 53 Noviss.2* Bl 133v.

68. Ibid. Also see Geck, 75.

69. Löwe's successor, Martin Colerus (c. 1620–1703), lacked sufficient skill for the composition of *Festspiele;* and Anton Ulrich shifted his attention more to solely literary projects; his sister Sibylle Ursula (who reportedly had helped in some capacity with the *Festspiel* librettos) had married and moved away from Wolfenbüttel; and the remaining siblings had never been involved in *Festspiel* productions. See Geck, 91–92.

70. Geck, 92–93.

71. An opera house opened in nearby Braunschweig in 1690.

72. Daetrius; also Geck, 94.

73. Geck, 95.

74. Ibid.

75. Daetrius.

76. The manuscript collections are the following: Cod. Guelf 52 Noviss. 8* (1633); Cod. Guelf 11a Noviss. 2* (1642?–1653); and Cod. Guelf 11 Noviss. 2* (1647–1655). See also Geck, 529.

77. Geck, 185.

78. Ibid., 268.

79. In the case of Sophie-Elisabeth's music, *Festspiel,* or *Singspiel,* was a rather broad term applied to a staged drama with music and spoken dialogue that was composed for a specific court occasion. This genre contrasted greatly with the Italian opera style of her day, which consisted of arias and recitatives in sung dialogue.

80. Geck, 353–57.

81. Set to a libretto by Georg Philipp Harsdörffer, the music of Seelewig consists of a mixture of chorales, continuo songs, and recitatives in the style of early Florentine recitative. (Bukofzer, 102, describes Seelewig as "a rather wooden allegorical play.") Much earlier (1627), Schütz had composed Dafne, considered the first German opera, but the music for this pastorale has not survived.

82. Geck, 79.

83. Ibid., 45–46.

84. Ibid., 78–79; also 356–57.

85. Ibid., 87–88.

86. An excerpt from this letter is cited in Friedrich Chrysander, "Geschichte der Braunschweig-Wolfenbüttelschen Capelle und Oper: vom 16. bis zum 18. Jahrhundert," in *Jahrbücher für musikalische Wissenschaft* 1 (1863), 150.

87. See Geck, 82–83.

88. Intimate friends, Löwe and Weiland even addressed poems to each other and collaborated on the composition of *Zweyer gleichgesinnten Freunde Tugend und Schertz-Lieder* (Two Like-Minded Friends' Songs of Virtue and Pleasantry). See Geck, 82–83.

89. Ibid., 84–86.

90. Ibid., 84–91.

Chapter 2. Elisabeth-Claude Jacquet de La Guerre

1. Before her marriage, Jacquet de La Guerre preferred to be known as simply Jacquet. But, to avoid confusion and accord with current library and publishing practice, I will consistently refer to her as Jacquet de La Guerre.

2. French National Archives Y11216.

3. See Catherine Cessac, *Elisabeth Jacquet de La Guerre: Une Femme Compositeur sous le règne de Louis XIV* (Arles: Actes Sud, 1995), 21.

4. Cyr's commendable scholarship includes editions of two volumes of Jacquet de La Guerre's *Collected Works: Sacred Works,* (vol. 3); and *Secular Vocal Works* (vol. 4). See *Elisabeth-Claude Jacquet de la Guerre: The Collected Works* (New York: The Broude Trust, 2005.)

5. (Musicological Studies 12) (Brooklyn, N.Y.: Institute of Mediaeval Music, 1966), 5–20.

6. The Indianapolis Museum of Art, Indianapolis, Indiana. See also Enzo Carli, *The Landscape in Art* (New York: William Morrow, 1980), 152–59.

7. Idem.

8. James R. Anthony, *French Baroque Music from Beaujoyeulx to Rameau,* rev. ed. (Portland, Ore.: Amadeus Press, 1997), 28.

9. Anthony, 17–18 and 34–35; also George Buelow, ed., *The Late Baroque Era from the 1680s to 1740,* (*Music and Society* Series) (Englewood Cliffs, N.J.: Prentice Hall, 1994), 6.

10. Alistair Horne, *The Seven Ages of Paris* (New York, Vintage Books [Random House], 2004), 100.

11. Ibid., 18.

12. Cessac, 33.

13. Bukofzer, 148 and following.

14. Anthony, 17–18; see also Buelow, 23, 147, and 175–81.

15. Bukofzer, 142; see also Horne, 100.

16. At the same time as these events, the French nobility and parliament were engaging in an ultimately unsuccessful xenophobic rebellion against the monarchy and its ministers, thus intensifying the chaos.

17. Marcelle Benoit, "Paris, 1661–87: The Age of Lully," in *The Early Baroque Era: From the Late 16th Century to the 1660s* (*Music and Society* Series) (Englewood Cliffs, N.J.: Prentice Hall, 1993), 266.

18. Cousin Claude Jacquet (1605–1661), a *maistre faiseur d'instrumens* and a *joueur d'instrumens de musique* (master instrument builder and instrumentalist), is not to be confused with Jacquet de La Guerre's father, also named Claude.

19. Cessac, 23.

20. Catherine Massip, "Paris, 1600–61," in *The Early Baroque Era,* 228; and Anthony, 19 and following. See also Cessac, 26 and following.

21. The renown of the Jacquets as instrument builders continued to the end of the eighteenth century. See Cessac, 29.

22. Sainte-Chapelle (on the Île de la Cité), as distinguished from the Chapelle Royale (on the Île Saint-Louis) of the court, was completed between 1699 and 1710. See Anthony, 28–30, also Cessac, 22.

23. Massip, 218.

24. Benoit, 252–55 and 266.

25. See Anthony, 29 and following, and Cessac, 102.

26. Cessac, 26, n. 1.

27. Horne, 82 and following.

28. Anthony, 411.

29. See Danielle Roster, *Allein mit meiner Musik:Komponistinnen in der europaeischen Musikgeschichte vom Mittelalter bis ins frühe 20. Jahrhundert* (Echternach: éditions phi, 1995), 65.

30. There is at present no record of her birth. See Cessac, 107.

31. Cessac discovered two of his compositions, published c. 1737; see Cessac, 43.

32. Cessac, 11, cites an archival death notice for him, this announcement also reporting that Nicolas, unmarried and impoverished, was forty-five years old at his death, which was caused by an unidentified illness.

33. Ibid., 40.

34. Patricia Ranum, "A Sweet Servitude: A Musician's Life at the Court of Mlle de Guise," *Early Music* 5, no. 3 (August 1987): 350–51; see also Roster, 78–79.

35. Cessac, 41–42. Could this duke perhaps have been Duchess Sophie-Elisabeth's grandson or grandnephew? See chapter 1.

36. Roster, *Allein,* 78–79 and 248; Ranum, 347 and 351; and Cessac, 42. One of the sons, Jean-Antoine, became an organist.

37. References to her age when she was presented to the king range from five to fifteen. See Mary Cyr, "Elisabeth Jacquet de La Guerre: myth or marvel? Seeking the composer's individuality," *Musical Times* 149 (Winter 2008): 79–87. At least in the eighteenth century, however, it was by no means rare that women—as well as men—composers and librettists had been child prodigies. See Jacqueline Letzter and Robert Adelson, *Women Writing Opera: Creativity and Controversy in the Age of the French Revolution* (Berkeley, Los Angeles, London: University of California Press, 2001), 16.

38. Cessac, 24–25.

39. Roster, *Allein*, 64–67; also Carol Neuls-Bates, ed., *Women in Music: An Anthology of Source Readings from the Middle Ages to the Present*, rev. ed. (Boston: Northeastern University Press, 1996), 62.

40. Roster, *Allein*, 64. Jacquet's earliest works, though performed at court, have not survived. See Cessac, 35–38.

41. Like the rest of the French nobility, in fact, Louis XIV's grandson Philippe Duke of Orléans (regent until Louis XV came of age) engaged highly qualified tutors for his own children in voice and harpsichord. See W. H. Lewis, *The Sunset of the Splendid Century: The Life and Times of Louis Auguste de Bourbon, Duc de Maine, 1670–1736* (Garden City, N.Y.: Anchor Books [Doubleday & Company], 1955 and 1963), 88–89.

42. Cessac, 108.

43. Barbara Garvey Jackson, "Musical Women of the Seventeenth and Eighteenth Centuries," *Women and Music: A History*, ed. Karin Pendle (Bloomington and Indianapolis: Indiana University Press, 1991), 201; also Julie Anne Sadie, "*Musiciennes* of the *Ancien Régime*," in *Women Making Music: The Western Art Tradition, 1150–1950*, eds. Jane Bowers and Judith Tick (Urbana and Chicago: University of Illinois Press, 1987), 191–223; and Roster, 62–63.

44. Although Jacquet de La Guerre was now married, her compositions continued to be performed among the higher levels of society. In the summer of 1685, the Marquis de Dangeau wrote in his journal, "A little opera was performed [at the home of the Dauphin], for which the little [Jacquet] had composed all the arias. She is, I believe, only twenty years old." In December 1691 the *Mercure gallant* commented, "Music lovers and—professionals agree that this extraordinary personality demonstrates as much taste as also skill in her vocal music." This commentary is written in the form of a poem, *Epistre de Monsieur de Lully à Mademoiselle La Guerre*, which claimed that "in France the highly celebrated Jean-Baptiste Lully wrote this ode on St. Cecilia's Day for Mademoiselle La Guerre—the first musician of the world—and sent it to her from heaven [implying where Lully was]." Lully had died on March 22, 1687.

45. Sadie, "*Musiciennes*," 211–12.

46. Évrard Titon du Tillet (1677–1762), *Parnasse français* (1732), 636, cited in Neuls-Bates, *Women*, 62–64. If she began her performances immediately after returning to Paris, they possibly took place in the couple's first home, on the Rue Saint Antoine; see Roster, *Allein*, 65.

47. Titon du Tillet, 30 and following; see also the *Mercure gallant* (December 1691), 231–42. See Roster, 66–69 and 248.

48. From 1673 on, in the era of the *tragédies lyriques* with their primadonnas, Lully himself trained gifted male and female students in the Académie Royale de Musique as preparation for professional careers in opera; this training also providing both genders with role models. See B. G. Jackson, 57–58; also Roster, *Allein*, 62.

49. The music of Sainte Chapelle (see n. 72, p. 208) was directed by the influential composer and organist Marc-Antoine Charpentier, who won this post over Jacquet's publisher Sébastien de Brossard. Sadie, "Paris," 155–56; also Cessac, 102.

50. Michel de La Guerre became organist of Notre-Dame at age fourteen (c. 1619). He was also considered an excellent lutenist, no doubt contributing to the influence of the lute on harpsichord music. Cessac, 33, n. 2.

51. The work was finally completely staged in the theater of the Palais Royale in 1657; see Anthony, 85; see also Cessac, 32–33.

52. Cessac, 33, citing seventeenth-century sources.

53. There were also La Guerre family ties by marriage and blood to the Bongards.

54. The extended Jacquet/La Guerre family also counted among its "members" René Trépagne, a clergyman and political activist in service of Louis XIV (1684–1697). He provided the verses for four of Jacquet's airs and wrote a paean to the composer, praising her as "Terpsicore, the classical muse of music and dance." Jacquet's publisher Henri Baussen was also related to the La Guerres by marriage. Cessac, 31–32, 169–70, and 191.

55. Massip, 231.

56. This date is given according to Titon du Tillet without substantiation. Her son's first name is not known.

57. See Cessac, 106.

58. This date, too, is given according to Titon du Tillet.

59. Cessac, 106–8.

60. Idem.

61. Cessac, 171–76 and 178–79.

62. Sadie, "*Musiciennes*," 199–201.

63. Four airs from *Les Amusemens* were performed in January 1711 by the Versailles court singer Marguerite-Louise Couperin, a member of a musical dynasty still considered remarkable today. See Cessac, 169–70.

64. Anthony, 36–38; also Massip, 231.

65. The church was built between 1532 and 1632.

66. As emphasized in other chapters of this book, in western European culture generally until the last one and one-half centuries, boys alone received their musical and academic training in institutional settings. For example, important composers "matriculated" from church choir schools, such as Dufay, Palestrina, Schütz, Haydn, Schubert, and Bruckner, to name only a few. By the seventeenth century in France, however, parents were gradually growing more aware of the advantages to be won for girls, as well as for boys, through intensive musical training from an early age as a direct path to significant professional attainments. As a result of this changing attitude, girls, at least in voice, were increasingly receiving improved vocal instruction. See Roster, *Allein*, 62.

67. Roster, "Elisabeth-Claude Jacquet de la Guerre," in *Annaeherung VI: an Sieben Komponistinnen* (Kassel: Furore-Verlag, 1995), 76–77.

68. Horne, 100 and 109; see also Bukofzer, 142.

69. Julie Anne Sadie, "Paris and Versailles," in *The Late Baroque Era*, 159–62; Anthony, 18; Lewis, *Sunset*, 45–48; Whitney Chadwick, *Women, Art, and Society*, 2nd rev. and expanded ed. (London: Thames and Hudson, 1990 and 1996), 139–43. For some of the general information on Versailles under Louis XIV, I have also relied on W. H. Lewis's classic *The Splendid Century: the Life and Times of Louis XIV* (Garden City, New York: Doubleday Anchor Books, 1957).

70. Anthony, 17–30, who also cites Norbert Dufourcq, ed. "La Musique française de 1661 à 1764," in *Musique, les hommes, les instruments, les sources,* vol. 1 (Paris: Larousse, 1965), 286.

71. Benoit, 247.

72. Until the mid-eighteenth century, women in France were prohibited as a whole from participation as instrumentalists in the chapels of the aristocracy, the church, or the king's court, and they were barred from joining any orchestras. Singers alone among women musicians could sometimes participate in court chapel performances toward the later seventeenth century. Unofficial artists, they were designated and paid only as *musiciennes ordinaires* or *extraordinaires* or simply as *filles de la musique.* While chapel choir members at first were amateur singers from parishes in Paris and the provinces, the court musical establishment (for which choral music functioned as a liturgical embellishment) increasingly appointed professional singers already active in secular music to its staff.

73. Bukofzer, 146.

74. In major churches of Paris such as Sainte Chappelle and Notre Dame, the royal choirmaster took charge of musical training—but according to the age-old practice, only for male child choir members at Versailles. Benoit, 246.

75. Sadie, "Paris," 140, 160; also *"Musiciennes,"* 177, 195–96, and 202.

76. Sadie, "Paris," 140 and following and *"Musiciennes,"* 195–96; see also Roster, *Allein,* 75.

77. Cessac, 58.

78. Ibid., 59–60, citing F. Couperin, *L'art de Toucher le Clavecin* (Paris, 1716), 12–13. Compare Mrs. Jameson's biological gendering of a much later era. (See p. 1.)

79. Cessac, 47.

80. Such lute scores used a type of musical notation in which symbols other than notes on a staff are given for the performer.

81. Cessac, 47. In France, the composition of lute music had waned since the death of Denis Gaultier in 1672.

82. Anthony, 306–7.

83. First published in January 1687 by Henri de Baussen. See Cessac, 35.

84. Bates prepared the first complete edition of the 1687 collection in 1986.

85. In the unmeasured sections, there is no set meter, the result being a freer rhythmic style of writing surrounding a more rhythmically persistent measured section that often ventures into the bass range, thereby stabilizing the harmony. The two free areas cover a striking range of pitches (with a great variety of note-values) following a predominately arpeggiated melodic course that is charged with emotional expression.

86. Cessac, 57.

87. Anthony, 288–99 and 306–12.

88. Cessac, 56–57 and 123–25.

89. August 1, 1707, cited in Roster, *Allein,* 72–73.

90. Cessac, 121.

91. French scholar Mary Cyr reminded me that Jacquet de La Guerre especially favored ornamentation and that her talent for improvisation was particularly noted by Titon du Tillet.

92. Anthony, 312, who also mentions a court performance of a piece of this nature in August 1729.

93. Ibid., 386–87.

94. Ibid., 133.

95. The name "Marchand" mentioned here possibly refers to the brothers Jean-Baptiste (1670–1751) and Jean-Noel (1666–1710). Roster, *Allein,* 73 and 249.

96. See Cessac, 87–89; see also Anthony, 307 and 386–87.

97. Cessac's conclusion, 36–37.

98. Cessac, 38.

99. Bibliotèque Nationale, ms. fr. 2217. See Cessac, 35–38.

100. Letzter and Adelson, 240. The dedication is in the Bibliotèque Nationale de Paris: BN ms. fn. 2217, as cited in Roster, 23 and 248.

101. Benoit, 266; see also Letzter and Adelson, 16 and 23.

102. Anthony, 39 and 235.

103. Cessac, 79.

104. Members of the nobility danced in Duchess Sophie-Elisabeth's dramatic works, as described in chapter 1.

105. Between 1670 and 1720, we know of only seven operas by three French women; between 1720 and 1770, twelve operas by seven women have been identified. In contrast to Jacquet de La Guerre, many eighteenth-century European women opera composers were aristocrats, or even members of the royalty, such as Maria Antonia Walpurgis, Electress of Saxony (1724–1780), Anna Amalia, Duchess of Saxe-Weimar (1739–1807), Wilhemine Sophie Friedericke, Margravin of Bayreuth (1709–1758), and Catherine II, Empress of Russia (1729–1796). The operas of women such as these—perhaps those having recourse to extensive court libraries for text sources—could be staged in their own court theaters. See Letzter and Adelson, 4 and 23.

106. *Céphale et Procris* has been revived and published in a performing edition. See Mary Cyr, "Representing Jacquet de La Guerre on disc . . .," *Early Music* (November 2004): 549.

107. Regarding the orchestration of French baroque arias, see Deborah Kauffman, "*Violons en Basse* as Musical Allegory," *The Journal of Musicology* 23, no. 1 (Winter 2006): 184–85.

108. As was customary with much of her music, Jacquet wrote a flowery formal dedication (printed in Ballard's published score) of her opera to Louis XIV, confirming her gratitude to him for taking time between his strenuous work schedule to hear performances of her music. Benoit, 266; see also Roster, 72.

109. No staging indications for the opera have survived. Ballard's published score contains only one or two tempo indications.

110. Cessac, 71–72.

111. Ibid., 72–79.

112. Ibid., 79.

113. See Roster, *Allein,* 72, citing Sébastien Brossard, Catalogue. Bibliotèque nationale de Paris N Ré. Vm8 21, 544, 264. Also see Michel Brenet, "Quatre femmes musiciennes I: Mademoiselle Jacquet de la Guerre," *L'Art* 59, no. 4 (October 2, 1894): 107–12; Jackson, 74 and following; see also Letzter and Adelson, 100.

114. Cessac, 137–38.

115. Two primary publications in this affair were those of the pro-Italian François Raguenet (1702) and the pro-French Jean Laurent Le Cerf de La Viéville (1704).

116. See Sadie, "Paris," 176; see also Buelow, 1, 15, and 143–45.

117. Anthony, 422.

118. Idem. Despite the antipathy of many French toward the cantata, Sébastien Brossard

(see p. 102) claimed that France could gain from the cantata, because it cultivated "that air of liberty, which distinguishes [France] from other nations. . . ." Cessac, 135, citing Brossard's *Dissertation sur cette espèce de concert qu'on nomme Cantate*, bib. n., fr. 5269, n.d.

119. Anthony, 422–25.

120. Letzter and Adelson, 102.

121. Roster, *Annaeherung*, 76; see also Adrian Rose, "Elisabeth-Claude Jacquet de la Guerre and the Secular *Cantate françoise*," *Early Music* 13, no. 4 (November 1985): 539 and following.

122. Benoit, 238.

123. Also see Ranum, 353.

124. Some French nuns, while active in convents, also sang sacred music in the royal chapel; and nun singers in French convents (joined by a few lay women singers) were highly recognized for their art. Lay women musicians at Versailles included the royal singer Anne-Renée Rebel (see p. 55), her two daughters, and François Couperin's cousin Louise Couperin, probably an organist at the royal abbey at Maubisson. (The Rebel family, like Couperins, was another important Paris/Versailles musical dynasty.) Though Versailles choir members initially were amateur singers drawn from church parishes in Paris and the provinces, the court singers were increasingly professional performers already active in secular music.

125. Catherine Gordon-Seifert, "From Impurity to Piety: Mid-17th-Century French Devotional Airs and the Spiritual Conversion of Women," *Journal of Musicology* 22, no. 2 (Spring 2005): 268–91.

126. Idem.

127. Among the earliest (1703–1713) male composers of cantatas in France, Cyr ("Representing Jacquet de La Guerre," 549) lists Nicholas Bernier, Jean-Baptiste Stuck, Jean-Baptiste Morin, André Campra, and Thomas-Louis Bourgeois.

128. Sadie, "*Musiciennes*," 209.

129. *Journal des Sçavans*, January 7, 1709, 13–14, and April 6, 1711, 216–18, as cited in Roster, *Annäherung*, 74.

130. Ibid., 249.

131. See Deborah Kaufman, "Violons-en-basse," *Journal of Musicology* 23, no. 1 (Winter 2006): 153–85.

132. The Saint-Germain theater had appropriated the traditions of the Comédie Italienne in style, repertoire, and such characters as Arlequin and Pierrot, along with allegorical figures. Vocal and instrumental pieces were inserted into the dialogues of the play. "But the presence of newly composed airs by Jean-Claude Gillier and Jacquet [de La Guerre]," Cessac remarks, " . . . is a true precursor of *opéra comique*." She also considers Jacquet de La Guerre's duet the first duet given at the Théâtre de Foire. See Cessac, 166. Gaining experience for her operatic work, Jacquet had served as a harpsichord accompanist for dramatic productions in private homes from her adolescence on. She also played the harpsichord at the fair.

133. Sadie, "Paris," 212, and Cessac, 164–65.

134. Cited in Anthony, 428.

135. Ibid., 425.

136. Laura E. DeMarco, "The Fact of the Castrato and the Myth of the Countertenor," *Musical Quarterly* 86, no. 1 (Spring 2002): 175. Anthony, 37, notes that in French baroque vocal writing, the *haute-contre* prevailed over the tenor voice.

137. Jackson, 71, citing Jean Laurent Le Cerf de la Vièville, *Comparaison de la musique italienne et de la musique françoise* (Brussels, 1704–1706).

138. Massip, 223.

139. Roster, *Annäherung,* 63, who also cites Marcelle Benoit, *Versailles et les musiciens de roi, 1661–1733: Étude institutionelle et sociale* (Paris: Picard, 1971).

140. David Lewin, "Women's Voices and the Fundamental Bass," *Journal of Musicology* 10, no. 4 (Fall 1992): 476, where Lewin refers to Jean-Phillipe Rameau's *Traité de l'Harmonie* (Paris: Ballard, 1722). Trans. Philip Gossett, *Treatise on Harmony* (New York: Dover Publications, 1971).

141. Abbate, "Opera; or, the Envoicing of Women," in Ruth A. Solie, ed., *Musicology and Difference: Gender and Sexuality in Music Scholarship* (Berkeley and Los Angeles: University of California Press, 1993), 256–58.

142. Many students of such *musiciennes* even helped stimulate and inspire their mentors' work as composers, on occasion leading to publication of their teachers' manuscripts. See Sadie, *Musiciennes,* 201.

143. Ibid., 57–58.

144. Jackson, 55.

145. It should, however, be kept in mind that there were possibly other equally talented French women performers and composers who may have worked in Paris or Versailles, or even elsewhere in western Europe, but whose music has never been published, leaving their works hidden in libraries waiting to be taken into account.

146. A multitude of songs by women, even songs of dubious worth, were printed in fashionable collections or in journals such as the *Mercure de France.* See Anthony, 311; see also Jackson, 72.

147. Roster, *Allein,* 75.

148. Ibid., 55.

149. Benoit, 247.

150. Massip, 227.

Chapter 3. Josephine Lang

1. Nancy B. Reich, "European Composers and Musicians, ca. 1800–1890," in *Women and Music: A History,* ed. Karin Pendle (Bloomington and Indianapolis: Indiana University Press, 1991), 97–122.

2. I have not found a connection between this Steffani and the Italian composer, cleric, and diplomat Agostino Steffani (1654–1728), long a powerful force in the musical life of both Munich and Braunschweig, especially as a salient force in the development of early German opera.

3. This institution was founded in 1725, during Jacquet de La Guerre's final years.

4. See Bertil van Boer, "The Travel Diary of Joseph Martin Kraus: Translation and Commentary," *Journal of Musicology* 8 no. 2 (Spring 1990): 272.

5. See Sabina Hitzelberger," *The International Cyclopedia of Music and Musicians,* ed. Oscar Thompson, 9th ed. Robert Sabin, ed. (New York: Dodd, Mead, 1964), 989 and 1165.

6. "Würzburg," *The New Grove Dictionary of Music and Musicians* 20, Stanley Sadie, ed. (London and New York: Macmillan, 1980), 551.

7. "Munich," *New Grove* 12, 783.

8. Peter (von) Winter (1754–1825), who held office from 1778 to 1784, was a popular,

prolific comic opera composer. His opera *Das Unterbrochene Opferfest* became very popular after its Vienna premiere in 1796. The Abbé Georg Joseph Vogler (1749–1814) held the *Kapellmeister* post from 1784 to 1800 and was a highly regarded composition teacher. Vogler numbered among his students the celebrated composers Carl Maria von Weber, von Winter himself, and Giacomo Meyerbeer. The composer Carl Cannabich (1771–1806) was *Kapellmeister* from 1800 to 1806. Like the Langs, the Cannabichs were one of several outstanding musician families active at Mannheim, who then accompanied its musical establishment when it was transferred to the Munich court. Idem.

9. Gerhard Allroggen, "Maria Antonia Walpurgis," in *The Norton/Grove Dictionary of Women Composers,* eds. Julie Anne Sadie and Rhian Samuel (London: Macmillan Press, 1995), 313–14.

10. It had been claimed by some that, in recognition of Regina Hitzelberger-Lang's artistry, Beethoven composed his song "An die Geliebte" (first version) for her in Vienna in December 1811. See Maynard Solomon, *Beethoven* (New York: Schirmer Books, 1977), 175–297.

11. The large-scale formation of choirs, themselves not of modest size, grew largely out of Germany's powerful, post-Napoleonic cultural-national movement attracting choral groups (with an essentially middle-class membership). Choruses sprang up even in the tiniest German hamlets, as did song festivals with performances by hundreds of massed singers. See Cecelia Hopkins Porter, "The New Public and the Reordering of the Musical Establishment: The Lower Rhine Music Festivals, 1818–1867, in *19th-Century Music* 3, no. 3 (March 1980): 211–24.

12. See Porter, "The Reign of the *Dilettanti*: Düsseldorf from Mendelssohn to Schumann," *Musical Quarterly* 73, no. 4 (1989): 5–11.

13. Roswitha Sperber, ed., *Women Composers in Germany* (Bonn: Inter Nationes, 1996), 26–27.

14. See Arthur Loesser, *Men, Women and Pianos: A Social History* (New York: Simon and Schuster, 1954), 291–92.

15. Rev. Dr. Storrs, "The Mother's Love," *Mother's Assistant* 9, no. 1 (July 1846): 8. Though given by an English, not German-speaking, commentator, this citation is contemporary with Lang's midlife.

16. See Riemann, "Josephine Lang," in *Dictionary of Music,* 426; see also Harald and Sharon Krebs, *Josephine Lang: Her Life and Songs* (New York: Oxford University Press, 2007), 11–12.

17. For Lang's connections with the Stieler family, see H. and S. Krebs, *Josephine Lang,* 59–60.

18. Now displayed in the Munich Residenz, Stieler's painting of King Ludwig I in coronation attire (1826) was commissioned to honor not only Ludwig's statesmanship but also his generous arts patronage. Hermann Neumann, *Die Münchner Residenz* (Munich and London: Presteln Verlag, 2000), 22.

19. A commanding force in German musical life, Hiller was a virtuoso pianist, a noted conductor, a prolific composer, a writer on music, and a close friend of Robert and Clara Schumann and other major musical figures. See Sperber, 26–27.

20. Nancy Reich says 1836, rather than the previous year. See Reich, "European Composers and Musicians, ca. 1800–1890," in *Women and Music: A History,* ed. Karin Pendle (Bloomington and Indianapolis: Indiana University Press, 1991), 103–4.

21. Idem.

22. H. and S. Krebs, *Josephine Lang*, 24.

23. In October 1831, Mendelssohn conducted a concert in Munich devoted entirely to his own works as part of his own musical affairs in that city. He directed his Symphony no. 11, "A Midsummer Night's Dream" Overture, and his new Piano Concerto no. 1 in G Minor with the composer as soloist.

24. For Mendelssohn's descriptions of Lang, see *Felix Mendelssohn: Letters*, ed. G. Selden-Goth (New York: Vienna House, 1945 and 1973), 175–77.

25. Idem.

26. See Gordon Craig, *The Germans* (New York: Penguin Books, 1982), 153–54.

27. *Felix Mendelssohn: Letters*, 177. Mendelssohn even arranged two of Lang's works for male chorus.

28. See H. and S. Krebs, *Josephine Lang*, 50.

29. Heller remained in Augsburg until 1838, when he moved to Paris and was quickly drawn into the city's brilliant orbit of salons displaying the superstar virtuosi in their midst. His popular pedagogical studies for piano *25 Études faciles*, Op. 45, no. 2, not infrequently exhibit a clearly vocal lyricism.

30. See Schumann's discussion in *Die neue Zeitschrift für Musik* 39 (1853), 185–86, cited in John Daverio, *Robert Schumann: Herald of a "New Poetic Age"* (New York: Oxford University Press, 1997), 123 and 454.

31. Daverio, *Robert Schumann*, 454.

32. See Riemann, 407.

33. Ferdinand Hiller, "Josephine Lang, die Lieder-Componistin," in *Aus dem Tonleben unserer Zeit* 2 (Leipzig: H. Mendelssohn, 1868), 120–21. Heller's circle of friends in Paris included Mendelssohn's close colleague Ferdinand Hiller.

34. George W. Bethune, *The British Female Poets: with Biographical and Critical Notices* (New York: Hurst, 1846), iv–v. As previously stated, Lang was guided through the music world first and primarily by her mother, Regina Hitzelberger-Lang, whose own mother had done the same.

35. One can reasonably imagine that at least the historic, restored town center of today's Tübingen looks similar to its physical appearance in Lang's day. During a research visit to Tübingen in 2003, the author observed that much of its renaissance architecture survives still. The town escaped World War Two bombing and is reachable even today only by ground transportation, making it seem as remote in space as in time. Everyday life in this Old World city still revolves around its university, the streets and cafés populated mostly by students, faculty members, and their families.

36. Curiously, there was apparently another Professor Köstlin active at Tübingen University: Karl Reinhold (1819–1894), six years younger than Josephine Lang's husband, Christian. Both Köstlins shared the middle name Reinhold and a father who was a theologian in Urach, home to an important German monastery school about twenty-five kilometers directly east of Tübingen. One therefore surmises that they were brothers.

37. Another outstanding example of soirée hostesses in nineteenth-century Germany was Mendelssohn's great-aunt Sara Levy-Itzig (1761–1854). Her salon exemplified the important position occupied by the salons of wealthy educated women in the cultural life of Berlin from the later eighteenth century through the nineteenth. See Peter Wollny, "Sara Levy and the Making of Musical Taste in Berlin," *Musical Quarterly* 77, no. 4 (Winter 1993): 651.

38. The daughter of an established composer, Emilie Zumsteeg (1796–1857) lived and

composed in Stuttgart, not far from Tübingen. It would be interesting to see if she ever attended Lang's salon. Mörike was a noted German lyric poet whose songs were set by many composers, some of them by Josephine Lang.

39. See Reich, 103–4.

40. See Heinrich Adolf Köstlin, "Josephine Lang [Köstlin]," *Sammlung musikalischer Vorträge,* 3, ed. P. Waldersee (Leipzig: Breitkopf & Härtel, 1881), 54; and Köstlin, *Die Geschichte der Musik; für die Gebildeten aller Stände* (Tübingen, 1875). Köstlin's other works include *Die Tonkunst: Einführung in die Ästhetik der Musik* (Stuttgart, 1877) and books on German Lutheran choral music, performances of which he himself conducted. See also Riemann, 407–8; and Thompson and Sabin, *International Cyclopedia,* 1128.

41. Reich, "European Composers," 101.

42. Ibid., 102.

43. A painter, sculptor, and photographer, Maria not only mended the great composer's socks and made him silk ties, but she even brewed his favorite broth and included him at family Christmas dinners. Maria also took many informal photographs of Brahms of inestimable value to historians. An attorney, her husband was director of the celebrated Siemens engineering firm. See Jan Swafford, *Brahms: A Biography* (New York: Alfred A. Knopf, 1997), 496–97; also Malcolm MacDonald, *Brahms* (New York: Schirmer Books, 1990), 234–39 and following.

44. Marcia J. Citron, "Josephine Lang (1815–1880)," *Historical Anthology of Music by Women,* ed. James R. Briscoe (Bloomington and Indianapolis: Indiana University Press, 1987), 109.

45. See Hiller, 116–36.

46. Reich, "European Composers," 118.

47. See Loesser, 268–70.

48. Uhland and Hölderlin had strong connections with Tübingen.

49. See Cecelia Hopkins Porter, *The Rhine as Musical Metaphor: Cultural Identity in German Romantic Music* (Boston: Northeastern University Press, 1996), 83–84.

50. Reich, "European Composers," 103.

51. Porter, *Rhine as Musical Metaphor,* 48–52.

52. The *Handbuch* lists the following songs of Lang from opus 10 through 15. "Abschied," (E. Schulze) for mezzo soprano (or contralto), Op. 10, no. 6 (Leipzig, Kistner), 5 Ngr; *6 deutsche Lieder* (L. Uhland and J. Kerner) ("Antwort," "Ruhethal," "Frühlingsahnung," "Abschied," "Sängers Trost," and "Im Herbst"), Op. 11 (Lpzg., Kistner), 15 Ngr; *6 Lieder* (C. Reinhold) ("Am Wasserfall," "Nachts," "Abermals am See," "O würst du da," "Der Herbst," "Die wandernde Wolke"), Op. 12 (Leipzig, Kistner) 25 Ngr; *6 Lieder* ("Abschied," "Der Wanderer an die Quellen," "Aus der Ferne," "Schmetterling," "An die Entfernte," "Namenlos") for soprano, Op. 13 (Mainz, Schott) 1 fl., 21 Kr.; *6 deutsche Lieder* (C. Reinhold) ("O sehntest du dich so nach mir," "Am Flusse," "Gedenke mein," "An den See," "Vögelein," "Auf dem See in tausend Sterne"), Op. 14 (Lpzg., B and H) 1 Kr. 5 Ngr; *6 deutsche Lieder* ("Den Abschied schnell genommen," "Mag da draussen Schnee sich thürmen," "In weite Ferne," "Lüftchen, ihr plaudert so viel," "Der Winter," "Sehnen"), Op. 15 (Lpz., B and H), 20 Ngr. (See Adolphe Hofmeister, *Handbuch der musikalischen Literatur oder allgemeines systematisch-geordnetes Verzeichniss der in Deutschland und in den angrenzenden Ländern gedruckten Musikalien; auch musikalischen Schriften und Abbildungen mit Anzeige der Verleger und Preise, Erster Ergänzungsband, die vom Januar 1844 bis Ende des Jahres 1851,*

neu erschienenen und neu aufgelgten musikalischen Werke enthaltend (Leipzig: Friedrich Hofmeister, 1852), 329.

53. See Daverio, *Robert Schumann,* 119 and 188.

54. Schumann, *Die Neue Zeitschrift für Musik* 2 (1835), 3, as cited in Daverio, 119.

55. *NZfM* 9, no. 43 (November 27, 1838): 174.

56. Oswald Lorenz, "Josephine Lang: *Sechs Lieder für Singst. m. Pfte.,*Op. 9—Leipzig, Fr. Kistner.—5/6 Thlr.—; *Sechs Lieder* f. mezzo soprano od. Alt, m. Pfte.—Op. 10—Ebendas.—5/6 Thlr.," *NZfM* (July-Dec. 1841), 15/4, (9 July 1841), 14.

57. See also reviews of Lang's songs in *Die allgemeine musikalische Zeitung,* Bd. 10, no. 3 (1841); Bd. 10, no. 8 (1846), 36–37; and Bd. 1, no. 1 (1848), 35.

58. See Marian Wilson Kimber, "The 'Suppression' of Fanny Mendelssohn: Rethinking Feminist Biography," *Nineteenth-Century Music* 26, no. 2 (Fall 2002): 113–29; and see the review of Hensel in *Die Wiener Allgemeine Musikalische Zeitung* 17 (May 8, 1847): 223.

59. Op. 14, *Sechs deutsche Lieder,* Breitkopf und Härtel, in the *NZfM* (July–December 1848) Bd. 29, 66; and Op. 14 and 15 NZ (January–June 1848), Bd. 28, 236. Other important critics in Leipzig in 1848 included C. F. Becker, Franz Brendel (when editor of the *NZfM*), Alfred Dörffel, and A. F. Riccius.

60. At this date one cannot determine the exact dates of the songs for which Lang gave only opus numbers—songs that she designated "composed before 1867."

61. Charles Rosen, *The Romantic Generation* (Cambridge, Mass.: Harvard University Press, 1995), 46.

62. See the discussion of this topic in Porter, *Rhine as Musical Metaphor,* chapter 1.

63. Kreutzer had been court *Kapellmeister* in nearby Stuttgart (1812–1816) and in Donauesschingen (1818–1822), and was also music director of the Vienna Court Opera (1822–1827 and 1829–1840). Silcher was an important folksong collector, a folklike style also pervading his own songs. He was music director of the University of Tübingen from 1817 to 1860; he also founded a singing society and oratorio choir.

64. See Harald Krebs, "Irregular Phrase Rhythm in the Songs of Josephine Lang," Lecture, Rochester, N.Y., University of Rochester, November 12, 2001. Also, references to hypermeter appear throughout H. and S. Krebs, *Josephine Lang.*

65. The songs discussed here are some of those I examined between 1998 and 2006 in the Bayerische Staatsbibliothek in Munich and the Württembergische Landesbibliothek, Stuttgart (the major collection of Lang's compositions and biographical sources); and three libraries in Vienna: the Österreichische Nationalbibliothek, the Stadt- und Landesbibliothek, and the Archiv der Gesellschaft der Musikfreunde. The Krebs' detailed database and information on locating the chief musical and biographical sources on Lang in Germany have been invaluable. Also helpful was the staff of the Musicology Department of the University of Munich and Dieter Spatschek at the Bayerische Staatsbibliothek, also in Munich. In 2003 Dr. Horst G. Weise arranged a backstage tour for me at the restored Bavarian State Opera (in the former royal Residenz) in Munich, where Josephine Lang and her family were court artists as both singers and instrumentalists. The theater was rebuilt after World War Two.

66. See Marcia Citron, "Josephine Lang," in *Historical Anthology of Music by Women,* ed. James R. Briscoe (Bloomington and Indianapolis: Indiana University Press, 1987), 109–12. The Krebses list it as Op. 6, no. 3. Lang sang it for Mendelssohn in 1831.

67. Württembergische Landesbibliothek: Mus.fol. 530 S7v-9r, first version; 1835 Mf 54a S38r-39v, second version.

68. Ibid., third version 34/49: Mus fol 53i S. 19b-21.

69. Krebs, 147.

70. *NZfM* 43, no. 16, 175.

71. See Krebs, 35–36.

72. Examples of these features in songs from 1838 include "Der Schmetterling," Op. 13, no. 4 (Graf von Giech) and "Namenloses," Op. 13, no. 6 (Maltitz).

73. See the Index of Rheinlieder, no. 146, in Porter, *Rhine as Musical Metaphor,* also pp. 18 and following.

74. Many forces were at work in the European situation of the 1840s; these included a strategic Rhine issue—part of the entangled European power-play over control of the Mediterranean. The French brazenly threatened in July 1840 to take the Rhine River, further sharpening German cultural-national sentiments. As a result of this turmoil, the appearance of the poem "Der deutsche Rhein" by Nicolas Becker, an obscure Rhineland attorney, inspired the composition and publication of more than one hundred musical settings of his verses alone. (More than four hundred Rheinlieder were composed and/or published in Germany during the 1840s decade.) Lang herself composed a version (see p. 99 regarding her setting). The popularity of the poem also sparked an intense competition between Berlin, Leipzig, and other German cities, even tiny villages, to choose the "best" setting. During this unsettled 1840s decade, Schumann composed nine *Rheinlieder* (including a Becker setting, which never won the prize); and Wagner gestated his Rhine-embedded Ring Cycle. See Porter, *Rhine as Musical Metaphor,* 38 and following.

75. Kinkel's compositions include stage works, choral cantatas, and song collections. See Rosario Marciano and Jorge-Sanchez-Chiong, "Johanna Kinkel," in *The Norton/Grove Dictionary of Women Composers,* 249–50. During her twenties in Berlin, Kinkel's compositions drew the admiration of Mendelssohn; later Schumann commended her songs. Her friends included Fanny Mendelssohn Hensel and Bettina Brentano, a member of a noted German literary family. As a newspaper publisher in Bonn, Kinkel, along with her husband, expressed political sympathies unfavorable with the powers that be during the *Vormärz* crisis of the 1840s. As a result, Kinkel, with her family, exiled themselves to London, where she gave up composing in favor of advocating women's rights. Ultimately she succumbed to a deep depression, committing suicide at the age of forty-eight.

76. See Krebs, 118–23.

77. See Jennifer C. Post, "Erasing the Boundaries between Public and Private in Women's Performance Traditions," in *Cecilia Reclaimed: Feminist Perspectives on Gender and Music,* ed. Susan C. Cook and Judy S. Tsou (Urbana and Chicago: University of Illinois Press, 1994), 35–36.

78. "Ancient Germans," Gordon A. Craig maintains, "lived in a society of tribal enclaves favoring male children—above all, for their fighting potential, making it no surprise that German women held a subordinate position compared with their menfolk. . . . The Roman historian Tacitus wrote that German women 'receive one husband, as having one body and life, that they may have no thoughts beyond, no further-reaching desires.'" In nineteenth-century Germany, both its women and its Jewish citizens expected the equal rights posed by the aristocracy of the enlightenment to continue. To the contrary, such eighteenth-century ideals faded with the turn of the century, as Napoleon devastated the German landscape; and the rising bourgeoisie were increasingly assuming leadership in politics and cultural life. (See Gordon A. Craig, *The Germans,* 147–48.)

79. Kimber, 124.

80. Ibid., 128.

81. Rosen, xi.

82. See Nancy Reich, *Clara Schumann: The Artist and the Woman* (Ithaca, N.Y., and London: Cornell University Press, 1985), 111–17 and 175–76.

83. Ibid., 111–17 and 175–76, and "European Composers," 97–122.

Chapter 4. Maria Bach

1. I am grateful to the Fulbright Commission for the Senior Scholar grant awarded me in 2000 to do research on this chapter in Vienna libraries. I would also like to thank the Kulturforum (formerly, the Cultural Department) of the Austrian Foreign Ministry in Vienna for additional research support in this project. Maria Bach's *Blitzlichter aus meinem Leben* (Vienna: Self-published, 1976) is Bach's account of her personal and professional life presented in a series of sixty-six vignettes completed in 1975. The original manuscript of the *Blitzlichter* is held in the Druckschriften department of Vienna's Nationalbibliothek. Another starting point for this chapter was the excellent study by Gerda M. Eiselmair, *Die männliche Gilde sehe sich vor! Die Österreichische Komponistin Maria Bach* (Vienna: Löcker Verlag, 1996). I also owe much to Professor Elena Ostleitner of the University of Music and the Performing Arts in Vienna for her support and information regarding twentieth-century Austrian women composers.

The original German of this citation reads: "Dieses junge Frauenwesen ist ausgesprochen begabt. Zwar glüht sie, stürmt und weiss nicht wohin! Können und Kindlichkeit hart nebeneinander. Zum Schluss wird es entzückend wüst! Aber tut sie das mit Talent. Wie klein Mariechen sich den Strawinsky vorstellt. Genie oder Philister, Heilige oder Teufelin, sie kann noch alles werden—vielleicht sogar ein ganz brauchbarer Komponist!"

2. "Die Reihe der weiblichen Komponistinen von Rang ist sehr dünn gesät. In allen Kunstarten haben die Frauen mit mehr oder minder Glück eine gewisse Gleichberechtigung dem Mann gegenüber, aber die Musik, als produktiver Kunstfaktor, blieb ihnen merkwürdigerweise verschlossen. Bis auf ein paar Ausnahmen." [He discusses only a large cantata for solo quartet, orchestra and organ—the work took up the entire concert—by Viennese composer and Maria Bach contemporary Johanna Müller-Hermann.] The critic adds that this work "zeigt neben einem imponierenden Können und Wissen um die technischen Dinge orchestraler Feinmechanik eine überraschend blühende Phantasie und Erfindung, eine Gestaltungskraft von bildhaften Anschaulichkeit und reichquellende Melodik."

3. Eleonore's sister Käthe was a pianist and a close friend of the noted Austrian composer Max Reger.

4. There was another Bach musician, a contemporary of Maria Bach: Vincent Bach, who was born in Baden on March 24, 1890. He was a brass instrument maker and a trumpeter and from 1914 on was first trumpet of the Boston Symphony Orchestra. He died in New York City on January 8, 1976. See "Vincent Bach," in *Lexikon zeitgenössischer Musik aus Österreich: Komponisten und Komponistinnen des 20. Jahrhunderts,* ed. Bernhard Günther (Vienna: Music Information Center Austria, 1997), 348.

5. *Blitzlichter* # 3.

6. *Blitzlichter* # 48; and reported by Margot Herz in the *Wiener Kurier* (May 1948).

7. *Blitzlichter* # 5.

8. *Blitzlichter* # 37.

9. Eiselmair, 23–25.

10. It is not known if this Bach was related to Maria's family. See Henri-Louis de La Grange, *Gustav Mahler: The Years of Challenge*, vol. 2 *(1897–1904)* (Oxford and New York: Oxford University Press), 355. See also Joan Allen Smith, *Schönberg and his Circle: a Viennese Portrait* (New York and London: Schirmer, 1986), 270.

11. The definition of "modernism" is a tangled and elusive one. Walter Frisch seeks to narrow it down for music in *German Modernism: Music and the Arts* (Berkeley, Los Angeles, and London: University of California Press, 2005). According to Frisch's study, "Historicist Modernism is represented most strikingly by Max Reger and Ferruccio Busoni. . . . In Historicist Modernism, musical techniques from the remote past are used prominently and vigorously as a way of achieving a distance from late Romantic styles. Historicist Modernism is not nostalgic or conservative in any traditional sense. It represents an attempt to bridge a historical gap without denying it, collapsing it, or retreating over it to return to the past. . . . Composers of Historicist Modernism . . . show little of the wit and detachment that we associate with the neoclassicism that emerged in the years just after World War I in composers like Stravinsky and Hindemith." I believe that, in Frisch's terms, the music of Maria Bach, her youthful friend Erich Wolfgang Korngold, and her composition teacher Joseph Marx are not examples of historicist modernism, for they use techniques of the past but in a sentimental and reflective way. See Frisch, 139.

12. See Oskar Kokoschka, *My Life*, trans. David Britt (London: Thames and Hudson, 1974), 35; also Carl E. Schorske, *Fin-de-Siècle Vienna: Politics and Culture* (New York: Vintage Books [Random House], 1981), 330–39; and Isabella Ackerl, *Vienna Modernism (1890–1910)*, trans. Erika Obermayer (Vienna: Federal Press Service, 1999), 14–38.

13. See Ackerl, *Vienna Modernism*, 30–33; see also Schorske, 212.

14. *Blitzlichter # 5.*

15. Ibid.; also see Eiselmair, 26–27.

16. *Blitzlichter # 19.*

17. Eiselmair, 29.

18. The vast Viennese network of musical families—connected by blood, marriage, and teacher-pupil alliances—calls for at least a chapter all its own.

19. The information about Koussevitzky was given to the author by Robert Mann, a noted American violinist, conductor, and founder–first violinist of the Juilliard Quartet.

20. *Blitzlichter # 23*, 10 and 36.

21. Eiselmair, 30–31.

22. *Blitzlichter # 11.*

23. Richard Newman and Karen Kirtley, *Alma Rosé: Vienna to Auschwitz* (Portland, Ore.: Amadeus Press, 2000). Sevcik, a brilliant concert soloist and conductor, was professor of violin at the conservatories of Kiev, 1875–1892, and Prague, 1892–1906. His most celebrated students included the violinists Wolfgang Schneiderhan and Jan Kubilek. The name Sevcik was also that of a music publishing house in Vienna. The author found several compositions by women contemporaries of Maria Bach brought out by the Sevcik firm.

24. The Russian pianist and composer Anton Rubenstein (1829–1894) has been considered the only rival of Franz Liszt in keyboard virtuosity.

25. Gordon Brook-Shepherd, *The Austrians: A Thousand-Year Odyssey* (New York: Carroll & Graf Publishers, 1996), 171.

26. See Robert K. Massie, *Dreadnought: Britain, Germany, and the Coming of the Great War* (New York: Ballantine Books, 1991), 865–79. See also John Keegan, *The First World War* (New York: Alfred A. Knopf, 1999), 48; Schorske, 24–26; and Brook-Shepherd, 113–123.

27. Brook-Shepherd, 249.

28. See Eve Blair, *The Architecture of Red Vienna, 1919–1934* (Cambridge, Mass.: MIT Press, 1999); see also Brook-Shepherd, 171–250.

29. See the account of the émigré Russian Princess Marie Vassiltchikov, a refugee from bombed-out Berlin and hospital nurse during the final bombardment of Vienna through March 1945, in her *Berlin Diaries, 1940–1945* (New York: Vintage Books [Random House], 1988), 261 and following. See also Sarah Gainham, *Night Falls on the City* (New York, Chicago, and San Francisco: Holt, Rinehart and Winston, 1967); and Alan Jefferson, *Elisabeth Schwarzkopf* (Boston: Northeastern University Press, 1995).

30. *Blitzlichter # 7.*

31. Ibid.

32. Eiselmair, 30–34.

33. Ibid.

34. Ackerl, 25.

35. This information is drawn from this writer's research—while on a Fulbright grant in 2000—in the Archives of Vienna's Gesellschaft der Musikfreunde.

36. See, for example, the cases of the painter Mary Cassatt and the writer Louisa May Alcott—some of the many given by Whitney Chadwick, in *Women, Art, and Society,* 2nd rev. ed. (London: Thames and Hudson, 1990 and 1996), 120 and following.

37. The author also surveyed music by Bach and these other Vienna contemporaries Frida Kern and Johanna Müller-Hermann in 2001 and 2006 in the Österreichische Nationalbibliothek Wien.

38. MICA *Lexikon zeitgenössischer Musik aus Österreich: Komponisten und Komponistinnen des 20. Jahrhunderts,* ed. Bernhard Günther (Vienna: Music Center Information Austria, 1997), 74.

39. The efforts of Alma Mahler (1879–1964) as a composer were reportedly stifled early by her first husband, Gustav.

40. See "Grete von Zieritz," *MaÖ* [MICA]; also Beate Philipp, "Grete von Zieritz," in *Annäherung VI—an Sieben Komponistinnen* (Kassel: Furore-Edition, 1995), 5–16; and *Women Composers in Germany,* ed. Roswitha Sperber (Bonn: Inter Nationes, 1996), 44–45.

41. Eiselmair, 34.

42. See Edda Fuhrich and Gisela Prossnitz, eds., *Max Reinhardt: The Magician's Dreams,* trans. Sophie Kidd and Peter Waugh (Salzburg and Vienna: Residenz Verlag, 1993), 105–40.

43. Marx was cited in the *Neuigkeits-Welt-Blatt* (November 1930) as one of two presidential advisers of the Österreichischer Komponistenbund. See Erik Werba, "Joseph Marx und sein Schülerkreis," *Musikerziehung,* Jg. 5/Heft 4 (June 1952): 214 and following.

44. Women could matriculate as composition students in music conservatories by the 1860s in Leipzig; the 1870s in Vienna, Stockholm, and London; and the first two decades of the twentieth century in Brussels, Frankfurt, Florence, Berlin, Cologne, Paris, Warsaw, and Moscow.

45. Werba, 214.

46. But there were earlier signs of success. Two programs at the Wiener Konzerthaus—in 1917 and 1920—included performances of some of Bach's music. (The Konzerthaus was second in importance after the Musikverein.) In fact, between 1917 and 1944, eleven concerts were presented with her music on the program, these events being presented nine times in the Schubert-Saal and twice in the Mozart-Saal. In December 1940 and December 1941, the evening's performances at the Konzerthaus featured Bach's music

alone. It is also striking to note that the first of the concerts in these years took place while World War I was still ongoing; and the last five during World War II, the final one (1944) being given late in that conflict.

47. Grümmer (1879–1965) became solo cellist at Vienna's Konzertverein and Court Opera in 1905 and taught at the Vienna Academy of Music until 1926, when he accepted a teaching position in Cologne and then Berlin until 1940. He returned to Vienna in 1940 and in 1946 began extensive concert tours with the celebrated Adolf Busch Quartet, which he had helped found in 1913. Grümmer settled finally in Switzerland. He edited many major works for cello, pioneered in the playing of the viola da gamba, and gained fame for his performances of J. S. Bach's music. See Walter Niemann, *Die Musik der Gegenwart* (Berlin: Schuster und Löffler, 1921), 47–49.

48. "Die männliche Gilde sehe sich vor." Though citing this quote, Eiselmair, 37, supplies no date or publication containing Korngold's opinion.

49. J. Korngold's review in *Die Neue Freie Presse*, May 5, 1930. In the 1950s Boutnikoff became director of New York's Ballet Russe de Monte Carlo.

50. Paris, February 8, 1933. See Eiselmair, 42.

51. See Eiselmair, 43–44. Austria's confiscation of Robert Bach's Polish properties during the 1920s had further depleted the family's holdings.

52. I found these addresses on some of her lieder autographs in the Wiener Stadt- und Landes-Bibliothek. I have seen her Kärntnerstrasse address: a handsome multistory apartment building in the heart of historic Vienna on one of the city's busiest commercial arteries.

53. Erik Levi, *Music in the Third Reich* (New York: St. Martin's Press, 1994), 210.

54. Levi, 211.

55. See Andreas Giger, "A Matter of Principle: The Consequences for Korngold's Career," *The Journal of Musicology* (Fall 1998): 547; see also Brigitte Hamann, *Hitler's Vienna: A Dictator's Apprenticeship,* trans. Thomas Thornton (Oxford and New York: Oxford University Press, 1999), 27 and following; and John Toland, *Adolf Hitler* (Garden City, N.Y.: Doubleday, 1976), 21–31.

56. See Fred K. Prieberg, *Musik im NS-Staat* (Frankfurt am Main: Fischer Taschenbuch Verlag, 1982), 295.

57. Eiselmair, 48–49.

58. *Blitzlichter* # 12; and see Eiselmair, 46.

59. The work was given in Vienna in 1932 and again in 1939 in a program also including "Draussen im weiten Krieg"; in New York City in 1940; and in Kobé, Japan, in 1942. Perhaps even more striking is the sensational success the Austrian composer Grete von Zieritz noted after a performance of her "Japanische Lieder" in 1921 at Berlin's Singakademie. See Clara Mayer, ed., *Annäherung VI,* 7–8.

60. The vocal and instrumental parts for this work have disappeared.

61. See Karl Ziak, *Wiedergeburt einer Weltstadt: Wien 1945–1965* (Vienna and Munich: Verlag für Jugend und Volk, 1965), 7–13, with its vivid photographs.

62. Ibid., 14.

63. See Vassiltchikov, *Berlin Diaries,* 262–63; see also Gainham, *Night Falls,* 538 and following; and Jefferson, *Elisabeth Schwarzkopf,* 40 and following.

64. Anthony Tommasini, review, "Plumbing Schoenberg's Inner Realm," *New York Times,* February 13, 2002.

65. Brook-Shepherd, 377–428.

66. Schorske, 346.

67. Eiselmair, 55.

68. Ibid., 66.

69. Eiselmair, 60–62; for the increasingly powerful use of the radio broadcast medium at this time in broadening the size of the audiences for contemporary music, see Andreas Giger, "A Matter of Principle: The Consequences for Korngold's Career," *Journal of Musicology* 16, no. 4 (Fall 1998): 545–64.

70. *Negroid, Japanischer Frühling, Silhouetten, Bengele, Narrenlieder* (titled *Il Giulare*), the opera *Il Glauco* (or *Glaukus*), *Sechs Altdeutsche Marienlieder, Marienleben* (retitled *Canti Maria*), *Arabische Nächte, Lieder des Hafis*, and *La Caravella*.

71. Concepts of fusion, as between visual properties such as color and music, were widely in fashion in the earlier twentieth century. Conversations in 1907 with his compatriot Nikolay Rimsky-Korsakov led to the Russian composer Alexander Skriabin (1872–1915), for example, involving himself deeply in exploring the possibilities of synaesthesia, linking the emotional effects of color with music. He was also associated with Alexander Mozer in contriving a color organ. An exhibit that this writer visited in Vienna's Jewish Museum in 2000 featured the use of a color orchestra devised by a Viennese music teacher in the 1930s for instructing elementary-age children in music.

72. Eiselmair, 70.

73. Ibid., 72.

74. The following discussion of her music is based chiefly on my study of this collection in the Wiener Stadt- und Landesbibliothek in 1998, 1999, 2000, and 2001; the examination of performance records in the Archive of the Gesellschaft der Musikfreunde Wien in 2000 and 2006; and studies of the collections of music—autographs and published scores—by Bach's contemporaries Frida Kern and Johanna Müller-Hermann in the Österreichische Nationalbibliothek in 2001 and 2006.

75. See Clemens Gruber, "Maria Bach," *Nicht Nur Mozarts Rivallinen* (Vienna: n.p., 1990), 41–45. Gruber notes that, as of 1990, Madeleine Delarue owned the rights to Maria Bach's *Nachlass*.

76. See Harald Goertz, *Österreichische Komponisten der Gegenwart* (Vienna: n.p., 1979), 13.

77. Robert Schollum, *Das österreichische Lied des 20. Jahrhunderts* (Tutzing: Hans Schneider, 1977), 106.

78. For this and the following quoted material, see Eiselmair, 65–66.

79. Eiselmair, 67–69.

80. Schorske, 9 and 152.

81. Giger, 547.

82. See Norbert Tschulik, "Musikkritik in Österreich," in Manfred Wagner, *Geschichte der Österreichischen Musikkritik in Beispielen* (Tutzing: Hans Schneider, 1979), 3–28; see also John Warren, "Viennese Theatre Criticism between the Wars," in *From Perinet to Jelinek: Viennese Theatre in its Political and Intellectual Context*, W. E. Yates, Allyson Fiddler and John Warren, eds. (Oxford, Vienna, and New York: Peter Lang, 2001), 191–202.

83. Leon Botstein, "Strauss and the Viennese Critics (1896–1924)," in Bryan Gilliam, ed., *Richard Strauss and His World* (Princeton, N.J.: Princeton University Press, 1992), 319; see also Sandra McColl, "Karl Kraus and Music Criticism: The Case of Max Kalbeck," *Musical Quarterly* 82, no. 2 (Summer 1998): 279–308.

84. Wagner, *Geschichte der Österreichischen,* 21 and following. See also Eduard Hanslick, *Music Criticisms 1846–99,* trans. and ed. Henry Pleasants (Baltimore: Penguin Books, 1950), 21.

85. Please note: All the reviews cited here are taken directly from the original Vienna newspapers, a few preserved on microfilm, in the Druckschriftensammlung of the Stadt- und Landesbibliothek in Vienna. These reviews appear in an appendix at the end of this chapter.

86. See Walter Frisch, *German Modernism: Music and the Arts* (Berkeley, Los Angeles, and London: University of California Press, 2005), 139, for example.

87. Eiselmair, 71.

88. Gary-Schaffhauser composed lieder (with varied instrumental accompaniments), chamber music, and choral and orchestral works, some of which were performed in Vienna during her lifetime. See "Marianne Gary-Schaffhauser," MICA, 184.

89. Eiselmair, 71.

90. In contrast, from the later decades of the nineteenth into the early years of the twentieth century, the majority of lower-class (that is, of lesser rank than the *haute bourgeoisie*) women musicians in Vienna and elsewhere in Europe in Bach's era were forced by their limited financial means to play in touring all-female dance bands and other orchestras hired for lighter entertainment purposes. See Dorothea Kaufmann, ". . . *Routinierte Trommlerin Gesucht*": *Musikerin in einer Damenkapelle—Zum Bild eines vergessenen Frauenberufes aus der Kaiserzeit* (Karben: CODA, 1997).

91. All translations from the German, given in the endnotes, are the author's. The original press versions of reviews as given in the Vienna press during Bach's lifetime are followed by comparisons with the versions as given by Maria Bach in her journal *Blitzlichter aus meinem Leben,* some of which is quoted in Eiselmair, *Die männliche Gilde.*

92. Reitler's original: "Richard Krotschak, der sympathische blonde Solocellist des Symphonieorchesters, gab mit Otto Schulhof einen feine hervorragenden kammermusikalischen Qualitäten enthüllenden Abend, von dessen Erfolg ein zarter Lichtschein auch auf eine offenbar von Josef Marx kräftig beeinflusste Cellosonate der jungen Maria Bach fiel." (Bach's version: "Es war ein Abend von dessen Erfolg ein zarter Lichtschein auf eine Cellosonate der jungen Maria Bach fiel.")

93. "Die Mitwirkenden, Henriette (Cello) und Maria Bach (Klavier), brachten eine ausgezeichnete Sonate für Cello und Klavier von Maria Bach zu Gehör, die weitgehende Beachtung verdient."

94. The original review, including Bach's lieder, by Hans Sachs in the *Völkischer Beobachter Wien* of May 20, 1939, is lost, but I consider my notes on it, together with Bach's own version of it, worthy of inclusion here. The review was written only one year after Austria's *Anschluss* by Germany, the same year as the Nazis' invasion of Europe. In Sachs's critique of a recital of lieder by several composers, Bach omits mention that a group of lieder by Hugo Wolf were described as "the peak of the program," and she omits the name of the poet of one of her lieder. Yet, in addition to omitting the names of the other composers represented at this concert (including lieder by her composition teacher, Joseph Marx), Bach omits Sachs's use of the words "[Bach] attempts," thus making her accomplishment appear totally successful; she reverses "without, however" to success in "content as in form"; and omits the reference to "dance and lied" and "improvisations." Bach also omits saying that the lieder were sung by Emma von Pichler and performed, along with accompanist Karl von Pichler, in the Figaro-Saal. In addition, Bach omits and

changes a few words given in the review of her "Draussen im weiten Krieg," omits the poet's name (Morgenstern) and changes *volksliedhafte* to *volksliedmässige*. The singer, accompanist, and recital hall are also not mentioned.

95. Schmidt's complete review: "Am Liederabend Emy von Pichlers zu hören.Hugo Wolf, Josef Marx und dessen Schülerin Maria Bach bildeten hier das Programm, in dessen Mittelpunkt die neuen Lieder der bekannten Komponistin standen. Marx' Schule lässt sich an allem, was Maria Bachs reiches in der Öffentlichkeit bekanntes Schöpfertalent gestaltet erkennen doch tritt überall, besonders in diesen neuen Liedern, die starke eigene Persönlichkeit vorteilhaft hervor. Emy von Pichler verstand es, begleitet von der Komponistin, den Gesängen mit schönen gesanglichen Mitteln und guter Einfühlung prächtige Wirkung abzugewinnen."

96. Maria Bachs reiches in der Öffentlichkeit bekanntes Schöpfertalent gestaltet besonders in Liedern starke eigene Persönlichkeit.

97. Fritz Skorzeny (1900–1965) was a Viennese composer of songs, chamber music, and orchestral works in a late romantic style. Poorly paid as a music critic and composer—and lacking no fixed professional title or place of employment—he earned a living in the age-old tradition by teaching private students. See MICA, 56, 109, and 180.

98. The original review: "Maria Bach ist unter den Wiener Tonsetzern kein unbekannter Name mehr. Wie schon oft, hat sie sich auch bei ihrem sehr freundlich aufgenommenen Kompositionsabend im Schubertsaal mit der Sängerin Emy von Pichler zusammengetan, die ihren klingenden Sopran und warmen Vortrag an eine lange Reihe von Liedern wandte. In all dieser aufgeschlossen-melodiösen Frauenlyrik spricht sich die kenntnisreiche Musikerin aus, deren Sinn für eindringliche Stimmungswerte sich schon in der Textwahl ausspricht: Trakl, viel Rilke (Portugiesische Sonette), AltJapanisches, während unter den zahlreichen Uraufführungen das feingesponnene Gewebe nach Karl Waches "Sehnsucht" oder die Lanjus-Vertonungen besonders ansprachen."

99. "In einem Grossteil der Lieder, welche Emy von Pichler mit aller gefühlsmässigen Hingebung und mit musikalischer Werktreue sang, lässt die Komponistin Maria Bach die Begleitung in gleichmässig rhythmisierten Akkorden von fesselnder Harmonik eingeschlossen während sich die oft ekstatisch gesteigerte Singstimme beweglich dem Tonfall einer sehr gehabenen Sprache anpasst. Japanische und portugiessische Lieder gewinnen ausserdem Lokalfarbe, so zwar, dass man sich bei den letzteren zuweilen an Puccini, fallweise auch leise an Hugo Wolf erinnert fühlt."

100. Original: "Weil wir bei den Liederabenden sind: Maria Bach, die liebenswürdige Komponistin melodischer, schön empfundener Lieder, hat uns an einem Abend mit einigen Gruppen ihrer zahlreichen Schöpfungen herzliche Freude bereitet. Lieder nach Rilkeschen und altjapanischen Dichtungen besonders zeigten die hochbegabte Frau wieder auf dem Weg ihres edlen Strebens, auf dem sie der Musikfreund schon lange verfolgte. Sind Lieder darunter, die es verdienten auch anderwärts gesungen zu werden. Emy v. Pichler, die mit seit ihrem vorjährigen Liederabend im Gedächtnis haftet, hat der Komponistin, die selbst die Klavierbegleitung gestaltete, einen schönen Erfolg ersungen."

101. "Von ganz besonderer Eigenart war der Kompositionsabend Maria Bach, die mit grosser Einfühlungsgabe Japanische, Altgriechische, Portugiessische und Persische Musik zu fesselnden Liedern und Instrumentalwerken eigener persönlicher Prägung verarbeitet. Die Grazer Sopranistin Emy von Pichler, das Grazer Michl-Quartett und der Cellist Wl. Knajasevsky waren ihre trefflichen Helfer zum starken Erfolg."

102. German original: "In Maria Bachs Schaffen binden sich mannigfache Elemente:

eine Exotismus, Rückkehr zum klaren, dem Volkshaften näher kommenden Klangbild (in uraufgeführten Tänzen aus dem Ballett *Bengele* und Liedern jüngeren Datums), Genreimpressionen für Klavier und Cello—alles in fortschrittlicher, harmonisch oft üppiger und fesselnder Schreibweise gestaltet, poetisch inspirierte Stimmungsmusik. Dass die Tonsetzerin ihr Handwerk beherrscht, dabei auch eine treffliche Pianistin ist, hat sie schon oft bewiesen, so auch an ihrem letzten Abend, dem Luise Brabées klangfülliger Sopran, Esta Maias reife Tanzkunst, der ausdrucksfähige Bariton Viktor P. Sedely und die empfindende Cellistin Elisabeth Rössler mit zum herzlichen Erfolg geholfen haben."

103. German original: "Maria Bach hat ihr zweites Streichquartett dem für Neuem interessierten Weisgärber-Quartett zur Uraufführung überlassen. Wieder meldet sich in diesen fünf im Sinne einer Tanzsuite sich folgenden Sätzen das an der Autorin wiederholt gewürdigte exotisierende Talent, sich in fremde Klangkomplexe einzufühlen und diese auf ihre stilisierende eigene Tonsprache zu beziehen."

104. German original: "Das Weissgärber-Quartett bot im Brahms-Saal eine aparte Vortragsordnung, die zwischen einem Boccherini-Quartett und einem Oktett von Svendsen die Uraufführung eines Streichquartetts von Maria Bach brachte, die auch in diesem Werk wieder ihre Vorliebe für fremdländische Rhythmik, Melodik und Harmonik merkbar werden lässt."

105. Although this writer has not yet been able to document any relationship, I think it possible that the critic Bruno Prohaska came from a musically noted Viennese family of Prohaskas: the composer Karl (1869–1927), the bass-baritone Jaroslav (1891–1965), and the noted conductor Felix (1912–1987), a son of Karl.

106. The Norwegian composer Johan Svendsen (1840–1911).

107. "Zwischen dem reizvollen dreisätzigen Streich-Quartett Boccherinis und dem wirksamen, klangschönen Oktett von J.S. Svendsen hörte man am zweiten Kammermusikabend des bewährten Weissgärber-Quartetts eine Uraufführung, nämlich ein Streichquartett der Komponistin Maria Bach. Die klangliche Grundlage entnahm Maria Bach wieder romantischer, vornehmlich spanischer und rumänischer Musik und führte die gewählten Themen sehr fein aus. Die Musiker um Max Weissgärber waren dem Werke treffliche Interpreten."

108. Original German: "Vom Weissgärber-Quartett ist ein neues Streichquartett von Maria Bach zu hören gewesen, in dem sich die Freude der Komponistin am Exotischen und Volkloristischen wieder interessant und anregend auswirkt. Voraus ging, immer erwünscht und als Abendeinleitung vorzüglich geeignet, delikat gespielt, ein Boccherini: der Neuheit folgte Svendsens Oktett (mit weiterin Philharmonikern)."

109. "Das Weissgärber-Quartett stellte vor zwischen das in seiner ganzen schwebenden Rokokograzie wiedergegebene op. 6 von Boccherini und das in der nationalen Frühromantik breit ausschwingende Oktett op. 3 von Svendsen, in dessen Aufführung sich noch vier ausgezeichnete Streicher lückenlos und einheitlich in den Klangkörper fügten, das zweite Streichquartett von Maria Bach. Mit erstaunlicher Einfühlung in die Eigenart rumänischer und spanischer Musik, die stellenweise auch gemischt erscheint, will die Komponistin hier sowohl inhaltlich als auch formal neues Blut in die Sonatenform giessen, ohne aber dabei über Tanz- und Liedgestaltungen beziehungsweise Improvisationen hinauszugehen." Johan Severin Svendsen (1840–1911) was a Norwegian composer, violinist, and conductor. His String Octet, Op. 3, dates from 1865–1866.

110. Original: "Nach längere Pause war Paul Marion, als ehemaliges Mitglied der Staatsoper in Erinnerung, wieder einmal hier zo hören; diesmal im Konzertsaal. Sein mächtig

raumfüllender, blühender Tenor lässt in jeder Beziehung italienische Einflüsse erkennen, namentlich in einem vollendet behandelten messa di voce, das hier, zum Prinzip erhoben, die Tongebung wunderbar elastisch macht, und immer von wohltuender Wirkung ist. In Arien und Liedern darunter fesselnden Gesängen von Maria Bach und andern seiten gehörten Stücken bewährte der Künstler, stürmisch ausgezeichnet, diese Vorzüge."

Chapter 5. Ann Schein

1. Author's interview with Schein, 2007.

2. Tim Page, chief music critic of the *Washington Post,* 2005.

3. Linda Schein Greenebaum, *Elizer's Troupe: Scheins in America, 1890–1999* (Amherst, Mass.: Linda Schein Greenebaum, 1999). Greenebaum is a professional violinist living in Amherst. Her three daughters collaborate with her in the Greenebaum Family String Quartet.

4. Lynch had previously had a daughter, Colleen, Schein's half-sister, by Lynch's first husband.

5. Greenebaum, 104.

6. Interview with Schein, 2008. Schein also notes that this boy coincidentally was the Yale roommate of Juilliard Quartet cellist Joel Krosnick's brother. See p. 184 concerning Krosnick.

7. Greenebaum, 49 and 98.

8. Ibid., 49.

9. Idem.

10. Ibid., 50.

11. Ibid., 50–52.

12. Ibid., 56–58.

13. Ibid., 57.

14. Ibid., 58.

15. Schein is now president of the philanthropic George Langer Shields Foundation, which provides financial support to educational, environmental, and cultural organizations.

16. Ibid., 105.

17. Ibid., 96.

18. Ibid., 97 and 100.

19. Ibid., 98.

20. I remember Hayes particularly because of my early days as a music critic for the *Washington Post.* He was a friendly and commanding figure with white hair and a statuesque bearing.

21. By the time Schein was about twelve, the family had settled into an elegant townhouse on Bancroft Place in the city's affluent northwest quadrant.

22. In 1950, Gunn would write of Schein in the *Times Herald:* " . . . She is a precocious child of 11, phenomenally talented. . . ."

23. Greenebaum, 101.

24. An unidentified critic for a Greenwich, Connecticut, publication wrote that he had heard Rachmaninoff himself play this concerto, the writer calling it "a great art experience, but not patently superior to that of Ann Schein." The reviewer also remarked that at

this performance, the audience gave Schein an ovation consisting of "extended stomping, clapping, and shouting."

25. Munz was a one-time student of Ferruccio Busoni and Egon Petri.

26. The performance, at 2 P.M. on December 13, 1954, was one event in the orchestra's series of Young People's Concerts.

27. Munz's close friend was Halina Rodzinski, the wife of the noted conductor Artur Rodzinski (1892–1958), who "adored Munz totally" and was the brother of Nela Mlynarski, Munz's wife, "who," Schein states, "was stolen from him by Rubinstein."

28. The school was then conveniently located near the Schein home.

29. Greenebaum, 102–3.

30. Author's conversation with Tim Page, the *Washington Post*, 2007.

31. Greenebaum, 103.

32. Every Saturday for five years, I trudged up the Avalon's long flight of stairs to study the piano with Peabody artist-faculty member Alexander Sklarevsky (a Russian immigrant). During my interviews with Schein for this chapter, I learned from her that she, too, often trod up these same stairs with her friend Linda Williams, who was taking ballet lessons in the same room where I was then studying the piano. In addition, Linda was the daughter of my previous piano teacher, Burris Williams, pianist (among several of his positions) of downtown Washington's Capital Theater Orchestra, which gave concerts between movie presentations.

33. In remembering this performance, Schein adds a personal note: "I loved this New York City setting, especially when I viewed the apartment buildings surrounding the stadium and the clothes on lines hanging from the balconies—a Gershwinesque scene and one in extreme heat."

34. As Schein's concert manager, Hurok was the chief negotiator for the Soviet Exchange of Artists program and the first impresario to bring Gilels and Richter (see p. 290) to the United States. He also engaged such renowned ballet companies as the Kirov, Sadler's Wells, and the Ballets Russes for performances in America.

35. See Harold C. Schonberg, *The Great Pianists* (New York: Simon and Schuster, 1963), 426; also 409–18.

36. Cliburn ended his career in 1970, acknowledging recently that he was burned out after twelve years of fame.

37. For an interesting update on Van Cliburn's career, see Anthony Tommasini, "Cold War, Hot Pianist: Now Add 50 Years," *New York Times*, Arts and Leisure section, March 9, 2008, 1 and 24.

38. Maria Watts, *Armchair World: World Perspectives*, 1996, www.armchairworld.com from the Internet.

39. Ross, "Madame X," *New Yorker*, November 12, 2001.

40. Besides Van Cliburn, Hurok's list of artists also included Andrés Segovia, Rubinstein himself, Gina Bachauer, Nathan Milstein, Isaac Stern, and Marian Anderson.

41. In fact, Rubinstein himself was preparing to record the Schubert, moved by the composer's profound emotional power. Revealing the depth of Schein's professional relationship with Rubinstein, Schein further recounts, "Rubinstein—unbelievably for me as he was on a concert tour—called me at one time in Washington, D.C., confessing, 'I don't want to record the B-flat Sonata' [for a recording in Los Angeles]." His recording producer Max Wilcox even told Schein that Rubinstein had been "completely overcome by this music." But much later, Schein reports, "he did record it."

42. Hurok was Schein's manager until 1968.

43. A paraphrase from *Die Neue Freie Presse,* Austria's most influential newspaper at this time.

44. Schonberg, 128 and 429.

45. Greenebaum, 105.

46. Idem.

47. This account is derived mostly from this author's interviews with the violinist between 2007 and 2008.

48. This program was established by cellist Claus Adam (d. 1983), also a onetime cellist of the Juilliard Quartet.

49. Earl's mother had studied at the Busch Conservatory in Chicago as a student of King.

50. Schuman was Juilliard's president from 1945 to 1962. Among his important contributions to the school and to American concert life overall was his establishing the Juilliard Quartet as the school's resident ensemble in 1949.

51. The Carlysses' first home together was a New York apartment on West End Avenue—on the thirtieth floor. "This was an ideal location," Ann recalls, "because no one lived near us, so there was no problem about practicing and we had a splendid view of the Hudson River."

52. Groves (1915–1992) was a highly respected British conductor.

53. Both Carlyss daughters were named after their grandmothers. Linnea's middle name comes from that of Schein's mother, Elizabeth ("Betty"); Pauline Evelyn Carlyss carries Earl's mother's name, Evelyn, as her second name.

54. This author wrote the program notes for the cycle.

55. Peter G. Davis wrote in the *New York Times* on April 1, 1981 about the concluding concert of Schein's Chopin six-part marathon: "It would be enough to content any pianist in search of a Mount Everest to conquer [to play Chopin's 24 Etudes, except for Op. 10, no. 1] . . . Merely noting that Miss Schein made her way through these thorny thickets with considerable proficiency is already saying a great deal." Davis continued with mixed feelings: "Miss Schein brought her overview of Chopin to an honorable conclusion, but without really putting a personal stamp on the music." For the first Chopin concert—his three sonatas—Bill Zakariasen wrote in the *New York Daily News,* October 14, 1980: "[Schein] presented these works with a virtually flawless technique and a reflective clarity of organization; one could come away from this recital with a feeling of satisfaction and a new realization of Chopin's stature." The critic concluded that the remainder of the cycle would "prove notable experiences for listeners curious to hear new and often unusual viewpoints on a beloved composer."

56. Schein in an interview with the author in 2007.

57. Adkins's sister Madeline is associate concertmaster of the Baltimore Symphony Orchestra; her brother Christopher is principal cellist of the Dallas Symphony Orchestra; and her husband, Edward Newman, is a distinguished pianist.

58. "In recent years," Schein once reminisced, "Jessye has turned to profound jazz evenings, including devotional music by Duke Ellington." Ellington was a Washington, D.C., native. Shedding more light on her own artistic outlook, Schein commented, "Jessye invited Earl and me to Lincoln Center for a jazz concert by John Coltrane in 2006 [or just Coltrane's music, considering that he died in 1967?] on the occasion of her birthday. The music we heard was one of virtuosity beyond instruments—one where music is *now* alive, visceral, transcendent." [The author's italics reflect Schein's own emphasis on that word.]

BIBLIOGRAPHY

Abbate, Carolyn. "Opera; or, the Envoicing of Women." In *Musicology and Difference: Gender and Sexuality in Music Scholarship,* edited by Ruth A. Solie, 225–58. Berkeley, Los Angeles, and London: University of California Press, 1993.

Ackerl, Isabella. *Vienna Modernism (1890–1910).* Trans. Erika Obermayer. Vienna: Federal Press Service, 1999.

Anthony, James R. *French Baroque Music from Beaujoyeulx to Rameau.* Rev. and exp. ed. Portland, Ore.: Amadeus Press, 1997.

Ärcke, Kristiaan P. *Gods of Play: Baroque Festive Performances as Rhetorical Discourse.* Albany: State University of New York Press, 1994.

Ault, D. S., and S. H. Steinberg, trans. and ed. *The German Hansa.* London and Stanford, Calif.: Macmillan, 1970.

Bach, Maria. *Blitzlichter aus meinem Leben.* Vienna: Self-published, 1976.

Benecke, Gerhard. *Germany in the Thirty Years' War.* London: Edward Arnold, 1978.

Benoit, Marcelle. "Paris, 1661–87: The Age of Lully." In *The Early Baroque Era: From the Late 16th Century to the 1660s,* edited by Curtis Price, 238–69. Music and Society series. Englewood Cliffs, N.J.: Prentice Hall, 1993, 238–69.

Bethune, George W. *The British Female Poets: With Biographical and Critical Notices.* New York: Hurst, 1846.

Blair, Eve. *The Architecture of Red Vienna, 1919–1934.* Cambridge, Mass.: MIT Press, 1999.

Blankenburg, Walter. "Amalia Catharina." In *The Norton/Grove Dictionary of Women Composers,* edited by Julie Anne Sadie and Rhian Samuel, 11–12. New York and London: W.W. Norton, 1995.

Blaukopf, Kurt, ed. Zoltan Roman, contributor. *Mahler: A Documentary Study.* New York and Toronto: Oxford University Press, 1976.

Boer, Bertil van. "The Travel Diary of Joseph Martin Kraus: Translation and Commentary." *Journal of Musicology* 8, no. 2 (April 1990): 266–90.

Bohlmann, Robert. "Die Zeichen oder Monogramme des Herzog Julius von Braunsch-weig." In *Festschrift für Paul Zimmermann,* 256–62. Wolfenbüttel: Bohlmann, 1914.

Booth, Ronald Earl, Jr. "Stephen Heller." In *New Grove* 8, edited by Stanley Sadie, 459–61. London: Macmillan, 1980.

Borroff, Edith. "Elisabeth-Claude Jacquet de la Guerre." In *The Norton/Grove Dictionary of Women Composers,* edited by Julie Anne Sadie and Rhian Samuel, 236–38. New York and London: W.W. Norton, 1995.

———. *An Introduction to Elisabeth-Claude Jacquet de La Guerre.* Musicological Studies 12. Brooklyn, N.Y.: Institute of Mediaeval Music, 1966.

Botstein, Leon. "Strauss and the Viennese Critics (1896–1924)." In *Richard Strauss and His World,* edited by Bryan Gilliam. Princeton, N.J.: Princeton University Press, 1992.

Bowers, Jane, and Judith Tick, eds. *Women Making Music: The Western Art Tradition: 1150–1950.* Urbana and Chicago: University of Illinois Press, 1986.

Brenet, Michel [Marie Bobillier]. *Les Concerts en France sous l'ancien régime.* Paris: Fischbein, 1900. Repr., Geneva: Minkoff, 1973.

———. *Les Musiciennes de la Sainte Chapelle du Palais.* Paris: Picard, 1910.

———. "Quatre femmes musiciennes I: Mademoiselle Jacquet de la Guerre." *L'Art* 59, no. 4 (October 2, 1894): 107–12.

Briscoe, James R., ed. *New Historical Anthology of Music by Women.* Bloomington: Indiana University Press, 2004.

———. *Historical Anthology of Music by Women.* Bloomington and Indianapolis: Indiana University Press, 1987.

Brockhaus Enzyklopädie 20, 9th ed. "Sophie Elisabeth," 479. Mannheim: F.A. Brockhaus, 1993.

Brook-Shepherd, Gordon. *The Austrians: A Thousand-Year Odyssey.* New York: Carroll & Graf Publishers, 1996.

Brosius, Dieter. *Herzogin Dorothea: Kopenhagen-Celle-Winsen (Luhe) und Umgebung.* Braunschweig: Heimat- und Museumverein, n.d.

Buelow, George J. "Protestant North Germany." In *The Early Baroque Era: From the Late 16th Century to the 1660s.* Music and Society Series. Edited by Curtis Price, 185–205. Englewood Cliffs, N.J.: Prentice Hall, 1993.

Buelow, George, ed. *The Late Baroque Era from the 1680s to 1740.* Music and Society series. Englewood Cliffs, N.J.: Prentice Hall, 1994.

Bukofzer, Manfred F. *Music in the Baroque Era: From Monteverdi to Bach.* New York: W.W. Norton, 1947.

Busch, G. "Herzogin Sophie Elisabeth und die Musik der Lieder in den Singspielen Herzog Anton Ulrichs zu Braunschweig und Lüneburg." *Chlö* 12 (1992): 127–43.

Butt, John. *Music Education and the Art of Performance in the German Baroque.* Cambridge, U.K.: Cambridge University Press, 2005.

Carli, Enzo. *The Landscape in Art.* New York: William Marlow, 1980.

Carroll, Brendan G. *The Last Prodigy: A Biography of Erich Wolfgang Korngold.* Portland, Ore.: Amadeus Press, 1997.

Carter, Tim, and John Butt, eds. *The Cambridge History of Seventeenth-Century Music.* Cambridge and New York: Cambridge University Press, 2005.

Chadwick, Whitney. *Women, Art, and Society.* 2nd rev. ed. London: Thames and Hudson, 1996.

Chrysander, Friedrich. "Geschichte der Braunschweigisch-Wolfenbüttelschen Capelle und Oper vom 16. bis 18. Jahrhundert." In *Jahrbücher für musikalische Wissenschaft* I, 147–286. (Leipzig, 1863).

Citron, Marcia J. "Josephine Lang," *Historical Anthology of Music by Women,* ed. James R. Briscoe. Bloomington and Indianapolis: Indiana University Press, 1987, 109–112.

———. "Josephine (Caroline) Lang." In *The Norton/Grove Dictionary of Women Composers,* edited by Julie Anne Sadie and Rhian Samuel, 264–65. New York and London: W.W. Norton, 1995.

———. "Women and the Lied, 1775–1850," In *Women Making Music: The Western Art Tradition: 1150–1950,* edited by Jane Bowers and Judith Tick, 224–48. Urbana and Chicago: University of Illinois Press, 1987.

Cook, Susan C., and Judy S. Tsou, eds. *Cecilia Reclaimed: Feminist Perspectives on Gender and Music.* Urbana and Chicago: University of Illinois Press, 1994.

Craig, Gordon A. *The Germans*. New York: Penguin Books, 1982.

Cyr, Mary. "Elisabeth Jacquet de La Guerre: myth or marvel? Seeking the composer's individuality." *Musical Times* 149 (Winter 2008): 79–87.

———. "On Performing 18th-century *Haute-Contre* Roles." *Music Theory* 118 (April 1977): 291–95.

Cyr, Mary, and Arthur Lawrence, eds. *Elisabeth-Claude Jacquet de la Guerre: The Collected Works*. 6 vols. New York: The Broude Trust. (As of 2010, four volumes had been published; two more are in progress.)

Daetrius, Brandanus. *Königes Davids Hertzens-Lust und Liebe zum steten Lobe Gottes: Als Der Weylandt Durchläuchtigsten Fürstinnen und Frauen/Frauen Sophien Elisabeth/ Veriwittibter Herzoginen zu Braunschweig und Lünenburg, Geborner Hertzoginnen zu Mecklenburg/ Fürstinnen der Wenden/ zu Schwerin und Ratzeburg/ auch Gräffinnen zu Schwerin/der Lande Rostock und Stargart, Fraün/ Unserer gewesenen hochpreisslicher Landes-Mutter hohes Herstammen/ glückselige Geburt/ Christlicher Lebens-Lauff und hochseliger Abschied. Verblichener Fürstlicher Leichnam, Den VI. Octobris nechst verflossenen 1676sten Jahres beygesetzet worden*. Niedersächsisches Landesbibliothek; Hannover: C 15782. Also published: Braunschweig: Christoff-Friederich Zilligern, 1676.

Daverio, John. *Robert Schumann: Herald of a New Poetic Age*. New York: Oxford University Press, 1997.

De Brossard, S. Catalogue. Paris, Bibliothèque Nationale Rés. Vm. 8.20, 367, 522, 526, 544, cited in Roster, 72.

DeMarco, Laura E. "The Fact of the Castrato and the Myth of the Countertenor." *Musical Quarterly* 86, no. 1 (Spring 2002): 174–85.

Dufourcq, N. "Notes et documents sur la capitation payée par les musiciens de Paris en 1695." *XVIIe siècle* 21/22 (1954): 485.

Edler, Arnfried. "Organ Music within the Social Structure of North German Cities in the Seventeenth Century." In *Church, Stage, and Studio: Music and its Contexts in Seventeenth-Century Germany*, edited by Paul Walker, 23–41. Ann Arbor and London: UMI Research Press, 1990.

Eiselmair, Gerda M. *Die männliche Gilde sehe sich vor! Die österreichische Komponistin Maria Bach*. Vienna: Löcker Verlag, 1996.

Erickson, Susan. "Elisabeth-Claude Jacquet de la Guerre." In *Historical Anthology of Music by Women*, edited by James R. Briscoe, 57–76. Bloomington and Indianapolis: Indiana University Press, 1987.

Fay, Amy. *Music-Study in Germany in the Nineteenth Century*. New York: Dover Publications, 1965.

Flaherty, Gloria. "Literary Perspectives on the Texts of Buxtehude's Abendmusiken." In *Church, Stage, and Studio: Music and its Contexts in Seventeenth-Century Germany*, edited by Paul Walker, 193–203. Ann Arbor and London: UMI Research Press, 1990.

Friedrichs, Elsbeth. "Josephine Lang." *Neue Musik Zeitung* 27, no. 10 (February 23, 1905): 220–22.

Frisch, Walter. *German Modernism: Music and the Arts*. Berkeley, Los Angeles, and London: University of California Press, 2005.

Fuhrich, Edda, and Gisela Prossnitz. *Max Reinhardt: The Magician's Dreams*. Trans. Sophie Kidd and Peter Waugh. Salzburg and Vienna: Residenz Verlag, 1993.

Gainham, Sarah. *Night Falls on the City*. New York, Chicago, and San Francisco: Holt, Rinehart and Winston, 1967.

Geck, Karl Wilhelm. *Sophie Elisabeth, Herzogin zu Braunschweig und Lüneburg (1613–1676) als Musikerin.* Saarbrücker Studien zur Musikwissenschaft; Neue Folge, Band 6. Saarbrücken: Saarbrücker Druckerei und Verlag, 1992.

Geiringer, Karl. "Johanna Müller-Hermann." In *The Norton/Grove Dictionary of Woman Composers,* edited by Julie Anne Sadie and Rhian Samuel, 340. New York and London: W.W. Norton, 1994.

Giger, Andreas. "A Matter of Principle: The Consequences for Korngold's Career." *Journal of Musicology* 16, no. 4 (Fall 1998): 545–64.

Goertz, Harald. *Österreichische Komponisten der Gegenwart.* Vienna: n.p., 1979.

Gordon-Seifert, Catherine. "From Impurity to Piety: Mid 17th-Century French Devotional Airs and the Spiritual Conversion of Women." *Journal of Musicology* 22, no. 2 (Spring 2005): 268–91.

Gorrell, Lorraine. *The Nineteenth-Century German Lied.* Portland, Ore: Amadeus Press, 1993.

Greenebaum, Linda Schein. *Elizer's Troupe: Scheins in America, 1890–1999.* Amherst, Mass.: Linda Schein Greenebaum, 1999.

Griffiths, Wanda R., ed. *Céphale et Procris.* Performing edition. Middletown, Wisc.: A-R Editions, 1998.

———. "Jacquet de La Guerre's Céphale et Procris: Style and Drama." In *Music in Performance and Society: Essays in Honor of Roland Johnson,* edited by Malcolm Cole and John Keogel, 250–68. Warren, Mich.: Harmonie Park Press, 1997.

Guérard, Albert. *France in the Classical Age: The Life and Death of an Ideal.* New York and Evanston: Harper & Row, 1928 and 1956.

Günther, Bernhard, ed. *Lexikon zeitgenössischer Musik aus Österreich: Komponisten und Komponistinnen des 20. Jahrhunderts.* Vienna: Music Information Center Austria (MICA), 1997.

Hamann, Brigitte. *Hitler's Vienna: A Dictator's Apprenticeship.* Trans. Thomas Thornton. Oxford and New York: Oxford University Press, 1999.

Hanslick, Eduard. *Music Criticisms 1846–99.* Edited and trans. Henry Pleasants. Baltimore: Penguin Books, 1950.

Head, Matthew. "Cultural Meanings for Women Composers in the German Enlightenment." *Journal of the American Musicological Society* 57, no. 2 (Summer 2004): 231–84.

Hiller, Ferdinand. "Josephine Lang, die Lieder-Componistin." In *Aus dem Tonleben unserer Zeit,* Bd. 2, 116. Leipzig: H. Mendelssohn, 1868.

Hofmeister, Adolphe. *Handbuch der musikalischen Literatur oder allgemeines systematisch-geordnetes Verzeichniss der in Deutschland und in den angrenzenden Ländern gedruckten Musikalien; auch musikalischen Schriften und Abbildungen mit Anzeige der Verleger und Preise, Erster Ergänzungsband, die vom Januar 1844 bis Ende des Jahres 1851, neu erschienenen und neu aufgelegten musikalischen Werke enthaltend.* Leipzig: Friedrich Hofmeister, 1852.

Holborn, Hajo. *A History of Modern Germany 1648–1840.* New York: Alfred A. Knopf, 1971.

Horne, Alistair. *Seven Ages of Paris.* New York: Vintage Books (Random House), 2004.

Hübler, Klaus Karl. *"Sie ist mir eine der liebsten Erscheinungen": Porträt der Münchner Komponistin Josephine Lang.* Munich: Bayerischer Rundfunk, 1985.

Jackson, Barbara Garvey. "Musical Women of the Seventeenth and Eighteenth Centuries." In *Women and Music: A History,* edited by Karin Pendle, 54–94. Bloomington and Indianapolis: Indiana University Press, 1991.

Jameson, Mrs. *Characteristics of Women: Moral, Poetical, and Historical.* London and Boston: William D. Ticknor, 1846.

Janik, Allan S., and Hans Veigl. *Wittgenstein in Vienna: A Biographical Excursion through the City and Its History.* Vienna and New York: Springer-Verlag, 1998.

Jefferson, Alan. *Elisabeth Schwarzkopf.* Boston: Northeastern University Press, 1995.

Journal des sçavans. Paris, January 7, 1709, 13–14, and Paris, April 6, 1711, 216–18.

Katzmaier, Martin. *Tübinger Spaziergänge.* Pfullingen: Günther Naske Verlag, 1977.

Kauffman, Deborah. "Violons en basse as Musical Allegory." *Journal of Musicology* 23, no. 1 (Winter 2006): 153–85.

Kaufmann, Dorothea. "*. . . Routinierte Trommlerin Gesucht": Musikerin in einer Damenkapelle: Zum Bild eines vergessenen Frauenberufes aus der Kaiserzeit.* Schriften zur Popularmusikforschung, Bd. 3, edited by Helmut Rösing. Karben: CODA, 1997.

Keegan, John. *The First World War.* New York: Alfred A. Knopf, 1999.

Keilitz, Alfred. *Die Wirkungen des Dreissigjährigen Krieges in den Wittumsämtern des Herzogtums Braunschweig-Wolfenbüttel.* Wolfenbüttel: n.p., 1938.

Kendrick, Robert L. "Devotion, Piety and Commemoration: Sacred Songs and Oratorios." In *The Cambridge History of Seventeenth-Century Music,* edited by Tim Carter and John Butt. Cambridge and New York: Cambridge University Press, 2005.

Kimber, Marian Wilson. "The 'Suppression' of Fanny Mendelssohn: Rethinking Feminist Biography." *Nineteenth-Century Music* 26, no. 2 (Fall 2002): 113–29.

Kokoschka, Oskar. *My Life.* Trans. David Britt. London: Thames and Hudson, 1974.

König, Joseph, ed. *Beiträge zur Geschichte der Stadt Wolfenbüttel aus Anlass der 400 Jährigen Widerkehr der Verleihung von Marktrecht und Wappen im Aufträge der Stadt Wolfenbüttel.* Wolfenbüttel: Stadtverwaltung Wolfenbüttel, 1970.

———, ed. *Wolfenbüttel: Wappen und Stadtgeschichte: Eine Ausstellung des Niedersächsischen Staatsarchivs in Wolfenbüttel.* Göttingen: Vandenhöck & Ruprecht, 1970.

Köstlin, Heinrich Adolf. "Josephine Lang." In *Sammlung musikalischer Vorträge,* 3, edited by P. Waldersee, 49–104. Leipzig: Breitkopf und Härtel, 1881.

Köstlin, Maria. *Das Buch der Familie Köstlin.* Stuttgart: W. Kohlhammer, 1929.

Krebs, Harald. "Irregular Phrase Rhythm in the Songs of Josephine Lang." Paper, presented at the University of Rochester, Rochester N.Y., November 12, 2001.

Krebs, Harald, and Sharon Krebs. Kompositions-Databank Josephine Lang.

———. *Josephine Lang: Her Life and Songs.* New York: Oxford University Press, 2007.

La Grange, Henri-Louis de. *Gustav Mahler, vol. 2: The Years of Challenge (1897–1904).* Oxford and New York: Oxford University Press, 1995.

Letzter, Jacqueline, and Robert Adelson. *Women Writing Opera: Creativity and Controversy in the Age of the French Revolution.* Berkeley, Los Angeles, and London: University of California Press, 2001.

Levi, Erik. *Music in the Third Reich.* New York: St. Martin's Press, 1994.

Lewin, David. "Women's Voices and the Fundamental Bass." *Journal of Musicology* 10, no. 4 (Fall 1992): 464–82.

Lewis, W. H. *The Splendid Century: Life in the France of Louis XIV.* Garden City, N.Y.: Doubleday Anchor Books, 1957.

———. *The Sunset of the Splendid Century: the Life and Times of Louis Auguste de Bourbon Duc du Maine, 1670–1736.* Garden City, N.Y.: Anchor Books (Doubleday), 1955 and 1963.

Loesser, Arthur. *Men, Women and Pianos: A Social History.* New York: Simon and Schuster, 1954.

MacDonald, Malcolm. *Brahms*. New York: Schirmer Books, 1990.

Marciano, Rosario. "Frida Kern," *Norton Grove Dictionary*, 248–49.

———. "Grete von Zieritz," *Norton Grove Dictionary*, 511–12.

———. "Maria Bach," *Norton Grove Dictionary*, 31–32.

Massie, Robert K. *Dreadnought: Britain, Germany, and the Coming of the Great War*. New York:Ballantine Books, 1991.

Massip, Catherine. "Paris, 1600–61." In *The Early Baroque Era: From the Late 16th Century to the 1660s*, edited by Curtis Price, 218–37. Music and Society Series. Englewood Cliffs, N.J.: Prentice Hall, 1993.

Mayer, Clara, ed. *Annäherung VI: an Sieben Komponistinnen mit Berichten, Interviews und Selbstdarstellungen*. Kassel: Furore-Edition, 1995.

McColl, Sandra. "Karl Kraus and Music Criticism: The Case of Max Kalbeck." *Musical Quarterly* 82, no. 2 (Summer 1998): 279–308.

Mendelssohn-Bartholdy, Felix. *Briefe aus den Jahren 1830 bis 1847,* edited by Paul Mendelssohn-Bartholdy and Carl Mendelssohn-Bartholdy. Leipzig: Hermann Mendelssohn, 1870.

———. *Felix Mendelssohn: A Life in Letters,* edited by Rudolf Elvers. Trans. Craig Tomlinson. New York: Fromm International Publishing Corp., 1984 (Trans., 1986).

———. *Reisebriefe*. Leipzig: HermannMendelssohn, 1862, 175–225.

Mercure gallant, Paris, July 1677, December 1678, January 1680, March 1687, December 1691, August 1707.

MICA Lexikon zeitgenössischer Musik aus Österreich: Komponisten und Komponistinnen des 20. Jahrhunderts, edited by Bernhard Günther.Vienna: Music Information Center Austria, 1997. Articles: "Frida Kern," 85; "Mathilde von Kralik," 52; "Johanna Müller-Hermann," 74; "Fritz Skorzeny," 109; "Grete von Zieritz," 70; and "Marianne Gary-Schaffhauser," 184.

Moser, Hans Joachim. *Heinrich Schütz: His Life and Work*. 2nd ed. Edited and trans. Carl F. Pfatteicher. St. Louis: Concordia Publishing House, 1959.

———. *Das Deutsche Lied seit Mozart*. Berlin: Atlantis, 1937.

Munck, Thomas. *Seventeenth Century Europe: State, Conflict and the Social Order in Europe 1598–1700*. New York: St. Martin's Press, 1990.

Murata, Margaret. "Image and Eloquence: Secular Song." *The Cambridge History of Seventeenth Century Music,* edited by Tim Carter and John Butt, 378–425. Cambridge and New York: Cambridge University Press, 2005.

Neuls-Bates, Carol, ed. *Women in Music: An Anthology of Source Readings from the Middle Ages to the Present*. Rev. ed. Boston: Northeastern University Press, 1996, 62–64.

Neumann, Hermann. *Die Münchner Residenz*. München, London, and New York: Prestel, 2000.

The New Grove Dictionary of Music and Musicians, edited by Stanley Sadie. London and New York: Macmillan, 1980.

Newman, Richard, and Karen Kirtley. *Alma Rosé: Vienna to Auschwitz*. Portland, Ore.: Amadeus Press, 2000.

Niedersächsisches Staatsarchiv Wolfenbüttel. Göttingen: Vandenhöck & Ruprecht, 1970.

Niemann, Walter. *Die Musik der Gegenwart*. Berlin: Schuster und Löffler, 1921.

Ostleitner, Elena. "Mozarts Rivalinnen? Können Frauen Überhaupt Komponieren?" Lecture, Augsburger Mozartfest anlässlich des 250 Geburtstag von Maria Anna Thekla Mozart, May 2009.

Pagel, Karl. *Die Hansa*. 4th ed. Braunschweig: Georg Westermann Verlag, 1952.

———. *Mecklenburg: Biographie eines Deutschen Landes.* Göttingen: Vanderhöck & Ruprecht, 1969.

Pendle, Karin, ed. *Women and Music: A History.* Bloomington and Indianapolis: Indiana University Press, 1991.

Philipp, Beate. *Annäherung VI,* 5–16.

Polisensky, Josef V. *The Thirty Years' War.* Trans. Robert Evans. London: B.T. Batsford, 1971.

Porter, Cecelia Hopkins. "The New Public and the Reordering of the Musical Establishment: The Lower Rhine Music Festivals, 1818–1867." *19th-Century Music* 3, no. 3 (March 1980): 211–24.

———. "The Reign of the Dilettanti: Düsseldorf from Mendelssohn to Schumann." *Musical Quarterly* 73 (1989): 476–512.

———. *The Rhine as Musical Metaphor: Cultural Identity in German Romantic Music.* Boston: Northeastern University Press, 1996.

Post, Jennifer C. "Erasing the Boundaries between Public and Private in Women's Performance Traditions." In *Cecilia Reclaimed: Feminist Perspectives on Gender and Music.* Edited by Susan C. Cook and Judy S. Tsou, 35–51. Urbana and Chicago: University of Illinois Press, 1994.

Prieberg, Fred K. *Musik im NS-Staat.* Frankfurt am Main: Fischer Taschenbuch Verlag, 1982.

Quittard, H. "La première comédie française en musique." In *Bulletin françois de la Société internationale de musicologie (SIM)* (1908), 377–96 and 497–637.

Ranum, Patricia. "A Sweet Servitude: A Musician's Life at the Court of Mlle de Guise." *Early Music* 15, no. 3 (August 1987): 347–60.

Raugel, F. *Les grandes orgues des églises de Paris.* Paris: Fischbein, 1927.

Reich, Nancy B. "European Composers and Musicians, ca. 1800–1890." In *Women and Music: A History,* edited by Karin Pendle, 97–122. Bloomington and Indianapolis: Indiana University Press, 1991.

———. *Clara Schumann: The Artist and the Woman.* Ithaca, N.Y., and London: Cornell University Press, 1985.

Riemann, Hugo. "Karl Reinhold Köstlin." In *Dictionary of Music.* Trans. J. S. Shedlock, 407–8. New York: Da Capo Press, 1970.

———. "Josephine Lang." In *Dictionary of Music.* Trans. J. S. Shedlock, 426. New York: Da Capo Press, 1970.

Rifkin, Joshua. "Heinrich Schütz." In *The New Grove Dictionary of Music and Musicians* 17, ed. Stanley Sadie. London and New York: Macmillan, 1980.

Rose, Adrian. "Elisabeth-Claude Jacquet de la Guerre and the Secular cantate françoise." *Early Music* 13, no. 4 (November 1985): 529–41.

Rosen, Charles. *The Romantic Generation.* Cambridge, Mass.: Harvard University Press, 1995.

Rosenwald, H. *Das deutsche Lied zwischen Schubert und Schumann.* Ph.D. diss., University of Heidelberg, 1929, 61 and following.

Roster, Danielle. "Elisabeth-Claude Jacquet de la Guerre." In *Annäherung VI an Sieben Komponistinnen.* Kassel: Furore-Verlag, 1995, 69–79.

———. "Elisabeth Jacquet de La Guerre." In *Allein mit meiner Musik: Komponistinnen in der europäischen Musikgeschichte vom Mittelalter bis ins frühe 20. Jahrhundert.* Echternach: éditions phi, 1995, and Vienna: Hora Verlag, 1995, 60–80.

Sadie, Julie Anne. "Braunschweig (Brunswick)." In *The New Grove Dictionary of Music and Musicians* 3, 391–92. London and New York: Macmillan, 1980.

———. "Musiciennes of the Ancien Régime." In *Women Making Music: the Western Art Tradition, 1150–1950,* edited by J. Bowers and Judith Tick, 191–223. Urbana and Chicago: University of Illinois Press, 1987.

———. "Paris and Versailles." In *The Late Baroque Era: From the 1680s to 1740,* edited by George J. Buelow, 129–89. Englewood Cliffs, N.J.: Prentice Hall, 1993.

Sadie, Julie Anne, and Rhian Samuel, eds. *Norton/Grove Dictionary of Women Composers.* New York and London: W.W. Norton, 1994.

Schildhauer, Johannes. *The Hansa: History and Culture.* Trans. Katherine Vanovitch. Leipzig: Edition Leipzig, 1985.

Schleifer, Martha Furman. "Mathilde von Kralik." In *The Norton/Grove Dictionary of Women Composers.* New York and London: W. W. Norton, 1994.

Schmidt, Carl B. Review of La Guerre's Céphale et Procris, edited by Wanda R. Griffiths. *Journal of Seventeenth-Century Music* 5, no. 1 (1999): 1–3.

"Schönberg in Wien," *Österreichische Musik Zeitschrift* 3–4, 1998.

Schonberg, Harold C. *The Great Pianists.* New York: Simon and Schuster, 1963.

Schorske, Carl E. *Fin-de-Siècle Vienna: Politics and Culture.* New York: Vintage Books (Random House), 1981.

Smith, Joan Allen. *Schönberg and His Circle: A Viennese Portrait.* New York and London: Schirmer, 1986.

Solie, Ruth A., ed. *Musicology and Difference: Gender and Sexuality in Music Scholarship.* Berkeley and Los Angeles: University of California Press, 1993.

Solomon, Maynard. *Beethoven.* New York: Schirmer Books, 1977.

Sophie-Elisabeth, Herzogin von Braunschweig-Lüneburg. Musikhandschriften. Cod. Guelf. 52 Noviss.8zero, 11a Noviss.2zero, 11 Noviss.2zero. Wolfenbüttel: Herzog-August-Bibliothek.

Spagnoli, Gina. "Dresden at the Time of Heinrich Schütz." In *The Early Baroque Era: From the Late 16th Century to the 1660s,* edited by Curtis Price, 164–84. Music and Society Series. Englewood Cliffs, N.J.: Prentice Hall, 1994.

Sperber, Roswitha, ed. *Women Composers in Germany.* Bonn: Inter Nationes, 1996, 26–27.

Spitzer, John, and Neal Zaslow. *The Birth of the Orchestra: History of an Institution, 1650–1815.* New York: Oxford University Press, 2004.

Swafford, Jan. *Brahms: A Biography.* New York: Alfred A. Knopf, 1997.

Thompson, Oscar, ed. "Sabina Hitzelberger." In *The International Cyclopedia of Music and Musicians,* edited by Robert Sabin, 989. 9th ed. New York: Dodd, Mead, 1964.

Tick, Judith. *Introduction to Josephine Lang: Selected Songs.* New York: Da Capo Press, 1982.

Tiersot, Julien. "Une Famille de musiciens françoises: Les de la Barre." In *Revue de musicologie* 12, nos. 9–25 (February 1928): 1–11, 68–74.

———. "Les testaments d'Elisabeth Jacquet de La Guerre." *Revue de musicologie* 40 (1957): 206–14.

Titon du Tillet, Évrard. *Le Parnasse François.* Paris: J.-B. Coignard fils, 1732, 635 and following, 637, & rev. ed., 1971.

Toland, John. *Adolf Hitler.* Garden City, N.Y.: Doubleday, 1976.

Tommasini, Anthony. "Plumbing Schönberg's Inner Realm," *New York Times,* February 13, 2002, review of Allen Shawn, *Arnold Schönberg's Journey* (New York: Farrar, Straus & Giroux, 2001).

Tschulik, Norbert, "Musikkritik in Österreich." In Manfred Wagner, *Geschichte der Öster-reichischen Musikkritik in Beispielen.*Tutzing: Hans Schneider, 1979, 3–28.

Vassiltchikov, Marie. *Berlin Diaries: 1940–1945.* New York: Vintage Books (Random House), 1985 and 1988.

Wagner, Manfred. *Geschichte der Österreichischen Musikkritik in Beispielen.* Tutzing: Hans Schneider, 1979.

Wedgwood, C. V. *The Thirty Years' War.* London and New York: Methuen, 1938 and 1981.

Werba, Erik. "Joseph Marx und sein Schülerkreis." *Musikerziehung* 5, no. 4 (June 1952): 214–46.

Werner, Eric. *Mendelssohn: A New Image of the Composer and his Age.* Trans. Dika Newlin. London: The Free Press of Glencoe (Collier-Macmillan), 1963.

Werner, Roberta Carol. *The Songs of Josephine Caroline Lang: The Expression of a Life.* Minneapolis: University of Minnesota, 1992, and Ann Arbor: UMI 9231091, 1992.

Wiswe, Hans. "Handel und Wandel in Wolfenbüttel vor dem Dreissigjährigen Kriegs." In *Beiträge zur Geschichte der Stadt Wolfenbüttel.* Wolfenbüttel: Stadt Wolfenbüttel, 1970, 11–31.

Wollny, Peter. "Sara Levy and the Making of Musical Taste in Berlin." *Musical Quarterly* 77, no. 4 (Winter 1993): 651–88.

Yates, W. E., Allyson Fiddler, and John Warren, eds. *From Perinet to Jelinek: Viennese Theatre in its Political and Intellectual Context.* Berne: Peter Lang, 2001.

Zeichner, Craig. "Elisabeth Belgrano and the Language of Passion." *Early Music America* (Fall 2005): 27–28.

Ziak, Karl, ed. *Wiedergeburt einer Weltstadt: Wien 1945–1965.* Vienna and Munich: Verlag für Jugend und Volk, 1965, 7–13.

Zimmermann, Paul. "Zur Biographie des Kapellmeisters Michael Praetorius." *Jahrbuch des Braunschweigischen Geschichtvereins,* 2 Folge, Bd. 3 Wolfenbüttel: Braunschweigischer Geschichtverein, 1930, 91–97.

Zohn, Steven. "Telemann in the Marketplace: The Composer as Self-Publisher." *Journal of the American Musicological Society* 58, no. 2 (Summer 2005): 275–356.

INDEX

Index

CECELIA HOPKINS PORTER is a longtime classical music critic for *The Washington Post* and the author of *The Rhine as Musical Metaphor: Cultural Identity in German Romantic Music* and articles in professional music journals.

The University of Illinois Press
is a founding member of the
Association of American University Presses.

_____

University of Illinois Press
1325 South Oak Street
Champaign, IL 61820-6903
www.press.uillinois.edu